Enhancing
Religious Identity:
Best Practices from
Catholic Campuses

Enhancing Religious Identity: Best Practices from Catholic Campuses

Edited by
John R. Wilcox and Irene King

Foreword by
Monika K. Hellwig

Georgetown University Press / Washington, D.C.

#43634393

Georgetown University Press, Washington, D.C.
© 2000 by Georgetown University Press. All rights reserved.
Printed in the United States of America

10 9 8 7 6 5 4 3 2 1   2000

This volume is printed on acid-free offset book paper.

Library of Congress Cataloging-in-Publication Data

Enhancing religious identity : best practices from Catholic campuses / edited by John R. Wilcox, Irene King.
        p. cm.
    Includes bibliographical references and index.
    ISBN 0-87840-813-4 (acid-free paper)—ISBN 0-87840-814-2 (pbk. : acid-free paper)
        1. Catholic universities and colleges—United States.   2. Catholic Church—Education (Higher)—United States.   I. Wilcox, John R. (John Richard), 1939–
II. King, Irene.

LC501 . E53 2000
378'.0712'73—dc21   00-026368

Dedication

To the memory of a passionate advocate of Catholic identity and best practices:

Monsignor I. Brent Eagen
(1929–1997)

Vice President for Mission and Ministry
University of San Diego

Contents

The Faculty and the Disciplines

grading salaries, and competing for students and faculty with prestigious secular institutions across the country. This activity turned attention in a new direction.

A third important reason for change has been the acceleration of technology in the communication of information and knowledge, with the impact that this has had on relationships between the generations, on the particular relationship between teacher and students, and on the way the entire heritage of the past is valued by the young as they face the future.

These are reasons for the meetings, discussions, summer institutes and seminars, books and papers that have been devoted to the topic of Catholic identity and the means to promote it. The effort is not to regain something we have lost but to give it new form to meet a new situation in a new time. We are looking for continuity in identity and adaptation in form. Many have thought about this and many have worked on it. This anthology of that work may be helpful to others as they undertake similar efforts in their own contexts.

Preface

Religious Identity: A Critical Issue in Catholic Higher Education

John R. Wilcox*

M any administrators, trustees, faculty, and students are still not sure what Catholic identity means and why it has become such an important issue. This anthology is a response to their puzzlement. On the one hand, the essays describe steps colleges and universities may take to enhance that identity. They make it clear why the topic is timely and important. On the other hand, the practical steps described will also help the reader better to understand what Catholic identity means.

Identity has taken on a higher profile since the Apostolic Constitution of Pope John Paul II, *Ex Corde Ecclesiae*.[1] While the document offers a rich description of Catholic intellectual life and the profoundly humanistic nature of Catholic higher education, it has also moved Catholic institutional identity into the realm of canon law and the issue of episcopal jurisdiction over colleges and universities. Meanwhile, the highly pluralistic nature of American culture and higher education continues to affect, both positively and negatively, the evolution of Catholic institutions.

While identity, *Ex Corde Ecclesiae*, and pluralism are not the only issues facing Catholic higher education, they are particularly important in both an American setting and in the Church universal, where these colleges and universities play a unique role in education. As a result, the reader will have a context for assessing "best practices" to enhance identity and help achieve the mission of Catholic higher education.

Why Religious Identity Is Important

"Without a vision, the people perish." That utterance in the Book of Proverbs (29:18) goes to the heart of the current controversy surrounding the

---

*John R. Wilcox is professor of religious studies at Manhattan College, Bronx, New York.

religious identity, and therefore the mission, of Catholic colleges and universities. In the debate, much attention has been devoted to the role of Pope John Paul II's Apostolic Constitution, *Ex Corde Ecclesiae*, in triggering controversy. However, this document reflects only one dimension of the hard thinking about Catholic higher education in the Church at large and in the United States in particular over the past 25 years, especially during the last decade.[2] The religious identity of colleges and universities became a critical issue in the 1970s, when the opportunity to receive public funding brought it to the forefront.[3] Even then, identity was taken for granted and was not a burning issue. Today, that is no longer the case.

Media emphasis and the ongoing discussion among the college presidents and Church hierarchy on the most controversial, complicated aspect of *Ex Corde Ecclesiae*—the local application of the General Norms in Section II—has greatly skewed the discussion. There is no doubt, however, that the linkage between Catholic institutions and the Vatican, as outlined in the General Norms, needs attention. Papal emphasis on both the teaching of doctrine in Catholic colleges and universities and the probity of those who lead, teach, or work in these schools must be taken seriously. Nevertheless, as we shall see, the identity of Catholic colleges and universities goes beyond a series of ordinances that spell out their relationships with Rome.

Concern about linkages between Church and academe is intensified by several other developments. Among these is the rapid decrease in the presence of founding religious orders and diocesan clergy in the classroom, on the campus, or in the boardroom. Furthermore, the high cost of private higher education, competition for a diverse student body, and the imperative of educational excellence, lead Catholic higher education today to be more competitive with the other private colleges and universities and the lower-costing public schools. As an unintended consequence, Catholic institutions may emulate secular standards in hiring and scholarship without regard to the religious vision intrinsic to their identity. Retention of a critical mass of administrators and faculty committed to maintenance and enhancement of Catholic identity has thus become another dimension of the problem.

The admission of a high proportion of Catholic students who are unchurched or theologically ignorant of their own faith as well as many non-Catholics has also made attention to religious identity an imperative. Most undergraduate students in American Catholic colleges and universities are still Catholic, but it is questionable how long this preponderance will last. Furthermore the depth of the religious commitment of the Catholic students who choose these institutions is of great concern.[4]

At the same time, questions about identity in higher education mirror questions about identity in the Church at large. American Catholic higher education is very much tied to the evolution of Catholicism in the United States. As David O'Brien observes, Catholic institutions come "from the heart of the American Church."[5] Thus, it is impossible to discuss the future of education without attending to the Church itself. Charles Morris notes that the American Catholic Church is the most successful national church in the history of Catholicism and the most influential church in the United States. His thesis is that "the story of American Catholicism is therefore the story of the rise and triumph of a culture, and of the religious crisis that has ensued in the wake of that culture's breakdown."[6] He assesses the recent problems facing the Church "as the floundering of an institution suddenly forced to make its way solely as a religion, shorn of the cultural supports that had been the source of its strength."[7]

Even those who are not restorationists can appreciate Morris's insight. It is unlikely that the Church can make its way solely as a religion—a belief system with its doctrine, myths, and rituals—without the cultural support of the shared values and ideals of a community. A guiding principle governing the selection of essays for this volume has thus been the extent to which each will assist a college or university in establishing a Catholic culture where "Catholic ideals, attitudes, and principles penetrate and inform university activities" (*Ex Corde Ecclesiae*, paragraph 14). We are convinced that a college or university possessed of a profoundly vital Catholic culture will be the Church's best chance to strengthen American Catholicism, and an effective means of evangelization—an area of concern in *Ex Corde Ecclesiae*. We also agree with Alastair MacIntyre that "what matters at this stage is the construction of local forms of community within which civility and the intellectual and moral life can be sustained through the new dark ages which are already upon us,"[8] while recognizing that colleges and universities cannot be gated enclaves keeping the world at bay.

The graduates of American Catholic higher education should be the lay persons envisioned by Arthur Simon, founder of Bread for the World. "Simon argues that Christians should be 'twice-converted' people. They are first converted from the world to Jesus Christ . . . but then they are converted to the world again, to love the world and relate to it, not as they did before, but through the heart and mind of Christ."[9] Catholic graduates should be leaders in both the Church and civic life. This is the vision of the university's place in the Church, toward which the mission and goals are directed.

Attaining this vision, which is in reality evangelization, is a complex task. On the one hand, Simon's twofold conversion is what one hopes for in the Catholic graduate. Conversion in this sense is evangelization. But the student must be drawn to it as an adult, freely and without indoctrination—such is the bedrock belief of American Catholic higher education. On the other hand, the Catholic college or university generally does not have an explicit focus on converting those of other faiths to Catholicism—even though we believe a distinctive Catholic culture will prove attractive to many students who are not Catholic and thus will also be a powerful form of evangelization.

Yet our mission gains direction from the vision of *all* graduates as leaders in civic society and practitioners of civic virtue. In graduate programs, where religious pluralism is most evident, this civic vision should guide students in their understanding of professional life. Thus, while the Catholic college or university neither proselytizes nor seeks to "twice convert" all, there is no doubt that all should be at least once converted: They should be committed to service to the community and enhancement of the common good. This is the essence of professional life.

If we are to maintain the Catholic culture that makes our colleges and universities unique, our ability to address these and other issues is vital. American higher education has already witnessed the erosion of religious identity in a host of institutions founded within the Protestant tradition.[10] The erosion was usually unintentional, though in a small minority of cases there was conscious disavowal of religious identity. The long tradition of Catholic intellectual life and a highly articulated social teaching have made many administrators, trustees, faculty, alums, and clergy intent on avoiding either erosion or disavowal.

The Role of *Ex Corde Ecclesiae*

In selecting essays for this anthology, we were very conscious of three concerns in Catholic higher education: (1) presidential and trustee leadership, (2) the faculty and their academic disciplines, and (3) student life. At the same time, we see the positive importance of *Ex Corde Ecclesiae* in making Catholic identity vital to institutional culture. The document provides a framework for implementing best practices by identifying four characteristics of Catholic educational institutions. Catholic higher education is (1) in service to both Church and society, (2) distinguished by a distinct pastoral ministry associated with religious and moral principles, (3) in dialogue with the larger society, and (4) a contributor to the Church's work of evangelization (*Ex Corde Ecclesiae*, paragraphs 30–49). We believe these concerns and characteristics are reflected in the essays chosen.

What makes *Ex Corde Ecclesiae* energizing is the dynamism that flows from the vision and values it expresses. The vision challenges the present the Christian message," the "personal fidelity of Catholic members," the fidelity of theologians to the Church, and "respect for the authority of the bishops." These are made more specific in the section dealing with General Norms and local ordinances. This anthology does not address ordinances. Still evolving, they have generated a body of literature requiring an anthology of its own.

All sections of this anthology address the importance of a substantive relationship between the university and the Church, especially in terms of Service to Church and Society (paragraphs 31–37) and the Pastoral Ministry (paragraphs 38–42) of the university. Cultural Dialogue (paragraphs 43–47) and Evangelization (paragraphs 48–49) within the university will further deepen the relationship between higher education and the Church itself. "Through this [cultural] dialogue a Catholic university assists the Church, enabling it to come to a better knowledge of diverse cultures, to discern their positive and negative aspects, to receive their authentically human contributions, and to develop means by which it can make the faith better understood by men and women of a particular culture" (paragraph 44). In terms of evangelization, "[the university] is a living institutional witness to Christ and his message, so vitally important in cultures marked by secularism, or where Christ and his message are still virtually unknown" (paragraph 49).

Pluralism and Catholic Identity

The pluralistic nature of Catholic colleges and universities, especially in the United States, demands special attention. Unless pluralism is taken seriously, there is little point in discussing Catholic identity.

Personal identity shows itself in a particular way of being, a style of living out individuality; *self-worth* leads the individual to take pride in that personal identity. Institutions similarly must strive to achieve a sense of identity and self-worth as well as a vital culture[13] that embodies both. Catholic identity is more complex because the future of Catholic higher education will not only be in the hands of lay persons, but a significant number, perhaps a majority, of these will not be Catholic, or at least not "practicing" Catholics. They will include "members of other Churches, ecclesial communities and religions, and also those who profess no religious belief" (paragraph 26). Yet all, regardless of religious persuasion, "are to be inspired by academic ideals and by the principles of an authentically human life" (paragraph 22).

A Catholic university, thus, "enables the Church to institute an incomparably fertile dialogue with people of every culture"(paragraph 6). This is especially the case when the university has a diverse faculty and student body. *Ex Corde Ecclesiae* does not, however, comment on the positive contribution those who are not Catholic make to the life of the university; it simply notes that "these men and women offer their training and experience in furthering the various academic disciplines or other university tasks" (paragraph 26).

If the Declaration on Religious Freedom is taken seriously, however, pluralism plays a more positive role in the search for truth than one finds in E*x Corde Ecclesiae*: "Truth . . . is to be sought after in a manner proper to the dignity of the human person and his social nature. The inquiry is to be free. . . . In the course of [teaching or instruction, communication and dialogue], men explain to one another the truth they have discovered, or think they have discovered, in order thus to assist one another in the quest for truth. Moreover, as the truth is discovered, it is by a personal assent that men are to adhere to it.[14]

Pluralism safeguarded by religious freedom is qualitatively different from mere toleration, as Franklin Littell says in his commentary on the Declaration: Religious freedom "derives, both historically and theologically, from a certain understanding of the nature of true faith. To tolerate dissent is today merely prudent; to respect the conscience and the person of another is noble."[15] It is noble because compulsion is alien to true religion.

The Declaration says further that the individual is bound to follow his or her own conscience in order to reach God (paragraph 3). Can embarking on such a journey be anything other than an insightful and positive contribution to the search for truth that *Ex Corde Ecclesiae* so emphasizes? Though *Ex Corde Ecclesiae* acknowledges the pluralism of the university, respect for pluralism is found only in the ideas of the Second Vatican Council: Pluralism is more than mere accommodation to the realities of contemporary higher education.

Pluralism has an intrinsic role in the search for truth because the search must respond to the individual's conscience: "In all his activity a man is bound to follow his conscience faithfully, in order that he may come to God, for whom he was created" (*Declaration*, paragraph 3). *Ex Corde Ecclesiae* does affirm this positive regard for pluralism: The university, it says, "is open to all human experience and is ready to dialogue with and learn from any culture" (paragraph 43) and "their authentically human contributions" (paragraph 44). "A faith that places itself on the margin of what is human, of what is therefore culture, would be a faith unfaithful to the fullness of what the word of God manifests and reveals, a decapitated faith, worse still, a faith in the process of self-annihilation" (paragraph 44).

Addressing pluralism, especially in the American context, is a challenge. Michael Naughton and Thomas Bausch discuss the nuances of this issue: "If in the name of pluralism Catholic universities fail to develop their Catholic identity, pluralism has become a platform for uniformity." Though distinctiveness should not be a victim of pluralism, Naughton and Bausch conclude that "Catholic universities walk a delicate line between retrieving what is particular to themselves as Catholic universities, and engaging this unique retrieval with contemporary culture."[16]

There are more than 200 Catholic colleges and universities in the United States. They vary in size from small liberal arts institutions to large research universities with many professional programs. They themselves constitute a pluralistic group and this book will not address all the needs of every institution. But we hope the essays selected will demonstrate how presidents and trustees, faculty, and student-life personnel can create a campus where Catholicism is "part of the woodwork," taken for granted in the best sense of the term, a motivational force and a frame of reference in decision making and personal relations, integral to the curriculum and to the ethos of student life.

Naughton and Bausch ask, "Should managers educated at Catholic universities examine layoffs and plant closures any differently from those executives taught at non-Catholic universities?" More generally, they ask, "Do faculty at Catholic universities teach management any differently from faculty at non-Catholic universities?"[17] Their answer is a decided yes, but the specific ways in which this happens will vary greatly.

How Best Practices Can Make a Difference

The overview that follows contains three essays, all of which address the issue of Catholic identity concretely. Next are reflections addressing Presidential and Trustee Leadership. They present a framework of moral responsibility for trustees as well as a case study analyzing board actions at a Catholic university. They challenge institutional leaders to address issues of mission in relation to identity, describe a process of cultural analysis and strategies for enhancing Catholic identity, and finally assess the sensitive area of hiring faculty in relation to mission. Although presidents and boards are not usually involved in hiring, they will find the final case study very helpful in analyzing their broader responsibilities for identity and mission.

In the section on Faculty and the Disciplines, you will find steps to elicit faculty involvement in identity issues through research intrinsic to their disciplines, a concrete example of that strategy, and several essays both on what it means to integrate academic disciplines with a Catholic world view and on the role of Catholic studies programs. The final essay analyzes academic freedom in a Catholic context.

The Student Life section addresses a number of issues: a social action model of university-community collaboration, the meaning of paradigms of justice and love in this context, the effect of paradigm shifts on a student life program. There are essays on religious diversity and a plan for spiritual growth.

The final section, Strategies for Change, presents an institutional values program and a method for assessing continuities and discontinuities between what is practiced and what is preached on campus.

Each section is designed to reinforce what is addressed in the other sections. These essays taken together, we hope, will help Catholic colleges and universities to strengthen their commitment to both Church and society. Administrators and boards can use the essays on retreat or in cabinet meetings. Deans can use them during faculty workshops and departmental meetings. Student life personnel will find much of interest in their increasingly difficult task of addressing the needs of a diverse student population. The growing number of programs in higher education administration and Catholic studies will have available in one volume essays that will be invaluable to graduate students. Bishops and clergy will appreciate the opportunity to grasp more fully what may be affecting Catholic education in their dioceses.

Catholic colleges and universities represent the last educational opportunity to challenge young adult Catholics to take their places of responsibility in the Church. They also offer a meaningful value system to students, all of whom, regardless of belief systems, will share responsibility for the common good through the practice of civic virtue. Thus, Catholic institutions have a significant role to play within the Church and American society. Let us hope that neither neglect nor secularization erodes the identity of these colleges and universities.

Notes

1. John Paul II, *Ex Corde Ecclesiae* [August 15, 1990], in Alice Gallin, O.S.U., ed., *American Catholic Higher Education: Essential Documents, 1967–1990* (Notre Dame, IN: University of Notre Dame Press, 1992), 413–37.
2. See Alice Gallin, O.S.U., ed., *American Catholic Higher Education: Essential Documents, 1967–1990* (Notre Dame, IN: University of Notre Dame Press, 1992).
3. On this point see Alice Gallin, O.S.U., *Independence and a New Partnership*

in Catholic Higher Education (Notre Dame, IN: University of Notre Dame Press, 1996).

4. On this point see Scott Appleby, "One Church, Many Cultures," *Church* (Summer 1998), 5–9. See also William Dinges, Dean R. Hoge, and Juan L. Gonzales, Jr. "A Faith Loosely Held," *Commonweal* (July 17, 1998), 13–18, and Gustav Niebuhr, "Young Catholics Found to Be Paring Back Beliefs," *New York Times* (July 18, 1998), A9.

5. David J. O'Brien, *From the Heart of the American Church: Catholic Higher Education and American Culture* (Maryknoll, NY: Orbis, 1994).

6. Charles R. Morris, *American Catholic: The Saints and Sinners who Built America's Most Powerful Church* (New York: Times Books, 1997), vii.

7. Ibid.

8. Alasdair MacIntyre, *After Virtue* (Notre Dame, IN: University of Notre Dame Press, 1981), 245.

9. Vincent J. Genovesi, S.J., "Is Jesuit Education Fulfilling Its Mission?" *America* (May 23, 1998), 5. See also John A. Coleman, S.J., "The Two Pedagogies: Discipleship and Citizenship," in Mary C. Boys, ed., *Education for Citizenship and Discipleship* (Cleveland, OH: Pilgrim Press, 1989), 35–75.

10. On this point see James T. Burtchaell, C.S.C., *The Dying of the Light: The Disengagement of Colleges and Universities from their Christian Churches* (Grand Rapids, MI: William B. Eerdmans, 1998).

11. Margaret J. Wheatley, "The Motivating Power of Ethics in Times of Corporate Confusion," in N. Dale Wright, ed., *Papers on the Ethics of Administration* (Albany, NY: State University of New York Press, 1988), 139–57.

12. Robert N. Bellah et al., *Habits of the Heart: Individualism and Commitment in American Life* (Berkeley, CA: University of California Press, 1985. See also Bellah et al., *The Good Society* (New York, NY: Alfred A. Knopf, 1991).

13. We rely on Kuh and Whitt's definition of culture: "the collective, mutually shaping patterns of norms, values, practices, beliefs, and assumptions that guide the behavior of individuals and groups in an institute of higher education and provide a frame of reference within which to interpret the meaning of events and actions on and off campus." George D. Kuh and Elizabeth J. Whitt, *The Invisible Tapestry: Culture in American Colleges and Universities*, ASHE-ERIC Higher Education Report No. 1 (Washington, DC: Association for the Study of Higher Education, 1988), 12–13.

14. "Declaration on Religious Freedom," in Walter M. Abbott, S.J., ed., *The Documents of Vatican II* (New York, NY: Guild Press, 1966), 680–81.

15. Franklin H. Littell, "A Response," in Abbott, ed., *The Documents of Vatican II*, 697–98.

16. Michael J. Naughton and Thomas A. Bausch, "The Integrity of a Catholic Management Education," *California Management Review*, Vol 38, No. 4 (summer 1996), 131. Reprinted on pp. 115–41, this volume.

17. Ibid.

Overview: Defining a Catholic University

Introduction

*Irene King** *

"My mischievous intent in writing this essay was to provoke your entanglement in these questions," writes Richard A. McCormick, S.J. We took the same approach in choosing essays. "These questions" are the essential queries that have been most recently raised by *Ex Corde Ecclesiae*[1], but they are also questions that all Catholic colleges and universities have struggled with since they were founded.

All the essays were chosen for their clarity of expression, articulation of the issues facing Catholic higher education, and distinctive viewpoints—and for their value as starting points for discussion and an authentic probing of the issues facing your campuses. This is particularly true of the three visions for Catholic identity at colleges and universities that make up this section.

In "What Is a Great Catholic University?" Richard McCormick, S.J., asserts the importance of finding "some minimal clarity" on the matter of identity in order to know our goal. Positing that a "great Catholic university should be measured by its product," he outlines eight qualities he hopes to find in the graduates of a great Catholic university: a Catholic vision, sensitivity to justice and injustice, appreciation of and thirst for knowledge, facility in spoken and written word, open-mindedness, critical capacity, ability to listen, and willingness to serve.

While McCormick eloquently describes these qualities, he offers no way to ensure their development or means of measuring their presence in

---

*Irene King is director of community partnership and service learning, Sarah Lawrence College, Bronxville, New York.

1

graduates. Ideas and programs in later sections will touch on the development and measurement of such qualities.

Michael J. Lavelle, S.J., begins his reflection in "What Is Meant by a 'Catholic' University?" with two central concerns raised by *Ex Corde Ecclesiae:* who is going to be in charge of what is taught and who is hired; and institutional Catholicity, "doctrinal purity, the teaching of theology and philosophy, and the Catholic ambiance and character of the school."

Lavelle identifies the central concern of Catholic education as "the complete formation of young men and women . . . to provide these students with an environment in which all components of their personalities will be developed—intellect, will, soul, and body." A Catholic university, he believes, is a place where a Catholic life can flourish, where young men and women can ask themselves the question that St. Paul, the Apostles, and the Church have asked throughout the ages: "Who is Jesus Christ, and where do I stand in relation to Him?" Lavelle thus concurs with McCormick that the ultimate mark of a Catholic institution is expressed in the qualities of its students.

Lavelle cautions readers of *Ex Corde Ecclesiae* against taking a purely juridical approach to developing and preserving Catholic identity. Universities, he asserts, must have the freedom to explore even viewpoints that oppose or differ from Catholic teaching. He reminds us that theology and philosophy courses are not catechism classes. Intellectual inquiry must be done with faith that the "Holy Spirit is guiding the Church."

Lavelle also cautions institutions against taking one of two polar stances regarding Catholic identity. The first would be to define Catholicity so narrowly "that it would be indistinguishable from a seminary." The second would define Catholicity so broadly that its distinctiveness would be lost. Religious identity would then be as amorphous in Catholic institutions as it has become in most Protestant universities. Lavelle challenges us to view the "inevitable demand for change . . . as an opportunity for greater enrichment and not as a betrayal of sacred trust."

In "The Sides of Catholic Identity," James H. Provost, a canon lawyer, offers few cautions about *Ex Corde Ecclesiae,* concerning himself rather with educating readers about the document's intent. He begins by deconstructing Catholic identity into "inside" and "outside" dimensions. He suggests that the heated debates about *Ex Corde Ecclesiae* arise in the outside dimension, "the relationship to hierarchy and official structures." He then contends that the National Conference of Catholic Bishops draft ordinances fail to address "the more significant aspect of *Ex Corde Ecclesiae,* its concern for the inner dimension of Catholic identity."

Provost advances two concepts, *church* and *vigilance,* whose misinterpretation, he says, has distorted *Ex Corde Ecclesiae's* intentions in many people's minds. He reminds us that *church* as it is used in relation to Catholic universities does not mean the hierarchy: "Church has a broader, more encompassing meaning here. The canons also affirm the right of Catholic institutions of higher education to conduct their own affairs without direct interference from church officials." Vigilance is a canon law concept that refers to "the pastoral concern bishops are said to have for everyone in their diocese." Vigilance is not something for universities to fear; rather, it can and should be an expression of support and communion.

Provost posits two central principles that will enable colleges and universities to enhance and develop their Catholic identity in concert with the vision of *Ex Corde Ecclesiae*. The first, persons, asserts that for an institution to be Catholic "a critical mass of people [ideally faculty] who are Catholics in full communion" must exist. A Catholic university must also respect individual dignity, reject discrimination, and "embrace all persons, with no distinction on the basis of age, race, national origin, or gender."

The second principle, procedures, concerns the hiring and orienting of personnel. Provost rejects the idea of a religious litmus test, but does question "where the authority to hire new personnel is located." Though it typically is located at the departmental level, Provost suggests that "higher level academic authorities may well wish to address this procedure if they desire to have an effective voice in the continued Catholic identity of the institution." Procedures might also encompass attention to appropriate orientation for new personnel, the choices made in creating a curriculum, support for certain types of research, and opportunities in every discipline for ethical reflection. All these provide opportunities for the expression of Catholic identity.

Note

1. *Ex Corde Ecclesiae* (Apostolic Constitution on Catholic Higher Education, Pope Paul II) 1990. *Origins.* Vol. 20, no. 17 (October 4, 1990), pp. 265–76. (Catholic News Service Documentary Service.) "The original was published in Latin by Libreria Editrice Vaticana in 1990. The English version was published by the same source as the Latin original and distributed by the Sacred Congregation for Catholic Education and reprinted by *Origins*." Quote taken from Alice Gallin, OSU, Editor, *American Catholic Higher Education: Essential Documents*, 1967–1990, p. 413. (Notre Dame, IN: University of Notre Dame Press, 1992).

What Is a Great Catholic University?

Richard A. McCormick, S.J. *

What is a great Catholic university? This may seem an otiose question, the type of thing that burned-out emeriti professors eagerly dissect when conversation falls mum at wine and cheeses. It may yet turn out to be that. But I hope not. If we cannot achieve some minimal clarity on the matter, we shall never know what we are to aim at; we shall never know our goal. Without a clear goal, confusion, stumbling, and failure are all but guaranteed. There may be isolated little victories here and there—almost accidental in their occurrence—but there will be no coherent and unifying dynamic that structures policies, shapes decisions, and guides the entire enterprise as a whole. We shall never arrive.

The dangers encountered in trying to answer the question stem from its terms: *great, Catholic,* and *university.* There is the temptation to understand these terms with one-sided, dictated, or inaccurate criteria. For instance, there are those who would interpret *Catholic* in terms of a rigid, narrowly defined orthodoxy, or in terms of the number of sponsoring religious priests and brothers and sisters on campus, or in terms of episcopal and/or Vatican approval. This last criterion was given some recent support in the encyclical *Veritatis Splendor.* In no. 116 we read: "It falls to them [bishops], in communion with the Holy See, both to grant the title *Catholic* to church-related schools, universities, health care facilities and counseling services, and, in cases of serious failure to live up to that title, to take it away."[1] Similarly, it is quite possible to collapse the notion of *university,* especially a great one, into its research component, or its connectedness to the business or professional world, as if ease of entrance into these worlds is synonymous with university excellence.

*Richard A. McCormick, S.J., was the John A. O'Brien Professor of Christian Ethics at the University of Notre Dame in South Bend, Indiana. The article is from Theodore M. Hesburgh, C.S.C., ed., *The Challenge and Promise of a Catholic University,* © 1994 by the University of Notre Dame Press. Used by permission.

perspective or point of view, whether that perspective be religious, political, philosophical, legal, historical, etc.

In the university context, openness concerns above all the search for truth. The American bishops have provided us with a powerful example in the open and revisionary process used in the development of their recent pastoral letters on peace and on the economy. They have welcomed all points of view, even dissenting ones. A similar example should be provided by the Catholic university.

The word *campus* is really the Latin word (*campus*) meaning "field." It designates the arena where armies settled disputes with lance and sword. College campuses exist in part to render such incivility obsolete. The vigorous exchange of ideas by the open-minded in the university setting is the way to reconcile our differences. That is why colleges have campuses, open forums for the discussion and clash of ideas. The word *campus* should stand as a reminder that the clash of swords, the targeting of missiles, and any use of force represent human failure, that vigorous but civil exchange is a form of loyalty to, and protection of, our humanity.

In this respect I should like to note that it always saddens me to meet people thirty to forty years out of college who view the contemporary church and world and their challenges in terms of what they were taught forty years ago by Father *X*. This means that what Father *X* gave them was not *philosophia perennis* but *philosophia paralizans*. To that extent, the university was defective.

6. *Critical capacity.* By *critical capacity* I mean the ability to think through a problem (event, possibility, piece of writing, policy, procedure, etc.), lift up the pros and cons, develop coherent reasons and arguments, and situate one's conclusions (or opinions) within a sufficiently broad context of human and religious values. So often, our convictions, solutions, actions, and policies root in biases, narrow self-interest, cultural distortions, etc., without our ability to recognize these origins. Unless and until these origins are recognized, our ability to think through events clearly is hampered. An excellent university education should leave a student at least several long steps down the road of critical thinking.

7. *Ability to listen.* The ability to listen is an absolute essential for continuing the educational process throughout life. The person who emerges from a truly great Catholic university should have picked up the art of listening because she or he saw it happening on a daily basis for four years on the part of educated and wise professors. I refer to the fact that an outstanding professor necessarily listens: to other professors, to her or his students, to people from other countries and cultures, to those with hands-on experience, etc.

From a student's perspective, one of the most supportive and confidence-building things a professor can do is show the student, by listening, that she respects the student and takes him seriously. In my own doctoral studies, I remember putting a question to the renowned moral theologian Josef Fuchs, S.J. He paused, then stated that my question was an excellent one, that he would think about it and I should too, that then we could discuss it later. Perhaps more than any single event in my graduate studies this incident was educational. In a very practical way it told me that I should trust my insights and have the courage to take my doubts and questions seriously. That taught me a great deal.

This kind of thing should be a daily experience in a fine university. When it is, the products of these universities will be listeners—and learners—in the world they inhabit.

The process of dialogical listening is threatened by authoritarian approaches, especially those that would attempt to stifle dissent. That is the danger in the current ecclesial context. The atmosphere is one of coercion. Elsewhere,[11] I have noted that a coercive atmosphere has the following effects: (1) weakening of the episcopal magisterium; (2) weakening of the papal magisterium; (3) marginalization of theologians; (4) demoralization of priests and other ministers; (5) reduction of the laity; (6) compromise of ministry; (7) loss of the Catholic lesson.

Coercion represents the cessation of the listening process. It represents a practical takeback of Vatican II's assertion: "Let it be recognized that all of the faithful—clerical and lay—possess a lawful freedom of enquiry and of thought, and the freedom to express their minds humbly and courageously about those matters in which they enjoy competence."[12] This affirmative assertion implies that authorities in the church need to listen. A coercive atmosphere takes it back. Where the church should be an exemplar of listening, its actual example moves in a different direction.

8. Willingness to serve. A university education in a Catholic context ought to foster a certain generosity of spirit that seeks opportunities to come to the aid of others in a multiplicity of ways: by education, by defending rights, by relieving suffering, by affecting public policy. This quality is close to the second noted above, sensitivity to justice and injustice, but is much broader and implies more than sensitivity. The Catholic university will foster and deepen this willingness by recognizing and honoring it, by supporting it spiritually and materially, by providing satisfying outlets for its exercise, and by reflecting it in its own structures and priorities.

These, then, are the qualities I would hope to find in the graduate of a great Catholic university: a Catholic vision; sensitivity to justice and injustice; appreciation of, and thirst for, knowledge; facility in spoken and written word; open-mindedness; critical capacity; ability to listen; willingness to serve.

Is this a hopelessly utopian recipe? Possibly. But I cannot see a single item I would remove from the list of qualities that a great Catholic university ought to inculcate. Indeed, if a Catholic university simply omitted or gave up on any one of these qualities, whether by oversight or intent, it would, I think, forfeit its claim to be a great Catholic university.

Two intriguing questions remain: Are there qualities that need to be added to the list? Are there any universities that meet the demands of the list? My mischievous intent in writing this essay was to provoke your entanglement in these questions.

Notes

1. John Paul II, "Veritatis Splendor," *Origins* 23 (1993): 331.
2. Michael J. Himes and Kenneth R. Himes, O.F.M., *Fullness of Faith: The Public Significance of Theology* (Mahwah, N.J.: Paulist Press, 1993), 82. A similar analysis is found in Richard P. McBrien, *Catholicism* (San Francisco: HarperCollins, 1981), 1180. It is developed even more fully in the revised edition of *Catholicism* (1994).
3. Himes and Himes, *Fullness of Faith*, 83.
4. Ibid., 85.
5. Lawrence S. Cunningham, *Sages, Wisdom, and the Catholic Tradition* (Tulsa, OK: University of Tulsa), 7. This is No. 27 of the Warren Lecture Series.
6. "Justice in the World," *Catholic Mind* 64 (1971): 29–42.
7. *Documents of the Thirty-Second General Congregation of the Society of Jesus* (Washington, D.C.: Jesuit Conference, 1975), 26.
8. Ibid., 17.
9. J. A. Plourde, "Making Justice a Reality," *Catholic Mind* 70 (1972): 7.
10. National Conference of Catholic Bishops, *Economic Justice for All* (Washington, D.C.: Author, 1986), ¶ 347.
11. Richard A. McCormick, S.J., and Richard P. McBrien, "Theology as a Public Responsibility," *America* 165 (1991): 187–88.
12. *Documents of Vatican II* (New York: America Press, 1966): 270.

What Is Meant by a "Catholic" University?

Michael J. Lavelle, S.J. *

On August 15, 1990, Pope John Paul II issued *Ex Corde Ecclesiae* ("From the Heart of the Church"), a statement on the relationship between Catholic universities and colleges worldwide and the hierarchical church. In the United States, a committee of bishops has consulted with a group of American Catholic college and university presidents on the practical implementation of this document. Bishop John Leibrecht of Springfield–Cape Girardeau, chairman of the implementation committee, has sent out a set of proposed regulations, on which all Catholic college and university presidents have been asked to comment.

One regulation indicates the various possible types of "Catholicity" of colleges and universities. The rest deal with such topics as an institution's internal review of its Catholicity, concern for promoting the teaching of correct Catholic theology, the authorization of a Catholic professor to teach, and the process of adjudication of disputes that may arise between competent ecclesiastical authorities and a particular college or university.

There are differences of opinion as to the meaning of these regulations and, indeed, as to the advisability of their being promulgated. Both bishops and university officials have concerns about the implementation of these regulations and about their implications for Catholic higher education in the United States.

What is at issue here? All the bishops and presidents are concerned about the future of U.S. Catholic life and faith. These concerns, as they are addressed in the sphere of higher education, may be focused differently by bishops and by presidents.

---

*Michael J. Lavelle, S.J., is president of John Carroll University in Cleveland, Ohio. The article is reprinted with permission of Michael Lavelle and America Press, Inc., 106 West 56th Street, New York, NY 10019. Originally published in *America* February 5, 1994.

Many U.S. Catholic bishops, along with some Vatican officials and the Pope himself, have two worries about Catholic higher education today. The first centers on control of the universities—that is to say, who ultimately determines what is taught and who is hired. Put more directly, who is going to be in charge?

The second anxiety has to do with the institution's Catholicity – its doctrinal purity, the teaching of theology and philosophy, and the Catholic ambiance and character of the school.

These two concerns of the hierarchical church, control of the universities and their Catholicity, are naturally my concerns as well, as president of John Carroll University. They are also concerns of every Catholic college and university president I know.

What, then, do I see as the purpose of Catholic education? I speak now of undergraduate education specifically. Catholic colleges and universities do not aim simply at presenting data, facts, or information to their students. They certainly also wish to provide these students with an environment in which all components of their personalities will be developed—intellect, will, soul, and body. No matter how we wish to explain it, our purpose in undergraduate education is the complete *formation* of young men and women.

This is where the second concern of the Pope and bishops comes in: maintaining the Catholic tradition and ambiance of the school. This is also where the interests of the Pope, the bishops, and Catholic college administrators and faculty again coincide. All these men and women are concerned to maintain and foster the Catholicity of the institutions.

Catholicity aims at the presentation of the Catholic past as it lives in today's world. It also aims to secure the presence on campus of Catholic religious life—through liturgies, retreats, and, more intangibly, the overall character of student life. It is concerned with the availability of counseling and the presentation of such service activities as the Jesuit Volunteer Corps and other volunteer works that traditionally have been connected with Catholic education and social action in the United States.

On a more academic level, for instance, concern for Catholicity would show itself in certain specific courses, seminars, lecture series, and workshops. An example would be the intellectual efforts most schools undertook after the U.S. bishops published their pastoral letters *The Challenge of Peace* (1983)[1] and *Catholic Social Teaching and the U.S. Economy* (1986).[2] We also expect a Catholic institution to have programs dealing with the history of Catholic spirituality. Depending on the founders of a particular school, one could hope for a course linking the traditions of the Jesuits, Dominicans, Benedictines, or Franciscans, for example, with the school's history.

A school may also preserve the Catholic tradition when it offers programs that have historically been of service to the immediate diocese or region in which they are located. Nationally known schools like the University of Notre Dame or Boston College have programs for the development of directors of religious education or summer seminars on religious education that draw participants from around the country.

All these are examples of what I mean by a school in the Catholic tradition. The presidents of Catholic universities consider it their job to maintain and foster the Catholicity of their schools. It is my impression, however, that *Ex Corde Ecclesiae* overemphasizes the issue of jurisdictional control of the schools. This runs the needless risk of pitting the hierarchical church against those who run the colleges and universities.

If we take a look at what these schools are doing today, we find that they share the worry and concern that parents, bishops and the U.S. church as a whole have about the development of Catholicism. For example, each of the 28 U.S. Jesuit colleges and universities has someone on its staff, usually a Jesuit, asking the question, "What is our mission today as a Catholic and a Jesuit school?"

At John Carroll, for example, we have seminars making explicit the Catholic and Jesuit nature of our institution. Other university concerns about our Catholic history and future are expressed in seminars, courses, workshops, general mission statements, and campus ministry and chaplaincy programs.

Recently, the University of Notre Dame issued a statement that looks to the year 2000 and beyond. In it we read of a commitment to the "cultivation of Catholic intellectual life . . . the determination of . . . centers and institutes that have a particular relevance to the service of society and the Church." This statement looks to strengthening the university in its mission both as university and as Catholic. Elsewhere Notre Dame affirms that "the University must pay special attention to the central elements of this religious heritage so that the inevitable demand for change might be seen as an opportunity for greater enrichment and not as a betrayal of a sacred trust." These statements sum up the hopes of all of us.

There is a keen desire to have the universities and colleges transmit and develop our traditions in a way that was not made so explicit 20 or 30 years ago. Perhaps we took for granted at that time that schools were transmitting these traditions. Now, we have become much more explicit in our desire to do so.

As a university tries to maintain itself both as an institution of higher learning and as a Catholic institution of higher learning, there are problems. First, there is the need for a university to be indeed a university—a place where there is freedom for differing and perhaps opposing views to be studied, expressed, and listened to in a charitable manner. This may

ments, and discipline (Canon 205). Other baptized persons are Christians who are not in full communion with the Catholic Church, but who share some communion with Catholics and their church in virtue of what we share in common as Christians. All Christians are called to express their commitment through mission and can collaborate in the mission of Catholic higher education.

For an institution of higher education to be "Catholic" implies a critical mass of people who are Catholics in full communion. What this critical mass is will vary depending on a number of factors. Clearly it is not necessarily the number of clergy or religious, but as their numbers decline the issue of critical mass has come more to the fore. *Ex Corde Ecclesiae* places the critical mass in a majority of the faculty being Catholic (article 4, ¶4). In some circumstances, other factors may be more significant. But provided the critical mass is active, committed, and effective, participation by others (Christians not in full communion and other persons) can enrich the genuine universal (and in that sense "catholic") character of the institution.

In addition to attention to the individuals who make up the community, a Catholic institution will also be marked by its careful implementation of Catholic social teaching about persons. Whatever people do (e.g., their work, occupation, profession) or have (rich, poor), all share a fundamental equality in the dignity of being human persons. Whatever one's role in the church (clergy, religious, lay), all share a fundamental equality in the dignity of being baptized Christians (Canon 208). For an institution of higher education to be Catholic implies a fundamental respect for the dignity of each person (students and faculty, staff and administration), and promoting a deep respect for human dignity among its graduates. Here, indeed, is a benchmark that can be used to evaluate whether the institution shows the effects of being Catholic.

Originally the term "catholic" was used to express that the Church embraces all, in contrast to sects that were exclusive, closed groups. Catholic still means to embrace all persons, with no distinction on the basis of age, race, national origin, or gender. It also implies service to all, so that practical concerns go beyond one's immediate circle and address the needs and concerns of all human persons and of creation itself. For an institution of higher education to be Catholic implies no discrimination, no "glass ceilings," and service to all precisely because the institution is Catholic.

2. Procedures

Given the central importance of personnel to identity, is attention to the institution's Catholic identity significant in procedures for hiring, orienting new personnel, and continuing attention of all personnel? The procedural issue is not whether there can be a religious test on the part of the applicant, but where the authority to hire new personnel is located. In many institutions this has been placed at a departmental or school level, effectively barring other officials of the institution from exercising their legitimate role in assuring the continuation of a Catholic identity among personnel in those fields. Although the department or school can exercise this function, to place the full burden of it there tends to Balkanize the institution precisely in regard to its central identity as a Catholic university. Higher-level academic authorities may well wish to address this procedure if they desire to have an effective voice in the continued Catholic identity of the institution.

Orientation of new personnel and continuing attention to Catholic identity by existing personnel have proven crucial to sustaining a Catholic mission in the health care field. Institutions of higher education are faced with similar challenges, and could learn something from the in-service programs in health care.

Specific to a college or university is the expression of Catholic identity in its curriculum. This is not limited to the importance of courses in philosophy and theology, or the provision for courses of ethical reflection in every field. It is also expressed in the fields an institution chooses to emphasize, the kinds of research it promotes, and the funding it provides for specialized academic efforts even in an interdisciplinary fashion. If there is no difference between the curriculum of any other school and a Catholic institution, where is the Catholic identity? Both the procedures for developing curriculum and the criteria applied to making these decisions are important opportunities for the Catholic identity to express itself.

3. Cautions

Catholic higher education would place itself at serious risk if it were to ignore the two-fold dimension of Catholic identity, inside as well as outside. To rely only on external controls, statements, and boards of trustees could turn an institution into an empty shell in terms of its Catholicity. To attend only to the inside, without regard for the greater church of which Catholics are a part, would deny an equally important dimension of being Catholic.

But the Catholic community must also not be reduced to one element, whether that of the hierarchy, of a religious institute with special ties to the institution, or of a committed laity. Attempts in this regard will equally evacuate the meaning of being Catholic and produce a hollow ring. Neither can theology be made to carry the Catholicity of an institution. This would isolate theology from its true integrating role and fail to appreciate the full meaning of the incarnation.

Academic authorities and hierarchy have a mutual interest in the continued vitality of Catholic higher education. Failure of either side to engage in a continuing constructive dialogue could well spell disaster for one of the Church's major presences in the world of culture. This is just the opposite of what canon law, apostolic constitutions, and episcopal conference ordinances are supposed to be designed to do in promoting Catholic identity.

Leadership and the
Board of Trustees

Introduction
Irene King

This section addresses the moral responsibility inherent in the role of a college or university trustee. The essays share the vision that trustee leadership extends far beyond preserving the financial integrity of an institution—a common misunderstanding of the role of a trustee. The authors challenge universities to charge their boards with responsibility to preserve and articulate the mission, values, and identity of the institution as well.

David Smith in "The Moral Core of Trusteeship" presents a clear vision for trustees, followed by a case study, "Conflicting Basic Duties." The case deals with Catholic University of America and Charles Curran; "the board at Catholic University of America was . . . torn between two foundational and, in themselves, compelling claims: academic freedom and Catholic identity." The case gets to the core of the role of trustees as conservators of the identity and mission of an institution. However, it does not provide an easy answer.

Smith outlines three principles that ought to guide trustee boards:

The fiduciary principle: Smith asserts that trusteeship is distinct from other kinds of fiduciary moral responsibility "by the fact that it is triadic . . . it comprises an entruster, a trustee, and a beneficiary." The trustee is charged by the entruster with the responsibility of governing the institution with "loyalty to the purpose for which the organization was created." Robert Bellah and colleagues refer to this role poetically as a "community of memory." Essentially, the trustee is a conservator of the original vision and objectives of the founders.

The common good principle: The trustee is also called to operate for the common good. Smith rightly anticipates that trustees may often encounter multiple options that might fulfill the vision of the founders. He asks, "Is one purpose as good as another?" In order to prioritize purposes, Smith asserts that trustees operate out of the common good principle – a concept admittedly fraught with ambiguity. Smith offers three questions for trustees to ask in discerning the common good:

- Is the organization's purpose morally worthy?
- Is the organization using morally worthy means?
- Is the organization actually able to accomplish its moral purpose?

The community of interpretation. The trustees are called to be reflective; the board's "major moral responsibility is to establish the identity or vocation of the organization." The peril of any interpretation is always literalism. To avoid this pitfall, Smith calls trustees to develop the "moral imagination, the ability sympathetically to identify with the needs of the beneficiaries or the problems of management." Such virtues are nurtured through the habit of listening. Finding the "right" trustee must take into account both personal attributes and institutional outcomes.

In "Conflicting Basic Duties," Smith presents very instructive guidelines for boards at Catholic colleges and universities, boards intent on preserving and enhancing religious identity in a highly charged area. At Catholic University in the Curran case, "the conflict was agonizing, a situation in which the sponsor's vision and identity conflicted with the identity of the sponsored activity." Indeed, this was a situation only the board could handle, for institutional identity was the issue. In the essay, Smith holds that "the board was obligated to give reasons for its actions that were credible to the Catholic community." He implies that the board did not do so. Nevertheless, Smith does not resolve the case. He notes that "one important contribution of a board as a community of interpretation is that it is a forum in which *conflicting* purposes can responsibly be discussed." The nub of the problem at Catholic University is that the board appears to have acted not for good reasons but with what appeared to be "mindless deference."

In "Centered Pluralism," Bruce Douglass records a collaborative vision and mission statement prepared by Georgetown University that provides a useful model for a community forum the goal of which is discernment of an institution's identity. The statement asserts that "tradition needs to be renewed and articulated in each age of the University's history, and that renewal is our responsibility today."

The identity statement was the year-long work of a broad seminar group of forty campus representatives, with faculty as the core. The goal was to create a report that would stimulate and foster discussion within the campus community about Georgetown's identity. The members of the group were concerned with locating their identity within the context of other Catholic universities and committed to articulating the Jesuit vision for Georgetown.

What emerged was a document that was critical, constructive, and affirming of the institution as it was currently construed. The committee agreed that "the religious vision behind this University is committed to knowledge that frees men and women for a more humane and just world. . . . The religious identity of the institution lies also in the free engagement of the faculty with this identity." These statements led to the characterization of Georgetown's religious identity in terms of centered pluralism, which is "respectful of the diversity that now characterizes this institution and yet convinced that the hard work of articulating an identity informed by our tradition is what will hold us together and enable us to thrive."

There are a multitude of statements that will be helpful to other institutions attempting to undertake similar projects. We advise a careful reading of this document and highlight only some of the more salient points.

The first concerns Georgetown's focus on a holistic approach to its identity. Correctly recognizing that universities are never solely academic entities, the writers affirm that a good university will accept its responsibilities to address the whole person they seek to educate—the religious dimensions, concern for the common good, the importance of participation of all members of the community, educational coherence based upon the institution's identity, and concern for the way members relate to one another.

The document covers six topics:

1. The role of institutional particularity in academic excellence
2. The promise—and shortcomings—of Georgetown's educational offerings
3. The role of Catholic thought and concerns in the University's current research agenda
4. The quality of campus life and its bearing on the University's performance
5. The procedures and policies used in managing the University's affairs and their bearing on its performance
6. The role of institutional particularity in a University dedicated to pluralism

"Integrating Mission into the Life of Institutions" by Mary Braebeck and her colleagues at Boston College presents a model of institutional leadership. Where Smith focused almost exclusively on the role of the trustees, this essay presents a collaborative approach to discerning and implementing institutional identity and mission. The team is comprised of the president, chancellor, and representatives from the schools of law, education, social work, nursing and management, and arts and sciences.

The team began by looking at the historical mission of the College, which stressed providing education to immigrants, commitment to the "action-knowledge link," and obligation to serve others. They continued reflection on all aspects of their educational system through an ongoing seminar format—always with the foundational belief that "working collaboratively makes us stronger."

Most disciplines within universities are autonomous; participants struggled to find creative ways to think in an interdisciplinary way that would allow them to honor the founders' vision for the institution and implement it in a new model true to the founders' intentions. With a vision of collaborative, interdisciplinary work articulated, the seminar team invited students and community members into their conversations. The goal was to create community partnerships that engaged Boston College faculty, students, and administrators in issues of social justice facing the locale where the College resides. The results have been an exciting and creative approach to integrating mission into the academic, social, and spiritual life of the College.

In "Hiring Faculty for Mission: A Case Study of a Department's Search," Father Feeney and his colleagues provide three perspectives on the hiring process at St. Joseph's University in Philadelphia, two from members of search committees and one from a non-Catholic hired by a search committee.

Feeney discusses myriad questions challenging a search committee. There is a desire to hire faculty and staff who support the college mission in an attempt to sustain its distinctive identity. This central concern leads search committees to struggle with such questions as: Will hiring for mission lower the quality of the faculty? Will good candidates be scared away? Will ecumenism or diversity be damaged? Are there legal implications? And how can mission-friendly professors even be identified? What sort of advertisement should be written?

The department met to outline seven guidelines for the search:

1. Institutional tradition urges a particular consideration for Catholics and/or alumni of St. Joseph's or other Jesuit colleges. Such a choice could offer the students identifiable role models of Catholic and Jesuit intellectuals.
2. Acceptable applicants should sympathize with institutional goals.
3. Such sympathy could probably be discerned through the interview process.

4. We would need to determine how our concern would be worded in our advertisement.
5. The advertisement should not put off viable candidates.
6. At issue is an act of departmental will to preserve the sense of institutional tradition.
7. Announcing ourselves as St. Joseph's University in the Jesuit and Catholic tradition would preserve the sense of tradition without eliminating potential candidates from other traditions.

During the interview process, some candidates raised the question of mission themselves. If the candidate did not raise the issue, the committee asked, "Why do you want to come to St. Joseph's University?" Answers ranged from location and size, to a commitment to social justice, a concern for others, and commitment to Jesuit education.

Feeney says, "There was no religious litmus test. . . . We carefully balanced a number of factors—professional, departmental, institutional, collegial, and personal—while never forgetting our mission and identity." The committee ultimately made decisions they were very happy with.

In the follow-up comments to Feeney's report, Owen Gilman as chair of the search committee recalls how a decade ago, when his department had a large number of faculty committed to the Jesuit mission, the idea of mission-friendly faculty was not a driving concern. The department now reflects a rich diversity of perspectives and religious affiliations. Under these changed conditions, the committee considered it important to conduct a search with an eye to mission and Jesuit identity. Still, Gilman states, "We knew all along that we would not compromise on quality, that we would serve the department and St. Joseph's poorly if we sacrificed talent simply to bring in someone who had the right religious credentials."

Jo Alyson Parker was hired by St. Joseph's during a time when the institution was not as concerned with mission and identity. At the time of her interview, she had very little knowledge of the philosophy undergirding Jesuit education. Parker remembers, "I was asked no questions about whether I had any devotion to the mission of the University, and, if I had been, I would not have known how to respond." Her story represents the fact that the lack of prior knowledge or commitment does not prevent the faculty member from becoming a committed and sympathetic member of a mission-oriented institution. Parker remarks how impressive the commitment to mission and the living out of it was to faculty, administration, and students.

When Parker eventually served on a search committee, "mission came up in the interviews not as some sort of religious litmus test, but as a way of informing candidates about the University's strong sense of its identity as an institution in the Jesuit, Catholic tradition and inviting them to discuss how their own 'mission' might correspond." What a wonderful and creative reconceptualizing of the concern for hiring mission-friendly faculty.

Vincent Genovesi, S.J., in "Is Jesuit Education Fulfilling Its Mission?" provides another Jesuit perspective on understanding and integrating the mission and identity of colleges. Genovesi articulates the outcome of a Jesuit education as the nurturing of "twice-converted people." He quotes Arthur Simon, founder of Bread for the World: "They are first converted from the world to Jesus Christ . . . but then they are converted to the world again, to love the world and relate to it, not as they did before, but through the heart and mind of Christ."[1]

Genovesi believes this concept of twice-converted summarizes the Jesuit educational mission: "The mission of the Society today is defined as the service of faith, of which the promotion of justice is an absolute requirement. The service of faith and the promotion of justice . . . cannot be separated from one another. . . . We must . . . prepare all our students effectively to devote themselves to building a more just world and to labor with and for others."

Genovesi affirms that most Jesuit institutions are finding ways to educate their students in "faith-justice," yet such efforts reach only a limited number of students. He fears that we are "simply career-oriented, and we leave unchallenged their desire simply to find a comfortable niche in society." He asserts that we must design curricula that allow for "serious, systematic and sustained reflection [on] the complex ethical questions that they will face in their careers."

Genovesi outlines three responsibilities that Jesuit education must inspire and educate students to meet, outcomes that will enable students to work through faith for justice:

1. *Competence*: Students must graduate with the knowledge and critical thinking skills needed for their field of study.
2. *Conscience*: Students must be challenged to explore ways in which they can use their knowledge base to promote the common good. This implies that students be versed in the skill of moral reasoning and reflection.
3. *Compassion*: Competence in one's field, coupled with a formed conscience, must "be seen and felt in loving hands."

"The Integrity of a Catholic Management Education" by Michael J. Naughton and Thomas A. Bausch poses a question essential to Catholic business programs: "Should managers educated at Catholic universities examine layoffs and plant closures any differently from executives taught at non-Catholic universities?" The historical mission of Catholic schools of management, Naughton and Bausch say, has been "moving an immigrant, blue-collar, inner-city class to a mainstream, white-collar, suburban class." The authors ask a thoughtful question about an unintended consequence of this mission: Did this focus inadvertently teach students to work for purely individualistic aspirations?

Business ethics courses have traditionally served as a corrective for the careerism that may arise in traditional business education. The authors believe, however, that such courses inadequately integrate a Catholic vision or sensibility into business education. They are often an add-on, not a theme that threads its way through all business courses at Catholic institutions.

Naughton and Bausch identify clear, specific contributions of a Catholic-based management education:

> The major contribution of management education in a Catholic university is not in techniques, but in developing criteria of judgment . . . informed with principles such as human dignity, the common good, and the priority of labor . . . greater disciplined sensitivity . . . the virtues of justice, practical wisdom, and solidarity. And it should produce a decision directed toward human development. . . . A driving question in a Catholic educational context is not only "what should I do?" but "who should I become?"

Naughton and Bausch posit four components necessary to Catholic identity in a school of management:

1. *Management as Liberal Learning.* Curricular requirements must integrate management education with the liberal arts; the authors suggest that 60 percent of the course work be in the liberal arts. Such a marriage of the two disciplines will ensure that business students are immersed in the history, philosophy, and religious context that sets the stage for work in the business world.
2. *Management as a Vocation.* Catholic institutions must find ways to connect the work of business with the work and vision of faith. The authors state that "a dialogue between faith and work deepens and widens the criteria of judgment. Work, seen through the eyes of faith, is a participation in God's creation." Catholic social teaching, with its emphasis on the distribution of wealth and worker rights, will no doubt conflict with some of the prevailing wisdom in the business world. These points of conflict must be examined if one is to integrate Catholic social teaching with business education: "To analyze financial, marketing, or production issues from only a quantitative perspective is to slip into an

economism that carries moral implications." The authors view such tensions as areas ripe for research and continued study.

3. *Management as Profession.* Naughton and Bausch are careful to honor management as a profession that has procedures, skills, and techniques that must be taught if students are to succeed in it. While the mastery of such skills is essential, such education must be learned within a Catholic context that values the dignity of the human person and addresses the moral implications of the skills and procedures learned. Management education must "engage the student in the essential dimensions of how their skills and techniques can be ordered toward human development. [If it] fails to engage students in this process, it would be like law schools teaching their students all about the techniques of trying a case but nothing about justice, or medical schools teaching their students all about human anatomy but nothing about care." Recognizing the difficulty of integrating such values into business education, the authors devote a section to "Infusing a Professional Ethic in Functional Courses." Although brief, this section sets an essential premise for business education: "technique as service to human development" rather than instrumentalism.

4. *Management as Service.* Naughton and Bausch pose an essential question to Catholic schools of business and management: "How can a Catholic university, particularly in its management education, serve the community, especially those who are marginalized?" The question gets to the heart of the tension between the core tenets of contemporary business education and Catholic social thought.

The first response of many Catholic colleges and universities is to encourage volunteerism. While such programs are valuable, they do not integrate Catholic social teaching into the heart of Catholic education—its curriculum and research. The authors support a "disciplined concern for the suffering in the United States and the exploited throughout the world" as part of basic Catholic education.

Volunteerism, in contrast, supports a vision of service as "performed in the private time of one's life." In most volunteer work, students do not learn to use their management education and skills in the service of social justice; they spend their time engaged in valuable, but unrelated activities like tutoring children or serving meals to the homeless.

Naughton and Bausch propose a "capstone practicum" for business students that would remedy the failings of a purely volunteer approach to integrating Catholic social teaching into business education. This would place business students in community businesses and nonprofit organiza-

Suppose that I want to do something about education or health care and that I want to have an impact that continues after I am gone. I know that I will not be around to make decisions forever, and I also know that someone must direct choices about policy and personnel if my cause is to prosper. Thus, for a long-range effect, I must designate an individual or a series of individuals to act on my behalf. Moreover, if the particularity of my vision is to be respected—if connection with my wishes is to be preserved—these individuals must have an essential fiduciary duty to my objectives. Unless I have the ability to empower a group of trustees, I will have three choices: personal, private consumption; a one-time gift to persons or individuals in need; or public control of my resources after my death.

Even though the fiduciary principle is well established in legal precedent and historical experience, it is possible to argue that individuals' power to affect society *should* end with their deaths. It is logically possible to design a society in which the hand of the past is powerless; we could confiscate all of an individual's amassed wealth or resources at the time of death. In effect, a state with that policy would be telling its citizens: "Use up what you have; pass on to your heirs whatever you can find a way to shelter; the state—on behalf of the public—reserves the right to determine the utilization of your residual wealth through normal governmental allocation processes." Notice that a society so conceived would give individuals powerful incentives for personal and family consumption. The simple pattern of trusteeship in which a specific donor empowers trustees to manage resources after his or her death, therefore, has a kind of prima facie credibility from the viewpoint of individual freedom and social utility.

This simple model of trusteeship is no abstraction. We see it in the establishment of foundations and colleges, in sponsored hospitals and charities. However, trusteeship also exists in many other complex and important forms. In some cases, the entruster may be a group, and its members may have no money but "only" a sense of mission, as when people band together to form a community service organization. In many self-help organizations and small nonprofits, it may be impossible to distinguish a board from founders, managers, or service providers.

What these groups have in common with the simple model is a sense of organizational dedication to providing a good to needy persons. The fact that this dedication stems from a group, or that members of the group may themselves be beneficiaries, is of secondary importance. We have an identifiable form of trusteeship whenever a cause or mission defines a group's identity, so that we can speak of a duty to beneficiaries that is created and constrained by the organization's sense of purpose or the cause it exists to serve.

On these terms, members of the board of directors of a business corporation are trustees with special fiduciary duties to corporate stockholders. If we grant that they also have duties to *stakeholders* (e.g., employees, residents of the communities in which the firm operates, or consumers), the differences between their role and that of trustees in the nonprofit sector may diminish. Nevertheless, they have an additional duty to make money for investors. Thus, their form of trusteeship differs from that of my main concern.

Another contrast worth noting is that between a trustee and an elected representative. Some writers on politics suggest that a representative (a member of Congress, for example) should be thought of as a trustee in the sense that her or his duties to constituents are clearly limited by the representative's own judgments about what is in the best interest of the state. This conception reflects Edmund Burke's notion of representation, and it remains helpful, but it leaves out of account the responsibilities of elected representatives to take special cognizance of the interests—indeed, the preferences—of their constituents. Those responsibilities are better captured when we think of the representative as a (sometimes instructed) delegate. I contend that trustees must consult the needs of beneficiaries. I do not want to argue for a radical dichotomy between governmental and philanthropic relationships, but there is a difference in priority: A delegate cares for common purpose because of duties to constituents; a trustee cares for beneficiaries' needs because of commitment to the cause or the trust. Trustees are not instructed delegates of their beneficiaries.

Debate over the balance between these principles is as old as the Republic. The issue was joined and partly resolved in 1819 in the U.S. Supreme Court decision in *Dartmouth College v. Woodward*.[7] In that case, the Court dealt with a question of who should govern or control a private university. The controversy over this point was not, in itself, novel. Struggles over who should control a university date back to colonial times in America and at least to the thirteenth century in Europe. Church and state, and various factions within those entities, struggled for control over universities in medieval Europe. Distinctive ways of reconciling these conflicts were worked out at Calvin's Academy in Geneva, at Oxford and Cambridge, and in the various colonial colleges and universities before the American Revolution.

The Dartmouth dispute began in 1815 when the Federalist trustees fired John Wheelock, the president of the college. Wheelock had wanted to reform religious worship and instruction along lines supported by the Jeffersonians. When the Jeffersonians won a majority in the New Hampshire legislature in 1816, they and Governor Plumer felt they had a mandate from the people of the state. They passed legislation designed to ensure state control of the college.[8] Trustee governance, Plumer and Jefferson thought, should not be allowed to stand in the way of the common good. They meant to defend Wheelock, whom they regarded as a social reformer, against a group of trustees who resisted change (in my terms, to insist on a common good or social justice principle as dominant over the fiduciary principle). Jefferson wrote:

> The idea that institutions established for the use of the nation cannot be touched nor modified, even to make them answer their end, because of rights gratuitously supposed in those employed to manage them in trust for the public, may perhaps be a salutary provision against the abuses of a monarch, but is most absurd against the nation itself.[9]

But the Federalist United States Supreme Court "decided the question of Dartmouth College's nature as a private or public corporation by looking to the private source of its original funds rather than to the public purpose for which it was established."[10]

Dartmouth College v. Woodward resolved the conflict between common good and fiduciary principles by suggesting that social space must be left for the latter. The college could not be forced to become strictly public, acting according to legislative or majority perceptions of need. The college's own perceptions and vision rightly were to have a determinative role. But the case tells us only what the college had a right to do, not what it should have done. Were the Jeffersonians right about the proper forms of religious worship in the college? Had the trustees worked out a consistent statement of the college's mission going back to its original objective as a missionary school for Indians? Boards of trustees have the right to make these choices, and they must take the responsibility for making them. It is clear that they have to think about something in addition to founding purpose.

The Common Good Principle

My analysis so far suggests that a key aspect of a trustee's role is loyalty to the cause or purpose for which the organization exists. Actually, I have oversimplified the issue of purpose in several ways. One very important oversimplification arises from the fact that a given founder or organization may appropriately have more than one purpose. Indeed, the only way in which purpose may be unified may be by stating it in such general terms that it becomes vacuous and uncontroversial. Hidden under the platitude are multiple, sometimes conflicting purposes. My whole point is that trustees are responsible for ensuring that these issues get sorted out—and conflicts resolved—in a responsible way.

First, however, it is important to address a second issue raised by the fact of differences between organizational purposes and other ends or goals cherished by the wider society: Is one purpose as good as another? What constraints are imposed on the ends for which trustees may act and on the means they may use to attain those ends?

Broadly speaking, my answer to these questions is that only just ends may be pursued and that only just means may be used in their pursuit. Entrusted organizations are nested in the larger moral matrix of their society. That matrix may be pluralistic and incomplete, but in any given society at any given time the concept of justice is not vacuous. Although we can easily find hard cases about which we disagree, we can meaningfully use words like fairness and honesty. The fiduciary principle does not exempt trustees from these ordinary moral constraints or somehow lift trustees above the basic requirements of social morality.

Trustees must deal honestly with management, professionals, and the general public; they must treat each other and all persons with respect. In particular they are constrained by a principle of universalization understood to imply nondiscrimination. Obviously, institutional choices are inevitably specific: Certain diseases will be attacked, courses taught, grants funded—but the grounds on which these decisions are made must be universalizable. Would the organization consider supporting all applicants who meet a given set of criteria in a given set of circumstances? I do not think this formal principle of justice is sufficient to specify what purposes trustees should select, but it is a necessary condition of any reasonable purpose.

Furthermore, a commitment to honesty means that it is entirely appropriate for the rationale underlying fundamental decisions about institutional policy to be a matter of public record. Sunshine laws are a legitimate constraint not only on publicly funded but also on privately endowed entrusted institutions. I do not draw the conclusion that all meetings and discussions must be open to the public: People do not have to think out loud, and neither do organizations. But openness to public review remains a legitimate requirement for institutions that exist for the public good. The public has a right to know what options were considered and what rationale guided the choices that were made.

I will call the idea that trustee action is rightly constrained by general social morality the *common good principle*. So far I have said something about the ways in which the principle constrains the means trustees may use. But it also imposes constraints on the ends they may pursue.

Inevitably, constituents or beneficiaries will want trustees to do—or to refrain from doing—something that is inconsistent with the organization's purpose. Trustees' sense of mission may conflict with beneficiaries' preferences, and the very fact of trustee power may strike beneficiaries as offensive. Trustee-governed institutions are a potentially patronizing form of benefaction. Is the idea of foundation giving, for example, "an anachronistic throwback to the lord of the manor bestowing his largess on the peasants and knowing what is good for them"?[11] Analogously, is it morally wrong for boards of colleges, hospitals, or seminaries to offer curricula, forms of care, or styles of community that were not chosen by students or patients? Must trustee governance inevitably be intolerably paternalistic? I argue that it need not be, so long as trustees attend to the goals, values, and expectations of the larger community.

I can best explain my reasoning by recalling a distinction used in the medical ethics literature between "soft" and "hard" paternalism. In soft paternalism, the paternalist does patients a favor that they *did not* choose but that he has reason to believe they *would* choose if they could (e.g., insisting on necessary but inevitably painful treatment for patients who plan and hope to continue to live). In hard paternalism, the paternalist provides care that patients actively reject (e.g., ordering blood transfusions for Jehovah's Witnesses). In soft paternalism, the paternalist acts on behalf of the patients' own values; in hard paternalism, the paternalist trumps or overrides not only the patients' expressed choices but their values. *Ceteris paribus,* soft paternalism is easier to justify.[12]

I suggest that trustee-governed institutions are not offensively paternalistic if they act on behalf of values that beneficiaries as members of society can reasonably be assumed to hold (that is, if their actions are analogous to soft paternalism). Thus, there is a limit to the extent that trustee-governed institutions may legitimately depart from the overall values of a society—whether one describes this departure as "leading" or "reactionary." Merrimon Cuninggim's description of foundations is true of all trustee-governed institutions to a degree. They exist "by the grace of the public . . . in order to serve the general welfare or some acceptable portion of it."[13] They "cannot justify their existence unless they accept as their own the virtues and values espoused by the social order of which they are a part."[14] When trustees act according to commonly held values, according to the common good, they are not acting in violation of human dignity.

One important implication of this analysis is that we cannot evaluate the degree to which trustee actions are paternalistic without taking into account the context and community in which those actions are taken. Compliance with the common good principle requires a certain degree of change and adaptation. Actions that seem inappropriately paternalistic in one community at one point in history might be consistent with the values of the same community at another point in history. As long as trustees attend to the ebb and flow of commonly held values within their community, we can say they are acting in conformity with the common good principle.

The evolution of trusteeship in American voluntary hospitals illustrates this point. Hospitals as we know them today are much younger institutions than colleges or universities. At the time of the American Revolution, the most common form of health care institution in this country was the almshouse, supported by church or state and designed to provide shelter and minimal care for the very poor. Because colonial society viewed illness and dependency as indicators of moral failing, almshouses were seen as depositories of the most fallen and despicable. Most physicians believed disease and volition to be linked:

> Certainly, the prostitutes and alcoholics who cluttered the almshouse hospital provided living proof that God chastised sin immediately and inevitably through the body's own mechanisms; one need not await the hereafter to encounter punishment for spiritual transgression.[15]

Hospitals arose as a response to the recognition that some morally worthy citizens nevertheless found themselves in need of institutionalized health care. The preferred site for health care delivery was still the home, but for those morally deserving and respectable individuals who, for whatever reason, could not be nursed at home, the hospital emerged as an alternative to the almshouse.

The hospital had a role in the spiritual and religious—as well as in the purely medical—life of the community. Physical health and moral standing were closely coupled in the minds of philanthropists. To distinguish the hospital from the almshouse, the trustees and founders of voluntary hospitals sought to impose moral standards and moral order within the hospital walls. Only those who could provide a written testimonial to their moral standing were admitted to some hospitals.[16] In other hospitals, as Rosenberg has written, "membership in a particular church, long service to a particular family, an appropriate demeanor—all served to separate the worthy sheep from the almshouse-bound goats."[17] Once admitted, patients were subjected to stringent rules and specific moral codes. They were required to attend religious services and receive religious advisers while refraining from smoking, drinking, swearing, card playing, loud talking, "crowding around the stove," and "impertinence."[18] Trustees served as the keepers of morality, and the rules and practices they instituted reflected a belief in their moral superiority within the hospital social system.

By today's standards, the actions and policies of these trustees epitomize "hard" paternalism. The more difficult question is: How were they regarded at the time? To the extent that trustees' actions reflected a concern for and awareness of commonly held values in early nineteenth-century culture—values in which decent behavior and good health were clearly linked—those actions were within the bounds of the common good principle. I am not claiming that they never crossed this line; the emergence of Catholic, Jewish, and other denominational hospitals makes clear that what must have seemed like a general consensus was in fact a specific set of standards that was offensive to many. But all sides agreed that moral and physical well-being were linked, and trustees understood their roles in terms of a linkage between health, morality, and piety. Patients may have disagreed about what piety entailed but trustees who found it relevant acted according to values their patients would have affirmed.

Obviously, our attitudes toward the sick and our understanding of what it means to help them have changed dramatically in the last century. The practice of medicine has become increasingly specialized and scientific; the hospital has become a citadel of technology. We are a much more diverse people—and much more self-conscious about our diversity—than we were 150 years ago. Hospitals have changed as trustees have adapted to new values and expectations about health care. To operate within the bounds of the common good principle in the 1990s means something very different from complying with this principle in the 1850s.

Requirements of piety would be unthinkable today in an American hospital (but not, perhaps, in other parts of the world), and today it would not be considered objectionably paternalistic for American colleges to require students to study mathematics or for hospitals to offer only conventional Western therapies. Conversely, it would be intolerable for a college to forbid the study of mathematics or for a hospital to offer only nonscientific treatment, no matter how much those practices might reflect the deeply held beliefs of founders, sponsors, or board. Should a hospital or college adopt such a course, we could rightly say, "You have no business imposing your ideals on us."

Thus, trustees should be constrained not only by the organization's donor or purpose but by the society in which they live. They must make their arguments over contested terrain within the moral community of citizens, appealing to considerations and values that the larger community finds plausible. Entrusted institutions should expect to meet indifference and opposition, for value disagreement and inertia constitute part of their reason for being. They do not have to settle hard questions by plebiscite. The expectation of controversy should not, however, give them a blank check. There is such a thing as immoral organizational purpose, and trustees cannot escape responsibility for judgments about the legitimacy of the ends they serve.

Trustee discretion is constrained by reasonable moral perceptions about what people need within the society; this constraint is necessary to redeem trustee governance from the charge of paternalism. My idea is that trustee governance is respectful of human dignity (i.e., is non-paternalistic) so long as trustees act on the basis of generally plausible reasons and perceptions of need. Trustees can and must take controversial stands, but they are not at liberty to set public policy on the basis of a rationale that the larger community cannot comprehend.

Obviously, this sense of the "common good" is an extremely vague concept. Clearly, specification of plausible or reasonable purposes is a difficult task.

Equally obviously, the fact that a board has this kind of constraint is not innocuous. The common good principle, at a minimum, means trustees must be willing to ask (a) if the organization's purpose is morally worthy; (b) if the organization is using morally worthy means; and (c) if the organization is actually able to accomplish its moral purpose. If the answers to any of these questions is negative, the trustees should ensure that action is taken. At the extreme, they should vote to dissolve the organization or resign.

The Community of Interpretation

Although both the common good principle and the fiduciary principle can have radical implications for the organization, they may push in opposite directions. Taken by itself, the fiduciary principle can exclude attention to new problems or action on the basis of improved perceptions of the good. Standing alone, the common good principle waters down the particularity and cutting edge of distinctive insights and points of view.

Thus, as a means of reconciling the demands of fidelity and common good, I propose a further requirement for moral trusteeship—the idea that the trustees should constitute a *community of interpretation*. A board of trustees must be able to interpret an institution's history in order to reconcile its essential distinctive vision with the overall good of society. The trustees must be able to select from the past so as to plan for the future.

Interpretation

Conflicting visions of an organization's mission can arise in a number of ways. As we have seen in the history of hospital trusteeship, the need for interpretation and reconciliation of the fiduciary principle and the common good principle may arise when the values in the organization's community change. In this sense, interpretation serves an adaptive role, bringing the interests and concerns of the founders in line with contemporary values and new understandings of the common good. Alternatively, the need for interpretation may arise from conflicting values embedded in the organization's founding purposes. Some organizations begin with missions and ideals that are inherently at cross-purposes, and trustees of these organizations find themselves constantly faced with the need to bring order out of chaos, to affirm diverse objectives, and to reconcile, interpret, and establish priorities as they shape the organization's mission.

The challenge of interpretation is a standard problem in scriptural religions and law. As in those contexts, the need for interpretation can be denied in either of two ways. One approach is literalism: a strict adherence to the donor's or founder's specific statements, exactly preserving the specific goals and procedures that were put in place at the time of establishment. This strategy simply denies the need to select and interpret. A board that makes this mistake ignores the fact that time changes human needs and human society—a fact that provides part of the rationale for the very existence of a board of trustees. A trustee cannot simply be an animated tool but must be free to judge which actions cohere with the aims of the founders. If those judgments were unnecessary, there would be no need for the trustee.

The polar error from literalism we might call modernism. In a religious context, modernism means ignoring any particularity of the founding documents that is not rationally justifiable in the present. Trustees make this mistake if they forget the specificity of the donor or the purpose for which the organization was created. Modernism is a kind of institutional amnesia, and it is wrong in principle because it betrays the fiduciary constraint that is at the very core of trusteeship.

This point is clear with reference to an organization's charter, a document written in a particular time and place with certain specific problems in mind. As time passes, it retains relevance to institutional policy choices, but at some point and to some degree the specific situation visualized by the founders will no longer be exactly pertinent. The situation will become what the philosopher Josiah Royce called a "lost cause," because the exact configuration of human needs and society will have changed.[19]

At that point the organization either should cease to exist or should transform its purpose into one that both (a) is congruent with the values and vision in place at the founding, and (b) serves a legitimate social purpose. These judgment calls will always be difficult. My claim is that it is helpful to think of the process of reasoning involved as one of interpretation. Sometimes this process may require drastic change, as when the March of Dimes shifted its focus from polio to birth defects; usually the process of adjustment is more subtle. In either case, it is an essential part of the trustees' responsibility.

In many organizations, the natural result of this interpretive process is the mission statement, which at its best relates founding purpose and community need. Mission statements rightly change over time—we should be worried if they do not—and they may have to be fairly general. But a mission statement that is not vitally related to the organization's life, or one that appears wrongheaded or meaningless to the trustees, is a symptom of serious pathology in the organization.

The history of umbrella organizations in America, particularly the United Way, illustrates trustees' critical role in interpreting and balancing a variety of mandates and objectives. In 1877, the Reverend S. H. Gurteen, an Episcopal priest, established the first Charity Organization Society in America in Erie, Pennsylvania. The design was based on the organizations of the same name in London.[20] As Eleanor Brilliant has pointed out, from the start organizations of this sort have embodied two goals or ideals that have not always been easily reconciled:

> On the one hand, there was concern about insuring that the needy were provided with appropriate assistance; on the other hand, charity was not to be given indiscriminately—it was to be given sparingly, and on a scientifically determined basis, avoiding duplication of effort.[21]

The goals were to meet needs and to establish administrative credibility and efficiency.

The United Way, which is the best-known modern version of the umbrella organization in the United States, has at its core a commitment to certain principles and ideas that sometimes conflict and erupt in controversy. On one hand, the United Way has frequently been criticized for its tendency to reinforce the status quo. Critics have found the organization too slow to respond to new kinds of community demands or needs, and they have seen it as a hindrance to the development of new nonprofit organizations. They have argued that all the nonprofits should be allowed to stand on their own, and that individual donors should make choices according to their own conceptions of the good.

On the other hand, organizations that have participated in the community-wide funding process for several years or several decades also have charged the United Way for faltering in its support of community-wide interests and concerns. Needs remain needs even if they are not currently on the minds of citizens. Adding new organizations to the United Way fund drive can threaten the funding of some unglamorous but essential service providers. If the pie remains the same size but is divided among more people, everybody gets less.

Thus, the trustees or board of a local United Way find themselves confronted by a distinctive set of challenges: They are pushed to be responsive to all—or at least many—of the community's pressing needs; they must balance competing visions of communal needs; they must negotiate power struggles among local agencies. To raise funds, they must appeal to a significant fraction of the community's membership. Yet they are responsible for providing resources to meet needs that some members of the local community may not recognize.

At the heart of the United Way is the belief that community-wide support for nonprofit organizations can be maximized as long as individuals believe their donations are being allocated fairly and rationally. The problem arises, of course, when different segments of the community find they have differing views of the outcomes a "rational" system would generate. In practice, the United Way's attempts to construct and preserve a defensible and rational system of allocations have resulted in the perception that the United Way is unresponsive to many community needs. As the United Way has responded to these issues by developing donor option plans that allow contributors to designate recipients of their funds, the idea of "rational allocations"—allocating money based on the analysis and consensus of a cross section of community members—has been compromised.

The need for trustees who can act as an interpretative community is apparent in this situation. The founding purposes of the United Way include ideals that sometimes conflict with each other; United Way trustees must constantly interpret or reinterpret the proper mission of their respective organizations. That is a difficult process, as I shall attempt to illustrate below.

Community

The fact that a board of trustees should see itself as a community of interpretation has very important implications for the life and ethos of the board. It must be a community in which persons can and do talk seriously with each other about organizational purpose. The boardroom should be the place where past and future, particularity and the common good, are reconciled. The board's major role is reflective: Its major moral responsibility is to establish the identity or vocation of the organization.

Thus, a good board will be prepared to do much more than undertake fund-raising or assume responsibility for public relations. I do not mean to suggest that these practical matters are trivial or that organizations can or should be oblivious to them. The relevance of the power to raise or give money may always be important as an asset in a board member. I simply assume the importance of the legal responsibilities of trustees, and my own experience is primarily with organizations in which the "trustee" must do the cleaning, type the correspondence, and raise the money.

My point is that thinking of the trustee's role primarily in economic terms, or as cheap labor, leaves out the very heart of the distinctive contribution that trustees can make. These conceptions are inadequate characterizations of what trusteeship is about. The board must become a reflective community of interpretation.

Indeed, as custodians of mission, trustees may well find themselves dealing with economic issues of a larger scope than those that can be resolved by writing a check. Standing for a truly unpopular mission will result in loss of financial support. Many nonprofit boards find themselves dealing with a hard question: Should we stand for our principles, or compromise and survive to fight another day? In the abstract, this question may be an easy one: The fiduciary principle can never be betrayed. But in the real world the issues are complex; the art lies in discerning the difference between a faithful compromise and a sellout. I do not have a recipe for resolving these problems. For now, my main contention is that engagement with this interpretative problem should be the core of a trustee's concern.

People often disagree about interpretation, and many of us find these disagreements hard to live with. The issues seem intractable or amorphous; resolving them takes time; we often find ourselves convinced that an alternative interpretation has no credibility whatsoever. It is natural for groups of persons to respond to this situation by avoiding discussion of mission, dodging fundamental questions of purpose, or delegating resolution of these troublesome issues.

These strategies are not necessarily and always wrong; anyone who (like the author) has a low tolerance for interminable discussion and endless meetings will sympathize. But if a group of people is to call itself a board, it *must* be prepared to take the time to engage in the discussion that is an inseparable part of this interpretative task. That is what it means to *be* a board.

In many organizations, the nominal or putative board may be distinguished from the "real" board, which may be an executive committee or some other group of players whose power is not publicly acknowledged. Those arrangements usually reflect problems with both the real and the nominal board. The gulf between them is symptomatic of an organizational pathology. The core of that pathology is failure to realize that if it is to play its fundamental role in organizational self-definition, the board must be a *community*. It must have developed the habit of and procedures for talking together about issues of institutional mission and purpose. A board too large or too small to play this role is in trouble, as is one whose members are chosen in ways that guarantee they will be unable to work together. A desirable board culture will have a tradition of open discussion of the most fundamental issues. Optimal board leadership will ensure that this discussion is friendly and candid, and that it comes to closure in a reasonable period of time.

Procedural Issues

An important set of problems confronts a board of trustees as it develops its own distinctive identity and mode of work.[22] One of these problems concerns relationships with the community outside the organization. Some of the best literature on trusteeship calls special attention to the role of the trustees as ambassadors or "boundary spanners"[23] between the organization and the wider society. This function is obviously important, but if the board is simply an agent of the organization's management, it has been disfranchised as a community of interpretation. Among other consequences, this disfranchisement will greatly weaken the board as it tries to perform necessary boundary-spanning functions.

At any rate, trustees must set foreign policy. Any organization must deal with other organizations: groups to which it makes referrals, groups that help it raise money, groups that determine public policies that affect it. These relationships inevitably bear on the trustees' interpretative function because they are important elements of the world in which the entrusted organization must live and work.

A second category of trustee relationships has to do with the rest of the organization. In particular, trustees must have a good and supportive relationship with the chief executive officer of the organization they govern. There is much truth in the old saw that choosing the CEO is the most important thing that trustees do, but it should not be all they do. Further, the kind of support the CEO most needs from them is the support of persons willing to identify with the organization, to monitor its mission, and to assess the needs it claims to be meeting. In some contexts, it may be important to maintain a sense of community between board and staff by retaining some "inside directors" (staff members) on the board.

The crucial balance to be struck in these situations concerns perspective and imagination. On the one hand, preservation of trustees' autonomous perspective may mean that they must maintain some distance from others within the organization (e.g., the founder, the founder's family, or the management of the religious or business organization that provides the resources on which the trustees rely). Without some outsider perspective, it may be impossible for the trustees to be faithful to the core intention of the donor or founding group or to the human needs they meant to address.

Trustees also must be able to distance themselves from the beneficiaries of the organization's services. If trusteeship is understood as representation, it is representation of a particular kind in which duties to people who elected or chose the trustee are qualified by a commitment to organizational purpose. I would not go as far as Hannah Pitkin, who has argued, "Accountability may be an important part of trusteeship, but accountability to the beneficiary of the trust is no part of it."[24] However, I do contend that *trusteeship* has disappeared when trustees think of themselves simply as instructed delegates of voters, management, or appointing bodies. Trustees must have more discretionary authority than some representatives, and the question of how trustees are chosen must be separated from the question of their responsibilities.

On the other hand, a crucial virtue for trustees is moral imagination, the ability sympathetically to identify with the needs of beneficiaries or the problems of management. Identification is greatly helped if the board develops a habit of listening. If a board is to reconcile institutional particularity and the common good, it must be informed: It must listen to beneficiaries and organizational staff, and to analysts of its environment. As they listen, board members should not be excessively guarded; they should allow their value commitments and uncertainties to show, for honest grappling with hard problems in good faith is most likely to engender trust and nurture a sense of community.[25]

Inevitably this discussion brings up a third issue: How should board members be chosen? Who should sit on a board? I have no stock answer to these very important questions; my instinct is to be pragmatic about selection processes, favoring those that seem likely to produce the best board members. That outcome will require very different processes for different organizations in different contexts. It is a bad mistake, I think, to begin with an abstract definition of "the right" process and then define anyone it produces as an adequate trustee. To the contrary, we should begin with the outcome we want—a trustee who will be a good member of a community of interpretation—and ask: How are we likely to get that sort of person?

On the whole, my impression is that we undervalue subject matter expertise and overvalue social standing or connections in our choices of trustees. Public credibility is an essential asset in a board member, but even a small town may have many publics, and knowledge of the industry is vital, so long as it is combined with perspective. We find too few faculty from other universities on university boards; too few physicians from other hospitals on the hospital board. We find ourselves opting for selection processes that give us no read on the caliber of contribution someone will make to board discussion.

These are little more than impressions. The main point is simple: The process used for selecting board members should be one that will produce knowledgeable persons who possess what the board needs to determine its mission—good members of a community of interpretation.

Conclusion

Fidelity to a cause, commitment to the common good, willingness to become part of a community of interpretation—these should direct the action of trustees. These ideas are not particularly novel. They amount to an attempt to distill some general principles from the history of trustee-governed institutions in American democratic society. I do not think that lack of novelty means that the principles are vapid, however. In setting the terms of discussion, they guarantee that certain items must appear on the agenda, and they rule out some options. I need to say more about the difficulties of specifying organizational mission, and about organizations committed to conflicting purposes; I want to discuss the relationship between the board and the rest of an organization, and the key virtues of trustees.

Notes

1. See, for example, Walter W. Powell, ed., *The Nonprofit Sector: A Research Handbook* (New Haven, CT: Yale University Press, 1987); Richard P. Chait, ed., *Trustee Responsibility for Academic Affairs* (Washington, D.C.: Association of Governing Boards of Universities and Colleges, 1984); Richard P. Chait, Thomas P. Holland, and Barbara E. Taylor, *The Effective Board of Trustees* (New York: American Council of Education/Macmillan, 1991), Clark Kerr and Marian L. Gade, *The Guardians: Boards of Trustees of American Colleges and Universities—What They Do and How Well They Do It* (Washington, D.C.: Association of Governing Boards of Universities and Colleges, 1989); and Miriam Mason Wood, *Trusteeship in the Private College* (Baltimore, MD: Johns Hopkins University Press, 1985).

2. H. Hansmann, "Economic Theories of Nonprofit Organizations," in W. W. Powell, ed., *The Nonprofit Sector* (New Haven, CT: Yale University Press, 1987), 28.

3. Lester M. Salamon, "Partners in the Public Service: The Scope and Theory of Government–Nonprofit Relations," in W. W. Powell, ed., *The Nonprofit Sector* (New Haven, CT: Yale University Press, 1987).

4. Richard Fraher, "The Historical Origins of Trusteeship and Charitable Foundations," unpublished paper presented at Poynter Center seminar on the duties of trustees, Bloomington, IN, February 16, 1989.

5. Robert N. Bellah et al., *Habits of the Heart: Individualism and Commitment in American Life* (Berkeley: University of California Press, 1985), 152–53.

6. John D. and Catherine T. MacArthur Foundation, "Facts about the John D. and Catherine T. MacArthur Foundation" (Chicago: n.d.).

7. *Dartmouth College v. Woodward,* 4 Wheaton 518 (1819).

8. See Leonard W. Levy, "*Dartmouth College v. Woodward,*" in Leonard W. Levy, Kenneth Karst, and Dennis Mahoney, *Encyclopedia of the American Constitution* (New York: Collier Macmillan, 1986), I, 537–39.

9. Andrew W. Lipscomb, ed., *The Writings of Thomas Jefferson,* Monticello Edition (Washington, DC: no publisher, 1904), XV, 46–47, as cited in Jurgen Herbst, *From Crisis to Crisis: American College Government 1636–1819* (Cambridge, MA: Harvard University Press, 1982), 236.

10. Herbst, *From Crisis to Crisis,* 234.

11. Merrimon Cuninggim, *Private Money and Public Service* (New York: McGraw-Hill, 1972), 78.

12. Formulation of the distinction is taken from James F. Childress, *Who Should Decide? Paternalism in Health Care* (New York: Oxford University Press, 1982).

13. Cuninggim, *Private Money,* 253.

14. Ibid., 254.

15. Charles E. Rosenberg, *The Care of Strangers* (New York: Basic Books, 1987), 17.

16. Ibid., 19.

17. Ibid., 24.

18. Ibid., 35.

19. Josiah Royce, "The Philosophy of Loyalty," in John D. McDermott, ed., *The Basic Writings of Josiah Royce* (Chicago: University of Chicago Press, 1969), II, 965–69.

20. Eleanor L. Brilliant, *The United Way: Dilemmas of Organized Charity* (New York: Columbia University Press, 1990), 18.

21. Ibid., 18–19.

22. See Wood, *Trusteeship in the Private College,* and Chait, ed., *Trustee Responsibility for Academic Affairs.*

23. Melissa Middleton, "Nonprofit Boards of Directors: Beyond the Govern-

ment Function," in W.W. Powell, ed., *The Nonprofit Sector* (New Haven, CT: Yale University Press, 1987), 129.

24. Hannah Pitkin, *The Concept of Representation* (Berkeley: University of California Press, 1967), 129.

25. Niklas Luhmann, *Trust and Power* (New York: John Wiley, 1979), 62.

Conflicting Basic Duties
David H. Smith*

Trustees may be confronted with deeply conflicting duties. Contradictions at the core of their organization's mission may become obvious only in particular times and places; they may arise as trustees reinterpret institutional mission to forge a new identity; they may reveal deep conflicts between the vision of the world at the heart of the organization and that of the larger society. On the whole, I will argue for a strategy of accommodation and compromise within some specific parameters.

It will be most helpful to begin with a situation in which the conflict was agonizing, a situation in which the sponsor's vision and identity conflicted with the identity of the sponsored activity. In this kind of conflict, a board's resources and integrity are tested most severely. Other governance mechanisms can handle everything else, including financial integrity. But an institutional identity crisis demands a board habituated to reflection and accountability. It is very easy for the board to surrender to one or another of the conflicting purposes; it is also easy to duck the issues. Trusteeship requires finding a compromise that can be embraced with integrity.

Catholic University of America
and Charles Curran

Finding its own proper vocation can be a serious challenge for a board, but the task can be greatly complicated in a climate of legitimate un-

*David H. Smith is director of the Poynter Center for the Study of Ethics and American Institutions and professor of religious studies, Indiana University, Bloomington. Reprinted from David H. Smith, *Entrusted: The Moral Responsibilities of Trusteeship* (Indiana University Press, 1995) with the permission of David H. Smith and Indiana University Press, 601 N. Morton Street, Bloomington, Indiana 47404.

certainty about the objectives of the organization, or if the organization has two objectives that push in conflicting directions. Some of the old moralists called the first of these issues the problem of *doubt*; it occurred when clear guidance or precedents were lacking. The second they called the problem of *perplexity*; in this technical sense, an individual or group is perplexed when clearly relevant precedents or principles exist but they pull in opposite directions. A structured moral dilemma exists.[1] The board at Catholic University of America (CUA) was perplexed, torn between two foundational and, in themselves, compelling claims.

Charles Curran is an extremely well-known Roman Catholic moral theologian who began teaching at CUA in 1965. During the late 1960s, Curran's comparatively liberal views on sexual ethics became a major focus of controversy at CUA and indeed in American Roman Catholicism. (He opposes universal bans on artificial contraception, on masturbation, and on homosexual acts.) The issue first arose in 1967 when the CUA trustees voted not to renew his contract; the theology faculty rallied behind Curran, a strike was called, and the university was effectively shut down. Some members of the College of Cardinals rose to Curran's defense. The trustees changed their minds and offered him a new contract with promotion. A year later, Curran rejected portions of *Humanae Vitae*, the papal encyclical on birth control[2]; his stance led to a second unsuccessful attempt to remove him from the faculty.

Partly in response to these events, CUA reformed its policies to clarify and reaffirm its identity as an American research university; still, it had been chartered by the Pope in the last century, maintained ecclesiastical faculties, and continued the tradition of having American members of the College of Cardinals serve on its board of trustees. In fact, the university's bylaws stipulate that the forty-member elected board should be composed of twenty lay and twenty clerical representatives, and that sixteen of the twenty clergy must be members of the National Conference of Catholic Bishops.[3] Of special relevance is the fact that members of the ecclesiastical faculties must have a "canonical mission" from the ex officio chancellor of the university, who is the Archbishop of Washington, D.C. In effect, the canonical mission is a license that certifies that the faculty member can "teach in the name of the Church."[4]

A popular teacher and prolific author, Curran was rapidly promoted and by 1971 was tenured, but controversies over his opinions on some church teachings continued. His high profile made him a natural target for those whose theology, ethics, or views on moral questions were more conservative. The Vatican officials responsible for oversight of doctrinal orthodoxy, the Sacred Congregation for the Doctrine of the Faith,[5] opened a dossier on his work, and speculation continued for decades within Catholicism and among observers of the Catholic scene about whether, when, or how he would be disciplined.

The Sacred Congregation finally announced the conclusions of its investigation of Curran in the summer of 1986. Nine months earlier, its head, Joseph Cardinal Ratzinger, had informed Curran of its conclusions and urged him to reconsider his views. While on a trip to Rome, James Cardinal Hickey, Archbishop of Washington and ex officio chancellor of CUA, attempted a reconciliation; Curran later flew to Rome to attempt to work out "a compromise whereby he [Curran] would continue to teach moral theology but not in the field of sexual ethics."[6] The compromise was rejected; in July 1986 Ratzinger wrote to Curran: "[T]he authorities of the Church cannot allow the present situation to continue in which the inherent contradiction is prolonged that one who is to teach in the name of the Church in fact denies her teaching."[7]

The letter was sent to Hickey, who held it for three weeks while Curran was on vacation. Hickey and CUA's board had some difficult choices to make. The core issue was simple enough. As devout members of the Roman Catholic Church, they were bound by its processes and procedures; those procedures had clearly produced a verdict. But the board was also responsible for the identity of an American university, and American universities have historic and plausible commitments to academic freedom. Which master did they serve?

In the event, when Chancellor Hickey presented this letter to Curran he offered his own conclusion that the Sacred Congregation's statement—which had been approved by the Pope—was "incontrovertible proof that you can no longer exercise the function of a Professor of Catholic Theology" at CUA. He informed Curran that he was "initiating the withdrawal" of Curran's canonical mission.[8] The chancellor suspended Curran, and the president canceled his courses.

At this point, CUA's Academic Senate and, more importantly for our purposes, the board entered the fray. An ad hoc committee of the Academic Senate held hearings on the case. They concluded that the chancellor was wrong to determine that Cardinal Ratzinger's letter from Rome was "directly and immediately controlling"[9]; for them, the question of church authority was more complex. They thought arguments against the Sacred Congregation might be advanced in good faith, and that withdrawal of the canonical mission would compromise both Curran's tenure and CUA's academic mission. They recommended a compromise in which Curran's canonical mission could be withdrawn if he were to remain able to teach theology, ideally in the ecclesiastical School of Theology.[10]

Informed by this committee's report, the chancellor and the president and—after hearing presentations from Curran and his attorney—the board accepted the senate committee's compromise recommendation in part. They decided that Curran's canonical mission should be immediately withdrawn, but they instructed the president to find an alternative teaching slot for Curran "within an area of his professional competence."[11] The senate committee strongly endorsed the idea of finding a spot outside the ecclesiastical faculties for Curran, but the committee did not want the canonical mission withdrawn until that alternative spot had been found. The committee chair argued that "The statement of Cardinal Ratzinger . . . is not controlling with respect to Professor Curran's ability to teach in any department outside an Ecclesiastical Faculty. In such departments the University must be guided by the American norms of academic freedom and tenure."[12]

Attempts to work out this compromise failed. Curran's competence clearly was in theology, even if his courses were listed under some other rubric. Curran could not pretend that he was not a theologian, and the CUA administration found the device of a self-proclaimed theologian outside the ecclesiastical faculties to be unacceptable. Curran resigned; he has subsequently held several major academic appointments.

The fundamental conflict raised by this history is reflected in the fact that two responsible and serious studies reach opposite conclusions. The American Association of University Professors, on whose thorough report I have relied, concluded that CUA had in effect "deprived [Curran] . . . of his tenure without due process . . . [and] violated Professor Curran's academic freedom" and that the board, in particular, had failed "to exercise their responsibility to protect the university's autonomy and the academic freedom of the faculty."[13]

In contrast, the judge who wrote the decision in the civil suit brought by Professor Curran found in favor of the university's position. He defined the issue not as one individual's academic freedom, but rather as the freedom of an institution to define its own identity. A faculty contract is set in terms of reasonableness, Judge Weisberg argued, and Professor Curran "could not reasonably have expected that the University would defy a definitive judgment of the Holy See that he was 'unsuitable' and 'ineligible' to teach Catholic Theology."[14] CUA, the judge continued, was "bound" to "accept the declaration" of the Vatican "as a matter of religious conviction and pursuant to its long-standing, unique and freely chosen special relationship with the Holy See."[15] It "could not have given up its right to accept and act upon definitive judgments of the Holy See in its dealings with Professor Curran unless it did so explicitly, which it certainly did not do."[16] The court found for the university, against Curran.

Fidelity versus the Common Good

My way of sorting out this conflict is to say that the CUA board was caught between the demands of the fiduciary principle, which push it to accept direction from the Vatican, and those of the common good, which entail some agreements about the goods sought by and the demands of justice in higher education. CUA has an identity as a part of the Roman Catholic Church, and it also has an identity within American higher education. The sometimes uneasy relationship between these two ways of understanding itself made the board's task of acting as an interpretative community particularly difficult.

The arguments in favor of the fiduciary principle are particularly strong in this case. If religiously related higher education is to have any integrity at all, the board must have the liberty to define the institution's identity, which means establishing criteria for eligibility to serve on its faculty. A Jewish, Protestant, or Muslim school, as well as a Catholic one, must be able to define the context in which instruction will be conducted. The fact that some members of the faculty, others in the religious community, or the general public, do not agree with those terms—or do not share the school's particular vision of the proper content and function of higher education—could override the fiduciary principle only if the particular college or university were the only source of the goods that higher education can provide.

That is not the case at CUA. Despite its special relationship to the Holy See, its degrees do not open even Roman Catholic doors that cannot be entered some other way. Many other colleges and universities, including Catholic ones, exist in Washington, D.C., and the general area. These considerations suggest the difficulty of denying the university's right to make up its own mind on the issue; it has rights of religious liberty.

On the other hand, identifying oneself with the common purpose of higher education comes at a price. The Catholic University of America is an American university, entitled to the recognition, privileges, and resources of the sort accorded to other American universities, including public financial resources. In *Tilton et al. v. Richardson*,[17] the United States Supreme Court sanctioned federal assistance to Catholic colleges on the grounds that they, in contrast to Catholic elementary and secondary schools, respected academic freedom and were not designed for purposes of indoctrination. Were the Curran case to lead the court to conclude that this distinction is one without a difference, all federal funding for Catholic higher education might be jeopardized.

CUA, with its pontifical charter and historically special relationship to the Vatican, might seem to be an exceptional case that raises unique problems. That is true to an extent, but Canon 812 in the 1983 revision of the Code of Canon Law gives local bishops authority over appointment of theologians to faculties in their dioceses. Should this authority be exercised, as it has *not* been in the Curran case, the problem of nonacademic control over faculty appointments would recur throughout American Catholic higher education. The very passage of the canon (over the objections of leaders of American Catholic higher education) creates a serious problem.

In principle, this conflict between religious purpose and academic self-understanding or autonomy could be disastrous for American higher education. The issues are clearest for sponsored (usually religiously sponsored) higher education. The right of groups to sponsor colleges and universities, and to shape their lives and mission to particular ends, has been asserted since colonial times and, as we saw in the preceding chapter, was established in the nineteenth century by the Dartmouth College case. On the other hand, members of an academic community may learn that ideas of the sponsor are wrong, imprecise, misleading, or destructive of character. The college's essential commitment to understanding means that those ideas must be discussed inside and outside the classroom.

Thus we have a first-level issue: How can the maintenance of a distinctive institutional identity be reconciled with the demands of a more broadly held value such as academic freedom?[18] This question may well turn into a second-level issue: a debate over the requirements of institutional identity. What does being a Catholic—or Jewish, or Presbyterian—university require?[19]

As they negotiate compromises at the first level, trustees must realize that the demands of both fidelity and the common good—in this case, freedom of academic inquiry—are legitimate. Sponsorship of an academic institution entails giving up something, namely the right to act in ways contradictory to the institution's identity as an institution of higher education. If the sponsor means to maintain an American college or university, it must recognize the rules of the game in which it has chosen to play. The owner of a baseball team cannot unilaterally declare that for his players four strikes are required for a strikeout. Sponsored higher education cannot both claim the rights and privileges the community offers to an academic institution because of its commitment to certain values and violate the community's accepted standards derived from those values. Rights entail responsibilities.

That does not mean that sponsored higher education cannot maintain a vital religious affiliation through elective course offerings, opportunities for religious worship, and sustenance of a campus culture with a distinctive identity. It may even use religious affiliation or religious views as criteria in making some appointments. At this point, the requirements of faithful representation of the tradition or sponsor are likely to come up. No one disputed that Curran taught Catholic moral theology; there were harder questions. Did he in some way distort the tradition? Could he legitimately claim that the views he defended were Catholic views? What, in fact, are the requirements of the fidelity principle?

Catholicism has a distinctive, comparatively clear mechanism and set of procedures for settling these issues. Part of Curran's strategy was to insist that the real issue was the adequacy of those procedures, i.e., to deny that judgments of the Sacred Congregation were controlling for Catholic consciences or institutions. (In religious communities with less formalized procedures, the distinction between procedural and substantive issues may be less clear.) Whatever the procedures, however, the possibility of conflict between the commitments of an institution and those of the larger society in which it operates remains.

A sponsored college or university confronts important constraints on its actions when it confronts one of those conflicts. It should not pretend to be something that it is not. It cannot advertise a position as if orthodoxy were irrelevant to an appointment when it is in fact central. It cannot constrain the honesty or quest for understanding of its students and faculty. If it takes such actions, it can no longer claim to be an American institution of higher education entitled to the benefits and privileges that college or university status entails.

These ideas can be generalized. If the rationale for trusteeship I have offered means anything at all, it means that the trustees of a private sector institution may take a stand in a social controversy and let that stance determine institutional policy. The hard question is what limits, if any, should be imposed on this organizational freedom.

Consider two very different examples in which freedom might be limited:

1. An organization dedicated to causes the reader must regard as unjust, such as mandatory infanticide of all impaired newborns or legally mandated racial segregation; and
2. An organization with a particular religious or other history and identity, which de facto, and perhaps despite its endeavors, finds that a diverse group of citizens depends on it to provide some essential social good such as education or health care.

In either organization, how much latitude should the trustees have?

In assessing the first type of organization, we must distinguish advocacy from action. Infanticide and racial segregation are issues on which our society has come to moral closure, and our consensus is reflected in our laws. Thus, our commitment to pluralism does not mean that trustees of an organization favoring legal segregation may themselves run a segregated institution.[20] On these issues, as on the importance of freedom of inquiry within the university, we have drawn a line; we have concluded that entrusting people with resources to act on those interdicted ends would be wrong.

On the other hand, we allow advocacy of illegal purposes. Because, on my terms, the fact of pluralism strengthens the argument for trusteeship in the nonprofit sector, it would be inconsistent to oppose the freedom of a nonprofit organization governed by trustees to advocate causes, however repugnant the common morality may find them.

We face a somewhat different situation in Case 2 (the dominant organization). Here the issue can arise even if the most fundamental requirements of justice are not violated; at stake may be two acceptable but radically conflicting visions of the good. The question is, "Whose values?" Case 2 raises the issue of paternalism that is always in the background with trustee governance. Should trustees be guided by fidelity to mission or act according to standards supported by their beneficiaries? Their options seem to be betrayal or disrespect.

My suggestion about these difficult situations is that trustees should begin with their understanding of the fiduciary principle and then ask about the justifiability of its implications in terms of values shared with the wider community. It is essential to distinguish among purposes that can be justified more or less well. For example, a religiously sponsored college or hospital must take seriously the mission of its sponsor, but it is also a *hospital* or *college* with a broader dependent clientele that properly expects it to provide health care or educational services. Persons who depend on these services have no right to ask the organization to betray its purposes or surrender its principles. However, insofar as the larger community depends on it for provision of services, the organization must make the case for its controversial policies in the public forum. A policy that departs from a common moral consensus is justified to the extent that case is plausible.

I have tried to illustrate the implications of this idea for the CUA board. To take another example, albeit too briefly for the stakes involved, consider a religiously sponsored hospital in which the sponsor's values impose some restrictions on the medical procedures that can be performed. A clear case is abortion, which is ruled out not only by Roman Catholic theology but by the convictions of Orthodox Judaism as well as those of some Protestant groups. In this situation, the institution faces an obvious and serious problem of hypocrisy if its practices are not coherent with its professed mission.

My inference is that the sponsored hospital's distinctive mission or vocation should limit the services it provides, *so long as they are not generally perceived to be health care necessities.* If services are perceived to be necessities, then the hospital must provide them or give up the social privileges that come with being denominated a hospital (tax exemption, receipt of public funds in payment, etc.). I define a necessity as something for which a generally persuasive public argument can be made. Thus, a hospital that hopes to receive public funds in the United States today must perform hysterectomies, tubal ligations, and autopsies, because there is agreement in the common morality about the fact that those services are medical necessities. But it need not perform abortions, because the morality of abortion is seriously contested terrain in our society.

Obviously, this formula is not a magical device for resolving conflict. It is a rejection of extremes and a call to conversation. Distinctive institutional identity and the fiduciary principle must be allowed some social space, but the standards of the society impose limits. As the Curran case shows, identifying those limits is a complex business that places great demands on a community. I now turn to those issues of process.

Community of Interpretation

I believe that one primary reason for having a board of trustees is the need to maintain a group of persons who are responsible for ongoing conversation about the hard issues of institutional identity. I also believe that board discussions should be open and that boards are well advised to share authority. The board must establish internal and external legitimacy; in the case of CUA that means it must be in real community with administration, students, faculty, and the American Catholic community. The CUA board seems to have maintained a good relationship with the administration, but what about faculty and students? The results of negotiations with the Academic Senate are not encouraging on that score.

At least as much to the point is the board's relationship to the wider Catholic community in the United States. Let us assume for purposes of argument that this question is strictly limited to CUA's *religious* identity—bracketing for a moment the *academic* identity issues. On this question, the board's public statements simply announce the conclusion that the Sacred Congregation's judgment settles the issue. But the conclusion is in no way obvious. The exact scope and extent of the power of the Holy See has been the major subject of contention within Roman Catholicism since the second Vatican Council of the mid-1960s. The notion that a papal fiat can legitimately compel all kinds of behavior by people all over the world is a figment of the non-Catholic imagination. On a daily basis, bishops, parishes, and schools have been coming to terms with the issue of authority for at least twenty-five years. They have worked out solutions that range from strict conformity with official teaching through benign neglect to open disagreement. One cannot simply wave a papal charter and dismiss this issue. CUA's trustees were forced to take a stand on the most fundamental issue in contemporary Catholicism: the locus and scope of authority in the Church.

In an interesting discussion occasioned by the Curran case, Joseph Komonchak observed that authority is power made legitimate by the "capacity" to give reasons bearing on a group's common purposes. Actual reasons need not always be forthcoming, but authority, he suggests, is trustworthiness that rests on a habit or history of producing credible reasons.[21] The Church, Komonchak concedes, must claim teaching authority because "Integrity of faith is to the church what territorial integrity is to a nation,"[22] but Church teaching is not exempt from the "logic of authority," i.e., the requirement of reasonableness or reference to a "set of meanings, truths and values which define the particular social body within which authority is functioning."[23]

The trustees in fact took a clear stance on the authority question. As Judge Weisberg pointed out, there is nothing surprising or unpredictable about the way the CUA board decided or about the substance of its decision.[24] Curran's "evidence describes the University he wanted to work for, maybe even the one he thought he was working for, but not the one with which he contracted."[25] The board's sense of its own identity and purpose was clearly expressed. It spoke consistently with one important—perhaps the most important—voice in the chorus that makes up Catholic identity, and in particular the identity of CUA.

Those standards may be adequate legally, but they are inadequate morally. To be a true community of interpretation, the board was obligated to give reasons for its actions that were credible to the Catholic community. It had to confront the issue of what it means to be a faithfully Catholic university. The alternative is what I have called trustee fundamentalism: failure to see that an important ongoing task of the trustees is interpreting the meaning of the founding documents and purpose in the present.

The CUA board must maintain itself as a community of reasonableness with reference to shared meanings in at least three constituencies: the CUA faculty and students, the wider Catholic community, and American higher education. If the board's legal authority is to be seen as morally legitimate in those contexts, it must appeal to meanings and values shared within those communities. The contexts are diverse, and disagreements can be assumed. The CUA board members could not find, and need not have tried to find, a position that would please everyone. But they needed to work at understanding and taking seriously these constituencies, and the process should have been open enough to reveal real reasoning and argument. About the only thing that everyone is certain to perceive as *un*-reasonable is an unexplained act of—or deference to—power.

I do not mean to argue that CUA's board should have *ignored* the papal charter or the judgments of the Sacred Congregation; they are certainly pertinent. I mean only to say that if they are treated simply as controlling, then the sphere of judgment, or the capacity to interpret, has been removed from the trustees, who ultimately become irrelevant. In fact, in the 1968 debate over *Humanae Vitae* the board appeared to assume more responsibility, accepting in toto a recommendation of a faculty committee that challenged the Vatican.[26] Whatever the reasons, the appearance, if not the reality, was different in the 1980s. If the board is unwilling to take responsibility for independent judgment, it becomes a facade behind which the real power operates.

Perhaps the CUA board discussed the issue of authority, resolved the issue to its own satisfaction, and then presented a united front to the public. If so, that was a procedural decision of great importance, for it offered the *appearance* of thoughtless obedience to a controversial conclusion. Perceived injustice may be worse if it is seen as delivered without accountability. A hard call is easier to accept if it is clear that all options have been considered.

So long as a pluralistic society carries pluralism to the point that it allows sponsored higher education, problems like the Curran case will recur. Indeed, they are not unique to Catholicism. They can be avoided by eliminating sponsorship or, alternatively, by simplifying governance so that the college is directly controlled by the sponsor—as was characteristic of American Catholic higher education in the first part of this century. That "solution," however, would remove one key unit for reconciling the conflict—the trustees—from the scene.

One important contribution of a board as a community of interpretation is that it is a forum in which *conflicting* purposes can responsibly be discussed. To serve as such a forum, however, the trustees must be able to take responsibility, offering plausible reasons and explanations for their decisions. Trusteeship is constituted by fiduciary duty to a founder, a purpose, or, as in this case, a sponsor, but it is incompatible with mindless deference. The CUA board could legitimately choose to agree with Rome, but the fact that it is a board meant that it had to assume responsibility for that decision.

In fact, a compromise reconciliation may have been possible at CUA. William E. May has suggested a distinction between theological and pastoral authority, arguing that Curran and other theologians rightly claim theological expertise and a related academic freedom, but that "theologians are not pastors in the church." Therefore, theologians are not free to present their arguments and conclusions as if they have been formally accepted by the community as a whole.[27] Dissent must be labeled for what it is. Curran's vision of the Church was broader, one in which his views were one of several acceptable options. And he surely would have felt that confining his views to the realm of academic debate violated his academic freedom. I do not want to take time fully to assess the proposal. I mean only to assert that this strategy is the kind that should have been discussed by the CUA board. And perhaps it was; if so, American higher education and American Catholicism needed to know that the board discussed it.

Conclusion

Trusteeship stands in an ambiguous relation to a pluralistic society. On the one hand, the fact of pluralism argues for the necessity of institutions with diverse moral identities in which governing authority is in the hands of trustees. On the other hand, the fact of pluralism can present problems for organizations with a strong identity, whose vision of the good may conflict with that of the larger society. We should not be surprised by disagreement about the proper resolution of these conflicts. Boards must get into the habit of working them through in a credible way.

Notes

1. Cf. Kenneth Kirk, *Conscience and Its Problems: An Introduction to Casuistry* (London: Longman's Green, 1927), 255–56.
2. Curran himself has written extensively about the issues involved. See *Faithful Dissent* (Kansas City, MO: Sheed and Ward, 1986) and *Catholic Higher Education, Theology, and Academic Freedom* (Notre Dame, IN: University of Notre Dame Press, 1990). *Faithful Dissent,* written while the controversy was most heated, includes more than 150 pages of documents. *Catholic Higher Education* is a more "academic" statement.
3. "Academic Freedom and Tenure: The Catholic University of America," *Academe* (September-October 1989), 27.
4. Ibid.
5. The former "Holy Office," here simply the Sacred Congregation.
6. "Academic Freedom and Tenure," 30.
7. Ibid.
8. Ibid.

9. Ibid., 32.
10. Ibid., 33.
11. Ibid.
12. Quoted ibid., 33.
13. Ibid., 38.
14. *The Reverend Charles E. Curran v. The Catholic University of America*, Superior Court of the Disrict of Columbia, Action no. 1562–87, February 28, 1989, 26.
15. Ibid.
16. Ibid.
17. *Tilton et al. v. Richardson, Secretary of Health, Education, and Welfare et al.*, 403 U.S. 672 (1970).
18. For a discussion of nuanced Catholic—and non-Catholic—suggestions on this issue, see Curran, *Catholic Higher Education*, chapter 3. The issue is in no sense closed. The Vatican has issued an Apostolic Constitution on the subject (*Ex Corde Ecclesiae*, August 1990) and a set of Ordinances for the American Church is being discussed. See the symposium, "*Ex corde ecclesiae* and Its Ordinances: Is This Any Way to Run a University or a Church?" *Commonweal* 120 (November 19, 1993): 14–26.
19. I mentioned some Methodist reflections on this issue in chapter 3 of *Entrusted: The Moral Responsibilities of Trusteeship*.
20. See *Bob Jones University v. United States*, 461 U.S. 574 (1982).
21. Joseph Komonchak, "Authority and Magisterium," in William W. May, ed., *Vatican Authority and American Catholic Dissent* (New York: Crossroads, 1987), 105.
22. Ibid., 109.
23. Ibid., 112.
24. *Curran v. Catholic University of America*, 26.
25. Ibid., 33.
26. See Charles F. Curran et al., *Dissent in and for the Church: Theologians and Humanae Vitae* (New York: Sheed and Ward, 1969).
27. William E. May, "Catholic Moral Teaching and the Limits of Dissent," in William W. May, ed., *Vatican Authority*, 99.

Centered Pluralism: A Report of a Faculty Seminar on the Jesuit and Catholic Identity of Georgetown University

*Bruce Douglass, convenor**

Planned by a committee of faculty and administrators, the seminar met monthly during the 1995–96 academic year. Participants were drawn from faculty and academic administrators across the University. **This document is intended as a basis for discussion.**

1. This statement addresses a matter of fundamental importance to the future of Georgetown University. The product of a year-long seminar attended by faculty and administrators, it attempts to relate Georgetown's new promise as an academic institution to its heritage as a school founded and administered by Jesuits. It clarifies the issues at stake in the University's quest for excellence, and makes the case for a particular way of proceeding.

2. What is said in these pages reflects a view shared by those who participated in the seminar, and it addresses issues we think need to be addressed by the University as a whole. Georgetown has reached a point in its development where it needs to become more reflective about its mission, and we are confident that serious consideration of the point of view expressed here can contribute to that end. (We have not, however, attempted to address all the questions of principle that can be posed about faith and learning, religion and science, or the church and the university. This statement does not pretend to offer final or universal positions. Instead, even its general conclusions are directed at the practical reality and concrete potential of this one school at a specific moment in its history.)

*Bruce Douglass is dean of the faculty at Georgetown College, Georgetown University, Washington, D.C.

3. We believe the University should deliberately cultivate its religious heritage. We recognize that some ways of reaffirming Georgetown's Jesuit and Catholic identity would be inappropriate for a university with the pluralistic character it now has. We are confident, however, that the Georgetown community can undertake such a project while maintaining or even strengthening the University's openness to people of diverse beliefs and backgrounds and its commitment to academic freedom.

4. We also believe that an informed and intelligent effort to cultivate the Jesuit and Catholic elements in Georgetown's heritage is one of the most important things the University can do to realize its academic promise. Much of what we have to say is devoted to explaining why we believe that is the case—and what we think it implies.

5. We favor the University being faithful to its historic identity, however, for more than just academic reasons. One of the more valuable lessons we have learned from our exposure to Jesuit and Catholic thinking is to deal with matters of the kind discussed in these pages holistically. Universities are never just academic institutions. They are surrogate homes, social communities, and business enterprises (among other things) as well. Being a "good university" thus involves more than just academic performance—which is a challenge Georgetown, insofar as it takes seriously its heritage, is well situated to meet.

6. Another part of what follows explains why we believe this to be the case, and attempts to provide some indication of what it might mean in practice. In that section of the document, as in other sections, we do not go into great detail. This is because we wish to focus on matters of principle before moving on, at some subsequent time, to matters of practice. But it is also because we did not want to present our views in an excessively lengthy form. Those who want a better sense of possible policy implications can review the items listed in Appendix I.

7. In elaborating our argument, we take up six major topics:
   a. the role of institutional particularity in academic excellence;
   b. the promise—and shortcomings—of Georgetown's educational offerings;
   c. the role of Catholic thought and concerns in its current research agenda;
   d. the quality of campus life and its bearing on the University's performance;
   e. the procedures and policies used in managing the University's affairs and their bearing on its performance; and

f. the role of institutional particularity in an institution dedicated to pluralism.

Excellence and Particularity

8. Though we respect and admire much that has been achieved by those who preceded us, we do not wish to return Georgetown to its past. Nor do we wish to romanticize the past. We take for granted that the University needed to undergo changes of the kind it has experienced in recent years (for example, welcoming a more diverse student body and faculty) in order to realize its promise as an academic institution. We assume it will need to continue changing in the years to come. What is at stake in this matter is not holding on to the past, but making the most of the future.

9. Georgetown prides itself on being "the oldest Catholic Church–related institution of higher learning in the United States." Because we assume the University's Catholic and Jesuit identity and because we take for granted the desirability (and irreversibility) of many of the changes that have occurred in recent decades, we assume that the University must find a new way to express its Catholic and Jesuit heritage. An institution that is increasingly populated by people who are not themselves Catholic can hardly be expected to function in the same manner as one that was largely a Catholic enclave. Either it will redefine its historic role in terms that make sense to a broader range of people, or it will cease playing that role.

10. Historically, some U.S. universities have committed themselves to a pursuit of academic excellence and, concomitant with that pursuit, have abandoned their religious identities. Knowing this history, some persons may assume that academic excellence requires a non-religious identity and ask, "Why not just accept that this is how good universities are built?"

11. There are several reasons. The most fundamental is that academic excellence does not have a single meaning or assume a single institutional form. The pursuit of higher learning has taken any number of different institutional forms over the centuries and it would be presumptuous to assume that the form that has caught on in this country over the course of the past century is the only way to go about pursuing excellence. To do so begs, moreover, the question of whether that form deserves to be considered the last word.

12. We think not. This is not because we disrespect what has been

achieved by the universities that are now recognized to be the academic leaders in American higher education. Many of us are products of those institutions. We model much of what we do as scholars and as teachers after what we experienced in their halls and we are prepared to see Georgetown follow their lead in much of what it is attempting to accomplish. But Georgetown has more to achieve, we believe, than just a replication of what others have done. And it has more to contribute than merely to become one more thoroughly secularized university.

13. Even the example of these universities can be used to reinforce our point. If one looks at the way in which the more distinguished research institutions got to be that way, one finds that it was more than just imitation. There was an element of imitation, to be sure. But there was also a good deal of innovation. The MITs and the Princetons did not become academically distinguished by following a common recipe (like fast food franchises), so that they are all now doing the exact same things in the same manner. Quite the reverse. The most respected universities achieved that status by committing themselves to a particular and even distinctive set of intellectual projects. Their willingness to specialize is, in fact, one of the main reasons they have been so successful in attracting talented faculty and students.

14. Georgetown needs, therefore, to devote itself in a disciplined manner to the pursuit of a distinctive set of tasks that it in particular is capable of performing well—an undertaking we find difficult to imagine being performed intelligently, much less imaginatively, without taking into account the University's religious heritage.

15. The value of that heritage is particularly apparent when one considers the challenges now facing higher education in the United States. For all the success our universities have enjoyed, many people are dissatisfied with their performance and, as a result, are challenging some of their more basic operating assumptions. The issues at stake in those deliberations have to do, more often than not, with matters that historically have been at the center of Jesuit and Catholic reflection on higher learning. They are foundational issues like the integrity of the curriculum and the relationship between research and teaching. The more we have reflected on what ideas like John Carroll's founding civic republican vision of Georgetown and the Jesuit ideal of "contemplation in action" have to offer in dealing with such matters, the more convinced we have become that such ideas are among the more valuable resources available to the University today.

Education

16. Georgetown's Jesuit and Catholic heritage is widely acknowledged to be an asset for its educational mission, particularly with undergraduates. Not only do the Jesuits have a well-established reputation for providing quality education that is rooted in a distinctive and respected philosophy of education, but Georgetown has been known primarily for what it has to offer as an educational institution. People have sensed, correctly, that this was due above all to the Jesuit commitment to providing education of a particular sort well.

17. It is also widely acknowledged that this is something worth preserving. Even those most eager to see Georgetown achieve the standing of a distinguished research university do not suggest that this should be accomplished at the expense of its educational mission. The proposals they make are meant to enlarge and enrich the University's performance, not subtract from it anything of real value.

18. It is also widely recognized that students are well served by the particular kind of education that comes from approaching it in the Jesuit manner. Knowledgeable people, both inside and outside the University, routinely refer, for example, to Georgetown's characteristic emphasis on "values" as a strength. Surely this is one of the reasons why the philosophy and theology courses required of all undergraduates are as well received as they are.

19. At the same time, what all of this means is increasingly vague. In recent years we have had too little discussion about the specifics of the Jesuit heritage in education and, in fact, little serious consideration of the intellectual coherence of the institution as a whole. The University has tended to finesse the more difficult issues of educational policy posed by the changes it is now undergoing, and as a result to define its educational mission in generalities that people can construe as they choose.

20. This does not mean that the quality of instruction has been declining. We believe that Georgetown is today attracting faculty who are more dedicated and gifted as teachers than ever. But it *does* mean that little attempt has been made to figure out how to make the most of the resource they represent. It also means that the environment is not very conducive to generating a sense of coherence between the claims of the various academic disciplines and the larger purposes the institution seeks to serve. Without such coherence, teaching easily becomes a series of solo performances connected by only the thinnest of ties.

21. This should not be allowed to happen. To keep pace with its chosen peers, Georgetown will need to become much more self-aware and self-critical about the curriculum and other aspects of its educational mission. And if it is to avoid the educational compromises that many other research universities have made, it will need to devote considerable time and energy to figuring out *how* that is to be accomplished. Making research and teaching truly complementary is one of the great educational challenges of our time, and we cannot assume that Georgetown will meet it well just because the University has a tradition of devoted teaching.

22. Even less can we assume that tradition alone is sufficient to cause the University to continue to provide an education that serves certain worthy moral and spiritual purposes. Traditions need to be renewed if they are to endure and those Georgetown traditions that merit preservation are no exception.

23. If one is familiar with the educational purposes Georgetown was created to serve and the way of thinking they reflect, one can easily appreciate what the University and its students stand to gain from such renewal of purpose. Jesuit thinking about education is rooted in a vision of God and the world that insists on the inseparable conjunction of the search for God with service to humankind. From its inception, Jesuit education has stood, therefore, for a distinctive way of pursuing intellectual achievement that combines openness to the transcendent with down-to-earth practicality. The university, in the Jesuit vision, is a place where praise of God in public liturgies is combined with both the rigorous critical questioning essential to the life of the mind and a commitment to service.

24. Now more than ever is this vision relevant to the conditions students face. For in practice it means: taking faith seriously as a dimension of human experience worthy of study; cultivation of the whole person; and paying attention to the moral implications of learning in such a way that students are equipped to make responsible choices and see that more is at stake in their studies than just self-aggrandizement. Recent documents of the Society of Jesus stress that Jesuit institutions should be committed to a faith that promotes justice, to a care of and service to the poor, and to the education of men and women committed to the service of others. If Georgetown were to dedicate itself to realizing more fully this vision, it could accomplish something quite special.

25. This is especially likely if the project were to be undertaken in such a manner as to permeate the curriculum and to call upon the resources of many disciplines. We value the contribution made by philosophers and theologians to the Georgetown curriculum over

the years and we take for granted that they would play a key role in what we are proposing. But we also think that Georgetown will miss a valuable opportunity if it fails to engage aggressively issues of moral and religious significance across the disciplines. Among our faculty are people from a wide range of disciplines who have an interest in tackling such issues in their teaching. We believe that this desire is one of the more important parts of the promise Georgetown has today as an educational institution.

26. The effect of the ever-increasing specialization of scholarly inquiry on education also merits careful consideration. Specialization, while to some extent inevitable and desirable, can easily lead to a fragmentation of learning. This is not nearly the problem at Georgetown that it is now at many other schools, thanks in no small measure to the Jesuit emphasis on the integration of knowledge. Still, the problem does exist here, and the lack of a strong tradition of interdisciplinary collaboration means that there is little to counteract it. Dialogue across the disciplines will have to be actively encouraged, therefore, if the University is to achieve anything like the coherence of educational purpose we have in mind.

Research

27. Ever since Georgetown first began to grant graduate degrees and become something more than a college, it has been taken for granted that to some extent the scholarly work done here would reflect its religious roots. In much the same manner that the Jesuit presence has influenced its educational offerings, the Catholic operation of the University has affected the scholarship that it has produced.

28. In the 1980s a decision was made to make Georgetown a more widely respected research institution. This decision, along with other factors, has produced a change in the composition of the faculty and in the character of its scholarly agenda. More and more, scholarly trends in the disciplines have dictated the kind of faculty that the University attracts and, as a result, their research tends increasingly to resemble that done at other institutions of comparable stature.

29. This is not to say that the University's Jesuit and Catholic heritage plays no role in defining its research agenda. The curriculum still affects faculty appointments in ways that clearly reflect the University's religious roots. Prominent parts of the research apparatus

have the same quality. Institutions like the Kennedy Institute of Ethics, the John F. Connelly Program in Business Ethics, and the Center for Muslim-Christian Understanding owe their existence, in large part, to Georgetown's continuing interest in fostering research of a certain kind, and much of the University's scholarly reputation derives from such initiatives.

30. At the same time, however, scholars who are willing and qualified to conduct research informed by Catholic thought and concerns (whatever their own religious background) are less well represented on the Georgetown faculty than they once were. Consequently, the University has less opportunity to be exposed to the contribution such people might make to its intellectual life, and it has less to contribute to conversations occurring in both the academy and the church about matters to which Catholic thinking is relevant. We think this is anomalous, and believe it impairs significantly Georgetown's ability to realize its promise as a research institution.

31. In proposing this should change, we do not mean to suggest that the composition of the faculty should be altered in any dramatic way. Nor do we envision any intervention in the scholarly life of the University that would jeopardize the right of faculty members to design and conduct research as they see fit. Instead, we have in mind an enlargement of the University's scholarly agenda to allow for greater attention to questions of direct concern to the intellectual traditions of Catholicism. We encourage Georgetown to provide opportunities that allow faculty to address such questions. We would also like to see places found in the ranks of the faculty for scholars who are able and willing to make this happen.

32. This vision of Georgetown's future implies that scholars who take such ideas seriously should have a definite place in realizing the University's scholarly ambitions. It means that Georgetown should become more fully a place where scholars of this kind gather, and are able to undertake projects that enrich the scholarly conversation. But it does not mean that Catholic ideas—or the people who advocate them—would be permitted to have a limiting influence on scholarly inquiry and discourse.

33. We take for granted that such scholarship will be undertaken with full respect for the autonomy essential to the academic enterprise. It will need to be done by people appointed for their scholarly qualifications, who enjoy the same freedoms in the conduct of their work as other members of the faculty. We assume, therefore, that they will not be of one mind or faith, and expect their scholarship to reflect the diversity of opinion in the relevant fields. In-

deed, we would hope that their presence in the University would stimulate an active and enlivening debate about the issues raised by Catholic teaching and practice that would attract the participation of people with a wide range of views. Given its commitment to academic freedom, the foundation of university life, Georgetown cannot tolerate any attempt to silence voices arguing for controversial conclusions, including those that may be contrary to those of the Roman Catholic Church. Only by open and free discussion of the most contentious topics can this University perform its scholarly function effectively.

Campus Life

34. A lot more defines the character of institutions of higher learning than just academic programs and scholarly research. Colleges and universities are also places where people relate to one another in ways that add up to a distinct pattern, if not a way of life. More often than not, the resulting ethos plays a significant role in defining the way the institution understands itself and presents itself to the world. Harvard has thus become one sort of institution, Texas A&M another, and Notre Dame still another, not only because of their particular curricula and research foci but also because of the differing ways in which they incline their members to relate to one another.

35. Some of the most important learning that takes place at a university comes about as a result of the character of the institution's associational life. Associational life covers the myriad ways in which members of the university community conduct a common life formed by a shared intellectual and social ethos. Associational life teaches students in particular how to conduct themselves as mature human beings and to relate to other human beings. In many cases, the informal learning that takes place in this way turns out to be as important as anything learned in the classroom—which is why the better schools have been reluctant to leave the matter to chance.

36. The better schools historically have prided themselves, in fact, on the quality of their campus life, and have emphasized that certain norms of behavior should be observed. They have actively encouraged their students and faculty to live up to prescribed standards in everything from personal attire to the conduct of scholarly activity. Typically, the standards in question were designed to do

more than facilitate the acquisition of academic skills and the advance of knowledge: They were expected to foster a way of life that was conducive to various moral and civic purposes.

37. In recent decades, however, this expectation has fallen on hard times. Though few (if any) universities have explicitly abandoned the premises on which it was based, they have developed serious reservations about the propriety of taking concrete action. While Georgetown has continued to try to nourish the quality of campus life, it has, we believe, allowed the associational character of campus life to evolve with too little input from faculty and administrators.

38. The problem with this practice is that it leaves to chance some aspects of campus life that are of real consequence. And, in a time when academic institutions are vulnerable to many serious social ills afflicting the wider society, relying on chance does not seem to be a responsible course of action, particularly if universities continue to make claims about the good things higher education does to the character of students.

39. All too often, moreover, such claims are belied by the realities of campus life. For on too many campuses, including Georgetown's, recent decades have witnessed a deteriorating common life. Manifestations of the deterioration have included excessive consumption of alcohol; irresponsible sexual behavior; a withering of intellectual life outside the classroom; cultural activities below what one might hope for at a center of learning; verbal and physical abuse; and a growing tendency on the part of some students to consider "getting ahead" the primary objective of their educations, no matter what the costs to other people or what important values (for example, academic integrity) they violate. Indeed, despite all the talk of "community," it is not uncommon to encounter behavior that reflects snobbery and indifference or even downright contempt for the well-being of others.

40. Increasingly, therefore, administrators see a need to establish greater control over the quality of campus life. Many faculty share their concern and in some places have devoted considerable time and energy to devising improvements. No small number of students have also been speaking in these terms, and the more this happens, the more evident it becomes that the search is on for a new way of taking responsibility for the character of the common life. This does not mean that people want to return to student parietals and faculty dress codes, but it does mean that many persons would like to achieve a richer sense of community and shared commitments.

41. In seeking to satisfy these concerns, Georgetown has a number of

strengths on which to draw. Its traditions include the widespread involvement of students in volunteer and public service activities, their participation in a wide range of performing arts programs, and the opportunities provided through intercollegiate and intramural athletics. The intellectual quality of the common life at Georgetown is, however, another matter, and is increasingly a subject of serious discussion. We wholeheartedly endorse such discussion. We especially approve of the work being done by the task force created by the Executive Faculty to look into the state of the intellectual life of the Main Campus.

42. But something more is at stake than just the manner in which the tenor of campus life does—or does not—enrich and enhance academic performance. The common life of a university (including a sense of community and shared commitments) affects more than people's ability to teach and learn scholarly subjects. Often, some of the key formative experiences shaping people's lives come from what they are exposed to in campus life. Careers, life-long friendships, marriages, political and religious commitments—all sorts of fundamentally important aspects of people's lives—take shape there. We believe that this wider effect needs to be taken into account just as much in thinking about how to improve the quality of campus life at Georgetown.

43. We think it is both fitting and instructive to approach this matter with the University's Jesuit and Catholic heritage in mind. Not only does it provide a good set of terms on which to understand what is problematic about the current situation but we have also found it instructive in thinking about the direction in which Georgetown needs to move. If there is anything a Jesuit school should be, it should be a place that upholds an affirming respect for the whole person. Its governing norms should encourage an honest, caring, and supportive learning environment. Its ethos should encourage intellectual and moral inquiry, and through such inquiry result in choices that serve others. A school claiming to take Catholic teaching—and Catholic thought—seriously should *lift* the sights and *expand* the horizons of those who are exposed to it. It should be a place where people learn to think of their lives as opportunities for service and routinely have the kind of experiences that incline them to be more responsible, just, and compassionate.

44. We are convinced that Georgetown can do this while continuing to welcome persons who are from many different backgrounds and bring with them a variety of beliefs and faiths. It would be inappropriate for anyone to try to compel all the members of such a

diverse community to conform their lives to church teaching. But Georgetown *should* be the kind of place where responsibility for the quality of the common life is taken with special seriousness, and where Catholic thought is treated as a highly valued resource available to those involved in exercising that responsibility.

Management and Governance

45. Universities have not always recognized that the way they make decisions, wield power, and do business affects the rest of their performance. The history of higher education in this country is replete with examples of less-than-exemplary business practices and decision-making procedures that would not withstand critical scrutiny. Fortunately, the days when these practices were taken as normal are largely over. The moral responsibilities of those engaged in management and governance are now well recognized, in principle at least. In the academic world it is now widely understood that what universities *do* as institutions needs to be as consistent as possible with the things they *say* in their public discourse. The more respected administrators insist on this, arguing that a university's methods of operation constitute an important part of the institution's message to society. The more reputable schools routinely worry over the ethical issues posed by investment decisions, devote much time and energy to making sure that employees are treated fairly, and seek to create decision-making procedures that make good academic sense.

46. Georgetown is no exception. But it has been, we think, a bit slow in accommodating itself to this trend, particularly with regard to procedures for governance. Relative to comparable schools, Georgetown does not have much of a tradition of self-government. There is, of course, variation from one campus and school to another, and within schools and departments faculty have increasingly been asserting their prerogatives. But in the wider University—and especially at the higher levels of administration—faculty members have played a much less influential role than they have at other like institutions.

47. This has persisted until very recently. While Georgetown has attracted faculty members of the same character as those of other major research universities, it has not allowed them to share power in the way they would elsewhere. Until the creation of the Executive Faculty, for example, no mechanism existed for faculty

on the Main Campus to have a formal role in the making of *aca-demic* (let alone other kinds of) policy. The Faculty Senate made it possible for faculty to play an advisory role by appointing them to a variety of standing and ad hoc committees established by the administration. But the power actually to make policy remained almost exclusively in the hands of administrators.

48. There is no denying that Georgetown, like many other universities and organizations, has a strong tradition of paternalistic government and has a history of involving few women in important decision-making processes and promoting few of them to positions of senior leadership. These are things that need to be frankly acknowledged. It should also be acknowledged that, at Georgetown, paternalism has been intertwined with, and at times supported by, the University's religious heritage. But this is not the whole story; Jesuit and Catholic teaching also provide resources for developing other forms of government more appropriate for a contemporary university.

49. Catholic thought—and, even more, Catholic practice—is hardly ambiguous on the matter of self-government, particularly in this country. American Catholicism has long been characterized by an attraction to democratic ideals, which is making itself felt today more strongly than ever. Georgetown, as an institution shaped at least as much by its American as its Catholic roots, will, we are confident, be governed in the years to come in a manner that is more in keeping with these ideals. But as this takes place, it will still have to face the question of how its affairs are going to be managed. It will still need to decide what kind of institution it wants to become in the material or economic sense. It will also need to decide what specific kinds of participation it wants to cultivate—and why. A great deal will be at stake morally in these decisions, and the value of approaching them from the perspective of Catholic teaching is that this will be made clear.

50. One of the most important things that thinking in such terms can be expected to bring to light is the need to resist allowing academic policy to be driven solely by market forces. This is bound to be a temptation, and it is one on which modern Catholic social thought, as the product of over a century of struggling with the moral issues raised by market economies, has much light to shed. The more we have reflected on what the church has had to say about this matter, the more convinced we have become that it has particular relevance to issues of academic governance today.

51. For example, the idea of the *common good*, as developed in Catholic teaching and used in such documents as *Economic Justice for*

All, the 1984 pastoral letter issued by the U.S. Catholic Bishops, carries implications for the decisions managers must make that speak directly to the challenges of academic life today. It entails a way of thinking that suggests that if one wants to understand well the functioning of an institution like a university, one should not think mechanistically, as though one were dealing with nothing more than a collection of parts. It suggests that one needs to think holistically because such institutions are, in principle at least, more than the sum of their parts, and they cannot perform well if they are not treated as such. Their affairs need to be conducted, therefore, in such a manner that the health and well being of all their component parts are kept in mind, and that they are woven together into an integrated whole.

52. This is not a way of thinking that requires equality of condition. But it does require that all people—and organizational units—involved in the enterprise, whatever their functions or condition, be treated with respect and have their legitimate interests protected. When augmented by the related idea of *social justice*, this perspective carries the implication, too, that practices that exploit some for the benefit of others are inappropriate. It leads to much the same conclusion about policies that are designed to achieve some larger good by preying on the vulnerabilities of those who cannot defend themselves. Ever since the late 19th century, Catholic teaching on these matters has been closely associated with ideas like the "living wage," and for that reason it has been opposed by those who would have managers think less protectively about their treatment of employees.

53. Add to this the strong emphasis in recent Catholic teaching on the importance of *participation* in governance, and one can easily see how much of a difference this way of thinking could make at Georgetown. One can also see how relevant these concepts are to the challenges of morally responsible management today. For these are the days of "downsizing" and "contracting out," and the more economic pressure academic institutions come under, the harder it is going to be for them to avoid falling back into the old ways of conducting their business affairs. As an institution that is not now blessed with a large endowment (as major universities go), Georgetown can hardly afford, for the foreseeable future, to chart an utterly different course. But it *can*, and should, make an *effort* to do so. It can make a good faith effort to avoid some of the practices that are now fashionable in the business world. It needs, in other words, to become *more attentive—not less—to the moral claims on its material resources coming from its*

serve to strengthen the University's performance—and capabilities—in this regard. This should become an integral part of the
process of academic planning across the University, and it
should be pursued by asking schools and relevant departments
to consider following the example set by the memorandum on
the subject recently adopted by the Department of Philosophy—a document that provides a clear, well-reasoned plan for
integrating specifically Catholic concerns into the wider research
agenda and hiring priorities of the department.

A73. As a general rule, faculty appointments made for the purpose of
facilitating such research should be underwritten by funds specifically raised and given for that purpose. Such appointments
should be made, in each instance, in the appropriate academic
units by procedures that conform to the standard hiring practices in those units. They should be open to qualified applicants
of any faith or belief.

A74. Faculty should be actively encouraged to undertake scholarly
projects that would contribute to the realization of such an
agenda (better realization of Georgetown's Catholic and Jesuit
heritage). Faculty interested in engaging in such research should
be encouraged to collaborate with one another and to devise
projects that draw broadly on the relevant resources available in
the Georgetown faculty. They should also be encouraged to educate one another—and the wider University—on their research.

A75. Particular consideration should be given to the possibility of developing research projects on subjects that are currently being
emphasized in the teaching of the Catholic church but do not
appear to have attracted much scholarly attention at Georgetown. Examples include such matters as the spread of poverty
and economic inequality in this country, the growing instability
of families, the spread of violence, the commercialization of popular culture, and the ongoing dispute about the role of religion
in public life.

A76. Academic programs that deal with relevant subjects—such as
Catholic Studies, Medieval Studies, and the Program on Justice
and Peace—should be actively encouraged, and faculty involved
in research that bears on the concerns of those programs should
be encouraged to lend their support to them.

A77. A University-wide seminar for faculty and other interested parties—*The Georgetown Colloquy*—should be created to provide a
forum for scholars of all disciplines and interests to discuss their
research with educated nonspecialists.

Campus Life

A78. Every effort should be made to integrate more fully into the life of the Georgetown community those programs that provide students with opportunities for service in the wider community. Examples include the Pediatric Mobile Van, Sursum Corda mentoring, and the Fourth Credit Option. The giving of time and energy to support such programs should be a relevant consideration in the evaluation of the performance of faculty and other members of the staff.

A79. Georgetown should be steadfast in its commitment to a policy of need-blind admissions. It should also continue to support the Evening Law School and to provide special services for persons with disabilities and the educationally disadvantaged.

A80. Since it cannot be taken for granted that the diversity (of a number of different sorts) that now characterizes the staff and student populations at Georgetown is itself a recipe for mutual respect, much less understanding, attention needs to be devoted to figuring out how to turn it into a learning experience and how to promote mutual respect.

A81. The University should thoughtfully evaluate and aggressively seek to improve the quality of interaction among its students, particularly undergraduates.

A82. The University should do more to meet the personal needs (for example, in the areas of housing and health care) of graduate students.

A83. Those who exercise fiduciary responsibility for Georgetown as a Catholic institution have a duty to insure that the determination of University policy in matters touching on the current teaching of the Catholic church is made in a manner that accords such teaching appropriate respect but without assuming that it will be treated as the last word. Those persons should be encouraged to engage in full and frank consultation with the appropriate bodies in the University.

A84. As an addition to Georgetown's tradition of liturgical ceremony isolated within each of several faith communities, a carefully considered plan of widely supported and well-attended academic and liturgical ceremonies (some ecumenical), could contribute significantly to an awareness of Georgetown's identity and mission, as well as to communal commitment to the University's goals. All constituencies of the University (including our alumni) might, for example, participate in an annual Founder's Day or Week that would combine liturgical and academic ceremonies with public fora dedicated to the reinvestigation and reaffirmation of our institutional heritage and goals.

A85. Review procedures should be created to verify that honorary degrees and medals are awarded only to persons whose accomplishments are consistent with the highest ideals to which Georgetown is committed.

Management and Governance

A86. The University needs now to make a dedicated effort to carry forward the process of democratization initiated by the creation of the Executive Faculty on the Main Campus. The administration must be willing, for example, to share relevant information on such matters as the University's financial affairs. The faculty must be involved with the development of major University initiatives at their inception rather than being invited to react to proposals already developed by the administration. And bodies such as the Executive Faculty need to be encouraged to develop reliable mechanisms for both deliberation and representation.

A87. Students, too, need to be drawn into the decision-making process in appropriate ways, and there are various other kinds of employees that have both interests and experience that also need to be represented if the University is not to go from one kind of "benevolent paternalism" to another. This whole matter of how the University ought to be governed is in need of serious review.

A88. The University should conduct a "values and practices audit" based on appropriate norms drawn from Catholic social teaching. This would entail reviewing its current structures, practices, and policies in the light of such norms to identify ways in which they can and should be improved. One can well imagine this being done by a task force drawn from the administration, faculty, and board of directors that could then be constituted as a standing advisory committee to advise the president and other appropriate officials—an academic equivalent of the ethics panels that now exist in many hospitals.

A89. The University should undertake a careful review of the way it conducts its business (hiring and compensating staff and non-tenurable faculty, out-contracting services). Few things matter more in determining the moral quality of an institution than the way it treats its less privileged members—especially employees.

Appendix 2: Seminar Participants

Anthony Arend
Government

Judith Baigis-Smith
School of Nursing

Marianne Borelli
School of Nursing

Paul Betz
English

Robert Bies
School of Business

John Breslin, S.J.
University Chaplain

Peter Byrne
Law Center

Wayne Davis
Philosophy

John DeGioia
Vice President, Chief
  Administrative
  Officer, Main
  Campus

James Donahue
Dean, Student Affairs

Bruce Douglass
Dean of the Faculty

John Glavin
English

Steven Goldberg
Law Center

Margaret Hall
Sociology

Monika Hellwig
Theology

Otto Hentz, S.J.
Theology

Michael Kelly
University Vice
  President

James Lamiell
Psychology

Mark Lance
Philosophy

Robert Lawton, S.J.
Dean, Georgetown
  College

Robert Lieber
Government

Sam Marullo
Sociology

William McElroy
Economics

Marilyn McMorrow,
  R.S.C.J.
Government

Donn Murphy
Art, Music & Theatre

Peter Pfeiffer
German

Elizabeth Prelinger
Art, Music, and
  Theater

Lamar Reinsch
School of Business

Alvaro Ribeiro, S.J.
English

Pietra Rivoli
School of Business

Carolyn Robinowitz
Psychiatry

Karin Ryding
Dean,
  Interdisciplinary
  Programs,
  Georgetown College

John Samples
Director, Georgetown
  University Press

Alexander Sens
Classics

Sheila Sparks
School of Nursing

Philip Tacka
Art, Music & Theatre

Jeffrey von Arx, S.J.
History

Kevin Wildes, S.J.
Philosophy

John Witek, S.J.
History

Stephanie Wright
School of Nursing,
  Georgetown College

Lisa Zuccarelli, O.P.
School of Nursing

Integrating Mission into the Life of Institutions

Mary M. Brabeck, Otherine Neisler, and Nancy J. Zollers*

Children and youth enter today's schools with complex and multiple needs. Of the nation's twelve million children under the age of three, 24 percent are living in poverty and that number is growing.[1] About 50 percent of the approximately 28 million children and adolescents in this country between the ages of 10 and 17 engage in two or more of the following high-risk behaviors: drug and alcohol abuse; crime and violence; school failure and drop out; unsafe sex and teenage parenting. Approximately 10 percent, nearly 3 million of America's youth engage in all four behaviors.[2] Dramatic alterations in family composition and stability, inadequate housing, and violence in neighborhoods, affect the ability of our nation's children and youth to learn.

Many professionals in the fields of medicine, education, social services, and law are concluding that they must collaborate in order to address the complex needs of children, youth, and families.[3] However, most of these professionals have been trained in isolation from other professionals. Lawyers seldom work with teachers; nurses do not collaborate with social workers; psychologists and social workers often work in isolation, and sometimes competition, with each other. At Boston College we are developing a new collaborative model of working across professions to address the complex health, legal, human services, and educational needs of children, youth, and families. We are finding that to succeed, we must collec-

*Mary M. Brabeck is dean of the Lynch School of Education, Boston College, Boston, Massachusetts. Otherine Neisler is assistant professor, Lynch School of Education, Boston College. Nancy J. Zollers is assistant professor, Lynch School of Education, Boston College. The article is reprinted from Regina Haney and Joseph O'Keefe, S.J., *Conversations in Excellence* (Washington, DC: National Catholic Education Association, 1997), 39–56.

tively claim a mission and integrate it into the life of the university and our individual efforts.

Collaborative Efforts within Boston College: Toward a Mission of Service

For the past four years the Boston College School of Education, Law School, Graduate School of Social Work, School of Nursing, Carroll School of Management, and College of Arts and Sciences have been working collaboratively in four overlapping and integrated efforts. In our educational effort, we are drawing from the knowledge bases of our diverse professions and disciplines to design curricula that will prepare professionals to work more effectively with children, families, and communities. Our community outreach effort creates partnerships with local schools, clinics, hospitals, and community agencies. Our scholarship effort builds collaborative, co-learning research agendas that address questions designed by community members (as opposed to university faculty). Finally, reflecting on our collaborative research and service delivery, we are developing policy statements to inform federal and local governments. Our efforts move the faculty out of the ivory tower of the university and into the real world of local schools and communities in ways that are consonant with the mission of Boston College.

Boston College, a Jesuit university founded in 1863 to provide a Catholic liberal arts education for immigrants, has had a long-standing commitment to the action-knowledge link and an institutional identity marked by an obligation to serve others.[4] We have carried this service orientation into our efforts at joining thought and action through interprofessional collaboration. We have organized and maintained a monthly faculty seminar to expand our knowledge of interprofessional collaboration, revised aspects of professional preparation programs, and altered curriculum to better reflect the knowledge bases of the diverse professions engaged in our discussions. We have created faculty and student work teams who go to schools and community agencies and work collaboratively. We have formed panels and written papers that describe our efforts and how this work achieves the mission of Boston College.[5]

J. Donald Monan, S.J., chancellor of Boston College and past president, described the mission of the University, which is rooted in Ignatian spirituality, as resting "not in a particular virtue or speculative principle but in the motive or intention of service—namely, in all things to better serve the Lord out of passionate love."[6] More recently, William P. Leahy,

S.J., current president of Boston College, stated in his inaugural address that Boston College must "develop appropriate responses to the issues of justice, faith, and fairness and in this way serve the common good."[7]

The Jesuit challenge, to find God in all things, has been at the core of the Boston College mission and is the foundation on which our interprofessional collaborative work rests. If faculty and students are to find God in all things, the university may not be separate from the world; rather, we must be engaged in it. We must encircle the lives of the children and youth and families most at risk in today's society and we must enlarge our circle of community to contain them.

The circle is the metaphor for our work at Boston College. We claim a holistic approach that views the individual, family, and community from multiple and interrelated biopsychosocial perspectives that require collaboration of professionals from law, psychology, education, health, and social services. Our model, illustrated in Figure 1, involves overlapping circles that reflect collaboration among the professional schools and College of Arts and Sciences and cooperation with delivery systems such as schools and clinics.[8]

When we first began our collaborations, we worked independently in isolated circles. Now our circles are beginning to overlap. As we learn more from working as a team, the borders of our independent fields have blurred, though not disappeared. No one of us can do the entire (or even large segments) of the job alone, but our team efforts bring our multiple expertises to any one case. The information flows along a spiral as we address the multiple needs of the student, and students feel less like they are being passed from one place to another, from one professional to the next.

The concept within the Catholic tradition that most vividly symbolizes our circle of community is the mystical body of Christ. This concept embodies the belief that we are all spiritually united, rooted together in a common bond, a community of love. All the good that any one of us does enhances all members of the community. All the pain that any one of us suffers is suffered throughout the mystical body of Christ.

This concept both supports and challenges us. It supports us in our recognition that working collaboratively makes us stronger and more capable of addressing the complex needs of children, youth, and families. It challenges us in our acknowledgment that we have a responsibility to improve the life chances of the most unfortunate members of our enlarged community circle.

Efforts to create collaborative partnerships across professions and with communities is a return to an earlier outreach mission of higher education. According to Ernest Boyer, the late historian of higher education, the goal in previous years "was not only to *serve* society but *reshape it*." The conviction that higher education has a moral obligation to improve

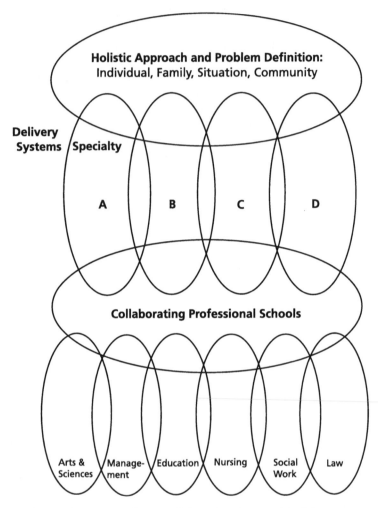

Figure 1. The Boston College Collaborative System Model.

society calls upon all universities to join in partnerships with communities to solve the problems that community members and agencies define.

In a special way, it calls upon Catholic universities whose mission is one of service. Father Leahy noted that nearly 30 years ago Riesman and Jencks wrote, "There is yet no university that manages to fuse academic professionalism with concern for questions of ultimate social and moral importance"[9]; he called on Boston College to be the counter-cultural university that addresses the eternal questions through "lives illuminated by faith discovery and service."[10] This is at the heart of the social justice mission at Boston College.

Social Justice and the Mission of the School of Education

The Jesuit character of the university, inspired by the order's self-understanding of social justice through its General Congregations and Superior General, entails a preferential option for the poor and an elimination of social, economic, and political structures that oppress people. This is the theological and ethical foundation on which the mission of the Boston College School of Education is being articulated.

While the social justice mission is central to the work of many School of Education and university-wide faculty, we have come to understand that social justice has many meanings. The multiple meanings have become a subject of weekly dialogue among the teacher education faculty in the School of Education. The entire teacher education faculty, including elementary, secondary, and special education, agreed to work toward understanding each other's and their own perspectives on social justice.

Dialogue across a diverse group of faculty members about university mission is complex and difficult work. We decided to engage in this work because we are interested in (1) how our mission of social justice is defined by each of us, (2) whether we can agree on some common understandings of social justice, and (3) how we envision incorporating mission into our work as teachers, advisors, and researchers. If these conversations are successful among teacher education faculty, we will have created a teacher education program that integrates mission into the work we do, including the research questions we ask, the decisions we make, the plans we formulate, and the priorities we set.

With support from School of Education administrators, our goal is to infuse social justice values into the School of Education mission. Such an effort is also occurring at the university level.

Integrating mission into the life of the school requires a deliberate dialogue to articulate a mission of service that promotes social justice. Consistent with the University mission,[11] faculty and staff have examined the mission of Boston College and the distinctive contribution our School of Education can make to society. Our discussion of how the mission is actualized in the work of faculty, staff, and students has led us to develop a shared language, essential for institutional change. Faculty and administrators speak of "preparing contemplative activists" by joining reflection and action, thinking and doing, in a way that will further the Ignatian mission to serve others and to find God in all things.

The emerging teacher education, school, and university missions are affecting our practice in schools and communities. Collaborative work in the community and in the schools, off campus and shoulder to shoulder with our neighbors, provides the faculty with clear opportunities to work with community members, children, and families to achieve social justice. While university teaching, advising young students, and scholarly research are complex enough to provide opportunities to live this mission, the outreach scholarship that faculty engage in offers stark and multiple opportunities for work with growing, hurting, or puzzled children.

Our work in Boston public schools has been in a community that has many needs and great hope. There are many children who are homeless, abused, failing in school, scared, or ignored. There are also children and families who are growing up healthy and bright. Boston is a community of resilient children, with wonderful cultural and language diversity. In both the families in pain and the children of hope, we are finding God, and working to achieve social justice through our outreach with, and service in, the schools.

Challenges and Barriers to a Mission of Collaboration

There are a number of challenges and barriers to this work and identifying them is critical to the development of mission. Among the challenges that we have identified, the most significant are the ones within each of us. Each of us was educated in a model of autonomy and independence and has little experience with interprofessional collaboration. We have our professional identities and these identities carry hierarchical valuing (e.g., teachers and lawyers do not have the same status). We all have the normal apprehension about exposing the limits of our knowledge, skills, and ability. Our biggest challenge has been to learn to trust each other. We continually learn that if we can keep focused on the mission of our work—to improve the lives of children, youth and families—we can make progress. There are many barriers to keeping that focus, including our language.

Naming is powerful when it describes or locates a problem. We had, for example, different opinions about the first sentence of this article, and discussed these different beginnings: "Children come to school faced with navigating the complex and multiple problems of our culture." "Children come to school with complex and multiple needs." "Children come to school with complex and multiple problems." Each of these sentences suggests a different approach to working with children in schools. Is the root of the problem in the children's behavior or in the society that does not provide adequately for these children? We recognize that these are not merely semantic problems and we place our language and that of our students as a central focus of our critical analysis. We hope to reveal and clarify the values and assumptions that direct the approaches to the work we collaboratively pursue.

Power is inherent in naming one's self, one's problem, or one's need, or those of others. Consider, for example, that at one multicultural curriculum discussion the moderator (an African American female who refers to herself as such but who also often calls herself black) referred to groups as black and white. A white female referred to herself as Anglo and a white male used the term European American. Another white male wanted the group to adopt a common term to be used by all. We decided to try to continue our conversations using the preferred terms for each person. Rather than becoming entwined in arguments about political correctness, we felt this was empowering to all and any compromise would have a reverse effect.

Definitions also hamper our progress. The word "confidentiality" has, for example, many meanings and operational definitions. When lawyers on our teams talk to students, those conversations are legally protected as privileged communications. Unless a student gives his or her consent, those conversations are not shared with any others on the professional team. Yet if a students tells certain information (e.g., reveals sexual abuse) to a teacher, that teacher is required by law to make a referral. Counselors, therapists, and nurses all face similar predicaments. It is, therefore, possible for members of a team of six professionals to have different information about a child and be unable to communicate that information to each other. Conflicts have arisen when a teacher makes a referral to another professional and is left out of the information and counseling process because of confidentiality. Our work is leading us to consider carefully policy concerning information flow in the schools.

While we all claim to embrace social justice in our work, our divergent understandings of social justice lead us to envision our mission from several different perspectives. One of the authors of this article believes, for example, that social justice depends on changing American values and mores. She sees the "culture of greed" and the huge disparity of income distribution as the root of all of our problems; that variation in values regarding sexual practice, pregnancy, abortion, welfare, the elderly, and downsizing create a climate that is nearly impossible to change in the schools. She believes that we can only address the symptoms but never cure the illness through our integrated services work. Others in the School of Education believe that our work should be to change the existing structures by working within them. They point to students who are able to create meaningful lives within today's complex world, and urge us to struggle toward both individual and structural transformation.

Recognizing that the root of the problem may be beyond the scope of our interprofessional team, our mission led us three years ago to make changes in our university curricula. In the School of Education we added a required course called "The Social Contexts of Education" at the graduate level and "The Child and Society" at the undergraduate level. The latter course educates students about the realities of social problems that impact student learning and development. This course also fulfills a new university core undergraduate requirement that all students at Boston College take at least one three-credit course that addresses issues of human diversity. Other courses also address social justice issues in accord with our mission; for example, one member of our faculty held a three-credit seminar designed to help our doctoral students understand and debunk the suppositions presented in *The Bell Curve*.[12] In many courses we encourage our students to become active in policy-making agencies in their communities and states and at the federal level.

The Boston College–Boston Schools Collaborative Efforts

While we have a great deal to learn about collaboration, we are trying to work in mutually supportive and respectful partnerships between the university and the schools, and we are learning to collaboratively deliver services in the schools and agencies. Our collaborative model assumes interdependence among individuals, organizations, and even whole systems, and our institutional mission and values provide a context essential for our ongoing commitment to the work.

We have developed integrated services/interprofessional collaboration teams within four inner-city Boston schools in a neighborhood community. While we have worked in two elementary schools, a middle school, and a high school, we focus here first on the high school and later on one of the elementary schools to provide some examples of our work and how our mission informs our work.

The high school serves approximately 1,200 students from working-class and low-income families. The diverse student body includes Hispanic, African American, Asian American, Caribbean American, and some Eastern European students. Many students are first- or second-generation immigrants. The faculty is predominately white male and female with a small number of African American, Asian, and Hispanic teachers. Built in the late 1890s, the building looks somewhat like a castle, with high ceilings and large windows, and is chronically in need of repairs and renovations. After being on probation because of inadequate facilities, including an inadequate library, the high school has recently regained its accreditation.

Community agencies, businesses, and universities are working with the school administration, staff, and faculty. Social service agency support is coordinated by student support teams, which develop action plans to address the needs of students. A local hospital works with the school in a health careers cluster, through which we train students for part-time work in the hospital. Many of these students are hired permanently after graduation. Our efforts are coordinated by the headmaster, who yearly holds a planning session to develop with deans and faculty a strategic plan that will facilitate greater exchange of information and coordination of efforts.

Our faculty and students entered the high school in many different ways. Counseling, guidance, and nursing interns began by participating in the student support teams with school personnel. Student teachers have been placed throughout the school in one of their three professional placements. We are in the second year of a legal services program in which law students and a law faculty member provide free legal and referral services to the high school students. Law students also teach Youth and the Law sessions in the tenth grade civics class.

Opportunities for collaboration also arise out of individual student or faculty interests, which pose different challenges and opportunities. A doctoral student is working with parents to develop strategies for greater parental involvement. She is also testing a parent guidebook developed by the Urban League, which houses its Department of Education in our School of Education. A master's student is working with students to determine what support services they want from the school and from their parents. His work is supported by a special education inclusion grant and by the Urban League Department of Education.

We are also collaborating in research. University-based research must be negotiated with and to the degree possible "owned" by school personnel, and must directly benefit the schools; for example, Neisler's research on the sociopolitical attitude development of adolescents evolved from her observation and participation in social studies classes.[13] Neisler found that students were expressing attitudes about society, politics, and each other but were not called upon to understand or examine their assumptions, their logic, or any related factual information. Teachers at the high school are using Neisler's research to modify their instruction.

In addition, one faculty member wrote a partnership grant with the special education coordinator to work with the social studies and the ninth grade cluster teachers on inclusion of special-needs students in the regular classroom. We are in the second year of funding of that grant. Our efforts to engage in outreach to an elementary school that was moving toward inclusion formed the basis for our inclusion grant at the high school.

A Context of Inclusion: The Elementary School

There is always a context within which we do our interprofessional work that derives from the culture, habits, and history of the schools and community, and the goals and mission of the schools that we enter. Our work with an elementary school that is inclusive illustrates how collaborators bring multiple perspectives to work on common goals and development of a joint mission.

The principal of the elementary school within which we are working is in her fourth year of creating an inclusion school. She sees the exclusion of children from regular classes into any pull-out models of special services as extremely problematic. For her it is a matter of social justice that everyone should be included in the regular class. She developed a model in which all special teachers who formerly had small classes in special education or remedial reading became classroom teachers in her building. This allowed her to achieve a class size for every teacher of fifteen to eighteen children, down from thirty or more. In this urban elementary school, there were so many children with language, learning, and behavior needs that the process of "sorting out" who was in need of special education became nonsensical. The small class size was designed to allow a more individualized approach to the classroom.

Through weekly meetings of an interprofessional support team consisting of Boston College faculty and school personnel, we address the needs of students who are at risk. The team includes the classroom teacher, school and community-based professionals, and university faculty. As we strategized with school staff about children in serious trouble academically, emotionally, or socially, we came to value the voices from diverse professionals. Interprofessional collaboration has the benefit of obtaining different perspectives on the social contexts in which we work.

As we worked collaboratively, we had the opportunity to understand that the inclusion model that the principal developed, based on notions of fairness and good pedagogy, was perceived in many ways: For some teachers, the idea of including everyone was frightening and made them question their own training and capabilities; for others, this model called into question their basic assumptions that specialists know more and can do different things for children; still others saw inclusion as increasing their teaching burdens; and yet others questioned whether inclusion in a regular classroom was adequately meeting the needs of the targeted students.

Inclusion allows a student the right to an appropriate education in regular classes with necessary services and supports. That right is violated when the supports and services are not available. Therefore, in the same school that made inclusion seem logical because of the large number of children in need, efforts at inclusion were thwarted because there were few resources to make it work smoothly. Working with too few resources and not enough support is a daily struggle, with or without one more complicated child.

Like all urban teachers, these teachers were asked to do more with less. Inclusion often takes more teacher time to accomplish and often requires teachers to reevaluate their current practices. This is one more obligation in an underfunded school. However, when the principal designed her inclusive school, she did not intend to dump children in any classroom without regard to what they needed to learn. She understood that inclusion means individualizing a common curriculum so everyone meets high standards of learning.

The goal of inclusion, when implemented in a poor school district with a faculty with a wide range of competence and commitment, allowed the school staff to talk about this mission and challenge it for the first time.[14] Having the university present encouraged the discussion that revealed these multiple perspectives. As this example illustrates, our collaborative work in schools has potential to illuminate school practices that require multiple perspectives to move toward a common goal. Our work in schools also helps bridge the theory-practice gap by allowing theorists to redefine theory for the practitioners and practitioners to react to the theoretical constructs out of their classroom experience.

Challenges and Complexities to University– School Collaboration

The challenge and complexities of interprofessional work was illustrated recently at a meeting of students who have a practicum in the school. Boston College student teachers, student counselors, student nurses, and student social workers met, as they routinely do, to discuss their work in the schools. A student from counseling psychology, who meets with small groups of children in the school to support and listen to them, asked how to handle the fact that she did not want the stories that were told "in group" to be retold back in the classroom. She was concerned about confidentiality and about maintaining openness and trust in the group. The student teacher was troubled that children might be sharing private stories that could be repeated. She also wondered if the families fully understood what these groups were, and questioned the value of taking children out of the classroom during academic time. A social work student thought the groups were very valuable to teach social skills the students badly needed. She saw them as skill-building groups, not counseling groups. Another student wondered what the impact was on the students when it was decided that they should go to group. She found some children reluctant to come with her when she arrived in class. Each Boston College student saw the work very differently from his or her professional perspective, and each perspective broadened the counseling student's understanding of the complexities of her work.

We see our work as evolutionary, defined by the direction the public school sets and influenced by our Jesuit University and School of Education missions. At times this leads to multiple and conflicting pressures. We find when the school-university relationship develops that there is no end to the requests we receive from schools. Urban schools have very limited resources and we become a powerful addition to their few resources. We are asked for student teachers, student counselors, student lawyers, student social workers, and student nurses. We are asked for books, to do workshops, to find literature, to gather information, and to judge the science fair. We are asked to write grants, meet school officials, talk with parents.

A university faculty could easily become drained by agreeing to the multiple requests of schools and communities. We could provide student teachers and tutors to teach use of the computers as well as literacy and second-language acquisition; we could distribute materials and conduct seminars about nutrition, drug use, violence prevention, or parenting skills; we could extend the legal services clinic to the parents of students, and provide nursing care, medical referrals, and social services. Setting priorities with the school is crucial to preventing burnout. Keeping our mission clearly in mind helps us make difficult decisions about where and how to use our human and material resources.

In order to accomplish our social justice mission to find God in the community, the traditional university role has to be turned on its head. To work together as partners the community needs to know that this collaboration would not be a traditional university relationship. Those traditional relationships often leave communities distrustful of our motives and our commitments. Boston College is dedicated to help meet the communities' needs, not merely the research needs of the university. We are in the schools every week to demonstrate that we are partners in tackling the everyday issues that the community faces. Using the school's agenda, working together often and over the long haul has resulted in an extraordinary collaboration built on trust. The result has been that our interprofessional work in the real world of schools has had important outcomes for both the schools and the university.

Results for the University

For the university faculty the outcomes have been many. We have the opportunity to feel exhilarated at living an activist life with the community, as its members struggle to improve their lives. This mission, described earlier, feels to us like good work: for some it is God's work. Second, our classes and our curriculum are profoundly and forever changed. We now teach very differently, incorporating what we know from our community work and knowing more clearly how our students must be prepared for their work in the future.

Our students might be the most fortunate of us all. They were able to join our interprofessional team in their schools and they observed their professors collaborating with each other and with the community professionals. They have been prepared in a new paradigm of collaboration among the professionals concerned with children and families at Boston College through their work in the schools.

Results for the Community

The community and the schools in which we work should speak to the results for them with their own voice, but our close partnership allows us to highlight a few outcomes as we see them. While no single activity can eradicate the conditions of poverty and school failure in urban centers, the Boston College partnership with the urban schools had direct and important impacts on many children and their families. In addition, the community professionals with whom we worked learned from us, as we learned from them. University faculty brought different perspectives, energy, and ideas to the work in the schools. Third, the school met in support teams to discuss children and families every week. The chaos of urban schools easily interferes with extraordinary activities, like meeting to problem-solve about children in trouble, as important as those activities might be. The fact that the team from the university was coming to the school each week solidified opportunities to discuss children needing attention, resources, etc., and possible solutions as we saw them.

Our impact has been so positive that the headmaster of the high school recently spoke to a group of twenty Boston College faculty and staff who work in her school. During the meeting she identified her concerns about the need for the ninth grade students to set goals and to develop strategies for their attainment, and said she hoped that we can form an inter-professional group to further support the ninth grade cluster. The principal at the elementary school has recently joined us in the fourth year of funded work on inclusion. The school, community, and university have recently collaborated to seek funding for an extended services school to address the needs of children and families after and before school hours.

We will continue to call on the Catholic tradition of social justice for strength, guidance, and sustained commitment to our individual and collective work. We believe that the Boston College story of integrating mission into the life of the university is a story that has lessons for Catholic schools that attempt to draw on their mission, so as to better serve the complex needs of children, youth, and families.

The university's outreach scholarship and the Catholic character of Boston College suggest a link between Boston College's collaborative service mission and a network of Catholic schools. Through the Selected Programs in Catholic Education (SPICE) the university provides a forum for practitioners to learn from practitioners, with the opportunities for reflection within the academy. Boston College is uniquely poised to identify and assess successful programs, and uniquely able to provide a forum in which these programs are shared through conferences on campus and through publications. Our efforts to realize our mission through interprofessional collaboration in service to urban children in public schools provides one such example.

Postscript

A short summary of this work was published in Momentum. *The work described here is due to the efforts of many faculty at Boston College and we acknowledge their role and contribution. The work has been funded by the Massachusetts Department of Education, the DeWitt-Wallace Reader's Digest Foundation through the National Center for Social Work and Education Collaboration at Fordham University, the U.S. Office of Education (Fund for the Improvement of Post Secondary Education; Patricia Roberts Harris Grant), and Philip Morris Companies Inc.*

Notes

1. J. G. Dryfoos, *Adolescents at Risk: Prevalence and Prevention* (New York: Oxford University Press).

2. R. M. Lerner, *America's Youth in Crisis: Challenges and Options for Programs and Policies* (Thousand Oaks, CA: Sage, 1995).

3. American Bar Association, 1993; American Academy of Pediatrics, 1994.

4. P. Byrne, *Paradigms of Justice and Love: Conversations* (St. Louis, MO: National Center on Jesuit Higher Education, 1995).

5. M. Brabeck, M. Walsh, M. Kenny, and K. Comilang, "Interprofessional Collaboration for Children and Families: Opportunities for Counseling Psychology in the Twenty-First Century," *Counseling Psychologist,* in press; M. Walsh et al., "Integrated Services/Interprofessional Collaboration and Related Areas" (Boston College unpublished photocopy, 1996).

6. J. Donald Monan, S.J., "From Palaces to Ghettos, a Jesuit Legacy of Action and Devotion," *Boston Globe* (April 22, 1991), 13.

7. William Leahy, S.J., "Rededication: The Inaugural Address," *Boston College Magazine* (fall 1996), 30.

8. S. Waddock, "An Emerging Model of Integrated Services and Interprofessional Collaboration: Working Together for Community Welfare" (paper presented at the Academy of Management Annual Meeting, 1996).

9. Reisman and Jencks (quoted in Leahy).

10. Leahy, "Rededication," 30.

11. "Advancing the Legacy," 1996.

12. R. J. Hernstein and C. Murray, *The Bell Curve* (New York: Free Press, 1994).

13. O. J. Neisler, "Inside Castleton High School: Development of Secondary Students' Sociopolitical Attitudes," unpublished dissertation (Syracuse University, 1994).

14. A. Hilliard, "Public Support for Successful Instructional practices for At-Risk Students," *School Success for Students at Risk* (San Diego, CA: Harcourt Brace Jovanovich, 1988).

Hiring Faculty for Mission: A Case Study of a Department's Search

Joseph J. Feeney, S.J., Owen W. Gilman, Jr., and Jo Alyson Parker*

As Jesuit schools puzzle about their identity, faculty hiring remains a recurring issue. The reason is clear: either Jesuit colleges and universities hire professors who support a Jesuit and Catholic identity, or they gradually will lose this identity and its appeal to prospective students. Yet the choice to hire such professors brings its own problems. Will such hiring for mission lower the quality of the faculty? Will good candidates be scared away? Will ecumenism or diversity be damaged? Are there legal implications? And how can mission-friendly professors even be identified?

In the actual hiring process, more problems emerge. What sort of advertisement should be written? Should issues related to mission be raised by the department or (as is now common) only by a dean or academic vice president? How can the mission affect the initial screening of dossiers and initial interviews with the search committee? If the question of mission is raised just with three or four finalists—often selected solely for professional qualifications—hasn't the whole process simply ignored the issue of hiring for mission? How can departments—who really make the effective choices—even engage the issue in conversations and meetings?

Within this framework, though without explicating all the issues, the English Department of St. Joseph's University set out in the fall of 1996 to hire two (later three) new professors. Since hiring for mission is a crucial yet little discussed issue at the department level, we offer here a case

*James J. Feeney, S.J., is professor of English at St. Joseph's University, Philadelphia, Pennsylvania. Owen W. Gilman, Jr., is chair and professor of English at St. Joseph's University. Jo Alyson Parker is assistant professor of English at St. Joseph's University. The article is reprinted from *Conversations on Jesuit Higher Education* 12 (fall 1997): 20–23.

study of our own hiring process. We write as three members of a five-person search committee—the three who did the interviewing at the Modern Language Association (MLA) convention. I should note that I am a Catholic and a Jesuit priest, while my two colleagues stand in different religious traditions. The chair of the search committee was Owen W. Gilman, Jr., later to be named the department's chair.

The departmental context is important. With fifteen members, the department's senior half was mainly Catholic, with five alumni of St. Joseph's; the junior half, selected for a needed diversity, was mainly non-Catholic with few Jesuit links. In the summer of 1996, two professors chose retirement or medical leave; a third planned his retirement in 1997. We clearly needed several new professors, and the discussions began.

A department meeting on September 10, 1996, caught the issues: (1) institutional tradition urges a particular consideration for Catholics and/or alumni of St. Joseph's or other Jesuit colleges; while avoiding parochialism, such a choice could offer our students identifiable role models of Catholic and Jesuit intellectuals; (2) acceptable applicants should sympathize with institutional goals; (3) such sympathy could probably be discerned through the interview process; (4) we would need to determine how our concern should be worded in our advertisement for the *MLA Job List*; (5) the advertisement should not put off viable candidates; (6) at issue is an act of departmental will to preserve institutional tradition; (7) announcing ourselves as St. Joseph's University in the Jesuit and Catholic tradition would preserve the sense of tradition without eliminating potential candidates from other traditions. After much discussion, our conclusion was unanimous: The advertisement should "identify the institution as Jesuit and Catholic," and of our next several hires, about half should be Catholics or St. Joseph's or Jesuit alumni. Such was the departmental will, and our advertisement read, "St. Joseph's University . . . an institution in the Jesuit, Catholic tradition."

As the applications rolled in—over 600 Americanists and 150 rhetoric/composition experts—many of us had to read the dossiers. In a memo the chair of the search committee summarized our need for lively, versatile people who could provide leadership in their fields through 2025, teach creatively and challenge our students, and make significant scholarly contributions to their disciplines. He continued,

As a department, at a meeting in September, we also accepted the goal of addressing the Jesuit mission in education as we consider applicants; consequently, be looking for applicants who already know about Jesuit education by personal experience . . . . We also agreed, however, that this particular objective could be met over the course of the next few hires, so we are not restricted in this particular search. We need to read wisely. There are many very talented applicants, from top-notch undergraduate programs and stellar graduate programs, who have not come out of Jesuit institutions and yet who could be perfectly suitable for the work that must be done here in the next few decades.

This was, I thought, a very fair summary of our needs and an open yet balanced statement on hiring for mission.

At the MLA Convention in Washington, D.C., we interviewed about ten people in each field; afterwards, back home in Philadelphia, we met with a few more Americanists. We tried always to put the candidates at ease, while doing highly professional interviews about the normal issues. As for hiring for mission, some candidates raised the issue themselves (they were Catholics, or committed to religion-based education, or wanted to work in the Jesuit tradition, etc.); those who didn't address the issue were asked, "Why do you want to come to St. Joseph's University?" Some spoke of a smaller school, quality students, good reputation, a strong liberal-arts core, the Philadelphia area, a beautiful campus, a balance between teaching and research, and a commitment to undergraduate education. Others were more explicit about mission and identity: a Catholic or Jesuit university, service-learning courses, a commitment to social justice, a care for others, the Jesuit educational tradition, and an interest in "belief and morality as issues." To our pleasure and perhaps surprise, we of the search committee agreed completely on the list of candidates to be invited for on-campus interviews with the full department and with the dean and academic vice president.

At this point—the end of the interviewing process—I end my narration, for reasons of courtesy, confidentiality, and perhaps legal prudence. I note, though, that there was no religious litmus test; rather, hoping within our next several hires to engage a number of Catholics or Jesuit alumni, we carefully balanced a number of factors—professional, departmental, institutional, collegial, and personal—while never forgetting our mission and identity. Our process, I believe, may offer help and perspective to other Jesuit colleges and universities in their own hiring.

I end with a story. Last November, at a national meeting on mission and identity in Jesuit education, I spoke of the need for a balanced complexity in faculty hiring. To be complete and honest, I noted that the choice might sometimes involve a Catholic with a good graduate degree and a less committed person with a better doctorate. A former administrator popped up, "Why the Catholic is of course better, for that very reason." My reaction—I was discreet enough not to express it—was that he epitomized precisely how not to make hiring decisions. Rather, I argue, we need the academic virtues of complexity, balance, frankness, and collegial trust so that we—non-Catholics and Catholics together—might hire with such integrity as to create the future solidly in the Jesuit and Catholic traditions. For that purpose, this case study is offered.

J.J.F.

The 1996–97 Search in Historical Perspective

A decade ago, I chaired another departmental search committee, which also happened to involve the rhetoric-composition field. In that search, there was no explicit mandate from the department regarding particular concern for institutional mission. We still encountered the issue, however, for several applicants had Jesuit college backgrounds, including one graduate of St. Joseph's. At that time the search committee noted that the department of English already had quite a few members with a home-grown sense of identity—and that the department might be best served by adding people with diverse perspectives, so long as they were comfortable with the particular mission of the institution as we outlined it for them. Consequently, as our deliberations proceeded from initial screening to interviewing about fifteen applicants at the MLA and then on to campus visits, we eventually focused on people who had no prior experience in Jesuit education.

Our other departmental search efforts over the past ten years have similarly not included any strong sense of urgency about adding faculty who would know the nature of the institution in advance through their own educational background. Over time, though, our situation has changed.

Undergraduate institutions with a strong sense of identity and mission have special strengths. There are distinct advantages in having people around who know an institution intimately—and who have a deep love for it. Undergraduates frequently acquire such a love in their years of study and growth at the institution where they matriculate late in their teens. The Department of English at St. Joseph's University has now reached a juncture where the number of members with long-term affiliations to it will change substantially. This process of change has already begun.

We currently have broad professional diversity in the department, a healthy mix of people who prepared for the work of teaching and scholarship in a rich variety of undergraduate environments. Under these conditions, it made good sense in 1996 to give special consideration to the issue of hiring for mission. We recognized the benefits in hiring someone with a strong, abiding devotion to the mission of the institution, although this matter had to be balanced delicately at every step with a host of other objectives and concerns. This past year, we knew all along that we would not compromise on quality, that we would serve the department and St. Joseph's poorly if we sacrificed talent simply to bring in someone who had the right religious credentials. As always, in filling each position, we looked for a person who would complement the current members of the department.

In the next several years, we anticipate conducting more searches. To maintain the sort of balance that has served St. Joseph's well in the past—and to sustain the sense of tradition that a place like this needs to flourish—each search process will incorporate the same judicious approach taken in 1996–97. We aspire to excellence in each search, and we are confident that our future efforts will reflect the same degree of success regarding the hire-for-mission concern that we realized this past year.

O.W.G.

A View from Both Sides of the Interview Table

I am one of the people hired within the last ten years, a period during which, in Owen Gilman's terms, there was no "strong sense of urgency about adding faculty who would know the nature of the institution in advance through their own educational background." Indeed, when I sent in my application to St. Joseph's, I had only a vague idea that a Jesuit education combined intellectual rigor with humanistic concerns—an idea that has been proved correct during my experience in the English department here. During my interview at the MLA convention, I was asked no questions about whether I had any devotion to the mission of the University, and, if I had been, I would not have known how to respond.

Thus I came to St. Joseph's with no actual sense of the Jesuit mission at all. Yet within my very first year here, I began to see that a sense of mission was an integral part of the intellectual fabric of the University. Quite frankly, I was fascinated at first by the ongoing discussion of mission that I encountered at St. Joseph's. I had done my undergraduate and graduate work at a large state university and had held a teaching position at another, and in neither place had the issue of mission been broached—not with regard to student needs or faculty aims. Here the issue was omnipresent, discussed at faculty retreats, student/faculty convocations, and faculty colloquiums. It was the focus of the semiannual "Gatherings" of faculty members from nearby Jesuit institutions. But, perhaps more important, a sense of mission informed the way things were done around here—students' embrace of service-learning courses, the faculty commitment to educating the whole person. Certainly, there was sometimes a gap between articulating the University mission and achieving it, but the very fact that articulating it mattered was impressive.

Although I do not profess to have become an expert on the mission of St. Joseph's University, by the time I served on the search committee I had come to understand it in part. From the perspective of an interviewer, rather than an interviewee, I think that our advertisement in the *MLA Job List*, our initial screening of applications, and our in-person interviews enabled us to strike a necessary balance in attracting and evaluating candidates between their professional qualifications and their devotion to the Jesuit tradition. Mission came up in the interviews not as some sort of religious litmus test but as a way of informing candidates about the University's strong sense of its identity as an institution in the Jesuit, Catholic tradition and inviting them to discuss how their own "mission" might correspond. I think that this search demonstrated—and I trust that future searches will demonstrate—that we had and will have the flexibility to consider alike those candidates trained in the Jesuit tradition and those who, like myself, learn over time to understand and appreciate its strengths.

J.A.P.

Is Jesuit Education Fulfilling Its Mission?

Vincent J. Genovesi, S.J.*

Arthur Simon, founder of Bread for the World, an organization committed to feeding the hungry, published in 1987 a book titled *Christian Faith and Public Policy: No Grounds for Divorce.* As the title suggests, Simon maintains that America's claim to be a Christian nation must be supported by the public policies it establishes. Convinced that unless Christian faith is active in the works of love—otherwise it is as dead as a body without a soul—Simon argues that Christians should be "twice-converted people. They are first converted from the world to Jesus Christ . . . but then they are converted to the world again, to love the world and relate to it, not as they did before, but through the heart and mind of Christ."

In effect, what Simon calls for is our entrance into a personal faith relationship with Christ, or a surrendering of our hearts to God in love. This love is the kind, however, that reveals itself in eagerness to put our minds and hands to work in fashioning a world that embodies justice; it is thus both more responsive to the rights and needs of others and more to God's liking. Understood this way, Simon's thesis raises serious questions for Jesuit schools, especially institutions of higher learning: How many of our graduates are such twice-converted people—people of faith who are working for justice? What are we doing to encourage and help more of our students to be twice converted, and what more can and should we do?

*Vincent J. Genovesi, S.J., is professor of theology at St. Joseph's University, Philadelphia, Pennsylvania. Reprinted with the permission of Vincent J. Genovesi, S.J., and America Press, Inc., 106 West 56th Street, New York, NY 10019. Originally published in *America* (May 23, 1998).

These questions are in no way idle or incidental concerns, for they arise from the very heart of the Society of Jesus's current understanding of its fundamental mission and purpose:

> The mission of the Society today is defined as the service of faith, of which the promotion of justice is an absolute requirement. The service of faith and the promotion of justice constitute one and the same mission of the Society. They cannot, therefore, be separated one from the other in our purpose . . . nor can they be considered simply as one ministry among others, but rather as that ministry whereby all our ministries are brought together in a unified whole.
>
> The educational apostolate . . . is to be valued as of great importance among the ministries of the Society for promoting today's mission in the service of faith from which justice arises. . . . We must in a special way help prepare all our students effectively to devote themselves to building a more just world and to understand how to labor with and for others. When dealing with Christian students, we should take particular care that . . . they acquire that knowledge and character which are worthy of Christians, and that animated by a mature faith and personally devoted to Jesus Christ, [they] learn to find and serve him in others. . . . Regarding all other students of other religions, we must take care throughout the whole course of studies and especially in the teaching of ethics courses to form men and women who are endowed with a sound moral judgment and solid virtues.

God's Reign

I know that Jesuit schools, for the most part, are trying to put some flesh upon the words used above to describe the Society of Jesus's present understanding of its basic mission. At the university with which I am associated, for example, we have a Faith-Justice Institute, several service-learning courses, and numerous community-action programs, but these courses and programs do not involve the great majority of our students. Furthermore, I dare to say that vast numbers of our students remain largely uninformed about the deeper meaning of a Jesuit education. They, of course, bear none of the blame for this. It is not their fault if they do not realize that for Jesuits education is an apostolate, a continuation of the work of the Apostles, and that the great gift of knowledge should finally be used for doing good, which means helping in some way to establish God's reign.

It seems to me that we allow too many of our students to be simply career-oriented, and we leave unchallenged their desire simply to find a comfortable niche in society. I fear that in the course of their studies many of our students gain only a minimal sense of social responsibility and little appreciation of the social teachings of the Catholic Church. Beyond this, I wonder how many students are required to take an ethics course that focuses on the moral issues associated with the careers they are planning.

I venture to say that in terms of our curriculum we leave too much to our students' "good will," and so fail to require that they give serious, systematic and sustained reflection to the complex ethical questions that they will face in their careers. I believe that students, at the very least, should first be helped to recognize, and then made to take a hard look at, the ethical concerns that are most closely connected to their chosen field of endeavor. Any hope that students will be motivated to do what is right must be based on our first helping them gain a clearer understanding of what "the right thing to do" is.

Head, Heart, Hands

On paper, Jesuit educational institutions are committed to encourage their students to the kind of faith in God that will inspire them to bring justice and love into their work and world. More specifically, it might be said that the Jesuit educational mission is to help students see that faith in God gives rise to a three-dimensional responsibility, which we educators must help them meet. In short, our students must seek and be encouraged to grow in three ways:

Competence: Every student should graduate as a well-rounded individual with a solid knowledge of a particular field of study. There is simply no substitute for an *informed head*.

Conscience: In addition, all graduates should have a better sense of how to use in a right and helpful way the knowledge they have gained. Correct information should be guided by a *warm heart*.

Compassion: Finally, understanding what is right, every graduate must find the courage to follow through in action and do what is right. Intelligence and talk of values should finally be seen and felt in *loving hands*.

It has been said that we make a living by what we get, but we make a life by what we give. Clearly, our students have a right to learn how to make a living, but they also have a duty to learn how to live. Jesuit schools must recognize and support this right of students, but they must also see to it that the students recognize and fulfill this duty. What other reasons do Jesuit schools have for existing?

The Integrity of a Catholic Management Education

Michael J. Naughton and Thomas A. Bausch*

When a U.S. manufacturing plant laid off 2,000 employees and moved its production facility to Mexico, a Catholic newspaper accused the company's executives, who were educated at Catholic universities, of violating Catholic social principles.[1] While the Catholic newspaper may not have been fully informed over the particularities, its story raises serious questions for Catholic universities: "Should managers educated at Catholic universities examine layoffs and plant closures any differently from those executives taught at non-Catholic universities?" Or more generally, "Do faculty at Catholic universities teach management any differently from faculty at non-Catholic universities?" In the words of Brian Daley, S.J., does the Catholicity of the university "really indicate a qualitative difference in the way a university teaches?"[2]

This episode highlights the problem of mission and integrity for Catholic universities and their schools of management.[3] Historically, Catholic schools of management have been instrumental in moving an immigrant, blue-collar, inner-city class to a mainstream, white-collar, suburban class. This shift has been a success in many ways. One can only hope that it will continue for the new immigrant classes entering this country today. But in providing economic and occupational success, did Catholic schools of management inadvertently teach their students to work with purely individualistic aspirations? Did Catholic schools of

*Michael J. Naughton holds a joint appointment in the departments of Management and Theology at the University of St. Thomas, St. Paul, Minnesota. Thomas Bausch is professor of management, Marquette University, Milwaukee, Wisconsin. The article is reprinted from the *California Management Review* 38 (4) (summer 1996): 118–40 by permission of the Regents of the University of California. Copyright © by The Regents of the University of California.

115

management contribute to the prevalence of careerism described by William F. May as a "glass-enwrapped privacy . . . where questions of public obligation and responsibility seem marginal and episodic at best, distracting and suicidal at worst?"[4]

A careerist and materialist indictment of Catholic schools of management would seem unfair in light of their liberal arts, ethics, and service requirements. Many Catholic universities should be applauded for not reducing liberal arts requirements, for introducing ethics requirements, and for making available service opportunities. However, a partial indictment is called for when such requirements fail to be more fully integrated with the curriculum and research of management education.

We believe that a Catholic school of management has great promise since it has all the essential elements to fulfill its mission, but its full potential is unrealized by its partial failure to integrate such elements. This integration lies at the heart of the integrity of a Catholic university and its school of management. With the integrity of any educational institution comes the ability to integrate those things that make it wholly consistent with itself, where students receive not two types of education but one. Business ethics courses, up until now, have played a critical role in attempting to provide this integration. Such courses are a help in the formation of a student's heightened sensitivity to ethical issues, but they are fundamentally inadequate in having any lasting impact as an integrating force in the education of management students.[5]

The penetration of the Catholic identity into its schools of management raises difficult questions of academic freedom, faculty integrity, diversity in the student body, independence of management methods and research, and so forth. Such issues need to be examined with sensitivity and flexibility, but they cannot be used to deflect the question John Paul II raises in *Ex Corde Ecclesiae:* How can "Catholicism be vitally present and operative" in the university?[6] This question suggests that a Catholic school of management can contribute to the diversity and plurality of management education if it takes its mission seriously. Lyman Porter and Lawrence McKibbin complain that they have found in many U.S. schools of management a "cookie cutter mentality," discouraging a diversity of approaches necessary to make progress in management education.[7]

Porter and McKibbin's argument was taken most seriously by the American Assembly of Collegiate Schools of Business (AACSB) when its accreditation standards were reformulated. The new standards are mission-driven and process-oriented. A school of management's mission must be consistent with the mission of the university, and management processes must continually reflect on the mission and its accomplishments. In other words, a Catholic university could lose accreditation if not Catholic enough, rather than endanger accreditation by being too Catholic.

We propose four integrating dimensions necessary for a school of management to maintain and sustain its Catholic integrity and identity, and to have a lasting impact on the intellectual and ethical formation of management students.[8] They are the following:

- *Management as Liberal Learning*: integrating liberal arts and management education. If management is to be studied at a Catholic university, it must be academically defined in part by the liberal arts context in which it finds itself. The liberal arts context must also be open to management education.
- *Management as a Vocation*: integrating faith and work. If management education is to serve the mission of the university, the fields of management and the Christian social tradition need to be better related.
- *Management as a Profession*: integrating principles and techniques. Management's own self-understanding at a Catholic university must be viewed within a professionalism and the various competencies that go along with a profession.
- *Management as Service*: integrating management and society. Catholic schools of management also must contribute to management's self-understanding and its role in the community, particularly a community where resources are poorly organized and distributed.

These four means of integration achieve the integrity (end) of a Catholic school of management, providing the conditions for students to address the integrity of the intellect, faith, profession, and service as a manager.

Management as Liberal Learning: Integrating Liberal Arts and Management Education

The AACSB has consistently maintained that management education must be based on a strong liberal arts foundation. It decries any attempt to reduce the importance of liberal arts. For years, the standards provided a corridor: not less than 40 percent nor more than 60 percent of a student's course work will be in the liberal arts. In a mid-1980s report on management education, the authors argue that business schools should shoot for 60 percent in the liberal arts rather than 40 percent.[9] This led to the change in the standards calling for a maximum of 50 percent business courses. There is general acceptance of Newman's dictum that "who has been trained to think upon one subject or for one subject only, will never be a good judge even in that one."[10] Management education is incomplete without a broader foundation of the liberal arts.

Yet this foundational view of liberal arts and management education and the departmental and school structures of universities have created a fault line, producing two kinds of education rather than one. As far back as 1959, the Carnegie and Ford Reports noted that "the work students do in liberal arts subjects appears to have little relation to their studies in business and economics and not infrequently consists of a certain number of courses to be gotten out of the way as quickly and painlessly as possible."[11] Or if any integration has been made, liberal arts becomes a list of skills that are instrumental to management functions.[12]

This so-called foundational approach should be more accurately called an "along side of" approach where integration is left up to the students.[13] While there are many reasons for this lack of integration, its root cause lies with the faculty and how they see themselves in the larger university. Porter and McKibbin explain that while "there are exceptions, the typical [business] school sees itself as pretty much a 'stand alone' operation; there is little interaction—or perceived need for interaction—with other academic units on campus."[14] Nor do the liberal arts faculties see much of a need to interact on an academic level with the school of management. This lack of interaction translates into a segmented curriculum that has lost a "vision about ways to achieve 'an amalgamation of the two.'"[15] Little emphasis relative to the students' education is devoted to the integration of their liberal and professional education. When a gulf between liberal arts and management curriculums occurs, it creates the impression in students that they are receiving two types of education: one that makes them more human, and the other that makes them more money, but they are unclear about how the two fit together.[16]

An important question for a Catholic school of management, as well as for any school of management, is *What makes management education liberal?* Liberal education must pervade the whole university. For this to occur, management education must be infused with the principles of liberal education, and liberal education must be open to engage management. While there are multiple ways to integrate the curriculum of liberal arts and management, we offer two courses, one in the management department that introduces students to the practice of management through historical and philosophical lenses, and the other that offers a modification of an existing course in the liberal arts—philosophical ethics directed toward managerial issues.

The Practice of Management: An Introductory Course

Management education should not only be based on liberal arts education, but should be seen as an extension of liberal learning. Since management's self-understanding depends on metaphysical notions of the human person, philosophical notions of justice, historical analysis of property, and so forth, management as a discipline cannot be reduced to techniques. To have a liberal understanding of management, these ideas must be integrated into the curriculum. This makes the first course in the school of management critically important. In this hinge course, students can begin to see management itself as a form of liberal inquiry by applying the historical and philosophical insights of liberal arts to management education. This course should begin to develop within students the *historical habit* of recovering the tradition of their professional practice, and in Newman's words, *the philosophical habit* "of pushing things up to their first principles."[17]

To be educated managers in the fullest sense of that term, students must begin to appreciate the tradition and the development of management as a practice.[18] However, this exploration into the history of management is not done simply out of an intellectual curiosity to show who thought what and when. A smorgasbord approach to history where one idea is as good as another can do more harm than good, representing the history of management as factoids that seem determined rather than freely chosen.[19] Rather, a historical search shows how management ideas and practices have shaped history. All management theory presupposes various first principles concerning the human person, motivation, community, work, property, authority, wealth, hierarchy, and so forth. These first principles shape organizational practices that shape people and their societies. A first course in management should introduce students to the significance of the practice of management they are about to enter. If management students do not understand the history and philosophy of their own profession, they not only become deficient in their professional understanding, but also in their self-understanding as future managers. Students are now shaping history, themselves, and others around them.

It is precisely this sense of a larger vision that Porter and McKibbin report is missing in today's management education. They argue that schools of management have adequately given students the necessary skills to perform entry level tasks, but they have not given students the larger historical and philosophical understanding necessary for effective future leaders. Restricting management to a series of useful techniques for today loses sight of the importance of management as a practice that shapes people and history for tomorrow. The curriculum in the school of management must provide students with a larger context in which they can understand the practice they are beginning to enter. If it does not, the student will most likely fail to understand the professional character of management and reduce the meaning of management to a game or series of profit-maximizing techniques. In preparing students for the organizational world, a school of management must give them some sense of the history and practice of management so that wherever they end up as managers, "they would have a conception of the whole and of their own particular parts in it."[20]

An introductory course in management should help students articulate a more explicit philosophy on which to understand the practice of management and the structure of organization. U.S. managers, in particular, need a practical philosophy to understand the work they do. The university is better equipped than most social institutions in forming that philosophy. As cultural institutions, colleges and universities have an important function in this area, and they should not abdicate it for any reason.

Philosophical Ethics for Managers

Many Catholic colleges and universities, unlike many of their state counterparts, require a course in philosophical ethics. At some universities, they have designated sections for business students in which they examine business issues within larger philosophical ethical traditions. Such a course is helpful since it challenges management students to examine their first principles in ethical decision making. All too often, students will approach ethical issues in an organization without an informed philosophical context. Either they will have some vague unarticulated intuition about what is good, or they fall prey to some crass cost/benefit calculation or cultural relativism that escapes the difficulty of the decision altogether. Even when students are given a course in philosophical ethics, they tend not to make the translation of what they have learned in philosophy to management. A course in philosophical ethics with special emphasis on managerial issues engages students with practical issues of management within various philosophical ethical systems. By making the main objective of the course the integration of philosophical ethics and management, the integral experience of students is not left to chance.

The danger of such a course is in whether the faculty members in philosophy fully understand the complexity of organizational issues. This can be overcome by encouraging philosophy faculty members to become further educated in managerial issues through faculty development programs, such as attaining an MBA or having the course team-taught with faculty from the school of management. A team-taught course would also alleviate the appearance of "letting the school of management off the hook" concerning ethics by placing the business ethics part of the curriculum in the liberal arts core.[21] A team-taught course, which raises a host of practical problems, must be supported by a significant amount of faculty development for its successful accomplishment. This would entail summer grants, release time, faculty partnerships, and so forth for business faculty to become familiar with philosophy and philosophy faculty with business. Liberal arts and management professional education can share a common commitment to an integral development of students "when their aims are unconfused and their sequencing coherent."[22]

Management as a Vocation: Integrating Faith and Work

In their document on the *Church and the Modern World*, the bishops at Vatican II stated that one of the greatest errors of the modern world is the "split between faith which many profess and their daily lives."[23] They explained that from a Christian perspective there could "be no false opposition between professional and social activities on the one hand, and religious life on the other." Catholic universities, more so than any other institution, have the opportunity to marshall resources and energy toward understanding—in both theoretical and practical ways—the relationship between faith and professional life. Yet, Catholic universities are in constant danger of equipping students for "a peaceful coexistence of privatized faith within a secularized world."[24] Not to engage faith in professional work is a distortion of the fullness of what faith means, and, in the words of John Paul II, "reveals a decapitated faith, worse still, a faith in the process of self-annihilation."[25] By penetrating the meaning of work within a faith context, there is also a simultaneous deepening of faith itself.

The engagement and encounter of the Christian social and spiritual traditions with management education can affect and broaden the discussion that takes place both in management and theology. A dialogue between faith and work deepens and widens the *criteria of judgment*. Work, seen through the eyes of faith, is a participation in God's creation. Every human work that contributes to an organization where people can develop is a participation in the ongoing creation of God. Christian faith and its intellectual tradition views work with different *key and determining principles* that recontextualize the role of profits, efficiency, property/ownership, work, productivity, wages, quality, and so forth.

Through the theological principles of creation and redemption, the moral principles of human dignity, common good, subsidiarity, participation, and preferential option for the poor, and the virtues of charity, justice, practical wisdom, courage, and solidarity, faith serves not only as a critical voice to maximizing profits and instrumentalizing employees, but as a constructive voice that sees work and faith as an integral whole.

Faith and its intellectual tradition can also be seen as a *source of inspiration* in its relationship to work, particularly on an international level that reveals a more complicated view of how religious and philosophical ideas have influenced managerial theory and practice. While liberalism has predominated in American and British managerial thought, various kinds of communitarian perspectives have influenced management in Europe (Christian social tradition), Asia (Confucian), India (Hinduism and Vedantic tradition), and the Middle East (Islamic).[26] In most of these religious communitarian traditions, management is viewed and practiced differently from the classical liberalism that has informed American and British management. A great deal of ecumenical convergence on the study of faith and work could be accomplished.

While it is true that some students are not inspired by religious faith, it seems more accurate to argue, as John Langan does, that "for most people in our society their sense of personal roots and their membership in significant groups along with the motivational strength that commonly accompanies such factors are connected with religious bodies rather than with philosophical or ideological systems."[27] Managers will more likely have questions of integration, conflict, and compatibility between their faith and their work, rather than utilitarianism or deontology and work. If a Catholic university does not provide ways to address questions of faith and work, it becomes deficient in its mission by failing to contribute theological and spiritual insights for an increasingly secular world. As Michael Buckley explains, a Catholic university can and should "demand from its students those foundational studies, theological and philosophical ethics, by which sensibility and knowledge are grounded in their presuppositions and brought into an integration with Christian life and the commitments of holiness."[28] This is certainly a large order, but one that lies at the heart of what makes management education at a Catholic university distinctive to its identity.

Faculty Research

A school of management at a Catholic university can serve a unique function in developing the Christian social tradition in relation to management theory and practice.[29] Unfortunately, this relationship between Christian social thought and management issues is undeveloped, and even at times apparently incompatible. Many businesspeople have been critical of the Catholic social tradition for its focus on distribution and worker rights, and for its failure to focus on the entrepreneurial and wealth-creating dimensions of business. If this is the case, then, as Terrence Murphy points out,

> There is no group better equipped to fill out the tradition by pointing out the contributions and claims of the productive side of the equation than scholars of business. If capitalism as we know it in the United States has made enormous contributions to human welfare and if those contributions have been somewhat overlooked in Catholic social teaching, then the persons to analyze the contributions, to bring them into line with other elements, to give balance and nuance to our social teaching, are the scholars who should be found in Catholic business schools.[30]

In its research capacity, a Catholic school of management has a unique opportunity in further developing this important connection, as well as understanding the complexity between the Christian social tradition and management practice.

Lee Tavis, a finance professor at Notre Dame, explains that the Catholic social tradition teaching on human dignity, the common good, justice, and preferential option for the poor provides a larger context and fuller analysis when examining improvements in efficiency, considerations in global resource allocation, global textile markets, and so forth. "As one whose early academic career was based on mathematical planning models for multinational corporations, I can attest to the challenge of including the poor in the analysis and in encouraging their participation."[31] To analyze financial, marketing, or production issues from only a quantitative perspective is to slip into an economism that carries moral implications.

The role of faculty research as it relates to the Christian social tradition does not mean restricting the research program of its management faculty to these issues. But it does mean that such research has a presence at a Catholic university. A Catholic school of management should have a significant portion of its research portfolio devoted to larger issues of human concern while at the same time recognizing the need for diversity in faculty research. Tavis explains that "the key is to find a balanced way to nurture the study of moral issues advised by Catholic social teaching in a manner that enhances and is enriched by technical research."[32] To guarantee the engagement between faith and management, Catholic universities must prioritize their faculty development programs to allocate funding in this area, establish research projects among Catholic schools of management as well as other interested parties, and develop centers or institutes in Catholic studies on faith and work that can serve as a network for other scholars.[33]

Management as a Profession: Integrating Principles and Techniques

Managing organizations take a great deal of skill and technique. Management education, just like any liberal arts subject, must teach skills that are proper to itself. Skills of reading a balance sheet, calculating cost of capital, providing statistical analysis, targeting and segmenting markets, managing group dynamics, generating creative thinking, initiating problem-solving techniques, mediating conflicts, and so forth are imperative. Such skills provide the *matter* of professional competence that has an important role in management education at a Catholic university. If Catholic schools of management fail to incorporate rigorous analytical skills necessary to run organizations, it would be as if an English department did not provide the necessary skills for a student to read a text or write a paper.

Skills provide the necessary basis for a competent manager. Without such skills and techniques, organizations will stumble, to the detriment of their own survival and to the common good.[34] Joseph Ratzinger points out that "a morality that believes itself able to dispense with the technical knowledge of economic laws is not morality but moralism. As such, it is the antithesis of morality."[35] An efficient and effective management system utilizes organizational resources that provide the necessary conditions that can increase the quality of life.

Yet just as dangerous if not more so is an approach to management that discards in its education a serious engagement with the human person and moral implications throughout its whole practice. Any notion of management "that believes itself capable of managing without an ethos misunderstands the reality of the person," as well as the reality of organizational life.[36] While skills provide the matter of management, they do not provide the *soul* of its professionalism. Skills and techniques are a necessary but insufficient dimension to management education at a Catholic university. But if management education is to be a form of professional and lifelong learning, then it must also engage the student in the essential dimensions of how their skills and techniques can be ordered toward human development.[37] If management education fails to engage students in this process, it would be like law schools teaching their students all about the techniques of trying a case but nothing about justice, or medical schools teaching their students all about human anatomy but nothing about care.

Here lies one of the greatest challenges of attaining the Catholic identity of schools of management. While courses in business ethics and theology of work contribute to the distinctive identity of a Catholic school of management, they will be marginalized if the rest of the management curriculum treats organizational activity as a series of techniques to maximize efficiency and profitability. To restrict the responsibility of ethics and anthropology in management to a philosophy class is to relegate the ethical dimension of management to abstraction, and create a false impression that "real" management is techniques. Only when disciplinary courses seek to integrate and engage more fully moral principles informed by a professional ethic will management education reflect its true professional character.[38]

According to Porter and McKibbin, most business schools have succeeded in providing students with the skills and techniques necessary to enter the organizational world. This task has been largely accomplished through functional courses like marketing, operations, finance, accounting, and human resources. They report that, overall, businesses are satisfied with the incoming skills of management graduates.

What is not as successful, however, is the contextualization of the skills in the broader purpose of the organization. The techniques of functional courses are powerful organizational tools having implications in the areas of property, authority, participation, and so forth, all of which have a tremendous effect on the human person. An important challenge for functional courses is to examine how their disciplines relate to the larger anthropological and moral questions of the organization and society, as well as how their disciplines relate to the common enterprise of the university.

Infusing a Professional Ethic into Functional Courses

Catholic schools of management must infuse a professional ethic throughout the functional courses of finance, accounting, marketing, operations, and human resources. What underlies this ethic is the reality "that to acquire knowledge and expertise is to acquire power, and no one should be allowed to wield such power without learning how to use it ethically, and in a manner that is socially responsible."[39] To accomplish this task will take a tremendous amount of cooperation among the management faculty, faculty development, and a person, such as a holder of an ethics chair, who can champion the cause. How this cooperation would be designed would depend on the particularities of each university. Instead of suggesting a design, we outline two critical dimensions that are essential for an infused professional ethic throughout the management functional courses.

Critically examine first principles of the function: Every functional area of management has first principles—those beliefs that serve as the foundation of the function. Too often first principles are left implicit and uncritically appropriated. For example, as the stepchild of economics (and economics a stepchild of philosophy), finance—more than most functions—still views itself as a valuefree science, a technique that would be tainted if questions of ethics, property, and anthropology were made more explicit.

The financial philosophy (and it *is* a philosophy) of organizational purpose (i.e., its first principle) is to maximize shareholder wealth. This purpose is based on principles of property, agency, contract, and a mechanistic understanding of justice through the market.[40] The finance classes we are familiar with take very little time uncovering the nature of the principles as well as the raging debate concerning these principles outside the function of finance.

The problem with the financial theory of the firm is not that it is taught; it must be, since the theory is presently an integral part of the function of finance. The problem with the theory is that in many cases there is no critical discussion of the theory within finance. Finance, marketing, or operations courses should create space for discussions to take place on first principles. An important quality of professional and liberal learning is "the freedom to think, to enjoy the argument wherever it might lead, to criticize and to question" especially on substantive questions concerning the first principles of a management function.[41] If a student passes through a finance course without discussing the conflicting dimensions in *theories* of the firm, it would be similar to a student in philosophy who only studied one theory of the person, or a student in theology who only studied one theory of the church, or a student in English who only studied one theory of interpretation. The first principles of all disciplines in an academic institution must be examined critically.[42]

A more insightful, explicit, and honest discussion of first principles leads to the second critical factor of implementing a professional ethic in the management curriculum: *Viewing the end of technique as service to human development rather than the reverse (instrumentalism).*[43] Within a professional understanding of management, profits, efficiency, productivity, and status are means, never ends. The professional manager must be educated in a context where he or she creates conditions for human development. For example, operations has traditionally defined itself in terms of designing efficient and productive systems through the best available technology. Workers are placed within these highly efficient systems and subordinated to its technical dimensions. Within operations, a priority of the technically efficient at times dominates over human development.

Recently, however, the sociotechnical movement has shown that designing only efficient and highly technical systems is not enough. Production processes must be social and human systems where people can develop. Technology, efficiency and productivity are necessary means to a successful company, but they are only means, never ends. At the heart of an operations manager's mission as a professional is the development of human workers within an efficient and productive system.[44] We would argue that such questions of technology and efficiency in relationship to human development in the production process must be addressed in courses concerning operations.

As future leaders of organizations, students of management will face issues of human development daily in their functional areas; unfortunately, many of the issues will be unseen because of their insensitivity and undisciplined education toward human issues (plant closings, job design, compensation policies, marketing policies, and so forth). As Tavis points out, "The real concern in the practice of management is the manager who simply does not see the moral component of the decisions he or she is called to make."[45] This includes not only the articulation of ethical reasoning, but the integration of such reasoning in the logic of the various management functions directed toward conditions that foster human development.

Management as Service: Integrating Management and Society

With all the resources at the disposal of Catholic universities and their schools of management, they can play a critical role to help alleviate the sufferings of this world, where economic, social, and political problems have caused an unprecedented amount of human suffering both locally and globally. Universities, and especially Catholic universities, must be actively involved in discerning the causes and solutions of these problems. Every Catholic school of management must take seriously the enduring duty of the Christian faith and ask: "How can a Catholic university, particularly in its management education, serve the community, especially those who are marginalized?" Catholic schools of management must face serious questions that get at the heart of their identity: Do they teach a "disciplined sensitivity" as a professional practice where those who suffer and are marginalized are given special consideration? Or rather do they teach a disciplined sensitivity that simply maximizes wealth-producing practices that reinforce "the social systems that do not benefit the poor majorities"?[46]

One's initial impulse here may be a generic call to volunteerism. Yet, this does not directly bring to bear the immense talent and skill of management. While management students are often asked to serve the poor through volunteer activities, they are not usually asked to bring their knowledge of management to alleviate poverty. Our comments here are not meant to undermine the volunteerism that has increased on colleges campuses, but rather to recognize its limited, although important role.

Volunteerism draws students, in a very real and concrete way, out of their own particular interests and can have life-changing effects.[47] Yet, for a university this is not enough for its role in the community. Buckley points out that "it is not enough—although it is marvelous—to have programs on the side, those open to the idealism and commitments of the young. But a disciplined concern for the suffering in the United States and the exploited throughout the world is still to become part of the basic education itself."[48]

While volunteer requirements and opportunities should constantly be fostered, the danger is that students learn how to serve society in volunteerism but not how to serve society through their role as managers. Volunteer opportunities express the Catholicity of a university, but by themselves they may actually provide a disservice to the Catholicity of the university by not connecting service to the heart of the university, namely, curriculum and research. Volunteerism without a disciplined basis to it may send the message that goodness is performed in the private time of one's life. Schaffer and Rodes explain that "if you spend the day on corporate takeovers and plant closings without thinking about the people you put out of work, you cannot make up for the harm you do by giving a woman free legal advice in the evening when her unemployed husband takes out his frustration by beating her."[49]

Capstone Practicum

Making service to the community an integral part of the curriculum might best be addressed through filling another void that most business schools experience, namely, practical experience. Unlike other professional schools, most schools of management do not include a practicum experience in their programs. While management should be seen as an extension of liberal arts, its field of study is different by its practical direction. An important dimension of management education is field work. Students of management cannot simply stay in the classroom. Unlike the traditional liberal arts, which can be characterized as the life of the mind, any professional program, especially one in management, is also a life of the hands and feet. Management must be done. And it must be done in a way that students experience management as a service to the common good.[50]

We propose a capstone practicum where students would learn the traditional capstone material with special emphasis on cross-functional integration. They would be organized in teams and placed in businesses and nonprofits in struggling economic areas in need of revitalization. In cooperation with community groups, the state, executive fellows of the business school, urban studies/experiential learning programs, Small Business Institutes, and a whole host of other programs that are already working in the community, students would provide strategic plans for businesses based on in-depth research that the entrepreneurs of these businesses do not have time for. Students would gain insight into the fuller picture of poverty in inner-city areas and would learn from experienced practitioners as apprentices. Students would have the opportunity to work side by side with people in the community whose business endeavors are part of efforts for neighborhood and community vitalization. A capstone practicum also provides a larger context in which to help students evaluate their whole education, not just their management education.

Whether the particularities of the program described would work or not, this idea of how the school of management can be connected to the community, particularly the poor, raises the larger question of the urban mission of a Catholic university. Catholic universities that find themselves in urban environments, with all the associated urban problems, can work as an intermediate association toward mitigating the problems through their unique resources of faculty and students in management. But this serves the common good in a very different way from traditional volunteerism and works of mercy. Management serves the common good by using in effective ways its own knowledge and skill. In the words of E. Abraham, "Rather than giving a glass of water to the thirsty, modern management and technology enable one to build the reservoir and manufacture the pump which will permanently quench the thirst of thousands."[51]

Conclusion: Some Reflections on a Decision-Making Process

The objection could be made that just as society is becoming more pluralistic, why should Catholic universities—and especially their schools of management—want to become more Catholic? And furthermore, not only is society becoming more pluralistic, but so are Catholic universities. With an increasingly diverse student body and faculty, is it realistic for Catholic universities to assert a distinctive identity?

If in the name of pluralism Catholic universities fail to develop their Catholic identity, pluralism has become a platform for uniformity. It is puzzling, Buckley points out, "to see distinctiveness ruled out in the name of pluralism. Pluralism is precisely the admission and celebration of distinctiveness and difference on every level of unity."[52] Catholic universities and their schools of management provide a basis on which to contribute to this wider pluralism and diversity in management education. They will best contribute to this diversity and pluralism as Catholic universities. They do so by maintaining their own integrity through the integration of liberal arts and management, faith and work, principle and technique, and service and management. If they fail to bring these integrating components together, they reduce their integrity, and lose a chance to contribute to the pluralism that should exist in management education.

Yet, while we have highlighted the dangers of not taking seriously Catholic identity, we are aware of the dangers of misinterpreting Catholic identity in relationship to management education. There is always a temptation when retrieving a rich tradition to become boxed in by that tradition. We call this sectarianism. A Catholic university exists in a pluralistic culture, and it must engage in dialogue with the plurality of the culture. It cannot remain in some intellectual vacuum demanding unquestionable obedience from its faculty and students to its denominational belief system or a rigid interpretation of liberal learning. Once a Catholic university becomes intellectually rigid, religiously dogmatic, or morally intolerant, it will not only fail to contribute to the wider culture, but it will also lose its identity as a Catholic university by failing to engage in its mission of learning. If Catholic identity is taken seriously in management education, this will create more conflicts and more debates over their relationship. Catholic universities must allow, in the words of Newman, elbow room for students to question and faculty to explore within the limits of human dignity and the common good.[53]

Catholic universities walk a delicate line between retrieving what is particular to themselves as Catholic universities, and engaging this unique retrieval with contemporary culture. In the words of Alasdair MacIntyre,

> If we do not recover and identify with the particularities of our own community, then we shall lose what it is that we have to contribute to the common culture. We shall have nothing to bring, nothing to give. But if each of us dwells too much, or even exclusively, upon his or her own ethnic particularity, then we are in danger of fragmenting and even destroying the common life.[54]

Catholic universities have much to bring to management education as Catholic universities, but they cannot contribute unless they are fully engaged with the realities of management in an open, dialogical, and critical way; nor can they contribute if they are unaware of the rich tradition they have to offer.

But will the U.S. economy look any different if Catholic schools of management take their institutional context more seriously? Or more specifically and back to our original question: *Should managers educated at Catholic universities examine layoffs and plant closures any differently from those executives taught at non-Catholic universities?*

We want to be very clear here that we do not believe Catholic universities monopolize the market on ethics and social responsibility; nor do we think that there is a Catholic cookbook for plant-closing procedures. The nature of Catholic education requires human judgement and sensitivity to the contingent nature of management practice, habituating students to encounter the complexity of the issues both in its ambiguity and its mystery. There is nothing in the formation of Catholic management education, for example, that prevents companies from moving plants to Mexico. The formation should not be that parochial, nor that imprudent.[55]

It also must be noted that a Catholic university is one among many cultural influences in a student's life. The management student may or may not take to its influence. And faculty in a Catholic university may not take their institutional context to heart, nullifying the four characteristics described above.

With these qualifications in mind, the major contribution of management education in a Catholic university is not in techniques, but in developing *criteria of judgment* that inform the first principles of management decision making. The decision-making process, at the level appropriate to the particular manager, should be informed with principles such as human dignity, the common good, and priority of labor. It should provide a greater disciplined sensitivity to the full ramifications of layoffs. It should be guided by the virtues of justice, practical wisdom, and solidarity. And it should produce a decision directed toward human development. While we cannot lay out in full detail all the implications of an informed decision-making process, we believe the four characteristics outlined above provide some direction in answering our original question.

Liberal Arts and the Skill of Synthesizing

Managers formed within the liberal arts tradition would see their decision to lay off 2,000 employees as a historical event reshaping the socioeconomic future of the community. Rather than a narrow economic decision confined by legalistic concerns, layoffs are historical events that change the pattern of community living. Like politicians and military officers, managers are historical change agents. If they do not view themselves in such broad and profound terms, they will most likely belittle their role in the community by not synthesizing the sociological, psychological, and spiritual consequences of their decisions. Educated within the liberal arts, the manager has the rudiments of the skill of synthesizing technical business skills within the broader context and environment in which business exists. Recently, for example, consultants have sprung up offering seminars on the techniques of firing and minimizing employer's legal exposure. Little attention, however, is spent on helping people cope with job loss.[56] Such consultants escape the skill of synthesizing altogether by dodging the complexity of the issue. They evidence a unidimensional approach to layoffs that Catholic management education should seek to transcend.

The Common Good and Conditions Prior to the Layoff

Robert K. Greenleaf writes that an executive forced to dismiss thousands of employees or face the destruction of the entire organization, with negative consequences for all employees, customers, investors, suppliers, and others does not have a choice, for there is no alternative other than the layoff.[57] The critical question that needs the most focus is not how to close the plant, important as it is, but "What conditions were created that would lead a company to layoff 2,000 employees?" For instance, in the case under consideration, most observers believe that in the good times management was too generous when bargaining with the union despite being in an industry where the product is highly vulnerable to Pacific Rim competition. A manager educated in a Catholic liberal arts tradition would possibly develop a better sense of the historical and technological forces that are the context of the industry as well as a deeper understanding of the stewardship that is the special role of the manager in promoting the common good across time. For instance, greater work rule flexibility and more aggressive investment in new technology or product development, in lieu of some wage increases, might have allowed a more stable job situation.

Another critical issue for the company is: How did management view its purpose? Was the purpose of the company to maximize shareholder wealth, resulting in a culture of instrumentalization? Or was the purpose the "common good," that is, the creation of those conditions that foster human development? Did managers see themselves as "distributors of justice" or technicians of productivity? Did they see themselves as "developers of employees" or manipulators of human behavior? These purpose questions have concrete implications in such things as the ownership structure of the company,[58] wage and incentive policy,[59] job design, the decision-making process, and evaluation procedures—all of which set the conditions of whether human development can occur in the organization.

It is in this context that managers, depending on their sphere of influence, must address the anatomy of the current crisis of laying off 2,000 employees. Within the perspective of a manager educated at a Catholic university, the closing of a plant is a profound failure of purpose. It might mean that even though management had in place the necessary conditions to keep it both efficient and an integral part of the community, a complex web of factors may still force the plant to close; or it might mean that management failed to achieve such conditions, viewing the company as an asset to be amortized, rather than a community to be built. The second explanation is a moral failure on behalf of management and employees, while the first is circumstantial failure outside of intentions of management and employees. While no one can guarantee continual employment, just as no one can guarantee continual profits, the conditions that management establishes in the firm speak volumes about what is valued.

Professionalism and the Last Alternative

At the end of the day, the firm may have to close the plant because the cost structure of the industry no longer makes it possible to build its product in Northern industrial cities. Not to close the plant in light of industrial cost structure would be imprudent, since it would put at risk the existence of the company. Profit is a regulator of a business—if broken, it breaks the business. But if they were formed as professional managers, and they may have been, management at the organization would have exhausted every alternative before laying off 2,000 employees, and it would have included employees and the community in the process of seeking alternatives. Like a professional military executive who sees violence as the last alternative before going to war, a professional business executive, informed by the priority of labor, should see plant closings and massive layoffs as the last alternative; and if managers have to lay off or close shop, their professional duty would call them to mitigate the effects of the closure on employees. Just as a military officer who realizes the catastrophic effects war has on people (we call the person who does not a warlord), a manager must realize the catastrophic effects of major job loss in the community (we call the person who does not a manipulator).

The willingness to give prior notification, stretch eligibility for pensions, provide appropriate severance packages, pay for aggressive job retraining and placement, including within other divisions of the organization, are all concrete actions applying the principle of the preferential option for the poor in a particular situation.[60] Unfortunately, as permanent layoffs become commonplace, willingness to ameliorate the suffering seems to be declining. Consideration of executive compensation and benefits could be another area of concern where the virtue of temperance as well as solidarity could be exercised through appropriate adjustments.

Given that the decision to locate in Mexico is unavoidable, there is another aspect to the decision, namely, the specific location in Mexico. Is the company considering the location that would foster the greatest improvement in the common good of Mexico? AT&T faced this decision and—after weighing the options between a location in a Maquiladora versus a location in Guadalajara—choose the latter.[61] While somewhat more costly, Guadalajara enabled the company to help preserve the family unit and community and lessened the pressure for illegal emigration to the United States. Such concerns for the poor, the family unit, and the community should be an integral part of management education at a Catholic university.

Disciplined Sensitivity to Human Suffering

A manager who must go through downsizing and plant closings is experiencing a profound human event that will affect, in one way or another, the human soul. Downsizing is an experience of human suffering that can make the person either more bitter or more humane and spiritual. If managers are formed within a university experience that provides only technical, legal, and economic resources to handle layoffs, the likelihood, depending on their other cultural experiences, will be that they will become bitter, insensitive, and hardened to the suffering of others. However, if their educational experience can bring to bear the rich and profound cultural resources within liberal arts, faith, profession, and service, an experience of downsizing and plant closures could be avoided by their long-term perspective, and if not avoided, the turbulence of closure could be one of growth by developing a sensitivity to the suffering of those employees who, made in the image of God, must be treated with dignity. A driving question in a Catholic educational context is not only "what should I do?" but "who should I become?"

Our reflection on the decision-making process of a layoff sheds some light on the economic and cultural crossroad at which Catholic schools of management find themselves. As cultural institutions, they have responsibilities to further the culture, particularly intellectual culture. As economic practices, they must be informed by the business environment so as to prepare students adequately. Existence in two worlds should not lead to schizophrenia but to a profound integration best captured in the words of Jacques Maritain, an avid proponent of professional education at Catholic liberal arts universities and colleges:

> Education, in its final and highest achievements, tends to develop the contemplative capacity of the human mind. It does so neither in order to have the mind come to a stop in the act of knowing and contemplating, nor in order to make knowledge and contemplation subservient to action, but in order that once man has reached a stage where the harmony of his inner energies has been brought to full completion, his action on the world and on the human community, and his creative power at the service of his fellow-men, may overflow from his contemplative contact with reality—both with the visible and invisible realities in the midst of which he lives and moves.[62]

Notes

We thank Helen Alford, Don Briel, Jeanne Buckeye, Kenneth Goodpaster, Tom Holloran, Robert Kennedy, Pat Kowalski, Msgr, Terrence Murphy, John Murray, Emest Pierucci, and Bob Wahlstedt, all of whose comments and suggestions were extremely helpful. We would also like to thank Michael Jordan and Fr. Dan Pekarske for suggesting the theme of integration as well as focusing on the four areas of integration. A very special thanks to Michael Jordan, who took the time to edit the article. Finally, we would like to thank David Vogel and others at the *California Management Review* whose comments and suggestions were very helpful in tightening up the article. An earlier version of this article was presented as a paper at the American Catholic College and University Conference (ACCU) held at the University of St. Thomas in St. Paul, MN (August 1995).

1. Leslie Wirpsa, "Briggs & Stratton Layoffs Tear Family Hope," *National Catholic Reporter*, December 2, 1994, 6–8.
2. There are 235 Catholic universities and colleges with 656,905 students. Of those, 163 have undergraduate business programs and 93 have MBA programs. With approximately 20 percent on average undergraduate students majoring in business, there are approximately 91,000 undergraduate busi-

ness majors in Catholic universities. The number of students in the 93 MBA programs was unavailable, but with approximately 150,000 students in graduate programs, 40,000 students in business does not seem to be an unreasonable number in light of the fact that two of the schools are listed in the largest ten part-time MBA programs (University of St. Thomas, MN—2,957, and DePaul University, IL—2,444).

3. For Catholic law schools, see Steven Barken, "Jesuit Law Schools: Challenging the Mainstream," *Conversations* (spring 1993), 6–15.

4. William F. May, "The Beleaguered Rulers: The Public Obligation of the Professional," *Kennedy Institute of Ethics Journal* 2 (1992): 25–41.

5. Some studies suggest that business ethics courses by themselves have no significant effect on ethical decisions among students. It would seem that business ethics courses, by themselves, are not effective in incorporating ethical principles in the practice of management. This should be of very little surprise, since if one course is focused on the ethical principles and the other ten are focused on techniques directed toward wealth accumulating, there is very little doubt what will win out in the program, particularly for an unformed mind. This is in contrast to legal education, wherein one study "meaningful change" took place in the students, but it appeared to be attributed to the whole program rather than to one legal ethics course. Donald McCabe, Janet M. Dukerich, and Jane E. Dutton, "The Effects of Professional Education on Values and Resolution of Ethical Dilemmas: Business School vs. Law School Students," *Journal of Business Ethics* 13 (1994): 699. For a more critical view of legal education, see Thomas L. Schaffer and Robert E. Rodes, "A Christian Theology for Roman Catholic Law Schools," *University of Dayton Law Review* 14 (1999): 5–18.

6. John Paul II, *Ex Corde Ecclesiae* (Vatican City: Libreria Editrice Vaticana, 1990), 14.

7. Lyman W. Porter and Lawrence E. McKibbin, *Management Education and Development: Drift or Thrust into the 21st Century?* (New York: McGraw-Hill, 1988), 314–15.

8. The specific recommendations in this article are far more tentative than the general need in each of the four areas. The recommendations we propose below are possible expressions of the principles articulated. Principles, if they are authentic, often lead to a plurality of particular actions, depending on the unique circumstances of each university. Yet any program in undergraduate management education at a Catholic university must be built upon the mission that is Catholic and liberal arts at its core. If a management degree program fails in this quest for multiple levels of integration, then it incompletely realizes its mission and integrity as a Catholic university.

9. Porter and McKibbin, *Management Education,* 317.

10. John H. Newman, *The Idea of a University* (Notre Dame, IN: University of Notre Dame Press, 1992), 131.

11. Porter and McKibbin, *Management Education,* 317.

12. Newman, *Idea;* Ernest S. Pierucci, "The Relevance of Maritain's Understanding of the Development of the Natural Intelligence through Great Books Education to Contemporary Business Management Education" (paper presented at The American Maritain Association Annual Conference, Charleston, SC, December 1, 1995). Pierucci points out that liberal education should not be viewed "as simply an exercise of the mind preliminary to, and in the service of, a practical education. Any notion that a student should, for example, take two years of general education and then—perhaps having become more clever or having acquired mathematical or rhetorical skills—get on with a business major, misses the significance of 'integration' and 'synthesis.'"

13. Richard Pring, "Personal and Social Education in Vocational Preparation," in Samuel Natale and Brian Rothschild, eds., *Work Values: Education, Organization and Religious Concerns.* The Netherlands: Rodopi International Publishers, 1995, 305–21; Robert Grudin, "Point of View," *Chronicle of Higher Education* (February 24, 1995), A48.

14. Porter and McKibbin, *Management Education,* op. cit.

15. Michael C. Jordan, "The Tension between Liberal Education and Career Education," in *Papers 1987: Faculty Seminar on the History of the College of St. Thomas.* (St. Paul, MN: University of St. Thomas, 1987).

16. There are many notable exceptions to this. For example, Kenneth Goodpaster has crafted Aspen seminars for graduate students in the MBA program at the University of St. Thomas that integrate the great books tradition and management. Also at St. Thomas, Michael Jordan of the English department teaches a course in the Master's of Business Communication curriculum entitled "Readings in the Liberal Arts Tradition"; and the Hartwick Humanities in Management Institute has developed leadership cases that engage classical figures with modern management leadership issues.

17. Newman, *Idea,* op. cit.

18. William J. Bennett, *The De-Valuing of America* (New York: Summit Books, 1992); Alasdair MacIntyre, *After Virtue* (Notre Dame, IN: University of Notre Dame Press, 1984). The theory and practice of management has a long tradition that students are unaware of. Books such as Marvin Weisbord's *Productive Workplaces,* Daniel Wren's *The Evolution of Management Thought,* and others are valuable resources in introducing students to the historical community of management.

19. Louis Dupre, *The Passage to Modernity* (New Haven, CT: Yale University Press, 1993).

20. Robert Bellah et al., *The Good Society* (New York: Alfred Knopf, 1991).

21. See Michael Naughton and Thomas Bausch, "Catholic Identity of an Undergraduate Management Education Survey: Summary and Conclusions"

(paper presented at The Third World Forum of Jesuit Business Deans and Directors, Yogyakarta, Indonesia, July 29–August 1, 1995).

22. Michael J. Buckley, *The Catholic University as Promise and Project: Reflections in a Jesuit Idiom* (Washington, D.C.: Georgetown University Press, 1998).

23. Michael Walsh and Brian Davis, eds., *Church in the Modern World Proclaiming Justice and Peace: Documents from John XXIII–John Paul II* (Mystic, CT: Twenty-Third Publications, 1985).

24. Gustavo Gutierrez, *A Theology of Liberation: History, Politics, and Salvation* (Maryknoll, NY: Orbis Books, 1973), 224 (quoted from Schaffer and Rodes, "Christian Theology").

25. John Paul II, *Ex Corde Ecclesiae,* #44.

26. See S. K. Charkaborty, *Management by Values* (Delhi: Oxford University Press, 1987); Ronald Dore, *Taking Japan Seriously* (Stanford, CA: Stanford University Press, 1987); Jonathan Boswell, *Community and the Economy* (New York: Routledge Press, 1990).

27. John Langan, "The Ethics of Business and the Role of Religion" (paper presented at the University of Melbourne, December 1, 1991). Langan goes on to argue that "it is, I suggest, one of the major limitations of a purely secular approach to business ethics that it leaves out the task of drawing on the motivational power of religious convictions in order to sustain morally correct behavior."

28. Buckley, *The Catholic University as Promise and Project.*

29. An important area of engagement that also needs serious attention is between contemplation and activity, or what some would call a spirituality of work. This is particularly necessary when organizations attempt to define spirituality as "a nondeified, nonreligious 'spiritualism.'" Richard T. Pascale and Anthony G. Athos, *The Art of Japanese Management* (New York: Simon & Schuster, 1981). In his comment on the passage, Goodpaster asks "why insist *a priori* upon what might be a self-defeating set of constraints on spirituality?" Kenneth Goodpaster, "Work, Spirituality, and the Moral Point of View" (paper presented at the Second International Conference on Social Values, Oxford, England, July 22, 1993). While a nonreligious spiritualism attempts to transcend the denominational division within Christian spirituality, in reality it has the opposite effect by adding to the division by advocating a new denomination that is nondeified. Any notion of a Christian or Catholic spirituality must have at its center the work of Christ, where the worker participates in Christ's work as a collaboration with God on "the promises and the demands of a world transformed by a God of justice and love." Brian Daley, "Christ and the Catholic University," *America* (September 11, 1933): 6–14.

30. Terrence J. Murphy, "Remarks" (presented at the First World Forum of Jesuit Business Deans and Directors, Barcelona, Spain, June 11, 1993).

31. Lee Tavis, "Professional Education in a Catholic University," in Theodore M. Hesburgh, ed., *The Challenge and Promise of a Catholic University* (Notre Dame, IN: University of Notre Dame Press, 1994), 329–38.

32. Ibid.

33. Yet, because of the interdisciplinary nature of this research as well as its theological and ecclesial dimensions, it may not be well received in the various managerial disciplines, nor will some journals find it acceptable. A Catholic university, then, must have different reward systems concerning tenure and promotion and research awards from state universities.

On the positive side, the AACSB mission-driven guidelines indicate that faculty research should reflect the mission of the institution. If the mission is teaching, there must be research in pedagogy. At a Catholic university, faculty who engage in their research in the area of the Christian social tradition would be in conformity to accreditation guidelines. Faculty in a Catholic school of management would find such interdisciplinary research between faith and work easier if they had faculty in the theology department interested in bringing to bear Christian social and spiritual traditions. The collaboration between such diverse disciplines is largely missing in today's academic scene. A Catholic university that promotes such interdisciplinary research will make a contribution to the life of the academy, business, church, and culture.

34. Porter and McKibbin, *Management Education*.

35. Joseph Cardinal Ratzinger, "Market Economy and Ethics," in Association for the Advancement of Christian Social Sciences, ed., *Ordo Socialis: Making Christianity Work in Business and Economy* (Philippines : Divine Word Publications, 1992), 62–67.

36. Ibid.

37. Lawrence Lowell, "The Profession of Business," *Harvard Business Review*, 1 (January 1923): 131.

38. See Peter Drucker, *The Frontiers of Management* (New York: Harper and Row, 1986). If one wants to see what a school of management would look like without a professional ethic as well as liberal arts, the following shows a disturbing alternative:

Most managers we know are judged by results, usually measured by dollars and cents. We suggest doing the same for professors. Faculty should be paid and promoted on the basis of (1) whether their students can save or generate money during their field experiences, primarily their summer internships, and (2) whether or not their graduates can get jobs, make good money, and in turn, afford to donate to the alumni association. A publishing record would be irrelevant, unless a faculty member either had something to say, had an unquenchable personal desire to become rich and famous, or both. Tenure makes no more sense for a school of management than it does for a business organization, and should be abolished in a teaching school.

William C. Giauque and R.E.D. Woolsey, "A Totally New Direction for Management Education: A Modest Proposal," *Interfaces,* 11 (August 1981), 30–34. Without a professional ethic infused throughout its curriculum, a school of management becomes an institution of pride and greed.

39. Dennis Dease, "1991 Presidential Address," University of St. Thomas, St. Paul, MN.

40. Daley, "Christ and the Catholic University."

41. Pring, "Personal and Social Education."

42. Stephen R. Watson, "The Place for Universities in Management Education," *Journal of General Management,* 19 (winter 1993): 14–42.

43. Pierucci points out that "the refusal to see knowledge as self-development presents an insidious obstruction to the attraction and retention of knowledge workers. If their work is not understood as self-development, then personnel policies will be based on the instrumentalization of the intimate human act of knowing, and, therefore, on an ever deeper alienation of the person from work." Pierucci, "Relevance."

44. "We may say, paradoxically, that if he [the engineer] had been able to consider people as though they were robots, he would have tried to provide them with less trivial and more human work." Howard Rosenbrock, "Engineers and the Work that People Do," *IEEE Control Systems Magazine,* 1 (September 1981).

45. Tavis, "Professional Education."

46. Jon Sobrino, "The University's Christian Inspiration," *Horizons,* 17 (1990): 280–96; see also Buckley, *The Catholic University as Promise and Project.*

47. Boswell points out that business people who had experiences with the marginalized in society tended to be much more sensitive and sympathetic to the social responsibilities of business. Boswell, *Community and Economy.*

48. Buckley, *The Catholic University as Promise and Project.*

49. Schaffer and Rodes, "Christian Theology."

50. A capstone practicum also begins to deal with two prevalent criticisms of management school faculty: "They are too narrowly educated in a functional specialty; and they frequently lack relevant work experience." Porter and McKibbin, *Management Education.* This criticism must be kept in the context that 30 years ago the Ford Foundation study on management education chastised schools of management faculty for just the opposite reasons—not enough specialty and not enough academy study. The truth lies somewhere in between. See *Journal of Business Ethics* (January 1996)—the whole issue is devoted to service and community learning and management education.

51. E. Abraham, S.J., "What's Specific about Jesuit Management Institutions?" (paper presented at the First World Forum of Jesuit Business Deans and Directors, Barcelona, Spain, June 11–13, 1993).

52. Buckley, *The Catholic University as Promise and Project.*

53. Newman, *Idea.* "Catholic" and "university," as the etymological roots of the

words indicate, are intrinsically related. They are not an oxymoron. Buckley points out that all inquiry seeks ultimacy. The very structure of inquiry seeks completion or resolution so that which is inquired about makes sense. At the same time, faith, the belief in the ultimate, seeks further understanding of its ultimacy. In faith the font of truth is known, but the fullness of truth is not. In a sense, faith and the academy start at different ends of the spectrum and work toward each other. Each brings to the other a completion that is not possible without the other. Buckley, *The Catholic University as Promise and Project.*

54. Alasdair MacIntyre, talk given at St. John's University, Collegeville, Minnesota, 1990.

55. It should also be pointed out that the development of effective measures to mitigate the devastating effects of plant closings and layoffs "must rely on the insights and expertise of many talented, committed people of diverse faiths and no faith at all." Pierucci, "Relevance."

56. Andrea Gerlin, "Seminars Teach Managers Finer Points of Firing," *Wall Street Journal* (April 26, 1995), B1.

57. Robert K. Greenleaf, *Servant Leadership: A Journey into the Nature of Legitimate Power and Greatness* (New York: Paulist Press, 1977).

58. See David E. Sanger and Steve Lohr, "A Search for Answers to Avoid the Layoffs," *New York Times* (March 9, 1996), 1, 10–11. They discuss the role of worker ownership as one of the conditions critical to preventing massive layoffs.

59. When companies set up massive executive incentive policies based on shareholder price, the purpose of the company becomes transparent.

60. For a fuller discussion, see Business Executives for Economic Justice, *On the Firing Line* (Chicago: ACTA Publications, 1990).

61. Joseph L. Badaracco and W. L. White, "AT&T Consumer Products," Harvard Business School Case #392108 (Boston, MA, 1992).

62. Jacques Maritain, *The Education of Man: The Educational Philosophy of Jacques Maritain,* eds. Donald Gallagher and Idella Gallagher (Notre Dame, IN: University of Notre Dame Press, 1962).

The Faculty and the Disciplines

Introduction

Irene King

The Board of Trustees has a pivotal role in directing the overall vision and mission of a college or university. The faculty, however, are where the so-called "rubber meets the road"—where the mission is integrated and translated into specific disciplines. Without the support of committed faculty, no board, no matter how eloquent its vision and articulation of mission, can achieve its ends. This set of articles focuses on the varied ways faculty implement the values and identity of an institution.

In "Catholic Higher Education: A Strategy for Its Identity," John Haughey stresses the centrality of connecting concern for mission and identity with faculty research. While *Ex Corde Ecclesiae* may be attempting to mold the religious identity of Catholic institutions of higher education, the "market" dictates that if they are to remain viable they must become as distinguished and competitive as other colleges and universities. Haughey lays out five premises:

1. A Catholic institution is Catholic only if its faculty teach "with some knowledge of, reverence for, and advertence to the story and tradition from which their institution came." This does not presume that the faculty member actually be a Roman Catholic, but he or she at the very least should be conversant with the tradition.
2. A faculty member's effectiveness and "quality" of education "will be in proportion to the depth and breadth of the faculty member's research."
3. Catholic identity will not truly flourish until it is integrated into faculty research choices—and the institution rewards faculty for such choices.

143

4. Such research must be done with a consciousness of the "metaethics or spirituality that undergirds" the research.
5. There is "virtually no Catholic college or university with a sufficiently compelling vision" to lead faculty to begin research with these concepts in mind; Haughey suggests how to inspire such a vision.

Haughey asserts that the research done at Catholic institutions must be qualitatively different from that done at other institutions—although most faculty would disagree. He believes that research should not be driven solely by "what gets funded" or the current trends in a discipline. He proposes that research at a Catholic institution be driven by a spirituality of research—and he outlines the components of such a spirituality, being careful to assert that the burden for creating a spirituality within an institution is only partly carried by the faculty.

Haughey reflects upon the number of faculty, religious or not, who have described their path to academic careers as a "calling." He argues that the continuation of the path in the direction of that initial passion and call should be instructive in choosing research topics. Borrowing from the work of Bernard Lonergan, he then posits that one's interior self must be the place from which one's research emerges.

Haughey envisions academic disciplines through a spiritual lens, considering them little sovereignties with their own histories, methods, conventions, "and particular boundaries that cordon them off from the other disciplines." For believers, these principalities have, as it were, a penultimate authority. For believers, the ultimate authority is God—and thus the telos of one's discipline is seen through that lens and from that perspective.

Haughey then asks whether there is indeed something called "pure research"— work that has no context. He challenges faculty to ask themselves who or what their work is for: "truth? career? tenure? institutional prestige? people? societal change?"

Concerned for the right use not only of time and energy, but also of the tremendous resources of information available to researchers, Haughey believes that faculty are stewards of these resources, which must be used for the common good, to benefit "many, not a few."

Finally, Haughey turns to the important spiritual theme of reflection—looking closely at one's motives and the source from which they spring. He advises faculty to examine the immediate fruits of their research in terms of impact on their closest relationships—to oneself, family, other primary relationships, and God.

It will take a "compelling vision" to motivate faculty to integrate this type of spiritual assessment of their work into their research process,

Haughey recognizes. This compelling vision must be articulated and lived by members of the community. Unlike the authors of some previous chapters in this anthology, Haughey does not believe such a vision will come from a committee. The "institution will have to act its way into the new way of thinking, since it is unlikely it will think its way into a new way of acting." He believes that surveys and discussions with faculty about their reflections on a spirituality of research will bear great fruit. He sets forth five questions that he believes will guide the choice of research projects that contribute to the "self-understanding and mission of the Catholic institution."

1. What does "Catholic" mean?

"Catholic," Haughey reminds us, has meanings that relate to unity, integration, "according or towards wholeness." Faculty research at a "Catholic" institution should, then, "help students move toward a greater integration of understanding." It should be done with an eye toward the ways in which such work is connected to the "whole," the work of others in varying disciplines.

2. What in your research might be a subject for further inquiry and dialogue with faith?

Haughey encourages dialogues between faith and reason—openness to the possibility that all knowledge is potentially revelatory, since "nothing human is alien to the church."

3. How is your research serving the cause of the human person? Are you taking into account the ethical implications of your discipline's methods and discoveries?

Haughey draws this question from *Ex Corde Ecclesiae*: "The cause of the human person will only be served if knowledge is joined to conscience."

4. Does the subject matter you treat deal with issues that the Church's tradition has addressed? Would it be appropriate for you to take a position on the Church's position?

5. How is the research you are proposing to do connected to the struggle against injustice? Would there be any advantage to the poor from your research?

Haughey asks us to consider whether pedagogy and research that remain separated from the marginalized will teach students to "think" their way into action on behalf of justice—when our witness as faculty is a passive one only.

In "The Catholic University Project: What Kind of Curriculum Does It Require?" philosophy faculty member Stephen J. Heaney reflects on the nature of curriculum at a Catholic college. Heaney takes perhaps the most straightforward approach to the assertion of Catholic identity of all the essays thus far. He believes that Catholic universities have the responsibility to expose all students—Catholics and non-Catholics alike—to the truth of the Catholic faith. In attending a Catholic institution, they must be educated about Catholicism and given the opportunity to choose whether this is a faith and a way of life for them. Will his statement shut down dialogue on campuses? He tempers it so that his approach seems simply provocative, one that will indeed reach the core issues.

Heaney poses six questions—questions that could easily form the agenda for a seminar on Catholic identity.

1. What is a university? What is a Catholic university?

Heaney posits that a university is a locus of education, which means literally "leading out." The essence of a university is its faculty, those responsible for leading the students out to a place of discovery and excitement.

In a Catholic university the great truth that has been discovered is Jesus Christ and the faith community connected to Him. "In light of this revelation, how we view the world takes shape; we see how to live, and to die, as complete human beings." Heaney boldly asserts that in "the same way that the truths of science cannot be ignored by the artist," so the Catholic university community must recognize the claims of Catholicism and the ways such claims affect disciplines and research. However, "This does not mean that every member of the project has to accept Catholicism, but simply that each member cannot simply ignore it, dismiss it, or attack it as a member of the [entire university] project."

2. Given this definition, is it the task of a Catholic university to lead students to "think Catholically," to have a Catholic awareness in whatever profession they enter? What would it mean to have a "Catholic awareness"?

Heaney believes that the "project of any university is not brainwashing; it is an invitation to 'come and see'." For him it is logical and appropriate to show students the world through the eyes of the Catholic world view: "to show what it means to be affected by the truth, to show how this knowledge reverberates through one's entire life, one's outlook, one's approach to other human beings and the world."

Recognizing the fear some will have of alienating students with this straightforward approach to Catholic identity because of perceptions of intolerance and restrictions on academic freedom, Heaney avers, "Is it not a falsification of the project to put aside the central core truth because it is inconvenient?" Then follows a characteristic conciliation: "Let us converse; this is the heart of the university project."

3. If this is the project, is it then the task of each area of the university to promote this goal?

Heaney dismisses ancillary or ambiguous definitions of a Catholic awareness; he is clear that "it is an academic task to encourage these habits of thinking in students." And the task extends beyond the realm of the religion department. Each discipline and faculty member, Catholic and non-Catholic alike, must be able to articulate the ways in which their field touches upon Catholic thought or practice. Heaney's goal, it seems, is to inculcate within students a "Catholic habit of mind." Such a habit will not be learned in one or two courses; it must permeate the curriculum.

4. How important is the curriculum to this task? How do individual disciplines engage this project?

Heaney believes that "one can form a Catholically aware student in virtually any curriculum respectful of the Catholic university project." Yet he posits that an ideal curriculum is one in which faculty are respectful and knowledgeable enough to articulate the intersections of their field with the Catholic world view. In a sense, this is an interdisciplinary way of teaching, combining one's discipline with Catholicism.

5. How does my discipline accomplish this task? What perspectives must the students investigate? What skills should they develop? What courses should be in place?

Each discipline must use the questions and structure of its field, Heaney asserts, as a starting point for inquiry into the most appropriate ways to integrate it with Catholic teachings.

6. What is the role of a Catholic studies program in such a university?

Heaney warns that a Catholic studies program "could act as a convenient shunt for faculty members who are discomfited by the idea of being part of the Catholic voice of the university." A Catholic studies program could compartmentalize rather than integrate Catholicism into the curriculum.

Heaney concludes, however, that a Catholic studies program offers a wonderful forum in which "to focus the development of the Catholic habit of mind for those students and faculty wishing to do so." It also provides opportunities for faculty to explore further the intersections of their field with Catholicism. Thus, it creates a space for faculty to become "learners" in creating a curriculum rooted in the Catholic worldview.

James Heft, S.M., conducted a faculty seminar at the University of Dayton that addressed the issues laid out so eloquently by Haughey. As at Georgetown (see "Centered Pluralism: A Report of a Faculty Seminar on the Jesuit and Catholic Identity of Georgetown University", pp. 69–90, this volume), Dayton's eight-month seminar hoped to bring faculty together for "serious interdisciplinary discussion and research." The goal of this collaboration of minds was to explore how "ethical and religious issues ought to form an integral part of their research and teaching."

Heft, like Haughey, affirms that the most important determinant of the identity of a university "is the faculty's vision of its scholarship as it relates to the mission of their institution." Again like Haughey, he affirms that faculty need not be Catholic to be engaged in the mission and vision of the Catholic institution, astutely noting that non-Catholics often make more of a contribution to an institution's identity: "Some of them, by the thoughtfulness of their interaction with the rest of the faculty, force the discussion of the mission of a Catholic university to be more carefully, honestly, and inclusively articulated."

The Dayton group came to agree on three themes to guide their seminar:

1. A historical understanding of the development of higher education in this country, particularly Catholic higher education
2. Exploration of key elements of the Catholic intellectual tradition
3. Understanding of how that tradition might pose questions, inform faculty research, and influence the teaching of professional educators

Heft discusses the nuts and bolts of conducting the seminar—which should be especially useful to other faculty and administrators interested in creating a similar structure: faculty selection criteria, the sequence of readings, themes that emerged during the seminar, and serendipitous insights for setting up similar seminars. The Dayton faculty realized the void within most disciplines regarding ethical and spiritual reflection, and the benefit of an interdisciplinary and integrating approach to their work.

Heft concludes that such seminars should compensate faculty for the work they invest in this task; include a balanced mix of reading, discussion, and research; and be interdisciplinary in order to lay the foundation for a more integrated campus community.

Michael Hollerich reframes what is truly at stake for Catholic higher education in his provocative article, "Academic Freedom and the Catholic University." He asks, "Could we not today accommodate greater institutional linkage between the Church and the university than we have in the past?" He answers, "I would like to suggest cautiously that . . . the benefits of an organic connection of some kind outweigh the risks."

Hollerich begins with a historical overview: "Catholic colleges had always had as a primary practical purpose the upward mobility of the Catholic population, which for a century between the 1820s and 1920s was largely an immigrant population striving to transcend its working class origins." In order to ensure this goal of upward mobility, it became extremely important for Catholic institutions of higher education to be as competitive and respected as their secular and Protestant counterparts. With the marked discrimination and prejudice against Catholics, it became desirable for such colleges to distance themselves from ecclesial authority in terms of academic scholarship, "especially given Catholicism's not undeserved reputation as an authoritarian enemy of freedom." This mindset is reflected in the 1967 Land O'Lakes Statement that "insisted unequivocally on the full institutional autonomy of Catholic colleges and universities if they were to serve their academic and professional ends."

Hollerich articulates three main points. First, he asks whether the concern for academic freedom and the thrust away from identification with the Church is appropriate today. Second, he asserts that the more "immediate and serious threat" to Catholic colleges is not Church authority but the loss of a Catholic identity. In his view, Catholic colleges did their job of protecting academic freedom almost too well during the 1960s. He states: "Our religious identity is far more fragile and at risk at the hands of our academic and professional goals," than the converse. Third, he proposes an alternative framework for Catholic higher education.

Hollerich's first point is an excellent discussion generator. After discussing academic freedom and some of the real threats to that freedom today, he states, "Academic freedom is not an end in itself. . . . Rather, it exists as a precondition for the successful flourishing of colleges and universities. It is not a freedom *from* so much as a freedom *for*."

He then argues that "we are beset by the most varied challenges and threats to our academic freedom, in comparison with which it is hard to see that posed by the Catholic Church as particularly urgent. Fixating on it as a uniquely threatening danger actually diverts us from much more immediate, perhaps intractable, problems." He sketches limits on academic freedom: "The pedagogical needs of our students, the standards and methods of the discipline or profession in which we are trained, and the over-arching awareness of 'the common good.'"

Hollerich then elucidates other limits on academic freedom, particularly the "university culture." He claims that, just as corporations have "cultures" related to dress, philosophy, and expression, so do universities. "Codes of speech and behavior can vary greatly from one school to another," depending on where the school is, its ethnic profile, the economic class affiliation of the student body and alumni, its funding sources, and the academic and professional programs, among other things. Such factors influence what is considered appropriate—even in faculty teaching—at a particular institution.

Hollerich cites other influences on academic freedom, such as budgetary pressures and student evaluation of professors and courses, remarking accurately on the "politicization of the contemporary academy." Political correctness, however it is interpreted at a particular institution, can deter free expression of beliefs that differ from the dominant positions: "Far from promoting civil argument, the net effect of the ideological policing of the academy seems to have been to stifle debate."

Hollerich believes that all of these influences are a far greater threat to academic freedom than Church teaching. The religious affiliation of an institution, he says "is far more at risk from the university's general educational mission than the other way around." Secular influences impose "a degree of uniformity and sameness on American higher education that would be keenly resented were it to come in the form of a hierarchically defined religious orthodoxy."

Hollerich reframes religious identity as an asset to academic mission rather than a hazard. He supports this alternative view with well-defined points that religious identity enhances academic pursuits by providing:

1. *An overarching sense of purpose*: Religious identity restores "proportion and balance" and "gives our mission a transcendent and cosmic grounding that goes far beyond the public purposes to which secular institutions are dedicated."

2. *A sense of historic continuity*: The Catholic Church is part of a "continuous tradition of teaching and study that goes back to the Middle Ages and to the philosophical and biblical traditions of antiquity. . . . The history of Western culture in a sense is our history."

3. *A vision of the human good not controlled by instrumental rationality*: Religious identity allows Catholic schools to raise questions about "purpose and the good" in the technology they teach.

4. *A community committed to recognizing and dealing with diversity*: "From Pentecost (Acts 2) to *Lumen Gentium* . . . Catholicism is far and away the most thoroughly international Christian church. . . .Vatican II declared the Church to be the sacrament of the unity of the human race."

5. *An architectonic wisdom*: Catholic identity includes "the aspiration to offer an integrated view of human understanding"; this is a foundation for interdisciplinary collaborations and a communal approach to teaching and learning.

6. *Local roots and connections in city and region*: The Church and its institutions have long served as community gathering places; what does that role mean in the current context?

Finally, Hollerich asks us to entertain the idea of a stronger relationship between the Catholic college or university and the institutional Church. He harbors concerns about the increasingly lay-led Church. Access to the institutional Church might guard against some of the perils Hollerich fears in a lay-dominated context.

Lest lay people be put off, Hollerich reminds us that "in a well-ordered church the rule of subsidiarity ought to prevail: tasks should be undertaken and decisions made at the level of competence closest to the local situation"—so, in most cases, the college or university itself would resolve its conflicts, with the local bishop called upon only in extraordinary circumstances.

In "Teaching Sociology in the Catholic University: Conflict, Compromise, and the Role of Academic Freedom" William J. Kinney describes the challenges of finding Heaney's "intersections" for his own discipline. Kinney speaks of the often negative sociological analyses of Catholicism and other religious perspectives—from Marx to the perception of religion as a "subjective human construction possibly devoid of grounding in objective reality." This analytical rather than reverential approach to religion can create tensions in sociologists who teach at Catholic universities: "It is rather like being an analyst (and very often a critical analyst) of one's own employer."

Additionally, sociology classes explore birth control, abortion, homosexuality, and many other issues on which the Church has taken strong, far from neutral, stances. How does a sociologist teaching at a Catholic institution remain faithful to both the discipline and the institutional mission?

Kinney cites *Ex Corde Ecclesiae* and a statement by the University of St. Thomas to illustrate his belief that the Church is attempting to strike a balance between the needs to preserve its nonsecular identity and to "guarantee" academic freedom. He believes that the Church has made good-faith efforts to meet the needs of faculty and students for an atmosphere of open dialogue and academic freedom. He asserts that faculty "have a duty to meet and respect the needs and nature of their employer—a fact . . . lost on many in academia in the wake of the social upheaval of the 1960s and early 1970s."

One of the ironies that Kinney sees is the fact that the concern for diversity so often excludes the particularity and diverse world view of Catholicism. He asks, "How is diversity enhanced by imposing a homogenizing secularization upon universities whose mission and practices are guided by a unique, Catholic view of society?"

Kinney believes the potential tensions between sociologists and Catholic institutions can be mitigated by "simple mutual respect." Though that solution sounds simple in theory, its lived reality may be far more complex. His article could be a springboard for exploring how mutual respect is currently and could be further embodied within a campus community.

Thomas M. Landy observes the growing numbers of Catholic Studies programs at Catholic colleges and universities, most of them more broadly focused than are theology or pastoral ministry programs: "They aim to introduce students both to Catholicism's place in the history of ideas and—more concretely and sacramentally—to manifestations of Catholic life in art, literature, music, and everyday culture."

In a brief but enlightening historical review, Landy points out that since Vatican II many Catholic universities have tried to make their view of Catholicism more inclusive; many have emphasized the particular charism of their order rather than the overall Catholic identity. Others created peace and justice programs as their expression of Catholicism. The publication of *Ex Corde Ecclesiae* in 1990 coincided with an increasing sense among many Catholic colleges and universities that they "no longer felt able to take the Catholicity of institutions for granted." The Catholic studies program is one model for addressing these concerns and for sustaining Catholic identity at colleges and universities.

Landy describes programs currently in place. It is interesting that most programs are lay-led and interdisciplinary, drawing on a wide range of fields. Landy is hesitant to evaluate the effectiveness of the programs in addressing the concerns of *Ex Corde Ecclesiae* and many Catholic institutions; the programs are simply too new to provide compelling data.

Landy feels confident that the emergence of such programs will not "ghettoize" Catholicism or exclude non-Catholics from a sense of real membership in Catholic institutions. He also notes that the larger programs have attracted students from a variety of faiths. Still, some institutions are hesitant about developing such programs, and "faculty members have suggested that the difficulty is precisely that the faculty does not want to confront contested notions of what constitutes the Catholic tradition." This fear is connected to the concern among some faculty that *Ex Corde Ecclesiae* represents an attempt at ecclesiastical oversight of Catholic colleges and universities in a way that limits academic freedom.

A second fear is the concern that a formal Catholic studies program will satisfy demands for a Catholic presence yet prevent that identity from pervading the institution. Landy reports that most Catholic studies program directors feel their initiatives will serve as "leaven for the whole university community." He quotes David O'Brien's view that these programs increase "the likelihood that Catholic colleges and universities can be places where the Church can do its thinking and engage its own and other traditions."

In "Catholic Studies at the University of St. Thomas," Don Briel details how a successful program works. He believes that while the recent emergence of these programs could signal either the failure of Catholic higher education to integrate its religious identity with academia, more positively, it can be seen as "another indication of the sophisticated genius of Catholic universities, able to adapt to changing conditions and unexpected opportunities."

The University of St. Thomas Catholic studies program is one of the largest in the country. The program evolved, as it seems so many identity-focused initiatives do, from the collaboration of faculty and a dean who organized a series of lectures and discussions on the history and philosophy of Catholic higher education. This series was a response to the awareness that growing numbers of students, though nominally Catholic, had little background in Catholic thought and practice.

The Catholic studies initiative also arose from a decision not to "ghettoize," in Landy's word, the Catholic identity of the institution by assigning the burden to the campus ministry, a "values-oriented" curriculum, or a theology department alone. The University of St. Thomas sought to integrate Catholic thought more pervasively throughout the curriculum. Once again the emphasis was on interdisciplinarity.

Briel, like Haughey, comments that that such a fundamental change in integrating Catholic thought throughout every aspect of the campus could not occur by committee. The crisis facing higher education was one not of intellect, but of imagination. Briel and his colleagues believed that change would not occur through the "juridical authority of the hierarchy or the internal decisions of administration or faculty." It would only occur if there were opportunities for all sectors of the campus to engage in dialogue, seeking creative ways to implement Catholicism's "pursuit of the unity of knowledge."

To begin this dialogue, the St. Thomas group used *Ex Corde Ecclesiae*'s statement of the characteristics of the Catholic university as their starting point:

1. *A Christian inspiration not only of individuals but of the university community.* Briel comments that "the burden of institutional identity cannot be fulfilled" by the "ghettoization" of Catholic thought, but must find ways to permeate and animate every sector of the campus community.

2. *A continuing reflection in the light of the Catholic faith upon the growing treasury of human knowledge, to which it seeks to contribute by its own research.* Briel comments that we are called to reconcile the search for truth with the Truth as we understand it through faith. Yet he recognizes the tension: "The two-fold commitments of faith and reason find expression in an optimism that there can be no final contradiction of truths, although as Newman has cautioned, this confidence does not free us from the real collisions and tensions that frequently deserve the metaphors of warfare." Briel believes this commitment calls us to create sustained opportunities for reflection on our academic work in the light of Catholic thought. He adds that there are both curricular and hiring implications—a provocative comment with no further analysis.

3. *Fidelity to the Christian message as it comes to us through the Church.* This, Briel says, calls us to guarantee that students will have access to Catholic teaching in their curriculum.
4. *An institutional commitment to the service of the People of God and of the human family in their pilgrimage to the transcendent goal which gives meaning to life.* Briel interprets this statement as emphasizing "the prophetic role of the Catholic university within the Church, requiring, as the Pope said, 'the courage to speak uncomfortable truths that do not please public opinion, but that are necessary to safeguard the authentic good of society.'"

With these principles as a guide, St. Thomas organized a five-year series of summer faculty development seminars around the history of Catholicism and related topics. All participants in these week-long gatherings were required to do extensive reading and to write a reflective essay. Participation was voluntary, but recruitment sought to include persons from wide-ranging disciplines. Although not stated, compensating faculty for their investment of time may have been seen as imperative to honor this as legitimate work done during the vacation period.

These series led to campus publication of faculty essays to provoke further reflection, a continuing series of lectures during the school term, and eventually creative plans for a Catholic studies program.

Briel details the particularities of the St. Thomas Catholic studies program as it developed—vital reading for all considering a similar endeavor. Perhaps most important is his reminder that interdisciplinary programs are fragile, depending on a small group of faculty "whose initial enthusiasm and commitment is difficult to sustain in an academic climate in which universities tend to reward highly specialized research on a narrow topic rather than the broad interdisciplinary scholarship we have sought to foster."

In "Graduate Business Faculty in the Catholic University," Ray MacKenzie suggests that it is tempting for some business educators to dismiss *Ex Corde Ecclesiae*; "after all there's no such thing as Catholic accounting." MacKenzie rejects the temptation; *Ex Corde Ecclesiae* calls even these disciplines to "closer relationship with the school's Catholic identity." This will not be accomplished by inserting a Catholic component into a course or even by requiring business ethics classes, but "by the particular intellectual qualities of the faculty."

For MacKenzie, the question is: What sort of faculty should a Catholic university be seeking" for all its programs? Should a Catholic institution be looking for qualities beyond the usual skills such as teaching ability, competence in one's discipline, research, and publishing? He agrees with *Ex Corde Ecclesiae* in asserting that religious uniformity is not the goal of Catholic universities.

While the faculty need not be Roman Catholics, they must possess a "Catholic mind." MacKenzie, echoing Walter J. Ong, notes that "the Catholic mind, like the Catholic institution of higher learning, is one that strives for inclusivity, for a permeation of the whole, for connection and relationship between cultures, races, ideas, fields of study." Here Mac-Kenzie echoes Haughey's call for a similar spirituality of academic work—one that integrates one's own field with other viewpoints wherever possible, including Catholicism. Heaney's challenge to find the intersections between one's work and Catholicism is also present in MacKenzie's vision.

MacKenzie correctly observes that the trend towards specialization arises as the market becomes more unstable for workers; one can no longer be loyal to an employer in a business world where downsizing and outsourcing dominate. Instead, loyalty to a discipline and continually honing the field's cutting edge skills and technology become the only source of job security. MacKenzie reflects on William F. May's discussion of how the definition of what it means to be a professional is changing; a professional formerly "had a commitment to the good of the public that he or she served. . . . Today a professional is better described as a careerist, committed only to maintaining the technical expertise of the field and to maximizing his or her own self-interest."

In contrast, MacKenzie asserts, a Catholic university "ought to be a place where the individual can go to begin to build some of the intellectual and social connections missing in so much of modern life." MacKenzie views Catholic institutions as radical in that they are committed to recapturing the root meaning of education in the professions; thus they stand as counter-cultural witness to an education that is holistic rather than compartmentalized. A Catholic institution "is one dedicated to searching out and building up intellectual, cultural, and spiritual wholeness . . . if we only minister to the student's need for expertise, we are engaged in training, not education."

MacKenzie recognizes that a shift in business pedagogy will require the support of the entire institution, with forays into new territory rewarded with stipends, sabbaticals, and time to work out syllabi that really teach students how to ask such questions. He acknowledges that such a venture will be initially "messy" and (heaven forbid in the business world!) seemingly unmanageable. Yet he believes it is just such holistic thinking that distinguishes a Catholic faculty.

In "Theology and the Integration of Knowledge" theologian Terence L. Nichols explores the call of *Ex Corde Ecclesiae* for the integration of knowledge within a theological perspective. Nichols laments, as do most of our authors, the fragmentation of knowledge and the ever-increasing specialization of disciplines. He posits that the disintegration of our thinking creates a growing social problem, "a society of atomized individuals each seeking his or her own personal good." Nichols asserts that Catholicism, like most religions, views reality as a unified whole consisting of spiritual and material aspects; so the approach to knowledge that dominates most universities stands in direct contradiction to this worldview.

Theology is the discipline that seeks to understand the whole—that is, the spiritual and material aspects of creation and their relationship to God. It is the discipline that begins with the broadest questions: What is the nature of ultimate reality? How is that reality related to humanity and the universe? A theologian has a "broad orientation to problems, within which further exploration can take place." Thus, concludes Nichols, a Catholic university is one of the few settings in which a truly interdisciplinary approach to learning can flourish—precisely because the Catholic worldview is integrated within a "whole," which is God. "The investigation of this whole is the task of theology," but such an investigation can take place only in concert with disciplines of every type.

Nichols provides some examples of how theology and the Catholic worldview could be integrated with other disciplines: Within physics, students might ask, "What caused the Big Bang? Why are physical laws and constants precisely balanced so that life can occur?" It is hard to imagine a non-Catholic physicist—no matter how respectful of Catholicism—engaging in such discourse in the light of a faith-based paradigm. The suggestions in this essay would seem to work only if the faculty themselves are believers, or possess the extraordinary courage to pose questions that other physicists might ridicule as "unscientific." It will take thought and work to refine the ways that the intersections between Catholicism and certain disciplines can be explored.

More useful is Nichols's suggestion that the ethical questions that arise in each discipline might lend themselves productively to the integration of Catholic thought: "I think each discipline is in a position to offer a theological and ethical perspective that is unique." Nichols believes that the unique holistic Catholic world view lends itself to "the quest for the integration of knowledge [that] ought to be part of the Catholic curriculum, and probably can only survive at a religiously based institution." He asserts that administrators can facilitate this by choosing "to rate interdisciplinary work on a par with specialized research and publication when evaluating faculty performance, promotion, and tenure. This could help shift the balance away from ongoing fragmentation."

"In the Beginning Was the Word" is Glenn A. Steinberg's contribution. His theme, too, is the integration of knowledge as the distinctive sign of a Catholic university. In *Ex Corde Ecclesiae* the Pope states that "it is necessary to work toward a higher synthesis of knowledge, in which alone lies the possibility of satisfying that thirst for truth that is profoundly inscribed on the heart of the human person." Steinberg asserts that one of the most important contributions of a Catholic university will be its synthesis of such knowledge in the pursuit of truth.

Steinberg refers to *The Closing of the American Mind* by Allan Bloom as a secular resource making a similar critique of modern culture. He points out that the critiques contained in *Ex Corde Ecclesiae* have been observed not only by the Catholic community but also by a broad, thoughtful spectrum of society. Because of the growing emphasis in higher education and the marketplace for technical education, a "highly trained computer specialist need not have any more learning about morals, politics, or religion than the most ignorant of persons . . . [and is unable] to distinguish between the sublime and the trash, insight and propaganda."

Steinberg raises the very difficult question of how Catholic universities can integrate knowledge in a fragmented postmodern age. With MacKenzie, he recognizes that trends in many fields, including literature, have tended toward a critical deconstruction of texts and have "in recent years come to assert the instability and impossibility of meaning." This has exhibited itself in insidious ways. Steinberg observes that students "do not really seem to believe or understand that words have meaning." He describes this phenomenon in unsettling detail.

Steinberg counters this meaninglessness in his English classes by making every effort "to encourage students to become conscious of how they ascribe meaning to the texts they read for my class and also of how others might ascribe meaning in an entirely different way." Steinberg also "insists upon precision in their use of language in their own writing, requiring that they go beyond clichés and commonplaces." Through this type of pedagogy, Steinberg hopes, his discipline can contribute to the Catholic university's search for meaning by laying the groundwork for faith in and reflection on the very process of making meaning.

Catholic Higher Education:
A Strategy for Its Identity

John C. Haughey, S.J. *

As Catholic universities seek to become more distinguished and competitive in the world of higher education, faculty members are increasingly pressed to produce quality research. This pressure is shaping the ethos of their colleges and universities as never before. At the same time, Catholic universities, including the Jesuit universities with which I am most familiar, are facing more directly than they have in years the "Catholic identity" issue. I want to connect these two pressing matters—faculty research and Catholic institutional identity—because I despair of any resolution of the Catholic identity question unless it is connected with faculty perceptions of their research responsibilities and choices.

These ideas about Catholic identity and the research peculiar to faculty of Catholic colleges and universities do not presume to be descriptive of how faculty see their research at present. Nor do they presume to have the force of the prescriptive behind them. They do not even presume that faculty members are Catholic. Rather, they are envisioning what is not yet. They look for a response to what might be.

The ideas herein are tied to several beliefs. First, a Catholic school is only as Catholic as its faculty think and teach "catholically." (Needless to say this does not mean "Roman Catholically" in a denominational or parochial sense, but that they teach with some knowledge of, reverence for, and advertence to the story and tradition from which their institution came.) Second, the faculty member's classroom effectiveness, in fact

*John C. Haughey, S.J., is professor of Christian ethics at Loyola University, Chicago, Illinois. This article is reprinted from *Current Issues in Catholic Higher Education* 16(2) (winter 1996): 25–32.

the quality of the education the institution gives, will be in proportion to the depth and breadth of the faculty member's research. Third, the issue of Catholic identity will be endless talk unless it gets down to the research choices of the faculty person and how these choices are rewarded by the institution. Fourth, although faculty spend much time inquiring into a limitless number of possible objects of their research, they spend little or no time on the metaethics or spirituality that undergirds their research. This paper will seek to stimulate faculty reflection on their research choices. The fifth belief is that there is virtually no Catholic college or university with a sufficiently compelling vision of what it is about to draw faculty attention beyond their own disciplines or lead faculty members to choose their research topics in light of such a vision. This paper will have some suggestions about some of the ingredients of such a vision.

Should the research done by faculty in Catholic institutions have a different perspective, come from a different motivation or inspiration, be done with a different outcome in mind than research done in non-Catholic universities? I believe the faculty's operational answer is no, while the institution's would presumably be yes. Should research in a Catholic university be evaluated by colleagues and the institution itself in the same way and with the same measures as research done in other universities? I believe the institution's answer is that increasingly the research is evaluated the same way but it should not be.

The reaction of most faculty to these questions will be: "Let's face it—most research is chosen on the basis of what you can get funded." They would contend that the state of the questions and the methods and developments within a given discipline should determine the research choices of Catholic faculty members just as they do for non-Catholics or for faculty at non-Catholic institutions. Further, most faculty probably believe that the mission of a Catholic university does not and should not affect the research choices of its faculty. Since at all universities what is rewarded is research—to some extent quality, and more often quantity—the fewer exogenous factors counted in the better, faculty would be prone to insist. So the idea of something like a university's understanding of its mission affecting one's research choices seems, to most academics, financially, professionally, and psychologically unreal, not to mention academically undesirable.

I reject these arguments, their spirit, and the understanding of research behind them. I proceed here to supply some of the categories for what could develop into what might be called a metaethics or spirituality of research. They are submitted in the hope that faculty will find them helpful in developing a clearer rationale for why they do what they do in their research.

Categories for a Spirituality of Research

Call. Over the years I have been fascinated with how many faculty members I have spoken with who informally describe themselves as having undertaken their academic careers with the sense of having been called to do so. Opportunity beckoned, yes, but their deeper sense of themselves was not opportunistic. In the inventory of reflection prescribed here, one would ask: What has explained my choice of discipline, my academic field of labor, from the beginning? Is it explained merely by my attraction to it, by the right circumstances, and by having the personal wherewithal to become credentialed in it? Or do I read the choice/attraction/ability in more vocational terms, like a call? If I have used "call" as a way of interpreting my choice of discipline, and maybe even my dissertation topic, would it not be consistent to see my ongoing research choices as needing to be a continuation of a unique call (charism?) that was there from the start?

If a faculty member's self-perception is based on a unique call, then his or her subsequent research choices and work will, or to some degree should, be original. These will not be set by the pack. If this is true, then conceivably one's research could be deemed "right" in the judgment of the discipline while it is "wrong" in the light of the call. And vice versa. The accuracy and value of one's research will necessarily be measurable to a degree within the discipline, but the discipline will not be able to take the full measure of it.

Self-appropriation or interiority. There are rich categories in the thought of Bernard Lonergan that bear on our research choices. These can come either from superficial or deeper layers of the self and from different exigencies. The exigency of recognition or approval of those who can include me, advance me, or honor me is a strong one and certain to trivialize one's choice. Recall that Lonergan's four fonts of meaning are common sense, theory, transcendence, and interiority. Suffice it to say here that interiority is the font from which research is ideally chosen, and that any of the other three would give evidence of a lack of self-appropriation.

While theory might appear to be the most promising font from which to choose and execute research, it is interiority that takes all three fonts into account and radically internalizes them. Research chosen from the font of interiority takes seriously the measure of oneself, one's call, idiosyncrasies, interests, talents, and experiences. By contrast, theory is where the discipline itself is at any given time. If theory *solo* dictates research choices, one could be on the way to gaining the whole world (of comprehension, inclusion, recognition, status) and suffering the loss of oneself.

The sovereignties of disciplines. Academic disciplines are principalities in the scriptural sense. They develop like little sovereignties, internally constituted by their histories, findings, methods, conventions, giants, and the particular boundaries that cordon them off from the other disciplines. A discipline/principality cherishes its own autonomy, as it should. But for those scholars who ply their trade within it and who are at the same time believers, the discipline would have at best a penultimate autonomy. It certainly has an intramundane role and finality in and of itself but it also has, or should be open to, a transcendent finality that connects it to pursuing and attaining truth beyond itself, indeed beyond reason.

Well-trained researchers who are also knowledgeable about their respective faiths would work in the light of a transcendent horizon. For Christians that horizon sees God as having subjected all things to Christ, who in the course of history is subjecting all things, their own principalities in particular, to God. From this more transcendent horizon, one should be able to work less enmeshed in or limited by the foreshortened horizon of the principality. The *telos*, therefore, of one's discipline would be seen both in terms of itself and in light of the further horizon supplied by religious faith. One's self-understanding, and the everyday particulars of teaching and research, will be affected accordingly.

The common good. Faculty members, whatever their institutions of higher learning, inevitably must ask themselves what their research is for. Is it for itself? truth? career? tenure? recognition? institutional prestige? people? societal change? simply to add to the store of human knowledge? Although the research need not be done to benefit people directly, it cannot, by the same token, be neighbor-numb. Research, an investment of personhood, time, and talent, can hardly be done blind to the inequities, the inequalities, the unevenness in the distribution of the good things of the earth. Consequently, the issue of who is benefiting from one's research cannot be irrelevant; it should become an object of explicit attention. If call were part of scholars' self-understanding, they would work for something larger than themselves and their discipline. Recall the Christian scripture that has some applicability here: "To each person the manifestation of the Spirit [i.e., charism] is given for the common good" (1 Cor. 12, 7).

In this connection one could examine the category of pure research. There is undoubtedly justification for pure research, that is, research that is simply concerned to know. But pure research can also be irresponsible, and claims about its purity can be used as a cover for not examining one's motivations more closely.

Stewards of the goods of information. Academics have a luxury enjoyed by few, namely, access to a trove of data that is increasingly astonishing, at least in its quantity. Stewards in the raw biblical sense are aware that the goods they have been commissioned to manage are not merely for their own interests, purposes, and uses. These goods were meant to benefit many, not a few. This slant on the meaning of steward again speaks to the beneficiaries of research. For whom are we doing it? Not unlike the more primal goods of the earth, the goods of information are to be used for the sake of the many.

A research project is an effort to bring order to the goods of information out of the chaos in which we found them. Is the medium we choose to communicate our findings the best one for those who would most benefit from them? Academe's social responsibility is to more than one another; it is to the community members who most need the goods of information it masters.

Discernment. Sorting out one's research choices presumes sensitivity to one's interior movements of attraction and disaffection. Research chosen and pursued on the basis of or at least in the light of these movements will be more carefully chosen. These affective movements are best examined by stepping back from the drawing power of the subject matter to see what the attraction is, or, conversely, what the disaffection or indifference is. Our motivations are complex, and knowing them is essential to developing a maturity about research choices by keeping a healthy distance from the internal draw of the field, not to mention the politics of the institution in which one plies one's trade. Discernment can assist both initial research choices and all the major choices called for in the execution of the project.

Taking stock of the effects of our research on our immediate relationships is one of the better ways of discerning our research. What is this work doing to my relationship with self, spouse, family, neighbors, God? Does it contribute to order or disorder within these relationships? The research must be judged accordingly if I am advancing in my field while weakening or losing the relational base that enabled me to come to this point of productivity.

Discernment is ever alert to the actual or foreseeable "fruits" of doing the research. Affective signs accompany one who is operating from one's call. These are "the fruits of the Spirit" in Paul's epistles—joy, peace, patience, mildness, patient endurance, and so on. In general, I would say intellectual consolation and a growth in being related to others, including those who will benefit most from the research, are two signs that the choice and manner of execution are appropriate. Conversely, the fruits of operating from an ethos that is self-generated (Paul's "flesh") are dissonance, agitation, ennui, blaming, complaining, division (Gal. 5, 19ff).

Developing and Awarding a Compelling Vision

What has been elaborated thus far needs another dimension, a second move, since so far it would appear that the faculty member is the only one on whom the onus rests for ensuring the distinctiveness of the Catholic institution of higher learning. That would be unfair. The best way of attracting faculty to act in the light of a horizon that includes but transcends their own interests and field of study is for the institution to develop a sufficiently specific vision of what it means to be Catholic. Only then could the faculty identify with this and align their research to it. No mission statements that I know of draw or lure faculty to think and act in a horizon of Catholic identity. Rather, the generic, nice, pusillanimous pieties of such statements faculty easily live with, but such statements usually evoke the vaguest of assents or, more often, ennui.

By whom or how a compelling vision will be articulated is difficult to say, but of two things I am sure. The first is that the vision will not come from a committee. The second is that the institution will have to act its way into the new way of thinking, since it is most unlikely it will think its way into a new way of acting. The compelling vision is more likely to emerge if action is taken on the several things faculty and administration are likely to agree on, which come from inventories and reflections done by faculty about their research (a spirituality of research). So rather than waiting for such visions to hatch, I will elaborate five of the characteristics I anticipate will emerge from faculty reflection and from the simple logic of a Catholic institution of higher learning.

The reason for spelling out these characteristics here is that research grants and research leaves could be awarded if faculty give evidence of wrestling with the horizon these characteristics hold out. As faculty choose their research subjects, it would seem right if their grants and leaves favored those who can make a case for the relationship of their research to the self-understanding and mission of the Catholic institution. These five are submitted in the spirit of a challenge to faculty, rather than as strict criteria for qualifying for leaves or as a way of constraining faculty in the topics they choose.

1. What does "catholic" mean? Something has a catholic characteristic if it lends itself to unity, to integration. In its root meaning, the word connotes "according to or toward wholeness." If there is a native dynamism in the intellect toward the unitary and toward ultimacy, members of a university professing to be catholic should not be content to leave their particular research's connection to these dynamisms unexamined or merely implicit. A faculty member should attempt to show how his or her research project assists students in moving toward a greater integration of understanding. Showing how one's partial contribution relates to the whole is probably more difficult as one gets to the hard sciences, of course, but faculty members of all departments, including the hard sci-

ences, should not be without a sense of how their particular discipline relates to the overall educational mission.

2. Catholic universities exist because of the presumption that "nothing human is alien to the church" and that knowledge that comes in discrete pieces ought to be part of a body of knowledge, which, in turn, should be open to being seen in the light of revelation. Since most disciplines do not employ faith data directly in their research or methods, a dialogue between faith and reason should be part of what scholars at Catholic institutions are open to undertaking with their colleagues for the sake of the completeness of their own scholarship. Hence the question: What in your research might be a subject for further inquiry and dialogue with faith?

3. "The cause of the human person will only be served if knowledge is joined to conscience." First of all, how is your research serving the cause of the human person? And beyond this, are you taking into account the ethical implications of your discipline's methods and discoveries? Is your own research addressing these? The research will seldom address these issues explicitly, but the implications of what one is doing cannot be ignored.

4. Does the subject matter you treat deal with issues that the Church's tradition has addressed? If so, would it be appropriate to advert to the tradition? Would it be appropriate for you to take a position on the Church's position?

5. "The struggle against injustice and the pursuit of truth cannot be separated, nor can one work for the one independently of the other." How is the research you are proposing to do connected to the struggle against injustice? Has the inspiration to pursue it come from your own perceptions of social injustice or from relationships with poor people or those marginal to the privileges of higher education? Would there be any advantage to this population from your research?

Presumably most of us faculty would strike out on this last category. The reason for this is that the kind of "conscientization" it presumes is that the preferential option for the poor has been made by us or our institution or our church. But it has never been on academe's value list; it has an uncertain future in theology, and the pace of its acceptance in church circles is slow. Further, it is probably the last thing on the minds of administrators as they seek to survive in the competitive world of higher learning.

I believe the main reason there has been no compelling vision coming from Catholic institutions of higher learning is because this fifth category is the least explored. At best we mouth pieties about forming people "for others," or about educating for service, while keeping the poor at a distance from us. It would seem that justice is not being done to students by educational theories, programs, and institutions that believe students will think their way into acting differently than we who train them. Rather, they and we must act with and learn from and be closer to the portions of society that are, ironically, both needier and more learned in the very things about which we, the more privileged, need to learn. Can a person be catholically educated if he or she does not know existentially, experientially, that blessedness, indeed the kingdom of heaven, can be where the poor are?

So what is being envisioned here is a pincer movement, a two-pronged strategy, one half moved by the faculty, the other by the institution itself. In one pincer, faculty research (presumably done no less competently than that done by colleagues in other institutions) would be undertaken from a different horizon than their counterparts in non-Catholic institutions. The other pincer would come from the institution itself, after it came to a deeper comprehension of its connection with the poor and the church, and articulated this in a vision that faculty could identify with. This thesis, this strategy, does not believe that the future of Catholicism in colleges and universities is necessarily contingent on hiring or tenuring Catholics. It is contingent on faculty seeing what the institution stands for, if it stands for something along the lines mapped out here, and opting in or out of it on the basis of that vision.

The Catholic University Project: What Kind of Curriculum Does It Require?

Stephen J. Heaney *

The topic of this seminar is, of course, The Curriculum in a Catholic University, or perhaps (to put it in question form), "What should the curriculum of a university that calls itself Catholic look like?" The implication in this question is that such a curriculum should have a special character, one that distinguishes it from the curriculum of any other kind of university. This implication seems correct to me, but to see it clearly one must first answer a series of other questions. Some of these questions were addressed in last summer's seminar, The Idea of the Catholic University (and so can be addressed perhaps with less depth here), while others are specific to the current topic. The questions, I think, are these:

1. What is a university? What is a Catholic university?
2. Given this definition, is it the task of a Catholic university to lead students to "think Catholically," to have a Catholic awareness in whatever profession they should enter? What would it mean to have a "Catholic awareness"?
3. If this is the project, is it then the task of each area of the university to promote this goal?
4. If this is the project, how important is the curriculum to this task? How do individual disciplines engage this project?
5. How does my discipline accomplish this task in the curriculum? What perspectives must the students investigate? What skills should they develop? What courses should be in place?
6. What is the role of a Catholic Studies program in such a university?

*Stephen J. Heaney is professor of philosophy at the University of St. Thomas, St. Paul, Minnesota. This article is reprinted from *Curriculum in a Catholic University: Summer Seminar* (St. Paul: University of St. Thomas, 1995): 33–37.

Question 1

A university, I think we would all agree, is a locus of *education*, which means, literally, "leading out." It is a place where people lead one another (to use Plato's analogy) from the dark cave of ignorance into the light of knowledge. The great masters of this art—the scientists, the artists, the philosophers, all the great leaders out of this darkness—have some common characteristics. They hit upon something startling, something that fills them with wonder, something that makes them see the world they live in, and their own presence in it, in a new way. This wonder is not a *"what if"* kind of wonder ("What if we had eyes in the back of our heads?"), but rather that wonder at having stumbled across *what is*. Filled with this new wonder and insight, they turn to anyone who will listen and say, in effect, "Hey, come here! You have to see this!" They have glimpsed some facet of the truth, and newfound truth is hard to suppress.

What are the *sine qua nons* of the university? First of all, a university is its faculty. Although a university would likely be a poorly run affair without administrators and staff, it would still have the *essence* of a university without them. It is the faculty, therefore, that is the necessary and sufficient condition of a university (although not the sufficient condition for a well-run one); however, a collection of people, no matter how intelligent or degreed, is not a university until it has a *specific project* (typically specified by the board of trustees, protected by its administration, and carried out by the faculty), *a goal to which the totality is committed*. For the university, that project is the pursuit of truth in the many ways truth can be sought. A university is not just a collection of scientists, or historians, or musicians, but a collection of men and women who, in all sorts of different areas of existence, say to us, "You have to see this! Now, *let's see what else we can find out.*"

What is a *Catholic* university? All of the above applies. After all, it is a university. But notice that the word "Catholic" modifies "university." It is a characteristic of this group of people, of this project. It does not modify the atmosphere, or a program, or the campus chapel, except insofar as these things are connected to this project. The great Catholic source of wonder, the truth that beckons us to "come and see," is the Truth itself, God made man, Jesus born of woman, Jesus crucified, Jesus raised from the dead and ascended to the Father, Jesus who left us His Church to guard and guide, so that we might not, like Pilate, wander in the darkness asking, "What is truth?"

In the light of this revelation, how we view the world takes shape; we see how to live, and to die, as complete human beings. In the same way that the truths of science cannot be ignored by the artist, or those of psychology by the philosopher, without falsification of the whole university project, so the truth that Catholicism claims cannot simply be ignored by any member, or any discipline, of the university without falsification of the claim to be a Catholic university. (This does not mean that every member of the project has to accept Catholicism, but simply that each member cannot simply ignore it, or dismiss it, or attack it *as a member of the project.*) A Catholic university stands committed as an institution to the truths of Catholicism in faith and morals, as that is interpreted through the teaching authority of the Magisterium. This Catholicism must inform the entire academic life of the university, in the ways appropriate to the various disciplines.

Question 2

If this description of the nature of the Catholic university is accurate, other propositions follow necessarily from it. It would be quite peculiar for a faculty that has seen this particular source of wonder, the very Font of Truth, to put that source aside as somehow irrelevant. So it would seem a natural, logical outgrowth of the project of a Catholic university to show each student what it means to be affected by the truth, to show how this knowledge reverberates through one's entire life, one's outlook, one's approach to other human beings and the world. One would hope to see the student take on a certain habit of mind, to have at his or her disposal a tool for approaching life.

This seems to me to be such a natural outgrowth of the project that it would require some serious justification *not* to do it. We may, for instance, be afraid of scaring off potential incoming students; we may be afraid of a certain loss of academic prestige, due to a predominant world view that thinks Catholicism is a bad habit of the weak-willed and simple-minded, craving answers from some strangely frocked authoritarian leadership. But should we be afraid of how the world views us? Is not Catholicism supposed to be "a scandal" to those who are strictly "of the world"? Is it not a falsification of the project to put aside the central core truth because it is inconvenient?

On the other hand, we may be afraid of offending non-Catholics, afraid of the charge of brainwashing rather than teaching, of improperly restricting academic freedom. We may simply be afraid of coming across as arrogant and intolerant. But the project of any university is not brainwashing; it is an invitation to "come and see." Catholicism has rational arguments; it can be rationally discussed. Let us *converse*; this is the heart of the university project.

Question 3

If it is the task of the Catholic university to bring a Catholic awareness, the "Catholic habit," to all its students, one must ask how this is to be accomplished. Is there something "in the air," a certain atmosphere, at a Catholic school, that our students can somehow inhale? Is it an extra-academic task for which, say, campus ministry is responsible? If it is an academic task, is it one that can be accomplished through one or two courses, or through the efforts of one or two departments? Does the Catholic university require some special program that the non-Catholic university could not have?

If a Catholic university has a "Catholic atmosphere," it is not the "atmosphere" that makes the place Catholic. The atmosphere of any university is an outgrowth of the particular project of that university. If the Catholic university has a Catholic atmosphere it is due only to the fact that the people involved in the project take that project, and the central truth involved, very seriously. Nor can any amount of atmosphere give students a clue as to its applicability in their particular disciplines or stations in life.

Similarly, an extra-academic function, such as campus ministry, is not the answer. A non-Catholic university can have a campus ministry. Nor can an extra-academic function bear the weight of this task, for it is not essentially concerned with "habits of mind"; this is the purview of academia.

Clearly, then, it is an academic task to encourage these habits of thinking in the student. And if our prior comments about the nature of the Catholic university project are correct, all academic departments of the university, all members of the faculty, would see it as their task to bring these habits of mind to their students; indeed, such a task would be joyously engaged by the entire faculty, for the members, in freely taking up the project, would hardly be able to contain themselves in their eagerness to show students "what they have seen." Even those who are non-Catholic, insofar as they have found the project valuable and have respectfully and freely adopted it, should be fully capable of pointing to the intersections between Catholicism and their own disciplines; indeed, they should be eager to do so, to arouse in their students the recognition of the tensions between Catholic belief and the great diversity of ways to view the world.

Equally important, however, is the realization that one or two departments cannot bear the load of developing this habit of mind. For one thing, to have one or two "Catholic departments" would mean precisely that: There are Catholic departments, but not necessarily a Catholic university. More essential, however, is the disciplinary nature of learning. Each discipline has a peculiar habit of mind, and a peculiar set of questions, that other disciplines are not competent to address. Identifying the intersections between Catholicism and the particular discipline is, therefore, a task properly suited to the particular discipline. Theology or philosophy, for instance, do not have it within their power to point out how the Catholic faith informs, and is informed by, the study of history, or biology, or music. It is only the Catholically aware historian, or biologist, or musician—or the historically, biologically, or musically aware Catholic—who can awaken that awareness in the student.

Still less is it possible to expect one or two courses to bear the weight of inculcating a Catholic habit of mind. Again, the logic of the terms is felt: One or two "Catholic courses" are just courses, not a university. Also, one is hard-pressed in a single course to instill a mental habit of any sort. Majors must take a number of courses to develop the discipline of mind appropriate to the subject matter; expertise is only gained through more study, more observation, a constant immersion in the subject and its processes, in order to see how it applies to diverse areas and topics. Should we expect anything less to bring a Catholic habit of mind to our students?

We do not expect all of our students to agree with us. We do not teach with the purpose of driving from their minds all opposition to our viewpoints, or of filling their minds only with our own positions. This would be brainwashing, not the "leading out" that we espouse. But like the philosopher in Plato's cave, we should want our students, even those who disagree with us, to at least *see* what it is we see so that they may judge for themselves. The Catholic university project, it seems to me, is a desire to at least get each student to see what the Catholic sees, wherever he or she turns, in whatever career calling or vocation he or she adopts.

Question 4

How important is the curriculum to this task? It depends on what one means by this question. Does the project require a *particular* curriculum common to all Catholic universities? I would think not. There may, however, be certain vital areas wherein a "Catholic awareness" is of particular importance, in theology or philosophy, for example. Aside from this, one can form a "Catholically aware" student in just about any curriculum respectful of the Catholic university project.

How do we execute this project within the curriculum? I cannot answer this question for all disciplines—I do not *have* their disciplines, their habits of mind, and so I am not in a position to give anything but general ideas about them. I would think that a faculty excitedly engaged in the project would be eager to look for intersections between each discipline and Catholicism. Clearly this task is easier in some fields than in others. The Catholic mathematician, it would seem, might have few opportunities, the Catholic philosopher many. Still, most fields have more opportunities than we might realize. The challenges to the faith by the findings of physics and chemistry come to mind—as does the challenge to the assumptions of the physical sciences by a Catholic world view. Theories of the person driving many of the social sciences have their assumptions challenged by Catholicism. History, literature, and art are full of stories about the Church, by the Church, and against the Church. How the Catholic needs to act in relation to business and economic affairs, education, and social work is a crucial aspect in the development of the career person.

Many of these intersections are best dealt with in moments—a brief aside, a single day. Some, however, cry out for development, and can act for teachers and students as a time of intense disciplinary and interdisciplinary activity. Courses dealing with these issues would be highly appropriate *to give students time to see the Catholic habit of mind at work* over a whole semester, and to attempt that same work themselves.

Question 5

Aside from theology, the clearest point of intersection between academic disciplines and Catholicism comes in the field of philosophy. As a philosopher, it is easiest for me to speak of what my own field can do in regard to a Catholic university curriculum.

As we have said, a university is committed to the pursuit of truth, in the many ways truth can be sought. Departments, specific disciplines, are committed to the pursuit of truth in certain areas, areas that are not properly analyzed by the methods and questions of other disciplines. Philosophy is no different. Using the data of all other disciplines, we seek more ultimate answers, answers to questions of ultimate meaning: the very possibility of the world, the place of human beings in that world, and the meaning of human life and human action. All these are sought from the starting point of experience and through the use of reason, not faith or revelation.

To that end, the philosophy student—especially the major—must be given the tools to be conversant in the myriad methods used to arrive at answers to these questions, and at the many answers given to those questions, in order that he or she may be able to make independent investigations into these questions of ultimate meaning, and (we hope) arrive at more satisfactory conclusions than previously accepted. In other words, the student is called to live "the examined life," and we must supply the means to make a meaningful examination.

All this would be true at any university.

A Catholic university, I have argued, is committed as an institution (though not necessarily all of us individually, except insofar as we freely commit ourselves to the project) not just to the search for truth in general, but in a special way to the truths of Catholicism in faith and morals, as that is interpreted through the teaching authority of the Magisterium. The philosophy department in a Catholic university, as a fully integrated part of that project, is committed to what that entails; thus, it seems to me, it is incumbent upon us philosophers to make our students—especially our majors—conversant in the problems and questions *proper to our discipline* that have been addressed by the Church, and the possible answers to those questions, especially those answers that have been embraced by the Magisterium (but from the starting point of experience, not revelation).

Such a commitment entails a department with at least a considerable knowledge of, and respect for, the Aristotelian-Thomistic tradition as a particular access to truth. It entails more than a cursory transmission of the highlights of Aristotle's or Aquinas's thoughts or methods. It requires that we be committed to making all of our students at least aware of the power and importance—and limits—of this tradition. The Aristotelian-Thomistic tradition is the very philosophical language of Catholicism. An ability to have some idea of what the Church *means* exactly when it speaks of the soul, transubstantiation, the intrinsic dignity of the human person, or moral absolutes is vital to the Catholic university project; further, it requires that we give our majors the opportunity to become conversant in the language of that tradition, able to bring that tradition to the questions of life and culture and apply it usefully. Such students would have the language and concepts for understanding what the Church teaches, for talking about these things to others, and defending their faith *from the position of reason alone.*

What kind of curriculum should we see from such a department? At the very least, each student in the university, in order to be conversant at all in the overall project of the university, would need to grapple with the questions of what it means to be a human being and how we ought to live (and in that order, for the second question cannot be answered without answering the first). These are the overall questions of philosophical anthropology and ethics. Each student begins here to encounter the complexity of the creature that is the human person, and the multitude of answers—including those compatible with Catholicism—to questions about body and soul, knowledge, freedom, and death, moving on in ethics to questions about happiness and how best to act in relation to it.

There are several other courses that would be important in such a department. Besides logic (which is a necessary component of any philosophy department, which must do its job based on reason alone), one would expect to find here a higher-level course working out the details of the language of the Aristotelian-Thomistic tradition, i.e., a course in the philosophy of nature and metaphysics, dealing with such topics as substance and accident, form and matter. It gives to advanced students who wish to pursue it a whole different way of approaching reality, which most other systems deny. One should probably also find in such a department a course in the philosophy of religion that discusses the power of philosophical proofs for God's existence, the nature of faith claims, and the problem of evil. Each of these courses would need to have an element of the Aristotelian-Thomistic tradition *in conversation with other world views.*

There are many other courses necessary to make for a well-rounded philosophy minor or major. Because the Aristotelian-Thomistic tradition is such an important one, it is a fairly easy task to place it in conversation with the other major philosophical traditions in just about any course being offered. It is equally easy to note the challenges to Catholic teaching, especially in matters of morality, encountered in these opposing philosophical views, and some plausible answers to those challenges.

Question 6

What role does a program in Catholic studies have in this kind of a university, which by logical consequence, it would seem, should have the kind of curriculum I have been describing? There is a danger inherent in a Catholic studies program, but also one overriding strength. The danger is that such a program could act as a convenient shunt for faculty members or departments who are discomfited by the idea of being part of the Catholic voice of the university. I imagine *Star Trek's* "Bones" McCoy, as a member of our faculty, snapping at his department chair, Captain Kirk, "Dammit, Jim, I'm a doctor, not a Catholic." For a faculty uncomfortable with the Catholic project, the Catholic studies program would be an opportunity to place responsibility for the Catholic habit of mind on other shoulders. The danger is that the project of developing this habit of mind becomes marginalized. Unless every student is a Catholic studies major, too many students miss the chance to "come and see" what we claim to be offering; the habit of mind fails to be developed, the burden of its development placed on too few professors.

Let us not, however, assume this of the faculty. Let us assume instead that this faculty is committed to the project, excited at the prospect of offering students a look at the intersections between the wisdom of the Catholic faith and their own academic fields. Here is where we find the great promise of a Catholic studies program, a strength that overrides the potential danger.

It seems to me that, in a university dedicated to the project as I have described it, a Catholic studies program offers yet another opportunity, a spectacular opportunity, to focus the development of the Catholic habit of mind for those students and faculty wishing to do so. It is an opportunity, not simply to "come and see" what it is that excites the faculty and drives the project of the Catholic university; not only to become conversant about the intersection of Catholic faith with the academic exploration of human life and culture; but further to seek fluency, a degree of expertise, in this vision of the world. Disciplinary and interdisciplinary courses, developed by a faculty eager to explore these intersections, can be cross-listed with the Catholic Studies program, giving the student great flexibility and expanding the faculty's invitation to partake in the project. Interdisciplinary courses are especially important in this regard, for they allow faculty members to become part of the project *as learners*. Faculty members, then, not only gain expertise in Catholic awareness, but also knowledge of other disciplines. By team teaching in an area outside their normal field, they also get a chance to learn how to think in that discipline. In other words, they model for students ways of learning, which is good for students and faculty.

Conclusion

These answers, I have argued, are the logically necessary outcomes of a claim to be a Catholic university, that is, of a commitment by the institution to the truth of what the Catholic Church teaches. I have witnessed the eagerness for this project in many of my colleagues. Lest some, however, find these outcomes frightening or threatening, I implore you: Look at your Catholic friends and colleagues. Do you trust them? In an era that calls us to celebrate diversity, can we not welcome the invitation to come and see the Truth that animates and guides them? Even should you not accept the conclusions the Church has argued for about the ultimate truth, we ask you to respect the intellectual and moral integrity of this 2,000-year-old project. Let us not, like Pilate, wash our hands of this invitation from the Truth that stands before us. Let us instead join hands and begin our work together. We have much to offer each other.

on the part of some faculty and administrators that academic excellence requires not only the absence of control by the Church but also the absence of any influence by it; and (4) various flashpoints caused by speakers invited to campuses (especially if they have pro-abortion views), by student organizations (such as support groups for homosexual students), and by debates over the appropriateness of giving honorary degrees to individuals with views contrary to established Catholic doctrine.

What gets too little public attention, and what arguably is the most important factor that determines in the long run the real character of any academic community, is the faculty's vision of scholarship as it relates to the mission of their institution.[6] At a typical Catholic university today, the majority of the faculty have received their graduate degrees from secular institutions. Those faculty who are Catholic often know little about current theological issues. What is more, they often have little understanding of Catholicism as an intellectual, literary, or artistic resource for living and thinking through their disciplines.

Arguably what is most important for Catholic institutions in the future will be recruiting, developing, and keeping faculty who are personally and intellectually interested in both what the Catholic tradition has to offer to their own disciplines and in the distinctive mission of their institutions. Faculty need not be Catholic to be supportive of a distinctively Catholic dimension of higher education. For a university to be distinctively Catholic, at least some of the faculty—variously described as a critical mass, a majority, an influential core, 50 per cent, and sometimes as only the president and the members of the theology department—some of the faculty must, in my view, be personally committed Catholics who are first-rate intellectuals, aware of how their disciplines and their faith tradition might relate to each other.

At the same time, faculty who are Christian but not Catholic, or who are from other faith traditions, or who may be humanists and agnostics, can and do contribute to the religious mission of the institution. In fact, some of them, by the thoughtfulness of their interaction with the rest of the faculty, force the discussion of the mission of a Catholic university to be more carefully, honestly and inclusively articulated.[7]

A Seminar on Ethics and Religion in Professional Education: An Overview

In an effort to begin to address the importance of the faculty's vision in relationship to the religious mission of the university, a series of seminars for faculty have been conducted at the University of Dayton, a Catholic university founded in 1850 by the Marianists (Society of Mary). In 1995, a two-semester seminar for seventeen faculty from all parts of the university read and discussed classic texts from the Catholic intellectual tradition. The seminar was led by members of the Forum on Catholic Intellectual Tradition Today, eight faculty who, with the support of the provost and dean's offices, continue to initiate conversations, encourage research and publications, organize conferences, and invite speakers to campus.[8]

During each semester of the 1995 seminar, participating faculty had one less course to teach, an arrangement that allowed them to devote more time to reading and discussing texts by Augustine, Aquinas, Dante, Newman, O'Connor, and others. The second semester examined the relationship of various disciplines to the Catholic intellectual tradition and to some contemporary theological issues. The seminar group has continued to meet regularly.

A foundation grant generously supported a second, somewhat different, seminar in 1997. Eleven faculty members of our professional schools—two from the School of Law and three each from the Schools of Business, Education, and Engineering, met weekly for two hours during the winter semester (January to early May). They also received summer research support ($5,000) to continue to explore together and on their own specific areas of interest as they related to the Catholic intellectual tradition. While some faculty study the religious dimensions of their disciplines without special financial rewards, the University underscores the importance of such research by providing real financial benefits.

In order to set specific goals for the seminar, one representative from each of the four professional schools met several times in the fall of 1996 with the University Professor of Faith and Culture, James Heft, S.M., who conducted the seminar. Minutes were kept for each meeting and circulated to the rest of the participants with a request for comments. Thus the participants set the direction of the seminar.

Three themes were chosen for the seminar: (1) historical understanding of the evolution of higher education in this country, particularly Catholic higher education; (2) exploration of key elements of the Catholic intellectual tradition; and (3) understanding how that tradition might pose questions, inform research, and influence the teaching of professional educators. The three themes were to be studied sequentially, beginning with the historical studies. In order to facilitate conversations between people in different disciplines, the representatives recommended that during the semester all eleven of them meet regularly as a group rather than as subgroups by profession. Finally, the key readings were set by November, to allow time to buy and read texts early. In this way, the seminar could begin in earnest right at the beginning of the new semester.

Faculty Profile

The leader of the seminar, who wrote the original proposal when he was provost, invited comments from the deans on a draft of the proposal. The deans agreed to invite faculty who were respected scholars, who were likely to be interested in such a seminar, and who would be capable of influencing their departments and their schools. Though a few of the invitees had questions about the seminar's goals and about the substance of Catholic intellectual tradition and their own relationship to it, every faculty member invited decided to participate. Two were Jewish, one agnostic, two Protestant, and six Catholic. There were six full and three associate professors, one assistant professor, and one lecturer who had recently completed a Ph.D. in business ethics; all but the last two had tenure.

The first challenge, one nearly as complex as evaluating the secularization hypothesis, was finding a convenient time for everyone to meet two hours a week.[9] Before starting weekly meetings, the seminar was oriented at a meeting at a nearby conference center that lasted from Sunday afternoon to Monday afternoon (Monday was a holiday). On Sunday afternoon, the participants got to know each other and talked about their academic interests, family and religious background, and hopes for the seminar. People were open about their own religious biographies, and expressed genuine interest in the tasks associated with the seminar. On Sunday evening there was an animated discussion of Leo Tolstoy's *Death of Ivan Ilych*. Monday morning, the group discussed a series of articles on the Catholic intellectual tradition. And on Monday afternoon, the group discussed the first 100 pages of George Marsden's *Soul of the American University*. Each segment had a different leader.

The two-day meeting provided an excellent opportunity for participants to get to know one another better, and to acquaint themselves with two of the three themes. The characters in Tolstoy's novel reveal some of the hazards of professionals; Ivan Ilych's life as a lawyer raised fundamental questions about the culture of professionalism and social class in late 19th century Russia, and prompted discussion about how professional people might think about their professions and lives today.

The group devoted the next two meetings to discussing the rest of *Soul of the American University*. Reactions to the book varied from genuine appreciation for the extensive documentation of secularization at several major, once religiously affiliated, American universities, to impatience with repetition of case after detailed case of similar universities going down the same path. Most seminar members thought the movement toward secularism was unfortunate, but also identified certain benefits:

greater freedom for many faculty to explore their intellectual interests and the rapid development of modern science, though its applications have been a mixed blessing. An expert in educational policy found in Marsden's thesis a fresh and challenging perspective on higher education and the public policy that ought to guide it.

To focus our discussion of Marsden's work more sharply, each participant was asked to extract ten of Marsden's main theses and discuss their importance. Reviews of the book were circulated, including a collection of essays entitled "God in the Academy."[10]

Over the next two months, the meetings looked successively at the mission of a Catholic university,[11] further readings on the Catholic intellectual tradition,[12] the shaping of the professions in the twentieth century,[13] one historical interpretation of the current challenges facing Catholic higher education in America,[14] and finally the nature of Catholic higher education.[15] The diverse readings often converged on important points that will be discussed here later.

The next two meetings focused on Sissela Bok's 1978 book, *Lying: Moral Choice in Public and Private Life*,[16] allowing the group to explore the value and limits of a utilitarian approach to ethical issues in the professions, especially law and medicine. We then returned to literature with May Sarton's novel, *The Small Room*.[17] This 1961 novel describes the experience of a woman who begins teaching at a small women's college in New England. The story raises issues of career, personal vocation, the nature of the teaching profession, and the different ways of knowing that some argue are characteristic of men and women. Once again, a work of literature helped the group get more effectively at some issues that straight expository prose often failed to raise.

In early May, the participants devoted an entire meeting to explaining to each other what they were planning to do in their summer research. Some had difficulty deciding just what to do; others needed assistance in focusing a topic they had chosen; and some were already deeply involved in their research. Many found it challenging to address the religious as well as the ethical dimensions of their topic and the interactions of both dimensions. The research sessions helped the group understand better how the readings and discussions of the semester could enrich their research interests. The issues raised by their research projects caused seminar participants to meet with other faculty who were helpful, and some became research collaborators.[18]

During the summer, most members of the seminar kept in contact with at least their colleagues from the same professional school, as well as with the seminar leader. In August, all the participants reviewed this article and submitted reports on their research and evaluations of the seminar. A final meeting followed by a dinner, to which spouses were invited, concluded the seminar. Research and work on curricular projects continues. The group has decided to continue to meet to discuss the research.

The Seminar Profile

Which faculty should be invited to participate in a seminar on ethics and religion? Some might be tempted to think that only Catholics, or at least only the religiously "devout," should be invited, though no calculus of "devotion" yet exists. Whatever doubts a few who were not Catholic may have had about participating in the seminar seemed quickly to dissolve. It took longer, however, for some to see how they might fully contribute to the seminar if they themselves were not either personally religious or personally committed Catholics. On the other hand, the honesty of all in the seminar consistently added to the quality of the discussions.

Fundamental questions arose from all members:

- Does one need to be religious to be ethical?
- Isn't it dangerous to assume that anyone has *the* truth?
- How can religion assume a strong public role in a religiously pluralistic society?
- Wouldn't some in Catholic universities really want only Catholic faculty if they could at the same time sustain and increase academic quality?
- What specifically does Catholicism have to contribute to intellectual life?
- Don't dogmas by definition clash with academic freedom?

Facing such questions squarely provided some of the most valuable moments of the seminar.

The particular mix of disciplines also proved valuable. For example, one liked Marsden's data-rich historical study of the secularization of universities. For this professor, Marsden "proved" his thesis. A lawyer did not like the book at all, finding it burdened by repetitive documentation. The lawyer thought that since history can be written from so many angles, no particular history will necessarily prove anything; in fact, history is more an interpretative art than an empirical science. The lawyer added, "I believe, however, that I must learn to appreciate and learn to evaluate like an engineer might if we are to have a rich and fruitful dialogue." The quality of listening and mutual appreciation deepened with time. Skills for dialogue across disciplines may well be one of the most valuable outcomes of the seminar.

Disciplines constitute in their own way diverse cultures; interdisciplinary conversations require a form of multicultural skill no less than the mixing of races.[19]

Significant Themes that Emerged

Professional Neutrality and Deformation: Ivan Ilych

Some of the most vexing questions raised in our discussion of Tolstoy's brief novel were whether neutrality as a professional was possible or even desirable; whether the professions have been served well by the "power differential" based on the idea that professionals possess expertise that ordinary people do not; and whether being a professional inevitably diminishes a person's capacity to be vulnerable before others. Finally, we asked, as so many have presumably asked in past centuries, whether one has to face death, as Tolstoy's character Ivan did, in order to see the most elementary truths about the human condition.

Only gradually, over the course of months, did we find it easier to understand each other. Nevertheless, during this discussion of Tolstoy's first novel at the seminar opening, the participants started showing each other who they were and what ideas they as professionals thought were important. They were also free enough to challenge each other. In particular, they debated professional neutrality versus "advocacy," degree of personal involvement, even of "friendship" with a client or a student. Does a professor teach a discipline, or students, or both? How objective can a professional be when personally involved with a client? Does love deepen or distort one's understanding of another? Is it ever appropriate for professionals to be vulnerable in the presence of those they serve? Does being vulnerable weaken a professional's effectiveness, or is another type of power made evident in one's admission of weakness? Many of the participants later spoke of the value of this particular discussion.

The Catholic Intellectual Tradition

Several obstacles needed to be overcome before discussion on the Catholic intellectual tradition could be fruitful. First is simply the realization that there *is* such a thing as a Catholic intellectual tradition. Very few "cradle" Catholics, even those with Ph.D.s, turn to their religious tradition for intellectual stimulation. There are, of course, many reasons for this, not the least of which has been how Catholicism has been experienced in both schools and parishes. For those who are not Catholic as well as cradle Catholics, their understanding of Catholicism has been disproportionately shaped by the media, which highlights the controversies that, in the United States at least, are almost always cast in the form of rigid hierarchies trying to control creative liberals, with little attention paid to the actual issue itself. Being faculty members at a Catholic university *can* help individuals enrich their understanding of a rich and diverse Catholic intellectual tradition, but enrichment by osmosis ought not to be presumed.

There is a wider and deeper set of reasons for the lack of understanding of the Catholic intellectual tradition: American culture has privatized religion, forced it to the margins of life, made it purely a personal choice, private and subjective, and finally—particularly relevant for universities—reduced the religious realm to the affective and the private, eliminating its cognitive character and barring its public role.

Over 100 years ago, major U.S. universities began exiling religion from any central role. If it remained at all, it was studied primarily as a moral code and a set of rituals, which were looked at "objectively" for their "appropriateness" or "reasonableness." Most faculty today do not believe that theology departments, as opposed to Religious Studies departments, concern themselves with "real" knowledge, or that they actually communicate valuable insights and skills for life—certainly not as valuable as those learned in professional schools and in the study of the sciences, through which a person is much more likely to make a living. Parents of (especially male) students who change majors from, say, engineering to theology ask, "Are you prepared to flip burgers the rest of your life?"

Catholic universities make a greater investment in theology and philosophy, and in the ethical dimension of most disciplines. At least, such discussions are encouraged. In an address at the installation of a new president of Boston College in 1996, Martha Nussbaum, professor of law and ethics at the University of Chicago, commented:

> In Catholic schools it is common to find discussion of such ethical questions [questions about what human beings are, what they need and what they should pursue] in the economics department and in science departments, as well as in philosophy and theology. Economists don't simply assume that human beings are machines producing utility; they engage in a lot of foundational criticism of standard models of growth, welfare, and development. This produces a rich deliberative community in which students are strongly encouraged to think about how their courses fit together in forming the skeleton of a full, complete and valuable life.[20]

The seminar participants thought Nussbaum's statement might not be true in enough Catholic colleges and universities. None disagreed with the assumption behind her statement—that ethics and religion ought to be a natural part of the content of many disciplines—but many doubted that such discussions about such matters happened regularly, even after encouragement by administrators and support from university documents.

Because religion in our culture—and in the academy—is not seen as an intellectual phenomenon, this depreciation immediately affects how professors, even Catholic professors, think of their religious traditions. Many faculty experience their religious tradition as a source of personal motivation to be ethical. How often does religion affect in any explicit way what people do as engineers, accountants, or lawyers? It rarely becomes a source from which they rethink assumptions of their academic disciplines, and question their lives as professionals. Few professional faculty use religion as an important source for problem-solving and reflection in their disciplines. As one member of our seminar put it, "What will professions of faith add to the academic debate?"[21]

One of the first challenges in the seminar, then, was to achieve a basic understanding of the Catholic intellectual tradition, its sacramentality, its respect for many forms of knowing (not just the form that is empirically verifiable), its attention to history and tradition, its emphasis not just on the individual but also on the community, not just on choice but also on the ability to love, and not just on freedom but also on commitment to truth.[22] An informed study of the Catholic intellectual tradition reveals a striking pluralism (one participant suggested that we speak rather of Catholic intellectual traditions), recognizes limits to what can be adequately expressed through dogmatic formulations, and provides an often unexpected sophistication about such current issues as the nature of human freedom, the purposes of human community, the principle of subsidiarity, and the limits of both socialism and capitalism. One member of the seminar was dumbfounded with how current the Pope's ideas on women are, as expressed in the encyclical *Mulieris Dignitatem*.

Work and Integrity: Sullivan's Plea

William Sullivan's book, *Work and Integrity,* reviews the history of the professions in the United States, describing their present state as largely bereft of any vision of the common good; it calls for a reinvention of the professions, a restructuring that would "suffuse technical competence with civic awareness and purpose."[23] He calls the professions now to expand their horizons beyond merely personal financial rewards, a move characterized best, he believes, by the word "integrity," which helps individuals mediate the tension between individual rewards and the common good. He almost never refers to religious reasons for assuming a broader perspective as a professional, though his arguments could easily be rooted in religious traditions.

All the seminar participants agreed that professionals should be motivated by more than just personal rewards. Most thought Sullivan's formulation of the larger perspective as the "common good" easily linked with Catholic social teaching. On the other hand, some thought that Sullivan may have underestimated the challenge of "reinventing" the professions. Today, there are literally millions of professionals, not just in the traditional professions (law, medicine and ministry), but also in segments of the work force never before presuming to call themselves professionals: e.g., fund raisers and garbage collectors. Not only have the number and types of professionals multiplied incredibly, but certain structures in the university's promotion and tenure processes discourage professors from doing community service. Sullivan gave few practical suggestions for how to go about reinventing the professions.

Lying: Consequences and Character

Sissela Bok's 1978 book, *Lying: Moral Choice in Public and Private Life*, became one of the most persuasive arguments for the establishment in the late seventies and early eighties of much needed ethics review boards. Her book asks only one question: What obligation do we have for telling the truth in public life? Finding little wisdom in the religious and theological literature on lying (though she includes excerpts in her appendix from the writings of Augustine, Aquinas, Bonhoeffer, and others), she turns to utilitarianism. She focuses on the consequences of lying, employing the "publicity test"—asking what most people think. Consequence and publicity are the two foundations for her theory and its applications.

While the participants found many of her cases interesting in themselves, they were generally critical of: (1) the publicity test, as in fact impractical; (2) Bok's focus on the collective rather than the individual; (3) her lack of any philosophical or theological reflection; and (4) her doing moral analysis only along consequentialist lines. The discussion raised the moral issue of the effect of lying to oneself, something Bok does not deal with.

Since she excluded philosophy and theology from her argument, many larger and deeper questions of personal identity and purpose were not addressed. These questions arise when people understand the difference between mere productivity and fruitfulness; fruitfulness goes beyond the utilitarian calculus. One participant asked whether, given the secularization of the professions, she should be responsible for her students' character, not just their competence. Others, though agreeing that professors ought to be concerned about the moral dimensions of their students' lives, found it difficult to agree on how to express that concern as teachers.

As important as Bok's book was for applied ethics in the late seventies, its exclusion of religious tradition and theologically based ethics as sources for reflection and analysis confirmed Marsden's thesis that religion is no longer an important academic source.

O'Brien's *From the Heart of the American Church*

O'Brien finds the state of Catholic higher education in the United States positive: "The first thing to say about Catholic higher education is that it is prospering."[24] In one chapter on the debates within Catholicism about secularization, he concludes that laicization need not mean secularization.

Members of the seminar immediately began to compare O'Brien's description of the current state of Catholic higher education to Marsden's description of the secularization of private universities like Harvard, Yale, and Brown. At the end of the semester, the members were given copies of Philip Gleason's magisterial history of Catholic higher education, *Contending with Modernity*,[25] a study that ends on a much more somber, not to say pessimistic, note than O'Brien's book.

The participants appreciated O'Brien's clarity and willingness to engage contemporary issues—a willingness absent in most historians. The last four chapters of the book provide a candid discussion of recent efforts to write a mission statement for his own college (Holy Cross), the difficulty Catholic higher education has had in conducting civil debates on abortion, the differences between Religious Studies programs and theological curricula, and the obligation of Catholic universities to graduate both disciples and citizens. When O'Brien shifts from historical analysis to overt advocacy, the link between the two stays evident.

The Legal, the Ethical, and the Religious

Just as it is sometimes necessary to distinguish between what is legal and what is moral, it is also necessary to admit that professional ethical codes, though helpful, go only so far. Most professions now have ethical codes. Few, if any, refer to people's religious practices and convictions. As an accountant put it in a particularly intense seminar discussion, "Most of us professionals know the rules, but few of us, even when we know it would be the best thing to do, go beyond them."

In other words, in most professions it is possible to do one's work in a way that is legally acceptable but that will never advance the field, challenge current prescriptions, or move it beyond formal professional obligations. Engineering professors can easily teach the basics of design and develop their students' technical competence but not be concerned with the character of their students or the impact of technology; business professors can teach students how to increase commercial profits without considering how such approaches affect others—laborers, the unemployed, the poor; educators can advocate attending to "the whole child," but never attend to the child's need for a spiritual life and a moral core; and lawyers can advise clients without considering the role that religion, their own and that of their clients, might have in the situation for which their service has been retained.

And what about the service one owes not just to individual paying clients, but to humanity as a whole? In May of 1997, Ralph Nader told the law graduates of the University of Dayton to ask themselves, "How much of your time are you going to spend representing your clients as attorneys and how much of your time are you going to spend representing the broader objectives of justice in society as lawyers?"

The Enlightenment sought to sever the link between the ethical and the religious. Some results have been unequivocally positive: a reduction in the number of religious wars (though by no means a removal of them) and greater self-regulation among the professions (though scandals continue). Nevertheless, the vital link between what we believe and how we ought to behave, that is, between religion and ethics, has been weakened. Marsden's question haunted the seminar: "What is it about the dominant academic culture that teaches people they must suppress reflection on the intellectual implications of their faith?"[26]

The seminar participants repeatedly asked themselves what positive difference the intellectual implications of faith would make to their research and teaching. No single answer arose—the sign of an excellent question. But many reflections were shared, some of which converged and formed a background, a set of assumptions with which most of the participants agreed.[27] The positive differences such a link could effect were often intuited by the participants rather than schematically developed. The seminar created a clearer awareness of the lack of religious dimensions and reflection within professional disciplines today, and a realization of the need to try in some noncontrived way to address these lacunae.

History and Agency

A little knowledge of history makes it clear that things were not always as they now are. If that is so, the way things are now need not be the way things will be in the future. A grasp of the history of one's discipline, profession, and institutional context—the academy—frees up the imagination to envision changes.

Several members of the seminar decided to do research that would lead to curricular changes[28]:

- Research into how medical and divinity schools improved the counseling skills of doctors and ministers led to the design of a similar seminar for law students, who, in the seminar participants' view, could benefit from greater sensitivity to the ethical and religious commitments of their clients.
- A seminar participant worked with another engineer not in the seminar to design an introductory course on marketing and its ethical and environmental dimensions. Their suggestions were initially opposed by some other members of the school, but the two professors made adjustments, pressed on persuasively, and have already offered the new course.
- The three business professors have taken on the challenge to design, for business majors, a set of courses from the School of Business and the College of Arts and Sciences that are more effectively integrated.

In each of these instances, the study of the history, either of their disciplines or of the religious dimensions that have been excluded from them, suggested more wholistic ways of doing their work as professionals. In short, the seminar participants learned to imagine different ways of doing things and took practical steps to realize new alternatives.

Conclusion

Toward the end of the seminar, the members often discussed secularization, what it might mean, what could be lost if it were to happen, how far along this path some institutions already have trod, and what could be done to prevent it at our university. Among the recurrent suggestions was giving faculty the opportunity to study and discuss with each other the sorts of topics we explored in this seminar. Fundamental convictions of Judaism about the world as created by God and about people being created in God's image established common ground between Christians and Jews, two of whom were seminar participants. We asked ourselves repeatedly how such deeply held convictions could help affect the way we conceive of our roles as professional educators, and affect the research we think relevant.

Catholic universities should begin in a more serious way to provide opportunities for faculty to reflect seriously on questions that their personal and professional experience have rarely included, particularly the academic ramifications of their faith. The faith of the faculty and its relationship to their intellectual work needs to become a factor in the hiring process, even though such a practice can be easily twisted into many unacceptable forms: (1) only Catholics need apply; (2) choose piety over scholarship; (3) hire people who will be faithful to the Church teaching, but never be capable of critiquing and developing it; and (4) overlook the value of having faculty with diverse religious perspectives.

Intensive faculty seminars that are well-funded and interdisciplinary; include study, discussion, and research; are intense; and last the better part of a year are one of the most effective ways to strengthen a distinctive vision among faculty, especially when some of the themes and central texts explore the religious tradition on which the university rests. An interdisciplinary approach allowed this seminar to examine neglected dimensions. What can be seen when several disciplines converge on matters of fundamental importance can be every bit as valuable as what can be seen through any one of them. In the long run, such seminars may lead to the creation of more integrated scholarship that will expand the present scope of the disciplines.

Appendix: Summaries of Research Projects

Infusing Ethical, Moral, and Religious Values into a Law School Curriculum

Can better teaching methodologies enhance the exposure of law students to ethical, moral, and religious issues and relate those issues to the real world of practicing law? My research explored approaches used by other law schools to incorporate ethical and moral issues into their curriculums. I also reviewed programs at medical and theological schools to determine if any of their methodologies were adaptable to law schools. In addition to the literature research, I conducted numerous interviews with professors who teach ethics at law schools, medical schools, and seminaries.

Based on my research I developed a model program for the University of Dayton School of Law that would increase law students' exposure to the kind of ethical and moral issues that arise during the professional life of a lawyer. The key elements are to: (1) incorporate ethical and moral discussions in most of the substantive courses of the law school; (2) use simulations and role-playing to introduce the issues to the students; (3) have a theologian or a philosopher participate in the discussions.

The ordinary approach to teaching law students about ethics and morality is to require them to take a two-credit course in professional responsibility. Exposing students to ethical and moral issues is left to the teachers of professional responsibility, who have to tackle the problem in classes of over eighty students. My proposal attempts to spread the teaching of ethics and morality throughout the curriculum, with every professor including an ethical component in each of their classes. Furthermore, it suggests a teaching methodology that emphasizes the use of simulations and that allows students to experience how ethical and moral problems arise in the practice of law.

Dennis Turner, School of Law
turnerd@udayton.edu

Decision-Making of School Administrators: The Dynamics of Power, Ethics, and Religion

A young girl in a Catholic junior high school is expelled from the school because of her nonconformity in appearance, behavior, and attitude. What will happen now to this student? A public school superintendent redirects financial resources toward maintaining scores on state-mandated tests rather than to a deeper set of learning challenges to students. How does one comply with mandates without neglecting the intellectual growth needs of children?

School administrators are professionals in positions of power, making decisions daily that affect the lives of children and their families in very profound ways. Each decision is laden with moral and ethical meaning. The research question driving this study is: What is the relationship among religion, ethics, and power for school administrators? How might school administrators be better prepared to construct their power in ways that take ethics and religious beliefs into account?

I am reviewing the philosophy of power, the literature on ethics (history, philosophy, education, and management), and Catholic and other religious thought related to these issues. Examples that parallel the ideas generated in this study will be related to other recent studies that I have conducted on leadership in schools.

A model (solidly grounded in the literature review) of the interrelationship among these constructs (power, ethics, religion) will be created, as well as a proposal for how to integrate this model into leadership preparation in the School of Education.

Carolyn R. Ridenour, Educational Administration Department
Ridenour@keiko.udayton.edu

Engineering, Gender, and Justice

Most universities train new engineers to become gainfully employed, rather than to encourage reflection on the relationship between the professional and the spiritual. Thus, engineering programs are generally preoccupied with teaching students how to analyze and design new products and processes. An ethics or religion course is not required for most engineering students because these subjects are considered useless in the art of landing a high salary. Ethics is often seen as "common sense."

Existing engineering ethics courses address issues such as whistle blowing, legal liability versus moral responsibility, and ethical design decisions. Little is said of the ethical or religious dimensions of, say, gender diversity. The engineering profession has been an overwhelmingly male pursuit and, unfortunately, remains so today. Undergraduate female enrollment in engineering programs has increased, but not long-term retention. Engineering schools have become better at filling the female pipeline to engineering careers, but have failed to address the issues of life after graduation. The objective of my study is to address why women leave engineering, to describe differences between male and female engineers, and to say why in the light of spiritual motivation we should care.

One important realization that I have had is that women and men really *are* different, and those differences in how they approach a complex design problem or manage a staff of engineers should be valued. Furthermore, we as Christians who are called to avoid discrimination against women being engineers (or any other type of professional!) should be concerned with the low numbers of women retained in the engineering profession.

I carried out my work by reading numerous writings of sociologists, psychologists, and authors in women's studies, as well as the encyclicals of John Paul II (*Laborem Exercens, Mulieris Dignitatem, Familiaris Consortio, Women of Peace,* and *Redemptor Hominis*).

Since I am not a sociologist, a psychologist, or a person who has ever previously read anything in women's studies, this project has expanded my views concerning women, engineering, and the intertwining of the spiritual and the professional.

Jamie Ervin, Mechanical and Aerospace Engineering
eervin@engr.udayton.edu

Wholistic Engineering

My experience in the Ethics and Religion Seminar has been personally stimulating and energizing. It has generated an internal desire to seek greater understanding in disciplines once remotely connected to my professional life—philosophy, theology, ethics, history, and sociology. As I have learned more, I have been inspired to imagine how my own teaching could be enhanced by these new connections and how engineering as a whole might benefit.

I have become convinced of the necessity of challenging engineers to recognize that creativity is not solely to be employed for developing new designs and products, but is also essential for imagining the full impact of such designs and products on individuals, communities, and the world. These transformations have framed the research that I have conducted to better understand the context and conduct of engineering and business, both past and present, and to further my understanding of both religious and secular moral foundations. I have sought to imagine the future challenges facing engineers, as well as how we might best deal with the challenges, trying to fend off my tendency to create binary solutions for the generally complex and intertwined web of problems.

My research thus far has been touched by the world of philosophy and history. I have listened to past thinkers describe what it is to imagine and create. I have come to recognize with a great shock that the post-modernist claim of biases impacting conclusions has relevance to virtually all of engineering. I have sought to understand what these biases are. I have listened to the messages of social responsibility by liberation theologians and, surprisingly, Pope John Paul II, and have been compelled to consider how the technology of the West has contributed to the impoverished state of the world's poor.

The fruits of my research, I believe, are beginning to ripen. With Malcolm Daniels (EE), I have developed a five-week module as part of a new first-year design course to introduce all engineering students to the design of electro-mechanical systems. In this course, we have sought to acquaint students with a holistic view of design so that they might see the context of design, the impact of design on society, and the opportunities that exist to engineer in a way that reduces the "revenge" impact of design. This course has been developed for Web delivery and can be accessed at (http://www.engr.udayton.edu/SOE/Depts/Mechanic/FacStaff/khallina/classes/EGR101Engineering_in_Society/)

Kevin Hallinan, Mechanical and Aerospace Engineering
khallina@engr.udayton.edu

Exploring the Relationship between Religious Values and Professional Ethics

With one or two notable exceptions, most of the published teaching materials used in professional responsibility (or professional ethics) courses in American law schools make no (or at best oblique) references to religion. This is also true with respect to the two major bodies of ethical rules—the Model Code of Professional Conduct and the Model Rules of Professional Responsibility—which have been adopted, in one form or another, by every state. In addition, relatively little of the academic literature dealing with significant issues in professional responsibility deals in any substantial or systematic way with religious values as a source of guidance or insight.

My research represents an effort to identify the ways in which religion has (and, importantly, has not) explicitly and self-consciously influenced the modern legal profession's conception of professionalism and professional role; to speculate about the reasons why religious values are so seldom invoked as a source of professional ethical and moral values; and to consider how religion might be taken more seriously as a basis for professional norms. I expect that this research will have an important effect on my own teaching and thinking about professional responsibility and, to the extent that it leads to published work, the thinking of others in the field.

Richard B. Saphire, School of Law
saphire@udayton.law.edu

The Epistemological Problem in Teaching Applied Ethics

Over the past two decades there has grown up considerable interest in the ethical dimension of education. This interest has resulted in, among other things, numerous educational ethics courses in professional formation programs. For the teacher of these courses, there is a pedagogical dilemma arising out of a fundamental epistemological problem. The postmodern intellectual climate prevalent in academe is skeptical of any credible form of knowledge with respect to moral questions. Should the instructor of educational ethics courses, then, simply engage the students in ethical discussions without any hope of resolution on a rational basis? The discussions would be interesting but not very satisfactory for guiding practice and policy in a coherent fashion.

The full paper will examine two texts in which the authors propose models for achieving reasonable conclusions in practical ethical inquiry. The first is Sissela Bok's *Lying: Moral Choice in Public and Private Life.* The second is *The Ethics of Teaching* by Kenneth A. Strike and Jonas F. Soltis.[29] Sissela Bok proposes a "publicity" model for intellectually resolving practical ethical questions. Her proposal assumes that a utilitarian calculation of consequences is the most promising approach to providing rationally defensible moral judgments. Because she acknowledges the difficulty of calculating practical consequences of action and the susceptibility to subjective rationalization, she prescribes that speakers subject their oral judgments to the "publicity test," asking what would the "reasoning public" calculate to be the most orally acceptable course of action with respect to the probable consequences.

Strike and Soltis, on the other hand, propose a "provisional reflective equilibrium" model that has multiple tests for the rational acceptability of moral judgments and principles. Since they liken ethical inquiry to legal reasoning, they maintain that oral certainty is unrealistic, but one can reach a "provisional reflective equilibrium," i.e., moral judgments and principles that are consistent with a multiple range of standards. These standards include the public moral philosophy, personal intuitions, consequentialist considerations, and non-consequentialist moral principles.

The core of the paper will consist in an explication and analysis of these two models with a special emphasis on the pedagogical implications for holding either of these two positions. I will then propose a more satisfactory model that incorporates the central insights of the two models while strengthening key tests and expanding moral considerations to other key tests. The overall objective of the paper is to propose pedagogical guidelines for teaching applied educational ethics that are based on sound epistemological premises.

William F. Losito, School of Education
losito@keiko.udayton.edu

Proposal: A More Interdisciplinary Business Thematic Cluster

Understanding the relationship of business operations to the goals, purposes, and functioning of the larger society is vital if business school graduates are to be able to deal effectively with the complex demands modern business organizations place on them. Therefore, business education programs need to explicitly include coverage of areas of connectedness between business operations and the societal areas that impact and are impacted by business activities. An ideal place for such connectedness to be explored is in a general education cluster oriented to the needs of business students. Although the clusters already in operation have done an excellent job of covering the interrelatedness of knowledge in disciplines outside of business administration, business students have indicated that they do not see the relevance of the coverage in the existing clusters to their future careers in business.

We propose developing a new cluster that is oriented to the needs of business students and emphasizes the areas of connectedness between business operations and the larger society. The cluster would not be just an extension of business education but rather would cover the liberal arts and social sciences where business and society relate. Developing and maintaining such a cluster would require extensive and regular collaboration between business faculty and interested faculty in the liberal arts and social sciences. This collaboration is one of the unique and necessary aspects of the proposal. Although the administrative structure of the cluster has not been worked out completely, two-person teams composed of a business and a liberal arts or social sciences faculty member to coordinate each course is a strong possibility.

James B. DeConinck, Management/Marketing Department
James.DeConinck@notes.udayton.edu

Victor M. Forlani, Management/Marketing Department
Victor.Forlani@notes.udayton.edu

Kenneth Rosenzweig, Accounting Department
rosenzwe@notes.udayton.edu

An Alternative Vision for Educational Policy and Reform

I took steps to integrate themes developed in the seminar into my research on educational policy and reform. First, during the period when the seminar was reading Marsden's *The Soul of the American University*, I drafted a proposal for a new book, *Refinancing the College Dream: Contending with the Complexities of Affordability, Productivity, and Employability*, a book I am now writing (with Eric Asker) for Johns Hopkins University Press. This book uses Marsden's critique of progressivism as a starting point for re-examining higher education finance in the United States.

During the summer, when plans for the research projects were developed, I decided to use these funds to support training for three University of Dayton personnel in the Accelerated Schools Project methodology. This team has begun working with the twenty-eight accelerated schools in Ohio, has received notification of provisional status as a satellite center from the National Center for Accelerated Schools at Stanford, and is initiating a national effort to adapt the accelerated schools reform approach in Catholic schools.

More recently, as I reflect on the seminar, I am drafting a proposal for a new book, tentatively titled, *Moral Consciousness in Action: Reclaiming Professional Responsibility*. This effort is very deeply influenced by the discourse in the seminar, and my consulting with Father Heft and other seminar members on the proposal.

Edward St. John, Educational Administration
stjohn@keiko.udayton.edu

Notes

1. See David Damrosch, *We Scholars: Changing the Culture of the University* (Cambridge, MA: Harvard University Press, 1995). See also James Turner's thoughtful review and critique of *We Scholars*, "Humbling the Lords of Epistemology" in *Books & Culture* (Sept./Oct. 1996): 26–28.
2. A number of authors, including James Turner, have welcomed the less radical aspects of post-modern epistemological trends as allowing for the possibility of more porous boundaries between disciplines, and indeed as a quite different and more fruitful way of organizing knowledge itself (see James Turner, *Catholic Intellectual Traditions and Contemporary Scholarship* [Notre Dame, IN: Cushwa Center for the Discussion of American Catholicism, University of Notre Dame, 1998]).
3. See, among others, George Marsden, *The Soul of the American University* (New York: Oxford University Press, 1994); Julie Reuben, *The Making of the Modern University: Intellectual Transformation and the Marginalization of Morality* (Chicago, IL: University of Chicago Press, 1996); George M. Marsden and Bradley J. Longfield, eds., *The Secularization of the Academy* (New York: Oxford University Press, 1992); James Burtchaell, "Decline and Fall of the Christian College," *First Things* (April 1991): 16–29, (May 1991): 30–38; Michael J. Lacey, ed., *Religion and Twentieth Century American Intellectual Life* (Cambridge University Press, 1989); David W. Gill, ed., *Should God Get Tenure? Essays on Religion and Higher Education* (Eerdmans, 1997); and Michael Baxter, C.S.C., and Frederick Bauerschmidt, "*Eruditio* without *Religio?* Dilemma of Catholics in the Academy," *Communio* 22 (summer 1995): 284–302.
4. See Isaac Kramnick and R. Laurence Moore, "The Godless University," *Academe*, 82 (Nov.-Dec. 1996); and Stephen Macedo, "Religion at the Margins of the Academy: Where it Belongs," *Academic Questions* (spring 1996): 21–25, part of "Symposium: God in the Academy," with George Marsden opening and closing the discussion.
5. See James L. Heft, S.M., and Leo O'Donovan, S.J., "A University that Evangelizes? *Ex Corde Ecclesiae* Six Years Afterwards," *Horizons* 23 (spring 1996): 103–12; and J. Heft, "Theology's Place in a Catholic University," in Patrick W. Carey and Earl C. Muller, S.J., eds., *Theological Education in the Catholic Tradition: Contemporary Challenges* (New York: Crossroads, 1997), 192–206.
6. The Collegium program, an annual eight-day gathering of about thirty-five Ph.D. students, thirty-five young faculty, and about six more senior faculty from Catholic colleges and universities who serve as mentors, has aimed over the past five years to strengthen interest in the relationship between faith and

the intellectual life, and had encouraged Ph.D. students to consider careers at Catholic colleges and universities.

7. It can also happen that questions by skeptics, humanists, and atheists weaken an institution's capacity to articulate its religious mission, particularly when they outnumber and outshine the faculty who are Catholic. While intelligence and academic competence are not the key to the Christian life, they are nonetheless an indispensable asset, especially for those faculty who dedicate themselves to their professional work with explicit religious commitment.

8. A newsletter, *Faith's Reasons*, is now published twice a year to draw attention to the wide variety of initiatives, especially faculty research.

9. It would have been easier had participants been selected before the teaching schedule for the January term was completed the previous September. We alternated between Friday afternoon and Thursday morning meetings. Most people were able to make Friday afternoons most of the time; the other time, at 7:30 on Thursday mornings, was difficult for those who had children to get off to school. Never underestimate the challenges presented by scheduling.

10. "God in the Academy, *Academic Questions* (spring 1996): 11–36, includes comments from Jacob Neusner, Stephen Macedo, Glenn Altschuler, James Nuechterlein, and David Roskies. It contains a useful distinction between secularism and secularization: *Secularism* excludes religion; *secularization* removes church control. Laicization need not lead to secularism, though historically, according to Marsden, it played a role in the disestablishment of religion from the academy.

11. Martha Nussbaum, Peter Steinfels, and Bryan Hehir, "Mission Statements," *Boston College Magazine*; three essays from William M. Shea and Peter A. Huff, ed., *Knowledge and Belief in America: Enlightenment Traditions and Modern Religious Thought* (Shubert M. Ogden, "The Enlightenment Is Not Over"; David Tracy, "Modernity, Anti-Modernity and Post-Modernity in the American Setting"; and Richard J. Bernstein, "Are We Beyond the Enlightenment Horizon?").

12. Andrew Greeley, "The Catholic Imagination and the Catholic University," *America* (March 16, 1991); Thomas H. Groome, "What Makes a School Catholic?" in T. McLaughlin, J. O'Keefe, and B. O'Keeffe, eds. *The Contemporary Catholic School: Context, Identity and Diversity*; D. Carr, J. Haldane, T. McLaughlin, and R. Pring, eds., "Return to the Crossroads: Maritain Fifty Years On," *British Journal of Educational Studies* (June 1995); James L. Heft, S.M., "Faculty Address," *Current Issues in Catholic Higher Education* [summer 1991]); and Robert Wilkins, "The Lives of the Saints," *Remembering the Past* (Grand Rapids, MI: Eerdmans, 1996).

13. William M. Sullivan, *Work and Integrity: The Crisis and Promise of Professionalism in America*; Paul F. Camenisch, "The Professions as Moral Com-

munities," in *Grounding in Professional Ethics in a Pluralistic Community*, and William G. Tierney, "Organizational Socialization in Higher Education, *Journal of Higher Education* (Jan/Feb 1997).

14. David O'Brien, *From the Heart of the American Church: Catholic Higher Education and American Culture* (Orbis, 1994).

15. James Heft, S.M., "Challenges and Opportunities: Graduate and Professional Education," unpublished faculty address; *Vision 2005: The Foundation* document (the University of Dayton's most recent mission statement); and Heft and O'Donovan, "A University that Evangelizes?"

16. Sissela Bok, *Lying: Moral Choice in Public and Private Life.*

17. May Sarton, *The Small Room.*

18. The participants briefly describe their research projects in the appendix to this paper.

19. James L. Heft, S.M., "Catholic Multiculturalism: An Oxymoron?" *Logos: A Journal of Catholic Thought and Culture*, 1:3 (fall 1997): 12–30.

20. Martha Nussbaum, *Boston College Magazine* (1997): 33.

21. This echoes the comments of one critic of Marsden's *Soul of the University*, Stephen Macedo, who wrote: "Marsden himself fails to specify exactly what it is that professions of faith will add to the academic debate." Macedo complains that though Marsden asserts that religious perspectives will enrich public and scholarly debate, he offers no examples. (Actually, he does provide a few in his lengthy study.) Macedo's complaint is more amply addressed in Marsden's next book, precisely to respond to that criticism (*The Outrageous Idea of Christian Scholarship* [New York: Oxford University Press, 1997]). See Macedo, "Religion at the Margins."

22. The academy today hesitates to use the word "truth," and positively avoids speaking of "*the* truth," for fear that once "the truth" falls into someone's possession, inquisitions and pogroms will follow. Such fears are hardly groundless.

23. Sullivan, *Work and Integrity*, xix.

24. O'Brien, *From the Heart*, 69.

25. Philip Gleason, *Contending with Modernity* (New York: Oxford University Press, 1995).

26. Marsden, *Outrageous Idea*, 6.

27. In retrospect, we should have made a conscious effort towards the end of the seminar to spell out as clearly as we could the assumptions on which we agreed. It would have been hard but fruitful work.

28. The research projects seemed to arise once it became clearer that religion and its potentially positive influence had been excluded from academic thinking and disciplines.

29. Bok, *Lying*; Kenneth A. Strike and Joseph Soltis, *The Ethics of Teaching*, 2nd ed. (1992).

Academic Freedom and the Catholic University: One Generation after *Land O'Lakes*

Michael Hollerich *

A New Situation

Discussions about academic freedom in Catholic colleges and universities seem fated to fight the last war all over again. During the 1960s there was a strenuous, broad-based effort to move Catholic institutions closer to accepted standards of academic and professional excellence. That meant approximating criteria for excellence as defined chiefly at the same elite private institutions that had always set the standards of higher education in America.

That these standards were rigorously secular was not recognized as a serious problem. Catholic colleges had always had as a primary practical purpose the upward mobility of the Catholic population, which between the 1820s and the 1920s was largely an immigrant population striving to transcend its working class origins. In the heady days after the Second Vatican Council, with its call to read the signs of the times and to enter into constructive dialogue with all forces working for human advancement, there was now also a theological motivation to become conversant with the natural and the human sciences that had contributed to modern humanity's "coming of age."

*Michael Hollerich is assistant professor of theology at the University of St. Thomas, St. Paul, Minnesota. An earlier version of this article appeared in *Academic Freedom and the Catholic University: Summer Seminar 1997* (St. Paul: University of St. Thomas, 1997).

To establish the academic bona fides of Catholic colleges and universities, few goals therefore seemed more significant than adopting the ideal of academic freedom recognized by secular institutions, especially given Catholicism's authoritarian reputation. It was not just that Catholic schools had to live down the mistrust and even contempt of secular institutions that took the Whig view of the history of freedom as gospel. Catholic academicians themselves often had good reason for wanting as much distance as possible between their schools and religious authorities, whether those were the local ordinary, the religious order that had founded and usually still ran their schools, or the Vatican itself. The generation that taught me in college certainly took this view. It would be unwise not to respect their concern, which often enough stemmed from unhappy personal experience.

Such was the context for the drafting of the 1967 Land O'Lakes Statement.[1] That document insisted unequivocally that Catholic colleges and universities had to enjoy full institutional autonomy if they were to serve their academic and professional ends. Similarly, theological study was declared to be an autonomous discipline with its own standards. Seen in their original context, against a history of largely mediocre Catholic academic achievement, these propositions are understandable, even admirable. Whether the same can be said thirty years later is more doubtful. I will argue here that the full autonomy called for by the Land O'Lakes Statement now appears to be a self-defeating ideal. It overlooks the primary challenges facing schools that today aspire not only to be successful academic institutions but also to keep faith with the religious traditions that nurtured them.

First, the weight of a sometimes sorry past keeps us from recognizing that our schools face far more immediate and serious threats to our academic integrity than those posed by the authority of the Catholic Church. "Academic freedom" tends to be seen as something we supposedly already possess and have to protect jealously, lest a clumsy exercise of the Church's authority grab it away from us. To think this way is to succumb to an out-of-date script that diverts our attention away from dangers closer at hand.

Second, given the demonstrable secularization in higher education, our religious identity is far more fragile and at risk at the hands of our academic and professional goals than the other way around. But our religious identity is worth fostering not just for its own sake but also as an enhancement of our distinctively *professional* ends.

Last, an organic institutional connection of the type envisioned by, e.g., the controversial Canon 812 of the Revised Code of Canon Law, while not without risks, may be appropriate given the decline of the religious orders that have historically been the chief carriers of the religious mission and the identity of Catholic colleges and universities.

Academic Freedom and Its Limitations

Academic freedom is not an end in itself. Its goal is not to create a safe haven in which people can say, teach, and write whatever they wish simply because it pleases them to do so. Rather, as a precondition for the successful flourishing of colleges and universities, it is not a freedom *from* so much as a freedom *for*. The 1940 AAUP statement on academic freedom firmly asserts the service of "the common good" as the rationale for academic freedom. Scholars are thus granted the freedom to speak, teach, and write without fear of reprisal for being wrong *because society has judged that the open and disciplined pursuit of the truth, in the manifold ways expressed in the modern university, serves the common good.*

Our freedom to speak, teach, and write as we wish is therefore rightly limited in many ways: by the choice of subjects to teach, by the pedagogical needs of our students, by the standards and methods of the discipline or profession in which we were trained, and by that over-arching awareness of the common good that is the ultimate rationale for colleges and universities. Very few would probably object to restraints of this order, though in practice they entail fairly extensive limitations on what we say, teach, and write. They are basic to any persuasive sense of academic freedom. Dismissing them means vitiating the very integrity of university education. But these are scarcely the only limits on academic freedom. Many others affect every aspect of our work as scholars and teachers, most of them in a grayer zone, and some downright worrisome.

Consider, for example, the matter of a university's "culture." Management types like to talk about corporate culture, how it varies from one company to another, and the problems that crop up when through mergers one corporate culture collides with another. Universities, too, have cultures. Codes of speech and behavior vary greatly from one school to another, depending on location, the ethnic profile and class affiliation of the student body and alumni, funding sources, the academic and professional programs, the presence or absence of a religious affiliation, gender balance, relation to public worlds outside the university (business, the military, the media, etc.). Codes of speech and behavior will be accordingly diverse, not just in their judgments of value but even in what they choose to consider important: Things that matter critically to professional success at one school may be utterly irrelevant at another.

Very often the codes are tacit and traditional rather than written and explicit, making compliance even trickier. It is true that procedural safeguards try to ensure that faculty members who deviate from the code do not suffer at tenure time—but this only means that schools do the real scrutiny and selection at the hiring stage, when questions of "fit" may be debated passionately.

What about the limits to academic freedom posed by the increasing budgetary pressures on all schools, state-supported as well as privately-funded? Will our programs be pressured to become profit centers, required to justify their place in the budget by the money they bring in via external grants, student enrollments, and the like? It does not take a paranoid imagination to see what a crushing concern for the bottom line could to do to our freedom to speak, teach, and write as we believe is appropriate. Or, to take an issue not far removed from the budgetary realm, what about the increasing influence of student response to professors and their courses, especially their standardized and anonymous evaluations? How far are these from becoming customer satisfaction surveys? What effect do they have on freedom in teaching?

What about the troubled world of scholarly publication? Will scholarly monographs lose their de facto subsidies? Will university presses take a page from commercial publishers and look for the academic, or pseudo-academic, equivalent of the blockbuster? The state of scholarly journals is not reassuring, either. The multiplication of journals seems driven more by extrinsic pressures to publish than by the intrinsic value of the research. With more journals comes further balkanization; prospects of publication depend increasingly on conforming to the methodological and substantive interests of the journal's sponsors.

What about the politicization of the contemporary academy? As John Searle noted in a recent talk at St. Thomas, the academy and the curriculum have always been "political" in the trivial sense that they had political consequences. But in the past generation political passions and agendas have metastasized. The academy, or at least the humanities sector of the academy, has turned its traditional relationship to American culture inwards and directed it against the academy itself. Politicization has tended to blur the line between argument and accusation. Far from promoting civil argument, ideological policing of the academy seems to have stifled debate. Fashionably skeptical epistemologies, scorning rationality and reducing all differences to matters of power, make the situation worse. But a fragile institution like the university is a poor place for adjudicating disputes about power, which ought to be left to the ballot box or the courtroom.

This list could be expanded, but I have said enough to make my point: We are beset by varied threats to our academic freedom, in comparison with which it is hard to see the one posed by the Catholic Church as particularly urgent. Fixating on the Church as a uniquely threatening danger actually diverts us from much more immediate, and perhaps intractable, problems, than that posed by the historic affiliation of the University of

St. Thomas with the Archdiocese of St. Paul. In fact, that connection can be far more beneficial than threatening.

The Pull of Secularization

The religious affiliation of an institution like St. Thomas is far more at risk from its general educational mission than the other way around, because secularization is integral to modern colleges and universities.

The various professional dynamisms driving an institution like ours will inevitably drive a wedge between the school and its religious foundations. The history of religiously affiliated colleges and universities in this country proves this. In the normal course of their development, such schools progressively divest themselves of their religious affiliation, barring some countervailing force, such as unusual administrative vision or an unusually close tie between the school and its ecclesiastical sponsor. The mechanics of this process are not mysterious. They have been documented in numerous books and articles by scholars such as George Marsden, Philip Gleason, and others, including now James T. Burtchaell's massive study, *The Dying of the Light: The Disengagement of Colleges and Universities from their Christian Churches.*[2]

The causes of secularization include such things as the desire to improve the professional quality of the faculty, which leads to lessened attention to religious commitment as a consideration in appointments; a distaste for the administrative measures necessary to keep a Christian presence on the campus a public reality in a maximum of ways, from worship to curriculum to student life; the recruiting of students who lack any interest in or familiarity with the school's religious character, either because of a need to keep up enrollment or to recruit the intellectually ablest; the secularizing consequences of the specialization of knowledge; and the proliferation of graduate and professional programs, which are strongly driven by specialization and autonomous professional criteria.

To these must often be added embarrassment and uncertainty about a school's religious character on the part of the very persons responsible for staffing and running the institution. They may distance their school from its church or confessional affiliation because they fear it will doom the school to second-class status within the academic guild—in short, they want to be accepted by their secular peers.

The process of secularization has been evident for the past century at dozens of once-Protestant institutions. I still remember my first sight of the dedication *Christo et Ecclesiae* inscribed in stone above the gates of Harvard Yard, and hearing Professor George Williams recount his unsuccessful defense of the ringing of bells for chapel at Memorial Church (the memorial for Harvard's war dead—*pro patria mori* being the secular university's highest measure of devotion; it includes the names of a couple of Harvard students who died fighting for the Kaiser). These are but the thinnest of reminders that Harvard University originated as a Puritan seminary. A history not unique to Harvard: To my knowledge, until the 1890s every private college began as some type of church-related or church-sponsored initiative.

By contrast with the formerly Protestant colleges, secularization has been slower to work its results at Catholic schools. Various causes account for this difference. Nevertheless, there is no reason to think that over time our destiny will be any different. It was discouraging to see how sure some authors are that "it can't happen here." Administrators and faculty at Catholic schools have been too slow to realize this, although anecdotal evidence, such as the proliferation of Catholic studies programs, suggests that "Catholic identity" is increasingly seen as something that cannot be taken for granted.

Why the tardiness to learn from our Protestant brothers and sisters? It may be simply lack of concern about religious identity, or even a secret wish to see it discarded (that embarrassment factor), but several other factors may be to blame. One is a parochialism that grows out of the very success of American Catholicism in creating its own massive institutional subculture. Our colleges and universities are so numerous as almost to constitute their own world. Furthermore, the administration at most Catholic institutions has historically been composed of priests and members of religious orders, whose own education and professional experience were probably not at secular universities. The result is an administrative version of *ex opere operato*: How can we *not* be Catholic? We have priests in every position of importance. (This, of course, is a situation that is changing rapidly.) Finally, a certain boosterish complacency seems endemic to American Catholicism: It can't happen here. We live with a sweet insouciance. What we need is the wisdom of the serpent.

A crowning irony of secularization is that it imposes, top down, a uniformity on American higher education that would be keenly resented were it to come in the form of a hierarchically defined religious orthodoxy. The current shibboleth of diversity should not be allowed to disguise this. When one hears the same slogans and programs invoked at one school after another, one rightly wonders just how much difference there really is. It is an odd type of diversity that results in each school aspiring to look very much like every other school.

The standardizing pressures at work are very strong. We would be foolish to underestimate them. They are grounded in the dominance of discipline-based professional associations and accrediting agencies and in the homogenizing effects of our system of graduate education. They exert their leveling effects in marketing strategies to offer an education with the broadest possible consumer appeal. And they receive powerful ideological validation from the democratic passion for equality, which, as Tocqueville observed over a century and a half ago, strives relentlessly to produce sameness at the expense of liberty.

But if educational diversity is truly to be embraced as a good, the conclusion is inescapable: The Catholicity of St. Thomas should be prized as its most fundamental and most valuable difference.

Religious Identity and Its Benefits

St. Thomas's religious identity is far more an asset to its academic mission than a hazard. It deserves the special efforts necessary to ensure that it flourishes. It is characterized by:

1. *An overarching sense of purpose*: The Catholic affiliation gives our mission cosmic grounding that goes far beyond the public purposes to which secular institutions are dedicated. St. Thomas is no *less* committed than they are to the conventional goals of liberal education for life and citizenship, of technical and professional training and competence, of research, and the like. But at St. Thomas all of these have a justification and meaning that is much deeper than the daily activities that keep the institution moving forward. We are no less susceptible to routinization than anyone else, but there are rich local stimuli, above all the liturgy, to direct us away from immersion in the quotidian and to restore proportion and balance to our work. My own most vivid experience of this was the university funeral mass for Maureen Brennan, a St. Thomas student who died of cancer in 1996.

2. *A sense of historic continuity*: We are part of a continuous tradition of teaching and study which goes back to the universities of the Middle Ages and to the philosophical and biblical traditions of antiquity. Christianity is the carrier of this tradition. The history of western culture in a sense is *our* history. To say this is not to make a superficial baptism of western culture for the sake of an ecclesiastical monopoly. Nor is it to succumb to cultural chauvinism: Christianity's history is much *broader* than western culture, and has been so from the beginning. The gospel spread to the east as well as to the west (see no. 4). But a case can be made that western

thought and education, from the Greeks to the emergence of the natural sciences, are unthinkable without Christianity.

And, at a more local level, St. Thomas is thoroughly embedded in the history of its city and state, thanks above all to the ambitious vision of John Ireland (see no. 6).

3. *A vision of the human good not controlled by instrumental rationality:* St. Thomas holds to an understanding of human life in which questions of utility and power do not have the last word. This should be an especially critical advantage in our professional programs, in which preoccupations with method and technical expertise so easily displace questions about purpose and the good. Our contemporaries endlessly wring their hands about the decline of ethics in public life. St. Thomas ought to offer a better way. I presume that this is what the current official touting of our "values-based" education is getting at. During our seminar discussions, Chris Melloy made a similar point in describing how her work with children fit especially well into a Catholic context. The same could be true in education, bioethics, business, economics, and social work.

4. *A community committed from the beginning to recognizing and addressing diversity:* From Pentecost (Acts 2) to *Lumen Gentium*,[3] Catholicism has always recognized and made room for human cultural diversity, with an inclusivity that has not always been admired by other types of Christianity. Catholicism is by far the most thoroughly international Christian church. Although the Roman passion for centralization and uniformity has sometimes sat poorly with this inclusivity, it does not seek to eliminate it. Given that Vatican II declared the Church to be the sacrament of the unity of the human race,[4] we could hardly ask for a firmer mandate for cultural inclusivity. Also, Christianity can give an account of its respect for human differences and human dignity; secular endorsements of diversity tend to stumble when asked precisely *why* different individuals and cultures should be respected.

5. *An architectonic wisdom:* This phrase, which I believe is from theologian Michael Buckley, may sound overblown given the actual divisions within our curriculum, but the aspiration to offer an integrated view of human understanding is part of Catholicism's intellectual charter. St. Thomas has a large and energetic theology department. It makes impressive efforts at connection and coordination with other academic sectors of the university. We may never get more than partway to resolving the complexities of constructing such an integrated grasp of human knowing, but in an

age that seems resigned to fragmentation and skepticism, how many institutions are even willing to mount the effort? It makes a difference to the intellectual atmosphere of a school when there is a vigorous and *public* effort to reconcile a divine revelation like Christianity, whose bearer and authoritative interpreter the Church claims to be, with what the disciplined ingenuity of human reason has disclosed to us about ourselves and our world—all of which, the biblical monotheisms teach, are the creation of the living God.

6. *Local roots and connections in city and region:* This is both historical and contemporary fact. The school is inseparable from the history of the church in this area; both are inseparable from the larger history of city and state. To treat this fact as merely historical in a museum sense and not as a living reality would be a serious mistake. We hear a lot these days about the future of St. Thomas as an urban institution. Such language needs to be attended to carefully; it may encode a redirection of the university from its historic character. If so, we risk distancing ourselves from invaluable sources of human, moral, and financial support.

Balancing the Risks

If the real situation of Catholic schools like St. Thomas is the one I have been describing, perhaps the bold declarations of the Land O'Lakes Statement need to be reconsidered. Could we not today accommodate greater institutional linkage between the Church and the university than we have in the past? Is Canon 812, for example, really beyond the pale of what is tolerable in America, as many Catholic scholars, theologians, and administrators have suggested? I suggest cautiously that it is not, and that the benefits of an organic connection outweigh the risks.

The benefits to the university come above all from having an outside court of appeal, should cases of truly unresolvable conflict arise within the university. Better the bishop's mediation than the civil courts. If this seems draconian, remember that in the past most Catholic colleges and universities could rely on the religious order that had founded the school to be the ultimate custodian of the school's Catholic identity.

The decline of most orders has created an unprecedented leadership vacuum. Dean Carrocci argued that today's Catholic laity are well qualified to be entrusted with this custodial mission. I have reservations about this claim. The reservations do not arise from doubts about the integrity or qualifications of lay faculty and administrators. My concerns have to do with the long-range consequences of a lay-run church in general (a recent *Commonweal* cover reads: *The Laity Have Won—Now What?*)[4]. We are in the midst of what looks like a novel situation in Catholic life: The contribution of religious orders and congregations is rapidly being enfeebled. In the past, the orders, often new ones, have been the main engine for reform and innovation, at least since the advent of monasticism in the fourth century. Despite "the emerging laymen," it was still true during the ferment and run-up to Vatican II. It is true no longer.

I wonder whether we have any firm grasp yet of the real effects of this change. I am not denying the obvious—the dominance of the laity. Nor am I impugning the integrity of any individual, let alone the whole class to which I myself belong. I am simply saying that the jury is still out on how beneficial this change will prove to be.

To acknowledge an organic link with the hierarchy admittedly carries risks. Much depends on the good will and prudence of the ordinary. One hopes, for example, that he can distinguish significant appeals from merely alarmist ones. Terry Nichols reminded us that in a well-ordered church the rule of subsidiarity ought to prevail: Tasks should be undertaken and decisions made at the level of competence closest to the situation. Under normal circumstances the ordinary would have no reason to intervene in the life of the university, which is best left to the faculty and the administration. Only when normal operations break down might intervention become necessary, and then only after careful investigation and discussion. Sister Sharon Howell spoke about the importance of regular and candid conversation between college and Church in order to build mutual trust and understanding. Everyone should benefit from this increased understanding.

I am a rather reluctant supporter of a closer tie to the church. As a rule, I prefer decentralization in both the Church and university. A particularly sad feature of the current situation is the decline of the religious orders and their educational apostolate, since the orders traditionally offered a measure of autonomy vis-a-vis the hierarchy. St. Thomas of course is a diocesan university, the product, I assume, of Archbishop Ireland's passion for uniform lines of authority, which semi-autonomous religious orders appeared to threaten. But I am willing to entertain episcopal oversight, properly defined, in a cultural situation where the playing field appears far from level.

Notes

1. "Land O'Lakes Statement: The Nature of the Contemporary Catholic University." As contained in Neil G. McCluskey, S.J., *The Catholic University*

(Notre Dame, IN: University of Notre Dame Press, 1970). See Gallin, op. cit., pp. 5–6. [Gallin, op. cit., contains the Statement.] Summarizing Gallin's commentary on the Statement: The Document was the product of a regional meeting of the International Federation of Catholic Universities. In this case the region was the US. Gallin notes: "The group . . . included some twenty-six persons representing nine major Catholic universities, members of the episcopacy, and well-known scholars and leaders of religious communities. . . . Land O'Lakes contained two phrases that became fundamental in the future dialogue: academic freedom and institutional autonomy." (5–6)

2. George Marsden, *The Soul of the American University: from Protestant Establishment to Established Unbelief* (New York: Oxford University Press, 1994); Philip Gleason, *Contending with Modernity: Catholic Higher Education in the Twentieth Century* (New York: Oxford University Press, 1995); and James T. Burtchaell, *The Dying of the Light: the Disengagement of Colleges and Universities from their Christian Churches* (Grand Rapids, MI: William B. Eerdmans, 1998).

3. *Lumen Gentium 1.*

4. Ibid.; also see *Gaudium et Spes* 42 and 44.

5. Eugene McCarraher, "Smile When You Say 'Laity': The Hidden Triumph of the Consumer Ethos," *Commonweal* 124 (September 21, 1997), 21–25.

Teaching Sociology in the Catholic University: Conflict, Compromise, and the Role of Academic Freedom

William J. Kinney *

In the context of a Catholic university or college, practitioners of a wide variety of academic disciplines are often forced to ask themselves a difficult question: To what extent does or should the Catholic mission of an institution of higher education affect the practice of a given discipline and the teaching of that discipline to students? For some, the dilemma is minimal; their subject matter is such that there is little potential for conflict between their teaching or research activities and a given institution's Catholic mission or philosophy. However, the content of many disciplines is such that faculty and administrators alike are forced to exert extra effort toward maintaining that delicate balance between academic freedom and institutional integrity. Sociology could well be considered such a discipline for two fundamental reasons.

The first of these is that since religion in general and Catholicism in particular are important components of the social world, they have been and continue to be the subjects of scientific study and investigation for sociologists. Some of the earliest and most influential works in the discipline[1] have focused on the profound impact that various religious philosophies—including Catholicism—have had on the workings and structure of society. When cast in the often-critical light of sociological analysis, these impacts (whether the focus of classical or of contemporary research) are frequently viewed in a less than positive manner.

*William J. Kinney is professor of sociology at the University of St. Thomas, St. Paul, Minnesota. This article first appeared in *The Idea of a Catholic University: Summer Seminar* (St. Paul: University of St. Thomas, 1994).

Another somewhat problematic aspect of this critical view of religion is that, just as sociologists are concerned with objectively assessing the impact that religion has had upon society, they are also concerned with how religions may be affected by society. Of particular concern in recent decades has been the modern trend toward "secularization," by which religion in general is supposedly losing power and influence in the social world because of a collective disregard for matters regarded as "supernatural" or "sacred."[2] In researching and teaching about this trend (and other trends related to the possible decline of religion in society), sociologists may be delving into matters that create alarm or discomfort for members of the Catholic community.

A final problematic aspect of sociology's critical view of religion relates to the basic nature and structure of religion. To many sociologists—though certainly not all—religion is viewed as a fundamentally subjective human construction possibly devoid of grounding in objective reality.[3] From such a perspective, the existence and functioning of a given religion is attributable more to the unique psychological needs of its adherents than to the true existence of a God or gods. Viewing God as a subjective social construction in the context of a Catholic university may present some cause for conflict.

As a result, whether sociology is focused on analyzing the impact of religion on society, the impact of society on religion, or the social-psychological essence of religion and of God, the sociological view of religion is a fundamentally analytical one. And, since religion is viewed as the subject of social analysis rather than as an object of reverence, one can easily see the vast potential for conflict in being a sociologist in an educational institution with a strong religious mission and affiliation. It is rather being an analyst (and often a very critical analyst) of one's own employer.

As problematic as this particular aspect of the relationship between Catholicism and sociology has the potential to be, an even greater potential for conflict arises over the wide array of issues and subjects studied and taught by sociologists. Any standard introductory text in sociology will contain discussions of controversial issues such as birth control, abortion, homosexuality, the death penalty, and feminism. The potential for problems arises when the conclusions of sociological research call for solutions to social problems that clash with policies advocated by the Church. Hassel describes the unique dilemma presented to the Catholic university when faculty specialized in a given field of secular knowledge are also part of a religious community: "How can the university escape a schizoid existence if it is both an institution of specialized knowledges–skills–arts and yet a community of wisdom that serves its various constituencies?"[4]

Of course, differences between the official policies and stands of the Catholic Church and those supported by given sociologists are not always attributable to the Church's disagreement with the scientific outcomes of sociological research. In the wake of the 1960s sociology acquired the reputation of being a somewhat "liberal" academic discipline. Therefore, wholly apart from the objective findings of sociological studies, sociologists themselves often bring a wide variety of personal biases into their teaching and research agendas.

On many issues, such as civil rights, social justice, and economic inequality, a liberal or radical sociologist may not feel too much discomfort in a Catholic academic setting, since the Church has taken what are perceived to be liberal stands on such issues. However, on birth control, abortion, homosexuality, etc., the views of a liberal sociologist are likely to clash rather dramatically with the official, "conservative," doctrines of the Church. The specialized knowledge of the sociologist, and the liberal norm that has apparently evolved within the discipline, therefore often put sociologists at odds with official stands the Catholic Church has taken on a variety of controversial issues.

These two fundamental aspects of sociology—its analytical view of religion in general (and Catholicism in particular), and the clash between the personal views of many sociologists (whether rooted in objective data or subjective opinions) and official Church doctrines on a variety of issues—may create difficulties between people recruited to teach and practice sociology and the religiously affiliated academic institutions that hire them. What, then, is the answer to the resolution, or prevention, of conflicts between sociologists and religiously affiliated academic employers?

On the Catholic Church's part, substantial efforts have been made to balance faculty demands for academic freedom with its own desire to preserve the nonsecular essence of the Catholic university. This attempt is apparent in *Ex Corde Ecclesiae*, Pope John Paul II's Apostolic Constitution on Catholic Universities:

> Every Catholic university . . . is an academic community which . . . assists in the protection and advancement of human dignity and of a cultural heritage through research, teaching, and various services offered to the local, national, and international communities. It possesses that institutional autonomy necessary to perform its functions effectively and guarantees its members academic freedom, so long as the rights of the individual person and of the community are preserved within the confines of the truth and the common good.[5]

A prime example of the attempt to implement John Paul II's call for academic freedom has occurred at the University of St. Thomas, in the form of the June 1994 *Statement Regarding the Addressing of Controversial Issues at the University of St. Thomas:*

> The university exists as an environment which not only allows, but encourages, members of its community to ask questions and openly explore challenging ideas in their personal search for truth. Open forums through which controversial issues may be addressed in a responsible and educative manner will be available. More important, the university will ensure that these dialogues occur in an arena free of fear of reproach or reprisal.

Through efforts such as this, Catholic universities around the country, and the world, are apparently making good-faith attempts to mediate fairly between their Catholic missions and the demands for academic freedom of faculty and students.[6] Sociologists and other social scientists may feel particularly heartened by such attempts, in light of the broad potential for conflict that affects this particular discipline. Administrators and other university officials may feel some trepidation in anticipation of exactly how such policies of tolerance may eventually be put to the test.

It must also be remembered, however, that the responsibility for managing potential conflicts between the Catholic university and social scientists cannot—and should not—be placed solely upon the Church. Just as the Catholic Church has made an effort to meet and respect the needs of its faculty, faculty working in a Catholic university have a duty to meet and respect the needs and nature of their employer—a fact that apparently became lost on many in the social upheaval of the 1960s and early 1970s.

Many scholars have researched the impact of the political radicalism of the 1960s on academia in general and Catholic institutions of higher education in particular.[7] Gleason observes, "The cultural earthquake of the late '60s could not help exacerbating the Catholic crisis. . . . Catholics heard it said that their church was corrupt and its leaders bankrupt . . . they heard that their country was a racist imperialist monster, its leaders war criminals."[8] In general, it is concluded that this kind of questioning and challenging of social institutions—whether religious or governmental—led to a general erosion of the respect that such institutions had previously held in society. Academia was affected by this erosion, as faculty and students alike came increasingly to question or challenge the authority and validity of various aspects of academic operation, such as institutional missions.

Accompanying this trend was and is a strong sympathy for the secularization of many religiously affiliated academic institutions.[9] Since religion was one of the prime social institutions called into question during this period, and since universities were often centers for radical philosophy and activity, pressures mounted to minimize the influence that "questionable" religious views could have over the operation of a given institution. Burtchaell proposes that Protestant universities were the first to feel the impact of this trend, but concludes that Catholic universities are now secularizing in a manner similar to that experienced by Protestant universities some 20 to 25 years ago.[10] As a result of this general phenomenon, Hassel concludes, "Christian philosophy is presently under a cloud; it is poorly known and respected."[11]

Together, these social trends became a powerful force in academia, and the discipline of sociology provided fertile ground in which sentiments such as these could grow. The 1950s and 1960s saw the rise of many "conflict" and "critical" theories that advocated a radical Marxian approach toward understanding and resolving a wide variety of social issues. Such theories also tended to view religion in general, and Catholicism in particular, as suspect at best and exploitative at worst.[12] Through the rapid growth of these "critical" and "conflict" perspectives, sociology came in many ways to typify the radicalization and secularization that have become troubling for Catholic universities.

The irony in these developments is that it is often the most radical members of a given university's faculty who demand and probably receive the greatest amount of academic freedom from their denominational employers, and yet it is often these same faculty who espouse philosophies that show little tolerance for religion. When such is the case, one could well argue that Catholic and other religiously affiliated universities have accorded far more respect to their faculty than some faculty members are willing to accord the religious missions of their employers.

It is also ironic that many of these same academics have enthusiastically embraced the current movement for diversity, and yet accord little acknowledgement for the contribution Catholicism makes toward the diversity of society. Indeed, it would seem that attempts to secularize the Catholic university are, in fact, an attack on the very diversity that such persons claim to advocate. How is diversity enhanced by imposing a homogenizing secularization upon universities whose mission and practices are guided by a unique, Catholic view of society? How is society itself improved by a reconstruction of religious institutions of higher education in the generic model of the secular public university?

While Catholic institutions of higher education are well aware of concerns over academic freedom and tolerance expressed by their faculty, many academics (including many sociologists) are often unwilling to accord a reciprocal respect to their Catholic employers and to the unique contribution the Catholic university offers a society striving to accept diversity. Such may be said of the relationship between academia and Catholicism in general, and of the relationship between sociology and Catholicism in particular.

Therefore, just as the Catholic Church has acknowledged in a variety of ways that the faculty in its universities and colleges deserve academic freedom, so the faculty (of any discipline) working in such settings should accord respect to the religious denomination that employs them. While this obviously does not mean that faculty could or should be forced to embrace or advocate a given religious philosophy, it does mean that the employing denomination should at least be spared the scorn or derision that the more radical members of a given discipline may direct its way.

Essentially then, while the relationship between Catholicism and sociology has great potential for difficulty, the key to preventing and working through difficulties would appear to be simple mutual respect. Just as the Catholic university must respect the academic freedom and perspectives of sociologists, so sociologists teaching and researching within the Catholic university—or any institution of higher education with a religious affiliation—should accord respect to, and tolerance of, the views and missions of the institutions that employ them. If respect is mutual, it would seem likely that the delicate balance between institutional and disciplinary integrity can be achieved and maintained.

Notes

1. Emile Durkheim, *The Elementary Forms of Religious Life* (New York: Free Press, 1965 [originally published 1915]); Emile Durkheim, *Suicide* (New York: Free Press, 1966 [originally published 1897]; Karl Marx, in T. B. Bottomore and Maximilian Rubel, eds., *Selected Writings in Sociology and Social Philosophy* (Baltimore, MD: Penguin, 1964); Max Weber, *The Protestant Ethic and the Spirit of Capitalism* (New York: Charles Scribner's Sons, 1958 [originally published 1958]).
2. Harvey Cox, *The Secular City* (New York: Macmillan, 1971).
3. Peter L. Berger and Thomas Luckmann, *The Social Construction of Reality* (Garden City, NY: Anchor Books, 1967).
4. David Hassel, *City of Wisdom: A Christian Vision of the American University* (Chicago: Loyola University Press, 1983), 5.
5. John Paul II, *On Catholic Universities (Ex Corde Ecclesiae)* (Washington, DC: United States Catholic Conference, 1990), 13.
6. See James J. Annarelli, *Academic Freedom and Catholic Higher Education* (New York: Greenwood Press, 1987).
7. See, e.g., Philip Gleason, "American Catholic Higher Education, 1940–1990: The Ideological Context," in G. M. Marsden and B. J. Longfield, eds., *The Secularization of the Academy* (1992), 234–58; Nat Hentoff, *Free Speech for Me—But Not for Them* (New York: Harper Collins Publishers

Ltd., 1992); and Roger Kimball, *Tenured Radicals* (New York: Harper and Row, 1990).

8. Gleason, "American Catholic Higher Education," 246.

9. James T. Burtchaell, "The Decline and Fall of the Christian College," *First Things*, 12; Gleason, "American Catholic Higher Education"; and David Hassel, *City of Wisdom*.

10. Burtchaell, "Decline and Fall."

11. Hassel, *City of Wisdom*, 185.

12. See, for example, Randall Collins, *Conflict Sociology: Toward an Explanatory Science* (New York: Academic Press, 1975).

Catholic Studies at Catholic Colleges and Universities

*Thomas M. Landy**

When students on three Catholic university campuses returned to classes in the fall of 1997, they found a new option, Catholic Studies, among the curricular programs offered them. Three institutions—DePaul University in Chicago, Marquette University in Milwaukee and St. Louis University—inaugurated new undergraduate Catholic studies programs this past semester, and Loyola University Chicago launched a master's program. These new programs bring to at least seven the number of Catholic studies programs now in place, and may well signal the beginning of a trend in how colleges and universities address their religious identity and pass along Catholic traditions to students.

While the programs may have different strengths and weaknesses, they all aspire to give students broad exposure to Catholic culture, imagination, heritage, and traditions. Unlike programs that focus primarily on theology or pastoral ministry, Catholic studies programs cast their nets more broadly. They aim to introduce students both to Catholicism's place in the history of ideas and—more concretely and sacramentally— to manifestations of Catholic life in art, literature, music, and everyday culture.

The establishment of programs in Catholic studies might come as a surprise to people who presume that interest in Catholicity is on the wane on campus, or to others who think that what Catholic studies propose to

*Thomas M. Landy is the founder and director of Collegium, a faculty development program on faith and the intellectual life that began with a summer institute in 1993 on the campus of Fairfield University in Connecticut. This article is reprinted with the permission of Thomas M. Landy and America Press, Inc., 106 West 56th Street, New York, NY 10019, from *America* (January 3, 1998).

do is no different from what Catholic colleges are already supposed to do. Even some of the faculty who have talked about Catholic studies for years seem surprised that the idea has really begun to be discussed more seriously. The number of new programs has grown for each of the past three years; in 1998, for instance, at least five colleges were in the advanced stages of developing undergraduate minors. Many more institutions are considering the possibility. Because of the increasing interest, David O'Brien, professor of history at the College of the Holy Cross in Worcester, Massachusetts, organized a conference held at the University of St. Thomas in St. Paul, Minnesota, in November 1997 on the future of Catholic studies.

Faculty members who have worked to establish Catholic studies programs have encountered an array of responses on campus. On the one hand, some faculty members hesitate about adding a particularly Catholic academic program. On the other hand, Catholic teachers and administrators have sometimes been slow to embrace the concept out of fear that the programs would lead to increasing marginalization of Catholicism in the overall academic program. Establishment of Catholic studies, they suggest, may make Catholicism just another option in the curriculum alongside women's studies, race and ethnic studies, environmental studies, and the like. Proponents of Catholic studies, however, see the programs as a new opportunity for faculty and students to explore in depth topics that might otherwise get lost amid other curricular responsibilities.

Background

The idea behind Catholic studies is not entirely new. In the middle years of this century, many Catholic colleges and universities offered courses in Catholic literature and (more often) Catholic philosophy, as well as courses in religion. Christopher Dawson, a historian who was the first occupant of the chair in Catholic studies at Harvard, argued for the need to use Christian culture as the unifying theme for undergraduate education at Catholic colleges. Dawson's ideal was widely admired, but his program was institutionalized only at St. Mary's College in Indiana.

In the last thirty years, moreover, most institutions moved farther from emphasizing the specifically Catholic element of their mission and were more directly concerned with opening themselves up to the world and shedding the constraints of ghetto Catholicism. Institutions were much more likely to emphasize the charism of their founding community— Jesuit, Benedictine, Vincentian, LaSallian or Mercy—than their Catholic identity. Identification with the sponsoring religious community provided a special religious identity, which was called upon as a way to make the institutions seem more open than exclusive. Paradoxically, "Catholic" was often taken to symbolize the opposite.

In most instances, it is probably fair to say, the effort to be Catholic was not really abandoned but was more often either reinterpreted or taken for granted. A variety of programs and institutes founded in those years did in fact relate to issues of Catholic concern. Peace and justice institutes, in particular, have long flourished alongside campus ministry, service programs and theology and religious studies departments. A few Catholic institutions sponsored endowed chairs in Catholic studies (as did an equal number of secular institutions). In 1976 the University of San Francisco launched the St. Ignatius Institute, a great books program intended to update the Jesuit *Ratio Studiorum*, emphasizing Christian philosophy, theology, and literature. Most significant, in terms of Catholic studies, was the University of Notre Dame's foundation of the Cushwa Center for the Study of American Catholicism.

The emerging Catholic studies programs seem to have begun at a time when faculty and some administrators no longer felt able to take the Catholicity of institutions for granted. Faculty discussion groups, set up before or in tandem with Pope John Paul II's 1990 Apostolic Constitution on Catholic higher education, *Ex Corde Ecclesiae*, began to discuss the mission of Catholic colleges and universities. (*Ex Corde* dealt with the need to preserve and develop the Catholic mission of Catholic colleges and universities.)

On the scholarly front, cultural studies like Paul Giles's *American Catholic Arts and Fictions* began to expand the intellectual basis for understanding Catholicism's coherence in diversity. The growing prominence of other areas of culture studies—including Jewish studies—led many faculty members to feel either remiss at the slowness of developing Catholic studies, or at least more confident about the legitimacy of trying to create such programs.

Current Programs

How these programs will continue to grow remains to be seen, especially since many are still on the drawing boards and most of the programs already in place are small and still inchoate. All of them are interdisciplinary, and thereby aim to explore the influence of Catholic culture, thought, and institutions on a variety of aspects of human experience.

Structurally, these programs range from full-scale Catholic studies centers offering majors (12 or 13 courses) and minors (6 to 8 courses) to smaller interdisciplinary setups that offer a minor or a concentration (6 or 7 courses). At the University of Dayton, Catholic studies is integrated into the general education requirement of the curriculum. This obliges undergraduates to choose one of seven interdisciplinary themes that aim to unite the courses from core areas that make up the general education requirements. In addition to themes like ecology, globalism, and social justice, students have been able for three years now to focus on the Catholic intellectual tradition.

Most faculty members are drawn from existing programs in liberal arts departments, but at some institutions science faculty and faculty from schools of business and education have joined in as well. Though some of the efforts seem to have been hatched in administrative offices, most are the result of years of faculty gatherings. Almost all the programs are lay led, and all of those now in place have non-Catholic faculty members in the program.

There is some variation among programs in terms of "distance" from the subject matter. As would be the case in any cultural studies program, all want to give students a strong understanding of the lived experience of the subject. Some, like DePaul's, do so from a religious studies perspective that presumes no particular faith commitment, but only a desire to understand—and a willingness to criticize—the thought and institutions it studies. In Cleveland, John Carroll University's proposed program is much more explicitly apologetic. At the University of Scranton participants gather for liturgy, and the organizers hope that the program will spur students to constructive projects.

The course offerings are where Catholic studies gets most interesting. All the programs begin with one or two required introductory courses, which are usually team-taught, like Scranton's "Inside the Catholic Tradition" and "Christian Classics." Most require additional philosophy and theology but leave plenty of room for electives. All the designs also require a synthesizing "capstone" experience in the form of a seminar or thesis paper.

DePaul lists 85 courses in its program. In addition to a wide range of courses in theology and Scripture (students can cross-register at Chicago's Catholic Theological Union), courses include "Catholicism in Africa," "Catholic Faith and Musical Expression," "The Catholic Church in World Politics," "Economics and the Common Good," "Catholicism and Race," and "The Life and Times of St. Vincent DePaul." At Santa Clara University in California, the elective courses include "Dante," "Theology and Science," and "The Church in China." At LaSalle University in Philadelphia, the proposal includes choices from the fine arts department like "The Cult of the Virgin and the Saints: Art, Architecture, and Religion" or "Creation and Evolution." Loyola College in Baltimore hopes to include "Women in the Christian Tradition" and "Literature and the Catholic Imagination."

Two of the programs now on the drawing boards seek to specialize. John Carroll University's focus is largely historical—on pre-Vatican II Catholic thought and life, including "Origins of Western Monasticism," "Origins of the Liturgy," and "British Catholic Authors."

A faculty committee at the University of Notre Dame has proposed an interdisciplinary undergraduate concentration (12 credits) in the Catholic social tradition. This aims to examine the biblical, conciliar, and encyclical sources of the tradition, but also hopes to extend study to its manifestation in the work of social welfare pioneers like Msgr. John A. Ryan, activists like Dorothy Day and Daniel Berrigan, S.J., and public philosophers like John Courtney Murray, S.J., and Michael Novak. This program, the faculty suggests, represents an unusual opportunity to engage Catholic social teachings as a distinct, coherent, and developing intellectual tradition within Catholicism, and to call upon students to examine how it is lived out in various social institutions and professions.

Possibilities and Pitfalls

Most of the current programs are small and enroll six to sixteen students. Small enrollments, however, are not unusual for minors and concentrations, and the figures do not include students who decide to take just one or a few of the Catholic studies courses. Moreover, most of the programs have not been around long enough to be well tested. Still, Georgetown's program, now five years old, has drawn successful enrollments in its core courses, which has led its faculty committee to propose upgrading it from a concentration to a minor. The developments at the University of St. Thomas in Minnesota, which launched its Catholic studies program four years ago, indicate even better the potential that well-organized Catholic studies programs have. St. Thomas's program has become the largest and perhaps most successful of the programs now in place, and it is growing into a multifaceted center for Catholic studies. Founded and directed by Donald Briel, a professor in the University's theology department, the program now offers an undergraduate major and hopes to expand into a graduate program. It attracts 50 majors and offers 25 courses. Many of these students have a double major, allowing the program to draw undergraduates with diverse interests like pre-med, pre-law, business, and the liberal arts.

Professor Briel has been seeing to it that the program influences the rest of the university and the surrounding community: A Catholic studies club draws some 200 students, and a Catholic studies floor has attracted eighteen undergraduate women. A similar men's floor is planned for the next academic year. The program even hopes to sponsor a Catholic Worker house. The University has developed outreach initiatives through the program to the archdiocese and the people of the Twin Cities. Perhaps most ambitiously, the program has launched a periodical, *Logos: A Journal of Catholic Thought and Culture*, which began publication in 1997.

Some of the most important efforts center on the faculty, which, Professor Briel suggests, is the key to success. St. Thomas's plan grew out of a series of faculty development initiatives and conversations; it still draws its intellectual vitality from these. The program became a reality because there were faculty members interested in making it come about, though not all were initially trained in, or up to date on, the subject matter of the courses they were interested in creating. The University, like several other colleges launching programs, is trying to furnish faculty with the resources and support needed to develop these new courses, as well as to provide funding for faculty research in areas germane to Catholic studies.

While some institutions are backing up their programs with major fundraising initiatives (St. Thomas is seeking $10 million), other faculty committees indicated that they had to justify their programs to administrations that were at best indifferent.

Occasionally the fear is voiced that Catholic studies is a restorationist project, bent on drawing colleges and universities back into a ghetto. This restorationist charge was certainly leveled against the St. Ignatius Institute, which has been fueled by a rather traditionalist ecclesiological vision. Despite the considerable success of the St. Ignatius program in developing a coherent great books program and attracting a large number of students, none of the Catholic studies programs founded in the last several years appears to model itself on the institute. (Nor, for that matter, does the institute describe itself as a Catholic studies program.)

At the institutions that are launching Catholic studies programs, ghettoization of the university once again seems rather unlikely, simply because the institutions have already changed so much. Compared to the tighter sequencing at the St. Ignatius Institute, most of the new programs seem decidedly more post-modern in structure, despite their integrative goals and capstone courses. Furthermore, since most of these programs are only available as minors, and all of them are optional, the fear of ghettoization seems unrealistic. The larger programs reported that they had attracted students from a variety of faiths. All the program directors suggested that the faculty committees were trying to avoid getting trapped by any single ideological bent.

At other institutions where Catholic studies has not gotten off the ground, however, faculty members have suggested that the difficulty is precisely that the faculty does not want to confront contested notions of what constitutes the Catholic tradition. A Catholic studies program would require confronting these notions directly. Some faculty members have expressed fear that any explicit effort to define and develop Catholic identity and mission tempts ecclesiastical intervention or oversight, and hence threatens the academic freedom integral to Catholic studies and the whole university.

Paradoxically, the second fear most often expressed concerns a different sort of ghettoization. By assigning the curricular responsibility for Catholic identity to a single small program, these faculty and administrators fear that the institution may abandon its sacramental responsibility to infuse the whole curriculum with a Catholic vision. All of the Catholic studies program directors I have spoken with have heard this argument, and all counter it with the hope that their program will serve precisely the opposite function, operating as leaven for the whole university community.

There is undoubtedly some danger that small, underfunded programs will end up ghettoizing Catholic identity. Yet Catholic studies programs can also be of great value when they spur faculty to engage in new areas of research and teaching. While some programs have not yet been able to move much beyond drawing existing courses into greater coherence, they are already spurring the development of an increasing number of promising new courses.

In terms of larger institutional identity, it is also true, I believe, that the presence of even small academic programs may help stir departments to think about hiring new faculty able to teach courses germane to Catholic thought, life, and mission. At present, graduate students who want to teach in these areas still find themselves facing rather limited opportunities. In addition to its implications for undergraduate students who take Catholic studies classes now, cultivation of these programs on Catholic campuses can help open up a whole new field and increase the scholarship on Catholic thought and culture and thereby encourage graduate students to take up this work.

Though several institutions have done so already, more might think about establishing endowed chairs in Catholic studies, which would spur senior scholars and give Catholic studies more permanence, weight, and profile. I am told it is the common wisdom among fundraising officers at Catholic colleges and universities that Catholic donors are not very interested in giving money to endow chairs. Bricks and mortar, scholarships, and athletics are the gifts of choice; academic programs and chaired professorships are a harder sell. Notre Dame's experience at endowing well over a hundred chairs would seem to belie that opinion; but if it is true that Catholics are not so inclined, it is almost certainly to the detriment of Catholic colleges and universities.

At a time when the presence of founding religious communities is waning, and will likely have to be discontinued on some campuses, we would do well to think about what kinds of programs are left in place as a permanent legacy. Catholic studies can help build the kind of core faculty these institutions will need. Clearly, more administrative support and ambition will help Catholic studies programs develop to their real potential.

While a Catholic studies model is undoubtedly not the only way to develop an institution's Catholic identity, it can serve as an important means for developing Catholic identity within the academic program. At Santa Clara, where the program aspires to expand to include art exhibits, concerts and theatrical productions, or at other institutions that have already begun such efforts, the impact can be significant on students and the whole community. As David O'Brien has noted repeatedly, Catholic studies programs increase the likelihood that Catholic colleges and universities can be places where the church can do its thinking and engage its own and other traditions. The next several years should prove a fruitful time for testing that possibility.

Catholic Studies at the University of St. Thomas

*Don J. Briel**

The growth in Catholic studies programs around the country has received considerable attention recently. Some have argued that the development of these programs simply confirms the failure of Catholic higher education in this country. Others have argued that the emergence of these voluntary programs is another indication of the sophisticated genius of Catholic universities, able to adapt to changing conditions and unexpected opportunities. In any case, as the programs are beginning to exercise significant roles in articulating new possibilities for Catholic intellectual life, it is useful to consider the practical and philosophical difficulties that have hindered their development at some universities as well as the promise of the programs that *have* been created.

The largest and arguably the most ambitious program in the country, at the University of St. Thomas in St. Paul, Minnesota, developed out of a series of lectures in the 1991–92 academic year on the history of Catholic higher education. The faculty who collaborated with the dean of the college in planning that series had been concerned that distinctive features of Catholic higher education were no longer well understood by an increasing number of students and faculty—who often, Catholic or not, had little formal training in Catholic thought. We hoped that a historical context would provide a foundation for a reconsideration of the nature and implications of Catholic universities in contemporary culture.

The lecture series also provided an occasion for a number of faculty to continue their work on a proposal for an undergraduate program in Catholic studies. There was growing concern among many faculty that the tendency, by no means unique to St. Thomas, to embed the Catholic identity of the university in general requirements in theology and philo-

*Don J. Briel is director of the Center for Catholic Studies at the University of St. Thomas, St. Paul, Minnesota.

sophy and an increased visibility of programs in campus ministry might simply reinforce the general trend in American culture to marginalize religious questions to restricted areas of inquiry and private commitment. The dichotomy of private religious values and secular public policy struck many of us as particularly problematic as we sought to reconsider the implications of Catholic thought, marked by a profound and consistent sacramental consciousness. It was our view that the Catholic intellectual tradition engages all of reality. We agreed with John Paul II and Newman that a concern for the unity of knowledge and the fruitful tension but ultimate complementarity of faith and reason are central concerns of Catholic higher education. We also sought to create a program that would allow interested faculty and students to consider the contemporary implications of the broad and diverse Catholic intellectual tradition within a large interdisciplinary context.

With Newman, we were convinced that the essential modern problem was not a crisis of the intellect but of the imagination, that we had largely lost a sense of the unity or integral relations of separate aspects of reality. It seemed to us unlikely that such a vision would be unilaterally reappropriated under the juridical authority of the hierarchy or through the internal decisions of administration or faculty. We certainly saw the increasing specialization of academic disciplines as posing a threat to the interdisciplinary character of so much of the best of Catholic thought. At the same time, we were persuaded of the significance of much of the new and highly specialized research that has been a principal product of nineteenth century academic reforms.

We sought, then, not to transform the climate of the university as a whole, but rather to create forums for sustained interdisciplinary conversations central to the Catholic pursuit of the unity of knowledge. We also sought to create a model for this kind of interdisciplinary teaching and research.

An essential source for our own reflections on Catholic identity continued to be *Ex Corde Ecclesiae,* in which John Paul II rejected the tendency to insularism critiqued by John Tracy Ellis and others in the 1950s, but also reaffirmed that the Catholic university "has to be a living union of individual organisms dedicated to the search for truth. . . . It is necessary to work toward a higher synthesis of knowledge, in which alone lies the possibility of satisfying that search for truth which is profoundly inscribed in the heart of the human person" (paragraph 16). In insisting on this basic priority, the Pope argued that there were four identifiable characteristics of the Catholic university:

1. A Christian inspiration not only of individuals but of the university community as a whole;

2. A continuing reflection in the light of the Catholic faith upon the growing treasury of human knowledge, to which it seeks to contribute by its own research;
3. Fidelity to the Christian message as it comes to us through the Church; and
4. An institutional commitment to the service of the people of God and of the human family in their pilgrimage to the transcendent goal which gives meaning to life (13).

The first of these characteristics suggests that it is not sufficient that individual faculty, courses, or disciplines be animated by and reflect a Christian inspiration; the university's academic life and teaching as a whole must reflect that inspiration. This does not necessarily mean that all courses or all faculty do so directly. The Pope insists several times that non-Catholic faculty, indeed nonbelievers, have a vital role to play in the Catholic university's search for truth, and that specific disciplines have their own appropriate methodologies and presuppositions for it. It does suggest, however, that the burden of institutional identity cannot be fulfilled simply in one or two disciplines. It must penetrate in various ways all the disciplines and academic programs of the university.

The second characteristic is a concrete expression of the Pope's earlier insistence that "a Catholic university's privileged task is 'to unite existentially by intellectual effort two orders of reality that too frequently tend to be placed in opposition as though they were antithetical: the search for truth, and the certainty of already knowing the fount of truth'" (1). Here the Pope argues in the name of a universal humanism that "the Catholic university is completely dedicated to the research of all aspects of truth in their essential connection with the supreme truth, who is God" (4). The two-fold commitments of faith and reason thus find expression in an optimism that there can be no final contradiction of truths, although as Newman had cautioned, this confidence does not free us from the real collisions and tensions that often deserve the metaphors of warfare.

This characteristic suggested the need for a curriculum that would provide sustained opportunities to reflect on human knowledge in the light of Catholic faith. All courses in a particular discipline need not reflect both of these elements in their fullness, but the university as a whole must commit itself, both within the curriculum and within its research activities, to this kind of sustained reflection. This seems to me to have both curricular and hiring implications.

The third characteristic suggests at the least that the curriculum ought to guarantee access to the Christian message as articulated by the Church. This would include the historical range of expressions of Christian life and thought, both in individuals and in communities, including the contemporary. It would also necessarily include sustained attention to formal magisterial teaching.

The final characteristic emphasizes the prophetic role of the Catholic university within the Church, requiring, as the Pope said, "the courage to speak uncomfortable truths which do not please public opinion, but which are necessary to safeguard the authentic good of society" (32).

We thought it clear that these characteristics, and John Paul's later description of four principles of research, presupposed an integrity of truth expressed in a broad dialectic of faith and culture that does not preclude an often jealous tension of disciplinary prerogatives, but rather in large measure, depends upon them. We were persuaded, then, that only the creation of something like a Catholic studies program would provide the means to realize this broad vision, for we saw no other institutional forum in which it might be achieved.

Because we knew that we would have multiple audiences, we sought to include a wide range of faculty, staff, and students in a variety of programs. We eventually concluded that although the initial series of lectures was useful in providing a broad overview of general questions, we needed a more sustained forum for eliciting a sense of the implications of these questions for the university as a whole.

It has been difficult to find a common language with which to address the complex questions of Catholic identity and higher education; we found that general discussions began and ended with prejudices that were rarely confronted or significantly nuanced. As a result, we proposed a five-year series of faculty summer seminars based on a model already in place at the University. The original seminars had been supported by the Bush Foundation, which had funded initiatives to give faculty opportunities to discuss a range of issues in week-long seminars.

We early decided on two key points: (1) The seminars would incorporate an extensive reading list to provide a context for the discussions, and (2) we would ask faculty participants to write an essay in which they reflected upon the topic of the seminar and its relation to their own work at the University.

We wanted to ensure that the seminars would be fully voluntary and that the number of participants would be limited to no more than twenty-five members in order to foster a genuine conversation. From the beginning, seminar participants represented a variety of disciplines and religious commitments. There were faculty from the humanities, the social and natural sciences, the fine arts, and the professional programs. But because we wanted all faculty in the University to have access to the discussions, we also arranged for publication of the faculty essays and their distribution on campus. Many of these essays have had a substantial impact on the University's understanding of its Catholic mission, and, perhaps more directly, on the burgeoning of the University's Center for Catholic Studies.

We also arranged for fall and spring lectures and associated faculty discussions each year. In the first year we considered the idea of the Catholic university in the context of both Newman's classic account and more contemporary analysis. The facilitator of the first summer seminar, Brian Daley, S.J., described the energy and mutual respect of this first discussion:

> The seminar group was as varied in interest and expertise, in Church member-ship, in age and length of service at the university, in overriding concerns and convictions—as one might imagine in any American academic institution; yet it was a group constantly characterized by graciousness, energy, patience, mutual respect, and a serious focus on the issues our discussions raised—a model, re-ally, of civil and informed interdisciplinary exchange at its best.

The summer seminars brought a new vitality to the broader conversa-tions about Catholic identity and a variety of initiatives resulted. Groups of faculty began informal discussions that produced interdisciplinary re-search projects and course proposals. New summer seminars included a two-week seminar on the contemporary relations of theology and science and two subsequent seminars on the history of the relations of sci-ence and the Christian faith. In addition, we designed a seminar on man-agement education in a Catholic university and cosponsored with the Graduate School of Business an Aspen seminar on classic texts of the Catholic tradition.

During this same period, a faculty committee was continuing to work on a proposal for a Catholic studies program that would build on and comple-ment the wide range of general curriculum requirements that had been re-vised but not significantly restructured in a 1995 review. We agreed on several points early in the process: (1) We would work toward a truly inter-disciplinary program but would begin with foundational courses arising out of core disciplines and seek to establish more fully their interdisciplin-ary connections (this was in large measure dictated by St. Thomas's disci-pline-based general curriculum); (2) the program would offer both major and minor field concentrations; (3) courses would not be restricted to the humanities and fine arts but would seek also to engage the natural and so-cial sciences and the professions; (4) the program would be voluntary for both students and faculty; and (5) the program would not stand alone but would be part of a much broader set of initiatives designed to revitalize the University's Catholic mission.

We saw only two real remedies for our situation: (1) administrative im-position of new requirements related to the Catholic intellectual tradition in all areas of the University's curriculum and hiring; or (2) a series of strategies and forums that would highlight the ongoing relevance of Catholic thought in contemporary culture, and encourage voluntary participation in them. Chief among these strategies would be a Catholic studies program that would be a model of an integrated Catholic understanding of the mutual relations of faith and reason in an age increasingly skeptical about their potential complementarity. We might then be able to reconsider the present significance of Catholic thought.

We were not entirely satisfied with the language of "Catholic studies" but we thought that the program needed to be both explicitly Catholic and entirely voluntary. The title of the program reflected both concerns. Of course, it struck many as paradoxical that a Catholic university would depend on a Catholic studies program to fulfill its mission. It is not uncommon today to hear arguments that the ultimate result of such programs will be a marginalization of Catholic identity. As a result, it is suggested, the university as a whole is freed from its obligation to demonstrate its Catholic character in all of its activities.

We shared some of these concerns and early argued for the creation of a Center for Catholic Studies that would coordinate existing programs related to Catholic identity and initiate new faculty development, curricular, and scholarly projects as catalysts for a revitalized Catholic life within the University as a whole. Although we thought it critical that the program have its own autonomy and integrity, we were also committed to initiating activities that would engage the entire University. We were determined that the new program not stand as the sole expression of the University's Catholic commitments.

We knew that many faculty continued to make sustained contributions to the University's mission in their departmental teaching, in their scholarship and service, but we also thought that it was critical to support opportunities for more explicit activity to realize the University's Catholic identity. General requirements in theology and philosophy aside, our curriculum had begun to resemble closely that of any secular university in the United States. The riches of the Catholic intellectual tradition in the fine arts, the social and natural sciences, literature, the humanities and history had largely been lost. This fact was not obscured by the recent tendency to emphasize a values orientation throughout the curriculum.

We began the program not with an integrated curriculum but with a small set of courses that reflected the intellectual passions of our best faculty. We did insist that the program should be characterized by a sense of community, not only of critical inquiry but also of commitment to the Church, and thus to a fellowship of faith. Faculty meet regularly for discussion and shared meals. We built into the program an expectation that faculty would understand the program as a whole and would draw upon specific offerings of the program as they taught their own courses. In evaluations, students consistently cite this integration of diverse perspectives as one of the most satisfying aspects of their experience in the program.

In its first year the program sponsored three courses: "Catholic Vision," cross-listed with the department of theology; "Literature from a Catholic Perspective" (English); and "Faith and Doubt" (philosophy). At the end of the first year, we had two majors and proposals for a number of new courses. At the end of the fifth year we had ninety majors and twenty-five minors and offered twenty-four courses.

At the initial review of the program by a faculty committee and the college senate, their questions reflected traditional academic concerns. The most common concerns were:

- *Did the program not suggest that only Catholic studies courses were authentically Catholic?* Indeed not. Not all faculty were inclined to pursue interdisciplinary teaching or scholarship; the program took for granted the important work that faculty were making in their disciplines and in specialized research.
- *Would Catholic studies not threaten the central role of theology in the undergraduate program?* It has always been our argument that a strong theology department is a necessary precondition for a Catholic studies program. We predicted, rightly as it turned out, that the program would not reduce the number of students concentrating in theology; nor would it substitute for general requirements in theology.
- *Did the program identify itself with a particular group within the Church?* It had seemed self-evident to us that a new generation of students was entering our institutions who had received very little formal training in Catholic thought. They were prone to ask for an account of the Catholic intellectual tradition in terms of its enduring convictions and commitments. As a result, they tended to be increasingly impatient with the tendency to define Catholic thought solely in terms of contemporary controversies over sexual morality, authority, or ministry. This prompted our conviction that the tradition must be seen not only through the lens of contemporary concerns but through a variety of other historical and cultural perspectives. We have continued to expect a respect for and critical reflections on the implications of formal Church teaching.

As the program was growing and the faculty development offerings were being implemented, the University announced the creation of a Center for Catholic Studies with a $10,000,000 endowment goal. The center was designed to coordinate existing programs and to create new collaborations across campus. These included joint programs with the Jay Phillips Center for Jewish Christian Learning and other programs of interreligious and ecumenical dialogues. The chancellor of the university, Msgr. Terrence J. Murphy, had developed a new foundation to support programs to promote the Catholic mission of the University. The foundation strongly supported the initial efforts to launch the Catholic studies program.

We had recently created an institute, now located within the center, to concentrate on Catholic social thought. This institute, originally concerned with Christian social thought and the management professions, was sponsoring innovative programs with the undergraduate and graduate programs in business administration; outreach programs with a central city parish, St. Olaf's; and national and international conferences in association with the deans of Jesuit Business Schools, including a 1997 international conference on "Management Education in a Catholic University," in Antwerp, Belgium, and a 1999 conference on "Rethinking the Spiritual and Social Life within Business" in Goa, India.

With the strong support of the president of St. Thomas, Rev. Dennis Dease, the institute has been enlarged and renamed the John A. Ryan Institute for Catholic Social Thought. In addition to the program on (1) Christian social thought and management, there are new programs in (2) Catholic Social Teachings and Catholic Education and (3) the *Casa Guadalupana* House of Hospitality. The second program was created to help implement recommendations of the National Conference of Catholic Bishops task force chaired by Archbishop John R. Roach that stressed the need for greater integration of Catholic social thought into Catholic education from kindergarten through university and seminary formation. The *Casa Guadalupana* project, strongly influenced by the Catholic Worker movement, will be coordinated with parishes in a predominantly Hispanic area of St. Paul.

We also incorporated a new emphasis into an existing program. Focus on Theology had been created by St. Thomas faculty to provide opportunities for theological renewal for teachers in archdiocesan schools and religious education programs. The program has now been adapted into a series of videotapes and a resource book available nationally from Liturgical Press. In 1997, we launched a quarterly journal, *Logos: A Journal of Catholic Thought and Culture*. That same year, students created the Catholic Studies Club and established a Catholic studies floor in a women's dormitory. A men's floor was built in 1999. The club sponsors a monthly newsletter, retreats, book discussions, social activities, and service projects.

Having affiliated with the Faculty of Social Sciences at the Angelicum, Catholic studies began a Rome program in the fall of 1998. Students may spend a semester or full year studying at the Angelicum and completing courses to fulfill major field requirements at St. Thomas. Faculty have also completed a proposal for an M.A. in Catholic Studies and expect to begin offering courses in the fall of 2001.

If the center is to grow, there will be a need to more fully institutionalize its programs and its faculty. Even successful interdisciplinary programs are inherently fragile. They rely on the dedication of a small group of faculty whose enthusiasm and commitment is difficult to sustain when universities tend to reward highly specialized research on a narrow topic rather than the broad interdisciplinary scholarship we have sought to foster. The initial promise of Catholic studies has largely been realized at St. Thomas, but significant new curricular and institutional structures need to be created if the movement is to bring the larger vision of Catholic higher education into concrete expression in Catholic institutions that, like our own, are marked by a rich but challenging secular culture. The fact that so many new programs and centers are emerging around the country suggests the creative possibilities now becoming available as we confront with greater seriousness the contemporary problems of Catholic identity and mission.

Graduate Business Faculty in the Catholic University

Raymond N. MacKenzie*

Pope John Paul II gave an urgency to the issue of a Catholic university's identity with his 1990 Apostolic Constitution, *Ex Corde Ecclesiae*. Its opening sentence insists upon the closeness of university and church by saying that the Catholic university is "born from the heart of the church." It would be far easier, of course, to ignore this relationship and to continue with the school's ordinary enterprise, because the relationship between church and university is not easily defined, or even perceived, when we move into a specific field—like business. And it is tempting to dismiss the issue altogether with some superficially valid formulation such as "after all, there's no such thing as Catholic accounting." Apart from a tendency to cross oneself when approaching the bottom line, this is probably true. But there are Catholic accountants, and there are people who teach and study accounting at a Catholic university. Accounting, or any other business field, must somehow be brought into closer relationship with the school's Catholic identity. This is to be done not by redefining or tinkering with the subject (Catholicizing it), or even solely by an emphasis on the ethics involved in the subject (though this is important), but by the particular intellectual qualities of the faculty.

The question then becomes, What sort of faculty should a Catholic university be seeking and developing for its graduate business education programs? Should this faculty be different from those in comparable programs in any other sort of university? Should we be looking for anything other than the usual criteria: competence in the field, solid teaching skills, and appropriate commitment to consulting, research, and publication?

---

*Raymond N. MacKenzie is professor of business at the University of St. Thomas, St. Paul, Minnesota. An earlier version of this article appeared in *The Role of Faculty in a Catholic University: Summer Seminar* (St. Paul: University of St. Thomas, 1996).

Those criteria are obviously of great importance, but if a university is to call itself Catholic there are other traits that its faculty should have as well, traits that, in turn, the university community and atmosphere should value, nurture, and enhance.

First, the one quality we should *not* be looking for is religious uniformity. A Catholic university as described in *Ex Corde Ecclesiae* is not a university staffed exclusively by Catholics; therefore, there is no question of applying a religious litmus test to the faculty, of retaining those who pass and firing those who do not. The faculty need not be card-carrying Catholics, but they should be Catholic in another sense, a sense suggested by the word's root meaning. Father Walter J. Ong points up this meaning when he notes that in ordinary speech we often confuse the issue by saying that *Catholic* and *universal* are synonyms. They are not. Ong contrasts the original meanings of the words *universalis* and *katholikos* to make the point: the etymology of *universalis*, he says,

> suggests using a compass to make a circle around a central point. It is an inclusive concept in the sense that the circle includes everything within it. But by the same token it also excludes everything outside it. *Universalis* contains a subtle note of negativity. *Katholikos* does not. It is more unequivocally positive. It means simply "through-the-whole" or "throughout-the-whole."[1]

Father Ong's point here is that the Catholic mind, like the Catholic institution of higher learning, is one that strives for inclusivity, for a permeation of the whole, for connection and relationship between and among cultures, races, ideas, fields of study. This is the sort of striving we should be seeking and encouraging in our faculty as well.

The faculty of a Catholic university ought to have an interdisciplinary frame of mind. This applies to all faculty, but my emphasis here is on business professors, who in this regard are probably not much better or worse than their colleagues in other fields. The faculty of a Catholic university should be people who are willing, even driven, to go beyond the boundaries of their particular disciplines, to find where the connections are, and where the gaps are. The institution must encourage them to do this, to enhance and enlarge their understanding of their field by exploring its place in history, the philosophical problems underlying it, the manner in which it is reflected in the arts.

An eagerness on the part of the faculty to carry out this exploration is especially needed today, when all professions, and especially those within business, are increasingly narrowing their scope and growing more specialized, more compartmentalized. This narrowing process is by no means simply a characteristic of university life; it both mirrors and helps create our increasingly fragmented society. And it contributes—insidiously, because it does so quietly, and with the full authority of most institutions and professional associations—to a far-reaching dehumanization that characterizes our contemporary culture.

William F. May has traced one important aspect of our modern dilemma in the changing attitudes toward what it means to have a profession or be a professional.[2] May notes that the word formerly implied that a professional had a commitment to the good of the public he or she served. Today, a professional is better described as a careerist, committed only to maintaining the technical expertise of the field and to maximizing his or her own self-interest.

The historical development of this trend is complex, going back at least to the eighteenth-century theoretical developments (in Bernard Mandeville and Adam Smith, for instance) that accompanied the rise of capitalism. But whatever its history, the trend has accelerated recently: Today, the sheer survival of the professional in an age of re-engineering and downsizing is an ever-present issue. It has become almost a cliche to say that one's loyalty is not to the organization, which will probably change dramatically and continuously, but instead to one's profession—to strengthening one's grasp of the cutting-edge tools and skills that will ensure that one can safely land somewhere else when the organization hiccups, as it inevitably will. This state of affairs only deepens the problem May outlines: Where is the place for public commitment when simply maintaining a job is a constant concern?

So as the old conception of professionalism contracts into careerism, and as professional expertise becomes increasingly specialized and always more technical, the individual's connection with the larger community dims. When this occurs within a society already bleeding from racial and ethnic divisions, the problem is dramatically compounded. A university—especially a Catholic university—ought to be a place where the individual can go to begin to build the intellectual and social connections missing in so much of modern life. A university founded on the katholikos principle is one dedicated to searching out and building up intellectual, cultural, and spiritual wholeness. Technical expertise is indeed a part of the picture, but if we only minister to the student's need for expertise, we are engaged in training, not education. Skills and techniques are expressions of the whole person, but they are not the person, and they can do little enough toward healing the spiritual and social wounds of our day.

There are of course strong and compelling reasons to emphasize skill and technique. Students want it, for one thing. One of the most enthusiastic students I have recently encountered proclaimed on the course evaluation that the best thing about the course was that "you can take what you learn in the class at night and apply it at work the very next day."

That sort of praise is fine, obviously, but less obvious is the implication that if the subject matter cannot be applied the next day, there is something wrong with it. And beyond the pressure students bring with them, the doctoral training of most faculty members will also have insisted on the centrality of technique, and on a narrow specialization. Even more broadly, the culture itself, especially contemporary intellectual culture, demands this same emphasis; our journals and associations look with suspicion on a scholar who combines disciplines or attempts to reach a wider audience. To write and speak so that we are read and heard by people beyond those of our own specialization is—well, unprofessional. Alasdair MacIntyre sees this narrowing, this movement from substance to technique, as a twentieth-century phenomenon:

> The success of the natural sciences has conferred prestige upon technique as such, and outside the natural sciences agreement on technique has often been allowed to substitute for agreement on matters of substance. In both the humanities and the social sciences what can be reduced to technique and procedures and to results stemming from technique and procedure has enjoyed its own kind of status. . . . So the values both of genuine technical expertise and of its simulacra have been accorded a central place.[3]

To be a professional, then, is to be master of a set of skills, of technique, in isolation from the larger community. This is reflected in modern professional associations, where the key term often used is *portability*—acquiring skills that can be transferred from one company to another. Obviously, having portable skills is very much in the individual's self-interest and to that extent a very good idea, but when the sole emphasis is professional survival, there is little time left for the development of the whole person, let alone that person's wider obligations to the community. To be a teacher in a technique-based, skill-based professional world is, all too often, to be a purveyor of such skills at the expense of any concern with the student as a whole person or as member of a larger community. But to be a teacher at a Catholic university, one ought to recognize these pressures for what they are and to resist them. A professor at a Catholic university ought to at least be able to raise these issues with students, and to give them the centrality they deserve.

The teaching of ethics in a school of business is naturally essential, and most business schools—by no means just the Catholic ones—have moved to do this after a series of business-related scandals and disasters we have witnessed over the last few decades. But here, too, pressures come into play, for what the business world (which, after all, mirrors the culture at large) wants is not ethical inquiry but codes, processes for solving ethical problems: Ethics must be, in MacIntyre's phrase, reduced to one of the simulacra of the natural sciences. Yet genuine ethical inquiry reveals—if one's experience has not already revealed it vividly enough—that human nature and behavior cannot be reduced to a set of processes handily managed by the right skills or the right code.

This truth is fundamental, and to the extent business ethics courses make it plain, just so far can they become the true cornerstone of real business education. A Catholic university is an ideal ground for such considerations and such courses (indeed, a secular school can be so wholly dedicated to the skill-based ideal that such considerations would be easily crushed by the weight of the whole institution).

A faculty that is truly interdisciplinary can bring into the classroom the fresh air that exists outside the narrow room of technical expertise. The result will be an educational enterprise that moves students toward a fuller understanding of the question of what it is to be human, a question carrying a huge subset of more particularized questions that are insufficiently addressed elsewhere: What is it to be a business person, in America, in the closing years of the twentieth century? What are our responsibilities? What might help the situation, and what might make it worse? What are the tensions between the acquisition of wealth and the demands of the community? How can the teachings of the Church, with its long distinguished history of ethical inquiry, help in illuminating and in guiding the everyday life of the business person?

None of these questions in any way precludes the acquisition of the necessary expertise—what it takes to be a competent accountant or writer or operations manager—but insisting upon such questions will enfold that expertise within a profound intellectual and spiritual context for the student, a context almost completely ignored elsewhere. A Catholic university, with a faculty dedicated to interdisciplinary inquiry, can help move students from skill to substance, from technique to fuller participation in their own humanity, and to a clearer and healthier relationship with the human community.

Trying to teach and learn along these lines is complex and difficult. Success is not assured. Asking faculty and students to explore new and foreign areas is fraught with problems, messy and—the worst term of all in a business context—unmanageable. It can only work when the institution as a whole is dedicated to the enterprise, when truly interdisciplinary work is rewarded with tenure, promotions, sabbaticals. Curriculum development must take interdisciplinarity as its goal; bureaucratic problems such as who pays professor X when she teaches a course outside her department must be managed so as to make the cross-disciplinary assignment as easy as possible. We have long paid lip service to the value of the interdisciplinary, but if we took it with full seriousness we would soon find a dramatic transformation at work.

Again, this enterprise would not be an easy one. Both we and our students would have to confront the complexities it presents, and give up the easy certainties of the narrow, skill-based model. Probably one of the first things to change would be our terminology, both in the university and in the business world. For example, we would have to return to thinking of employees as people rather than "human resources." (When a layoff was threatened at a local software company, one of the programmers sardonically said the company was calculating how many "carbon-based coding units" it would need.) We would have to confront the web of connections between business and community, between community and world at large, with no guarantee we could organize and codify the connections and predict outcomes of all our business decisions.

It would be easier not to do any of this—for that is the greatest allure of the technical-expertise model, that it promises to make things easier. But its allure is false, as a glance at our current social and cultural condition will demonstrate. The opposing model is that of the Catholic university, an institution that, as John Paul has said, "assists in the protection and advancement of human dignity."[4] The opportunities for conducting business education within such an institution are remarkably rich and diverse. They require a faculty who can appreciate them, a faculty willing to range far more broadly than they would be able to in any other sort of school.

Notes

1. Walter J. Ong, S.J., "Yeast: A Parable for Catholic Higher Education, *America* (April 7, 1990), 347.
2. William F. May, "The Beleaguered Rulers: The Public Obligation of the Professional," *Kennedy Institute of Ethics Journal*, 2, no. 1: 25–41.
3. Alasdair MacIntyre, *Three Rival Versions of Moral Enquiry: Encyclopedia, Genealogy, and Tradition* (Notre Dame, IN: University of Notre Dame Press, 1990), 225.
4. *Ex Corde Ecclesiae*, I, 1.

Theology and the Integration of Knowledge

Terence L. Nichols *

In his *Apostolic Constitution on Catholic Universities,* John Paul II argues that a Catholic university is committed to exploration of the whole truth about persons and the universe, and that the integration of knowledge is of critical importance. He writes as follows:

> In a Catholic university, research necessarily includes (a) the search for an *integration of knowledge,* (b) a *dialogue between faith and reason,* (c) an *ethical concern,* and (4) a *theological perspective.* . . . It is necessary to work toward a higher synthesis of knowledge, in which alone lies the possibility of satisfying that thirst for truth which is profoundly inscribed on the heart of the human person. Aided by the specific contributions of philosophy and theology, university scholars will be engaged in a constant effort to determine the relative place and meaning of the various disciplines within the context of the human person and the world that is enlightened by the Gospel, and therefore by a faith in Christ, the Logos, as the center of creation and of human history.[1]

In this essay I will consider the implications of this statement for the curriculum of a Catholic university. In particular, I will suggest a possible model for the integration of knowledge, and consider the role of theology in that integration.

Any such integration is especially difficult today when research and publication in most disciplines, including theology, requires greater and greater specialization, and hence leads to greater and greater fragmentation of knowledge, not only across disciplines but even within disciplines. This fragmentation makes any kind of integral vision of human persons

---

*Terence L. Nichols is professor of theology at the University of St. Thomas, St. Paul, Minnesota. An earlier version of this article appeared in *Curriculum in a Catholic University: Summer Seminar* (St. Paul: University of St. Thomas, 1996).

and their place in the universe increasingly tenuous. But the lack of such an integral vision contributes to a society of atomized individuals each seeking his or her own personal good, with little knowledge of any unifying metaphysic or common good. We see this today at virtually all levels of society, from the highest to the lowest. Individualism is desirable, but can only flourish within a society held together by some unifying vision of a common reality and common good, without which society disintegrates into alienated self-seeking individuals and competing factions, and even relatively simple problems (e.g., balancing the budget) cannot be solved.[2]

Given its commitment to specialized research, the modern secular multiversity appears to be unable to provide an integrating vision for society; rather, it is part of the problem. Disciplines typically are isolated by their particular assumptions and methodologies and usually contribute to the problem of fragmentation. Let us consider some examples:

- Economics routinely eliminates variables that do not lend themselves to calculation; thus, modern economic projections of growth do not factor in the draw-down in resources (loss of topsoil, ground water, minerals, coal and oil, etc.) or environmental pollution and the cost of cleanup. These so-called "externals" are instead left to the discipline of ecology. The Valdez oil spill actually increased the GNP because of the expenses of cleanup.
- Routinely it is taught in finance that the purpose of publicly held companies is to maximize shareholder wealth. If that means firing one-third of the workers, or polluting the environment, so be it; the unemployment problem can be dealt with by the discipline of social work, and the pollution problem by ecology.
- Chemists produce some 5,000 new synthetic compounds each year, many of which are employed in industry with no research on their impact on the environment. And so on.

It need hardly be said that this fragmentation of knowledge is confusing to students, who usually take over the views of their majors uncritically, so that their world view is shaped by the assumptions and methods common in their field. If one is a molecular biologist, working daily with the model that biological processes are determined by genetic and molecular input, the temptation is great to assume that genes and molecules account for the whole of the human person.

Within this fragmentation, different types of integration of knowledge are possible. The simplest is reductionism, the belief that things can be explained by reducing them to their elementary components and explaining the laws of the components. Reductionism is an indispensable method of scientific research. But often that method becomes a metaphysic or total world view that claims that everything can be explained by reductionism. This might be called metaphysical or ontological reductionism: Nothing exists but material particles and energy, to which all else can be reduced. Thus Harvard biologist Edward O. Wilson, one of the founders of sociobiology, argues that social behavior can be explained by biology, biology by chemistry, and chemistry by physics. Eventually all higher disciplines will be reduced to nothing but the laws of chemistry and physics.[3] Some years ago Wilson told the National Conference of Catholic Bishops that science would soon render religion otiose and put the bishops out of business. Similarly, Nobel Laureate Francis Crick has argued that the goal of the sciences is to reduce all knowledge to the laws of chemistry and physics.[4] In *The Astonishing Hypothesis* he claims that the human person is "nothing but a pack of neurons," a collection of neural networks and their associated molecules, without free will or any spiritual aspect; once these networks are explained, we will be able to explain all human behavior.[5]

Reductionism succeeds in integrating knowledge by arguing that all higher knowledge can be reduced to a knowledge of elementary physical particles and molecules. This is not a Christian or Catholic view. Catholicism, like virtually every other religion, believes that reality, especially the person, is a complex interaction of both material and nonmaterial (or spiritual) dimensions. Ignoring the spiritual dimension, ontological reductionism promotes a partial and oversimplified picture of reality and a dehumanized picture of the person.

A holistic science of reality must wrestle with the problem of describing both the material and spiritual aspects of reality, their interaction, and in what sense they form a true whole. As John Paul writes: "A Catholic university is distinguished by its free search for whole truth about nature, man, and God."[6] In a Catholic view, therefore, it is critical to integrate knowledge of the physical world with knowledge of spiritual reality, lest our view of reality be too limited, too dehumanized, or too fragmented (e.g., we imagine that matter and spirit are dissociated and do not interact).

A natural way of organizing the disciplines that preserves their autonomy but also helps to integrate them is to organize them in a hierarchy of levels corresponding to the complexity of the systems they investigate; thus, at the simplest level, physics investigates atomic and subatomic particles and the laws that govern them. Above physics is chemistry, which presumes and incorporates the laws of physics but investigates larger molecular systems and so develops its own unique concepts, theories, methods, and laws. Above chemistry, but incorporating it, is biology, which investigates yet more complex systems—living systems—based on cells, and so develops its own set of concepts, methods, and laws. Above biology are the sciences that describe the behavior of living organisms, such as ethology and psychology. Finally, there are the disciplines that study human culture—the most complex system of all—such as anthropology, sociology, economics, the humanities, and philosophy. In this model the disciplines are arranged like a series of maps of increasing scale. At the most elementary level, physics provides a map of immense detail and atomic and subatomic-sized scale; at the most general level are maps of large scale, surveying human behavior and culture.

It is important to note that at each higher level of systemic complexity new properties and characteristics emerge; thus, wetness is not a property of a single water molecule, but is a property of many water molecules together. Reproduction is not a property of atoms or small molecules, but is a property of cells and living systems. Consciousness is not a property of atoms, molecules, or cells, but is a property of higher animals and humans. This is a major reason, apart from scale, that each discipline must construct its own concepts, theories, and methods, just as an engineer must construct different tools for different types of machines and tasks.

Again, many thinkers argue that at each higher level new kinds of wholes are formed, which in turn influence the parts of which the wholes are composed. For example, elementary particles, such as photons, can be obtained in twin pair sets, in which the spin of one is identical with the other. But the spin of either particle is not determined until that particle interacts with a measuring device (or another particle). Recent experiments have determined that the measurement of spin of one particle precipitates the spin of its twin apparently instantaneously;[7] thus, even if the two particles are separated by a light year, the measurement of the spin of one particle still will immediately precipitate a determinate spin in the other particle. The two particles, even though separated by a great distance, nevertheless behave as one system, a whole, which cannot be explained by reductionistic methods: Some kind of holistic cause would seem to be operating. Again, considering properties in a more complex system, psychologist Roger Sperry argues that the mind, though an emergent property that cannot exist apart from the brain, nevertheless is a quasi-autonomous whole that influences the behavior of the individual neurons, thus allowing free choices;[8] the parts influence the whole but the whole also influences the parts. It is precisely this that reductionists deny: They say the parts influence, indeed determine, the whole, but the whole does not influence the parts; thus, the human person is nothing but a pack of neurons, and free will is an illusion.

The hierarchy of disciplines that I have been describing from a scientific view culminates in two different but related wholes. One whole is human culture, which is due to the interaction of many human persons, the most complex physical systems known. The other whole is nature, the ecosystem of the earth and the universe, a whole that influences the parts of which it is composed.

One way to integrate the various disciplines, then, is to arrange them in a hierarchy of complexity corresponding to systems or wholes of increasing complexity. Many disciplines must combine to give us a complete description of nature. Many more must combine to give us a description of human persons and human culture. In this integration each discipline preserves its own autonomy—using its own concepts, theories, and methods; higher disciplines, because they describe higher level wholes, cannot be reduced to lower disciplines as reductionists like Wilson aver. But in addition to being autonomous the disciplines are loosely united in that many of them build on, incorporate, or are interrelated to other disciplines (chemistry builds on physics, biology on chemistry, psychology on biology and chemistry, etc.) All are necessary to describe human persons, human culture, and humanity's place in the cosmos.

From a Christian and Catholic point of view, however, the most comprehensive whole is not just the human person, or human culture, or even the earth's ecosystem or the physical universe. For human persons are individually and collectively parts of a larger spiritual and physical whole. Different religions describe this whole differently. In Catholicism, it might be described as the whole creation, including living and dead persons, related to God through Christ and the Holy Spirit. It is *God* who forms the ultimate environment for nature and persons. A complete picture of human persons and their environment must therefore include the relationship of persons to God, as well as to the ambient creation. The same is true for nature; nature in Catholic thinking is neither self-sufficient nor self-creating; like persons, it comes forth from God and returns eventually to God, who creates it and holds it in being. The *whole* truth about nature, man, and God, to use John Paul's language, must therefore include the relation of persons and nature to God. This requires a theological perspective, for theology is that discipline whose task it is to talk about God (Gk *theos* = God, *logos* = word, study, science), and God's relation with creation, i.e., with nature and humanity.

Many people think that Catholic theology is like catechesis—just a matter of repeating ancient dogmatic formulas. This is a misperception typically based on little acquaintance with theological practice. Theology begins with broad questions such as: What is the nature of ultimate reality? or How is that reality related to humanity and the universe? A Catholic theologian works with the faith assumption that ultimate reality, God, has been revealed through the Hebrew prophets and more fully in Jesus the Christ, and this revelation has been passed on through the church in doctrine and tradition (including a long tradition of theological reflection). If a Catholic theologian came to the conclusion that ultimate reality was *not* God, or that God had *not* been revealed in Christ, or that the Church had in fundamental ways falsified that revelation, he or she would probably, to be honest, have to leave the discipline.

A Catholic theologian, then, works within a paradigm. It is not that the theologian already has all the answers (a charge Bertrand Russell levelled against St. Thomas Aquinas), but that she has a certain broad orientation to problems, within which further exploration can take place. But this is true of any discipline. Biologists, for example, have a commitment to evolution, and to mechanism (as opposed to vitalism); within this framework they continue to search for more knowledge. Any biologist who rejected this overarching framework, i.e., rejected evolution or was a vitalist, probably could only teach in sectarian colleges, and could not publish in refereed journals. But it is also true that theologians, like biologists and other scholars, are continually returning to, examining, and re-verifying the foundational assumptions of their discipline (indeed, "foundational theology" is a recognized subdiscipline of theology).

From a Catholic theological perspective, then, the complex whole on which all disciplines converge is the whole made up of God, humanity, and nature. It is creation existing in God, and God immanent in creation. Let us call it God/Creation. This is like other wholes in the hierarchy of being, in that the active principle of the whole, God, affects the constituent parts, perhaps in a way similar to the action of the mind on the body. And the investigation of this whole is the task of theology. But, clearly, theology cannot by itself provide an adequate account of this whole. Only theology in cooperation with the natural sciences, social sciences, and the humanities can begin to give us an adequate representation of this complex whole. Each discipline by itself can provide only a facet of the whole picture. But all working together can provide a more complete, though never entirely complete, model. This, I would argue, is the ultimate rationale for the integration of knowledge. For an adequate understanding of God/Creation is the whole point of Christianity and Catholicism (and for that matter of Judaism, Islam, Bahai, Hinduism, and most Eastern religions, though they may not use the term God to describe ultimate reality); it is important to our wholeness, holiness, and fulfillment as persons; it is important for our relationship with God and our ultimate salvation.

To try to bring the disciplines together in such an integration—an integration that preserves the unique method and concepts of each discipline, but that also shows how the disciplines can be related to a larger whole—is a long-term task; it may require generations, not just years. It will certainly require a significant modification of the current orientation toward research and specialization. But, as the saying goes, "A journey of a thousand miles must begin with a single step." There are already signs of an emphasis on wholeness and integration emerging within the sciences, as the work of the Santa Fe Institute shows.[9] Integration of knowledge is also an emphasis in the fields of theology and science. A logical extension is to further this work in the setting of a Catholic university, whose mission, as John Paul insists, is to include a search for the whole truth about God, humanity, and creation.

To think of the whole to be known as God/Creation sheds some light on how particular disciplines might be taught within the setting of a Catholic university. Let us consider some examples.

Most of any physics course will be devoted to teaching the rather formidable content of physics, but in any course questions could be raised about how physics relates to the larger whole of God/Creation. Indeed, such broad questions naturally emerge from within physics. What caused the Big Bang? Why are physical laws and constants so precisely balanced that life can occur in the universe? And so on. A major in physics might end with a course on how physics could be integrated with other disciplines, including philosophy and theology, and so bring its unique perspective to the ultimate mystery of God and God's relation with creation.

Similar questions arise in other natural sciences, such as chemistry, biology, and geology. Within the psychological and social sciences, questions naturally emerge concerning the ultimate environment of the human person: Can the person be fully understood as the product of natural forces alone (as reductionism claims)? Or is the person open to transcendent spiritual influences as well, which might be factors in shaping human psychology, history, and society?

In fact, I would maintain, the mystery of God and God's relation to nature and humanity can be touched on by almost any discipline, and each discipline can bring a unique perspective to this mystery; indeed, much of the best theology of nature right now is coming not from theologians but from natural scientists, who are better positioned to appreciate the wonderful design found in nature than are theologians.

In the same way, ethical questions arise within each discipline, questions that ask what the relation is between the contents and methods of the discipline and the ultimate good of human persons and society. Such questions would involve both philosophy and theology, insofar as the ultimate good of persons involves fellowship with God.

Thus it seems to me that within any discipline, both theological and ethical questions arise. Essentially these questions concern how that discipline, with its assumptions, contents, and methods, relates to the larger whole, God, humanity, nature. Each discipline is in a position to offer a theological and ethical perspective that is unique and important to all who are concerned with theology and ethics.

I agree, then, with John Paul, that research (and I would add teaching) in a Catholic university should include a quest for the integration of knowledge, an effort to relate faith and reason, a consideration of ethics and a theological perspective. These are all interrelated—for considering the ethical or theological perspective implicit in one's discipline is one way to relate it to the larger whole that is the aim of all knowledge, and so to integrate it with other disciplines.

I must admit, however, that the question of how individual disciplines fit within the larger whole discerned by a Catholic vision of reality has not been a concern of most scholars and teachers, even in Catholic colleges. The overriding emphasis has been on research and publication within a specialty, on learning more and more about less and less, on methods and assumptions that define a discipline in contradistinction to others, rather than on methods and assumptions that would serve to show how that discipline is related to a larger whole.

I am not optimistic that this will change in the near future. The pressures for hyperspecialization and reductionism are too strong. But I do think that a shift is occurring in the sciences and elsewhere, and the necessity of integration is coming to be recognized. I am convinced that the quest for integration of knowledge ought to be part of the Catholic curriculum, and probably can only survive at a religious-based institution. One way that administrators could foster this quest would be to rate interdisciplinary work on a par with specialized research and publication when evaluating faculty performance, promotion, and tenure. This could help shift the balance toward integration and away from ongoing fragmentation.

Notes

1. *Ex Corde Ecclesiae*, pp. 14–15 (emphasis in original).
2. See Arthur M. Schlesinger, Jr., *The Disuniting of America* (New York: W. W. Norton, 1992).
3. Edward O. Wilson, *Sociology: The New Synthesis* (Cambridge, MA: Harvard University Press, 1975).
4. "The ultimate aim of the modern movement in biology is in fact to explain all biology in terms of physics and chemistry." Francis Crick, *Of Molecules and Men* (Seattle: University of Washington Press, 1966), 10.
5. Francis Crick, *The Astonishing Hypothesis* (New York: Charles Scribner's Sons, 1994), 3.
6. *Ex Corde Ecclesiae*, p. 9.
7. On these experiments, see Paul Davies, *God and the New Physics* (New York: Simon & Schuster, 1983), ch. 8, and P.C.W. Davies and J.R. Brown, *The Ghost in the Atom* (Cambridge, UK: Cambridge University Press, 1986).

8. Roger Sperry, "The New Mentalist Paradigm and the Ultimate Concern," *Perspectives in Biology and Medicine,* 29, 3, Part I (spring 1986): 416–17.
9. The approach pioneered by scientists at the Santa Fe Institute is the exact opposite of reductionism; it seeks to explore the behavior and emergent properties of whole systems as wholes. These scientists, who include many Nobel Prize winners like Murray Gell-Mann, "believe they are forging the first rigorous alternative to the kind of lienar, reductionist thinking that has dominated science since the time of Newton." M. Mitchell Waldrop, *Complexity* (New York: Simon & Schuster, 1992), 13ff.

In the Beginning Was the Word

Glenn A. Steinberg*

Early in *Ex Corde Ecclesiae*,[1] Pope John Paul II clearly states what he perceives as one of the most urgent obligations and challenges for Catholic universities in our time. The Pope writes:

> In the world today, characterized by such rapid developments in science and technology, the tasks of a Catholic university assume an ever greater importance and urgency. Scientific and technological discoveries create an enormous economic and industrial growth, but they also inescapably require the correspondingly necessary *search for meaning* in order to guarantee that the new discoveries be used for the authentic good of individuals and of human society as a whole. (paragraph 17)

In essence, the Pope perceives in the contemporary scene an urgent need for meaning to counterbalance the dangers of runaway, inhumane technology, and he looks to Catholic universities to assist the Church in discovering and imparting that meaning. As a result, the Pope sees *integration of knowledge* as a necessary foundation for all research and teaching in an authentically Catholic university (paragraphs 15–20). As the Pope observes, "It is necessary *to work toward a higher synthesis* of knowledge, in which alone lies the possibility of satisfying that thirst for truth which is profoundly inscribed on the heart of the human person" (paragraph 16).

This higher synthesis gives meaning to all specialized knowledge and is the basis for understanding and implementing technology in ways that are morally and anthropologically sound. The Catholic university, by applying itself to the work of such synthesis, renders invaluable service to

---

*Glenn A. Steinberg is professor of English at the University of St. Thomas, St. Paul, Minnesota. An earlier version of this article appeared in *Curriculum in a Catholic University: Summer Seminar* (St. Paul: University of St. Thomas, 1995).

the Church and the world, since the "present age is in urgent need of this kind of disinterested service, namely of *proclaiming the meaning of truth*" (paragraph 4).

In perceiving an urgent need for contemporary universities to emphasize truth over technology and meaning over information, the Pope is not alone. In *The Closing of the American Mind*, Allan Bloom sees our society and our students as growing progressively "flatter" because of the decline of "real learning" and the rise of narrowly defined, narrowly executed "technical education."[2] In the current academic climate, Bloom writes, a "highly trained computer specialist need not have had any more learning about morals, politics or religion than the most ignorant of persons."[3]

In reaction to this state of affairs, Neil Postman argues in *Technopoly* that "perhaps the most important contribution schools can make to the education of our youth is to give them a sense of coherence in their studies, a sense of purpose, meaning, and interconnectedness in what they learn."[4] The lack of such coherence and meaning, Bloom says, "simply results in students seeking for enlightenment wherever it is readily available, without being able to distinguish between the sublime and trash, insight and propaganda."[5]

Clearly, then, the Pope is not alone in seeing our age as one in urgent need of meaning and integration, especially in the realm of education. But in this time of apparent crisis, what specifically should Catholic universities do to fulfill the mission of "proclaiming the meaning of truth" that the Pope envisions for them? How can they overcome the many difficulties and obstacles in the work of integrating and imparting knowledge in our fragmented, "post-modern" age? How can they keep their curricula from oversimplifying competing claims to knowledge or from rationalizing away the potentially reactionary implications of favoring integration of knowledge over relativism? Most important for me personally, how can I, as a professor of English at a Catholic university, encourage my students' experience of coherence and meaning in their studies when my discipline itself has in recent years come to assert the instability and impossibility of meaning? As Postman writes, "We must not overestimate the capability of schools to provide coherence in the face of a culture in which almost all coherence seems to have disappeared."[6]

As a way of attempting to answer these very difficult questions, I would like to focus on a particular need that I have perceived among my students—a fundamental need that deprives them of much meaning (and of much potential integration) in their lives and education. I have observed that most of my students do not really seem to believe or understand that words have meaning. When they read the works of literature I teach, they read for large, sweeping patterns and generalizations—the plot, theme, "big picture." They consistently resist looking at the concrete, constituent elements of a piece of writing. They glide right over the long, descriptive passages in novels, for example, without working to piece together a cohesive meaning out of the resonant images and emblematic tableaux that those passages are carefully crafted to develop. Such images and tableaux are "just words" to them—meaningless, insignificant, bothersome. What's more, the professor who tries to draw out motifs and symbols in a novel's descriptions is simply "reading too much into it." The words of the novel cannot contain or embody their own meaning. The professor necessarily imposes an arbitrary meaning on them.

The problem is not only one of reading. In their writing, too, students manifest a marked lack of faith in the meaningfulness of words; indeed, they frequently glide right over the literal meaning of the very words they are using, producing tantalizing "bloopers" ("His expectations for papers were at a higher multitude compared to my other professor's") and meaningless filler ("The theme of relationships that occurs between the characters plays an important role in the two texts"). In fact, students seem to write primarily by stringing together commonplaces and cliches without paying attention to the shape or meaning of the actual words they employ. As George Orwell has observed,

> Modern writing at its worst does not consist in picking out words for the sake of their meaning and inventing images in order to make the meaning clearer. It consists in gumming together long strips of words which have already been set in order by someone else, and making the results presentable by sheer humbug.[7]

According to Orwell, "prose consists less and less of *words* chosen for the sake of their meaning, and more of *phrases* tacked together like the sections of a prefabricated hen-house."[8]

We are all guilty of this kind of writing from time to time. As Orwell points out, "It is easy. It is easier—even quicker, once you have the habit—to say *In my opinion it is a not-unjustifiable assumption that* than to say *I think*";[9] indeed, some of the most prominent recent theorists in the fields of linguistic and literary study argue that the process of writing inevitably works this way—that is, by piecing together stock phrases that by themselves convey little if any meaning. To Roland Barthes, for example, every text is the product of "a ready-formed dictionary" of cultural and linguistic cliches. A writer "no longer bears within him passions, humours, feelings, impressions, but rather this immense dictionary from which he draws a writing that can know no halt." Barthes asserts,

> We know now that a text is not a line of words releasing a single "theological" meaning (the "message" of the Author-God) but a multidimensional space in

which a variety of writings, none of them original, blend and clash. The text is a tissue of quotations drawn from the innumerable centres of culture.

For this reason, Barthes proclaims, the author is, for all intents and purposes, dead, little more than an insignificant compiler of commonplaces at the mercy of his or her own language and culture; by the same reasoning, meaning—"the 'message' of the Author-God"—is also dead. Instead of being the locus of a "single 'theological' meaning," texts are meaningless jumbles of contradictory, competing commonplaces.[10]

Some scholars and critics (among them, M.H. Abrams and E.D. Hirsch) have attempted to counter such attacks on "the stable determinacy of meaning,"[11] but for my purposes, the best defense of meaningfulness comes from a scholar who characterizes himself as one who preaches "the instability of the text and the unavailability of determinate meanings."[12] Stanley Fish argues quite forcefully that "unintelligibility, in the strict or pure sense, is an impossibility."[13] Every utterance, every text, every word has meaning to the person who hears or reads it. We all immediately and inevitably create meaning out of the words that surround us. As Fish says, "Words that are uttered are immediately heard within a set of assumptions about the direction from which they could possibly be coming."[14] As a result, they are ascribed a meaning—regardless of whether that meaning is what the speaker or writer of the words intended. Although my students may think that long descriptive passages in novels are meaningless, such passages are not in fact meaningless even to them but rather have very specific meanings and purposes—as part of the deadwood that makes the novel long and, therefore, a novel rather than a short story, for example, or as the trivial details that, taken together, produce the "atmosphere" of the book.

But the perception among students that such passages are meaningless—that words are meaningless—persists. Such a perception is dangerous. If we are unaware or careless of the meanings that we ascribe to the words and objects around us, we make possible the abuse of those words and objects—as Orwell has pointed out so well and so often in his fiction. In *Animal Farm,* all things are created equal but some things are more equal than others, and in *1984,* Ministries of Disinformation become Ministries of Information through the abuse of language and meaning. This same type of abuse also potentially occurs in the realm of technology; it is precisely what the Pope fears when he writes of the dangers associated with the "rapid developments in science and technology" in our day, the developments for which the "search for meaning" is so important (paragraph 7). Consequently, if such abuse is to be avoided in the political and technological spheres, in our classrooms every day we must counter habits of mind that assume meaninglessness or stifle reflection on meaning.

For this reason, as a professor of English, I generally attempt to design my classroom curriculum to emphasize meaningfulness as opposed to meaninglessness. I make every effort to encourage students to become conscious of how they ascribe meaning to the texts they read for my class and also of how others might ascribe meaning in an entirely different way—because we all possess different skills, different values, and different beliefs as part of our context for interpretation. In addition, I insist upon precision in their use of language in their own writing, requiring that they go beyond cliches and commonplaces, beyond dead, meaningless phrases, beyond the vague and general. In this way, I hope to contribute meaningfully to the university's "search for meaning"—by laying the groundwork for faith in and reflection on the very process of making meaning itself.

Specifically, this semester, I am having my freshmen reflect on their literacy—on their amazing ability to make meaning out of written language, which we all take for granted. I asked guest speakers from the Minnesota Literacy Council to come into my classroom to talk about functional illiteracy and its effects on the lives of individuals and the community. For one of the papers in the course, students have the option of volunteering in a literacy program and of writing about how their experience of teaching someone else to read has changed their perception of their own reading skills and responsibilities. In this way, I hope to make clear to the students just how meaningful their lives are and, even more importantly, how essential words and books are to the enrichment—and the creation—of meaning in all our lives. From there, we will spend the rest of the course exploring more and more specifically how literary scholars make very specialized meaning out of the literature they study—through literary analysis, explication, and evaluation.

This approach attempts to respond to the Pope's challenging vision for Catholic universities by assisting students in their own personal search for meaning in their lives and education—offering them a chance to explore their assumptions and values through service learning. It provides a broader context for their literary studies as freshmen at the University of St. Thomas by relating those studies to the community at large (and to the issue of literacy in America). Perhaps most importantly, it challenges habits of mind that allow meaning to lapse into meaninglessness—fostering habits of mind that potentially have application everywhere in the students' lives. My wish is for my students to be endlessly amazed at their own ability to understand what words mean and for them to become ever more curious about what everything around them—both in books and in the world—means. By encouraging curiosity and reflection about words and meaning, I hope to give them the impetus—and the necessary skills—for their own work in the search for meaning and the integration of knowledge within a Catholic university.

Notes

1. John Paul II, *Ex Corde Ecclesiae* (Washington, DC: U.S. Catholic Conference, 1990).
2. Allan Bloom, *The Closing of the American Mind: How Higher Education Has Failed Democracy and Impoverished the Souls of Today's Students* (New York: Simon & Schuster, 1987), 59–60.
3. Ibid., 59.
4. Neil Postman, *Technopoly: The Surrender of Culture to Technology* (New York: Vintage, 1992), 185–86.
5. Bloom, *Closing of the American Mind,* 64.
6. Postman, *Technopoly,* 186.
7. George Orwell, "Politics and the English Language," in Sonia Orwell and Ian Angus, eds., *The Collected Essays, Journalism and Letters of George Orwell,* Vol. IV: *In Front of Your Nose: 1945–1950* (New York: Harcourt, 1968), 134.
8. Ibid., 130.
9. Ibid., 134.
10. Roland Barthes, *Image–Music–Text,* trans. Stephen Heath (New York: Hill and Wang, 1977).
11. E. D. Hirsch, *The Aims of Interpretation* (Chicago: University of Chicago Press, 1976), 1.
12. Stanley Fish, "Is There a Text in This Class?" in *Is There a Text in This Class? The Authority of Interpretive Communities* (Cambridge, MA: Harvard University Press, 1980), 305.
13. Ibid., 307.
14. Ibid., 316.

Student Life

Introduction
Irene King

Patrick Byrne's approach to Catholic identity at colleges and universities is to discuss the impact of their predominant paradigms. A *paradigm* is defined here as "what a community . . . shares as incommensurable ways of seeing the world . . . an interrelated set of shared beliefs, values, instrumentations, exemplars and what Thomas Kuhn called 'symbolic generalizations.'" A paradigm is powerful because it is often "largely unarticulated" in the structure of our constructed reality. Yet it is possible to change a prevailing paradigm by giving people opportunities to experiences anomalies—things that don't "fit"—within the existing paradigm. This leads to a crisis within the community that adheres to the paradigm, which in turn leads to re-formulation of the paradigm in a way that makes sense of the anomaly.

Byrne contends that most universities predicate their pedagogy, programs, and identity on an academic paradigm that emphasizes facts, not values. Yet beneath this veneer of the importance of facts lies the Enlightenment ideal that "reason reveals the truths about the highest values, such as justice and love." Colleges and universities thus impart implicit paradigms about what is "most important." Catholic universities, in particular, need to be conscious of the paradigms they are working within—and whether they fit with their mission.

Byrne posits that service learning addresses the issue of Catholic identity, both facts and Catholic values, through "the combination of service praxis and academic reflection." To illustrate his points, Byrne uses twenty-five years of lessons learned by the Boston College service learning program, PULSE, and the work on paradigms by Thomas Kuhn.

Byrne observes two predominant paradigms held by most students at Boston College when they enter the PULSE program. These two paradigms, the conservative and liberal, are but two ways of viewing the world and the problem of human suffering, justice and love: "To put things simply, PULSE is primarily concerned with bringing about a change in students' paradigms of justice and love." Byrne describes student progression through paradigm, crisis, and then often a shift into a more encompassing paradigm. The objective, for a Catholic college, is to "do what Christians down through the ages have always done—to draw upon all the intellectual and interpersonal resources we can to unveil narrowness, and to broaden student awarenesses about all that is truly entailed in both love and justice in the fullest senses."

Karen Caldwell and her colleagues delineate the vital Neighbor-to-Neighbor Program at Saint Louis University. The authors posit that university-community partnerships shape our "understanding of the university's mission by emphasizing service to the community". . . "and refine our insights into what it means to be a university committed to service for others for the greater honor and glory of God." The Neighbor-to-Neighbor Program is one way that Saint Louis University lives its Catholic identity.

Reflecting national momentum, accelerated by federal programs, for collaboration between education, health, and social services, Neighbor-to-Neighbor brings together nine university departments and three community organizations to create a mutually beneficial service learning program.

The article discusses three processes inherent in community partnerships that can shape and re-vision higher education:

1. Practicing a praxis methodology
2. Building relationships on principles of mutuality, capacity, and resilience
3. Creating interprofessional strategies for addressing community issues

The authors define *praxis* as "the critically lived communion of theory and action that leads to refined theory and more deliberately chosen action." Praxis is intimately connected, first, to a university or religious order's mission and, second, to the relative value given to ways of knowing.

The first dimension of praxis, the mission of Saint Louis University, is to "transform society in the spirit of the Gospels" through education. What makes education distinctively able to motivate and train people to transform society? The authors quote David O'Brien in saying that it is the questions we ask, not our methods that make faculty at Catholic universities distinctive. Jesuit education is distinctive within Catholic higher education because it has integrated into the process of education a "faith that does justice." Education in the Jesuit tradition is "an act of justice because it is an act of collaborative liberation." Through this vision, and a service learning pedagogy, Saint Louis students, faculty, and the surrounding community reflect together on issues of mutual concern.

A second important dimension of praxis is our attitudes about different ways of knowing. The authors draw on the work of David Kolb in citing the traditional preference for knowledge that is abstract and analytical, "where objectivity is highly privileged, specialization is encouraged, having "hard" data is all that counts, and distance is required to gain perspective." Service learning instead values an approach to knowing "that builds on connection and relationships, a knowing that is contextual and develops in dialogue." This praxis incorporates the Jesuit and Catholic values of work with the marginalized, the importance of subsidiarity (letting those closest to the situation make choices about their lives), and a vision of the university as servant.

The authors ask, "how then do we build just relationships among university and community participants?" They respond that universities, particularly those in urban areas, need to "take to heart that the plight around them is their own plight."

To effectively engage with the plight of the community Saint Louis University had to let go of any paternalistic views of education and service. They adopted the Capacity-Focused Alternative Model for Developing Community Capacity by McKnight and Kretzman at Northwestern University. This model would address community needs with policies and activities based on the capacities, skills, and assets of people in the neighborhoods. Thus work with the community is not so much service, and more collaboration. "We can no longer see persons as the objects of our inquiry or as compliant recipients of services." This vision aims to create reciprocal, just relationships.

That includes relationships within the university community. If we want mutual, interdependent, holistic relationships with members of the local community, we must learn how to build them within our own university community. "If university faculty do not model collaborative attitudes and behaviors, it is unlikely that future providers (students) will . . . be prepared to function in emerging systems that are community-based and empowerment-oriented."

Caldwell and her colleagues recognize that the dominant culture at most universities is a culture of professionalism that hinders faculty from seeing connections between their disciplines. Departments become more isolated from one another as specialization increases. "Yet, most of the pressing questions of society do not fit nicely into single disciplines. . . . Interprofessional education is needed to emphasize the common denominators of vision, mission, knowledge, language, values, norms, and skills for all the professions dedicated to relieving pressing urban problems."

Overall, the authors of this article eloquently articulate the distinctiveness of Catholic identity for pedagogy—a way of teaching and knowing that embraces the marginalized, values relationship, and affirms the dignity of each person.

Margaret Kender's article, like Paul Stark's later offering, is a very hands-on, how-to approach to integrating Catholic identity into student life. In 1986, Allentown College of St. Francis de Sales initiated a ten-year plan. An important goal emerged: "to develop greater social awareness and a heightened moral consciousness among students"—a reflection of the mission of the college, which, as did St. Francis de Sales, emphasizes humankind's innate capacity to love: "He insisted that the ordinary person has the potential for doing great good, for leading a life of transcendent meaning centered squarely in the world."

A planning committee was charged with deciding how to inculcate these values into students' lives. Kender describes the process of creating a program that was very inclusive of all sectors of the campus community. A consultant helped the committee in reviewing the history of moral development approaches; committee members were asked about "what we need more of" on campus. They agreed on four concerns: for self, for personal relations, for civil society, and for relations to the Church.

The College used a values inventory to set a baseline for these goals and values and to measure the effectiveness of this program. Kender's description of the process, the inventory that emerged, and the resulting recommendations offer valuable ideas for other campuses.

Joan Penzenstadler's article poetically articulates the challenges to a college of welcoming religious diversity while maintaining religious identity. She quotes Lonergan to identify the "entry point that allows all students admittance, regardless of their religious backgrounds": "Deep within us all, emergent when the noise of other appetites is stilled, there is a drive to know, to understand, to see why, to discover the reason, to find the cause, to explain."[1] Penzenstadler believes that Catholic beliefs can be taught in a way that responds to this drive to understand as long as a college creates a space "where serious conversation, from varying perspectives, constantly challenges and refines the articulations."[2]

Penzenstadler offers three aspects of Catholic faith that can be taught in a way that invites students of different religious perspectives:

1. The principle of sacramentality
2. The juxtaposition of faith and reason
3. The value of unity in diversity

For each of these, Penzenstadler illustrates a way of engaging students in the core meaning of the issue, often through secular or scientific works or texts from other religious traditions. She also explicates how each of these topics deepens teaching. For example, she describes a course, "The Search for Meaning," in which students learn to define sacramentality as "a reverential way of attending to life," cognizant that the infinite dwells within the finite. The course uses the research of a biologist, Barbara McClintock, whose work is with chromosomes.

Penzenstadler quotes Einstein to strengthen her connection between a "sacramental attentiveness" and science: "The state of feeling which makes one capable of such achievement is akin to that of the religious worshipper or of one who is in love." Viktor Frankl and Alice Walker are other authors whose worldviews can be considered sacramental without being Catholic.

Penzenstadler explores the tensions between faith and reason by exploring the similar struggles of others. She quotes Simone Weil: "Christ likes us to prefer truth to him, because before being Christ, he is truth. If one turns aside from him to go toward the truth, one will not go far before falling into his arms."[3] This articulation of Weil's struggle demonstrates "the interplay between love of God and critical reflection, an interplay that is a hallmark of Catholic higher education."

Penzenstadler encourages teachers to draw from the innate desire of students to know, to explore what truth is. Students exposed to the search of others, such as Frankl, McClintock, Weil, Thomas More, or Job, see their own questions and struggles mirrored in the lives of others. Faith becomes not a monolithic belief system but a very human process of trying to understand the meaning of one's life: "Many students . . . begin to see that Job's fidelity rests in his refusal to collapse the tension between his love and his intelligence." When she poses questions like "Are reason and love compatible?" she no doubt intrigues Catholics and non-Catholics alike.

Penzenstadler challenges teachers to become intentional about the atmosphere they create in classrooms, agreeing with John Henry Newman that the classroom is the place "in which the intellect may safely range and speculate, sure to find its equal in some antagonistic activity, and its judge in the tribunal of truth."[4] She correctly recognizes that we must create an environment where it is safe for students to participate, disagree with each other and the teacher.

Discussing unity in diversity, Penzenstadler continues to make connections between a Catholic belief and the search for meaning of any human person—regardless of spiritual affiliation. She reminds us that "welcoming those not considered part of the accepted system was one of Jesus's main activities in establishing God's reign . . . they were meaningful contributors to the vision of a community based on love, justice, and peace. From this principle of community that is inclusive flows a way of being, teaching, and learning." She shares beautiful material from the writings of Etty Hillesum, Martin Luther King, Jr., and Barbara McClintock.

Penzenstadler believes that "forms of teaching that flow from the desire for inclusiveness search out ways to help students connect with ideas that have not yet come to light and enhance the joy of learning together." She firmly believes that both teacher and student must collaborate in the search for meaning so that both have the opportunity to be transformed.

Paul Stark, like Byrne, recognizes that to communicate Catholic identity to students one must evoke within them a paradigm shift. By attending a Jesuit university, in this case Saint Louis University, students are entering a community of Jesuits—a religious community whose mission is nothing less than "to change the world." Stark believes the only way to truly include students in the Catholic (here, Jesuit) mission is to "provide them with a stake in society, and to re-establish the credibility of the organizations and the institutions they often feel have failed them: our families, our businesses, our churches and schools, our universities."

The mission of Saint Louis University is to transform students into people who are "fully prepared to contribute to society and to be effective leaders of social change" based on ethical values and principles. Stark outlines three goals to realize this mission:

1. To *inform,* "to develop an intellectual competence"
2. To *form* "our students, our faculty, staff and administration, with character, values and respect for each other, with a heartfelt, integrated understanding of our connectedness."
3. To *transform*: "St. Ignatius of Loyola had no less than the transformation of the world as his goal. Isn't that—can't that be—our goal? Isn't that the most profound legacy we can leave those who follow us?"

Stark then discusses how we develop competence, conscience, compassion, community, and commitment within students, helpfully summarizing the student life programming and policies in place at Saint Louis University that help engender the qualities needed for transformation. These range from community service to mornings of recollection, retreats, the discipline process, and residence hall activities. The University offers a multitude of activities and programs that all work toward the same goal—the transformation of the individual and the community.

Notes

1. Bernard Lonergan, *Insight: A Study of Human Understanding* (San Francisco: Harper and Row, 1957), 4.
2. See B. Daley, "Christ and the Catholic University," *America* 169 (1993).
3. Simone Weil, *Waiting for God,* tr. by Emma Craufurd (New York: G. P. Putnam's Sons, 1951), 69.
4. John Henry Newman, *Idea of a University.*

Paradigms of Justice and Love

Patrick H. Byrne*

"Service learning doesn't belong in an academic curriculum." Twenty-five years ago I repeatedly heard words like these when I was involved in setting up Boston College's PULSE Program. Much has changed since those days, but the basic challenges remain the same: Is there a legitimate, properly academic role for service learning in the curricular offerings at our colleges and universities? Are the dual commitments of the Jesuit tradition—to excellence in scholarship and to Christian service—merely two parallel, not intersecting, tracks? Or is there an intrinsic unity between the two? What kinds of curricular structures might embody this unity—if indeed it is a unity?

Looking back over the twenty-five years since the founding of the PULSE Program, I believe that its model of service learning has something to offer in response to these questions, because the PULSE model rather uniquely emphasizes the *combination* of service praxis and academic reflection. The benefit of this type of combination was put into words by a senior PULSE student, Russell Turk, who has since gone on to a career in medicine. Russell says that he never considered himself to be "very contemplative," but the PULSE program gave him "no real choice to be otherwise":

> It's not that an idea taught in a classroom cannot be as profound [as learning through an experience]; it's simply that when you live through the principles discussed in class, they become imprinted in you, and become more integrated and permanent in your life. I now see that philosophy is not something that should only be learned in special experiences like a classroom or the homeless shelter where I volunteer. Philosophy should be learned everywhere you go, and applied to everything you do.

*Patrick H. Byrne is associate professor of philosophy at Boston College, Boston, Massachusetts. This article first appeared in *Conversations on Jesuit Higher Education* (spring 1995): 5–17.

The PULSE Program's emphasis on the combination of service praxis and academic reflection originates in two decisions made at the inception of the program: that students would receive academic credit for participation in an off-campus field project in combination with specially designed academic courses; and that the program would concentrate on field projects that have a social-service or social-action focus rather than, say, a pre-professional training focus. In choosing these as our working principles, we were deliberately opting not to follow simpler paths suggested by two more familiar ideas. First, we decided that PULSE would not adopt an internship model, in which academic credit is awarded for solely pre-professional, non-academic activities. Second, we intentionally adopted a position counter to the prevailing conception of the contemporary university—that its proper province is the cultivation of critical thinking alone, with all other functions consigned to an ancillary status. We were motivated by a conviction that there is an intrinsic connection between theory and practice—that careful study of our intellectual and religious traditions can inform and transform practice in profound ways, and that appropriately structured forms of praxis can add depth to the comprehension of theoretical issues.

Over the past thirty or so years, we have witnessed a great transition in the academic standards and structures at our Jesuit colleges and universities, and our standards now may be said to emulate those of the great secular universities. Their ideal of higher education received its most influential contemporary articulation from Max Weber, whose well-known fact-value dichotomy has led to a correlative divorce, in principle at least, between the academic quest for knowledge and public pursuit of practical ends.[1]

Unfortunately, this way of conceiving of the purpose of the university tends to obscure the fact that the great modern emphasis on science and higher learning was itself derived from the Enlightenment's hope that modern forms of reason would liberate human life. That is to say, behind the academic ideal of the fact-value split lies an implicit value commitment: Higher learning is for the sake of forming liberated human beings. In the Enlightenment ideal, reason reveals the truths about the highest values, such as justice and love.

It therefore remains as true today as ever that, more than anything else, what students acquire in institutions of higher learning are "paradigms" about what is most important in life—paradigms of justice and love. From this point of view, I would contend that there is a serious crisis in higher education, and that it derives from the desperate shallowness of the paradigms of justice and love our students are currently acquiring in their classrooms as well as in their dormitories and through extracurricular activities.

Of course there are narrow and pernicious views of the relations between theory and practice, which contend that the university must subordinate its thinking to the needs judged "relevant" to contemporary times. We were well aware of this danger when we were developing the PULSE Program, and explicitly eschewed any model that would subordinate academic inquiry to ideological or narrowly conceived "practical" goals. Still, we did not possess a clear alternative model for several years. The PULSE model did not emerge full-blown at the moment of its inception but took shape gradually, through a process of trial and error as we learned from the many valuable things that happened (and failed to happen) in the hearts and minds of students enrolled in the program. In this article I would like to describe the model that eventually did emerge, in the hope that this may contribute to a larger discussion about the prospects and possibilities of service learning in general.

One way of understanding the PULSE model's efforts at integrating theory and practice is to focus on the problem of transforming students' paradigms of justice and love. Since I am adapting Thomas Kuhn's term, "paradigm," to the problem of service learning, I shall begin by explicating what Kuhn means by that term and by showing how it relates to the communal identity of natural scientists. In the sections that follow I shall extend the term in order to analyze some of the prevailing paradigms of justice and love that influence our students, and the sorts of communities with which they identify. The final sections will reflect on some of the limitations of those paradigms, and consider the possibility of facilitating a conversion to a paradigm that transcends those limitations.

Paradigm and Community in Kuhn's Writings

Possibly the most influential publication in this century devoted to topics in the philosophy of natural science has been Thomas Kuhn's *The Structure of Scientific Revolutions.*[2] It has sparked three decades of animated debate and disagreement among philosophers of science, and has stimulated the thinking of many outside that field. It is not my purpose here to take up a critical study of Kuhn's work (although on one point alone I shall have something to say in the last section of this article). I wish simply to draw upon his ideas in order to highlight salient features of the PULSE model.

Kuhn adopted the term "paradigm" to analyze the complicated processes through which scientific knowledge changes. What he referred to as "normal science" is a more or less continuous process of accretion accomplished by a community of scientists who share one and the same paradigm. There is also a discontinuous process—"extraordinary" or "revolutionary science"—in which a scientific community abandons a previously held paradigm in favor of a new and incommensurably different paradigm (Kuhn 1970, 4–9).

Kuhn's use of the term "paradigm" is ambivalent, as his critics have noted, and as he has acknowledged (1970, 174–87). In its most basic sense, however, a paradigm is what a community of scientific investigators shares and what constitutes it as a scientific community (1970, 4, 10, 179). Kuhn speaks of paradigms as "incommensurable ways of seeing the world and of practicing science in it" (1970, 4). Paradigms consist of an interrelated set of shared beliefs, values, instrumentations, exemplars, and what Kuhn called "symbolic generalizations" (1970, 4, 10, 181–87). His most succinct statement about paradigms runs as follows:

> Effective research scarcely begins before a scientific community thinks it has acquired firm answers to questions like the following: What are the fundamental entities of which the universe is composed? How do these interact with each other and with the senses? What questions may be legitimately asked about such entities and what techniques employed in seeking solutions? (1970, 4–5)

The most important aspect of paradigms, in Kuhn's view, pertains to the task of puzzle-solving, the effort to explain phenomena. Kuhn takes puzzle-solving to be the fundamental activity of any scientific community. Even the most impressive solutions by innovative thinkers, however, do not by themselves form an adequate basis for a scientific community. It is also necessary that these solutions be "sufficiently open-ended to leave all sorts of problems for the redefined group of practitioners to resolve" (1970, 10).

Many of the open-ended puzzles that confront a scientific community gradually give way to solutions. But some resist solution for long periods of time, and certain new phenomena or ideas may resist integration into the paradigm (1970, 52–76). Scientific communities are aware of the existence of such "anomalies," and yet generally remain untroubled about their existence. These anomalies are simply regarded as puzzles whose solutions will come as a result of future intermediate accomplishments, and are set aside for the time being (1970, 77–82).

Occasionally, however, "an anomaly comes to seem more than just another puzzle of normal science" (1970, 82), and in such cases the scientific community enters a discontinuous, revolutionary period. In such a period, clarity about just what the paradigm is—which beliefs, values, rules, and so on are essential and which are dispensable—itself becomes a problem (1970, 83). Some scientists become willing to abandon the paradigm altogether and seek a new one. Eventually one is found that gradually attracts the allegiance of great numbers of people from the former scientific community and becomes the basis for a new community of scientific practice. When this sort of large-scale shift in allegiance takes place, according to Kuhn, a scientific revolution has occurred.

Paradigms in the Contexts of Justice and Love

I would now like to indicate briefly how Kuhn's notion of a community grounded in a shared paradigm can be used to interpret the ways people think about justice and love, and to identify issues in service learning. In the first place, to use "paradigm" in this connection is to draw attention to justice and love as problems. Ultimately, concerns for justice and love come down to questions about how to act justly or lovingly in the concrete situations in which one finds oneself. Students pose these questions and seek answers, I believe, within the context of something like paradigms of justice and love.

Second, just as scientists learn their community's paradigm in their professional education, so also we acquire our paradigms of justice and love from the communities to which we belong—family, neighborhood, peer group, college or university, church, country, and the like. In Kuhn's terms, this means we acquire shared beliefs, values, instrumentations, exemplars, and symbolic generalizations. Of course these terms mean something different in relation to problems of justice and love than they do in the context of natural science. Here, "symbolic generalization" refers to terms such as "freedom," "evil," "rights," "happiness," "sacrifice," "passion," "care," and "helping," and to how they are concretely understood and applied to different people and different circumstances. "Exemplars" are people, institutions, or events that show what it is to act justly or lovingly according to a particular paradigm. "Instrumentation" would refer to methods and techniques, both acceptable and not acceptable, employed as means for achieving justice or love. "Values" here primarily refers to the scale of priorities according to which various goods are arranged—expressed, for example, in a phrase like "People are more important than things." Finally, "beliefs" denotes the most fundamental views regarding human nature and the ultimate significance of the universe held by a community.

In order to give a clearer indication of what I have in mind in adapting Kuhn's ideas to justice and love, I shall first describe two "incommensurable" paradigms of justice that prevail among virtually all students when they first come to the PULSE Program. These paradigms roughly correspond to what we mean by "conservative" and "liberal" in this country. I shall then offer a kind of topography of paradigms of love held by our students.

Two Prevailing Paradigms of Justice

The conservative paradigm places a high value on the system of rewards inherent in the organization of American economic institutions. Most students sharing this paradigm have come to college to enter that system at its most prestigious and glamorous levels—as professionals, as governmental officials, or as business managers. They believe that this system will reward them for their talents (and few doubt that they are sufficiently talented) and for their hard work. In this paradigm, the system of economic rewards holds the key to happiness (which in this case means absence of privation) and freedom (possessing the means to do what one wants and to go where one pleases). Even though certain other qualities—such as friendships and family intimacy—are included in this paradigm's vision of happiness, economic rewards are considered indispensable for these as well.

The system is, therefore, perceived as just, since talent and hard work are rewarded with the highest human goods: freedom and happiness. Students in this paradigm share the belief that these goods are available to every member of our society and, if people do not achieve the desired level of happiness and freedom, it must be because they lack talent or ambition. This does not mean that these students—especially those who enroll in the PULSE Program—are insensitive to those who do not attain high levels of success. They recognize certain imperfections in the existing system; but they perceive these imperfections as anomalies that will be overcome in time by means of the paradigm itself. Above all else, however, this paradigm's most fundamental belief is in being realistic, pragmatic, and practical; and, if some people do not succeed, the realities of nature and human nature dictate that this is the way things must be.

As these students get older, they begin to articulate their paradigm in terms of property rights and a system of free enterprise. Yet initially the paradigm is understood in terms of an exemplar—usually one or both parents—who did work hard and sacrificed in order to achieve happiness and freedom. Finally, justice is conceived of principally as a matter of problem-solving, of improving the system's efficiency by removing obstacles (ignorance, crime, government bureaucracy) to its smooth functioning.

In a certain, somewhat dim, sense, these students tend to think of themselves as contributing to solving problems of justice in their field projects, insofar as they can offer instruments (such as education) to, or instill values (such as hard work) in, those they meet. To conclude, let me stress that students holding this paradigm are *not* insensitive to injustices; they perceive themselves as being deeply concerned with what *they* regard as justice.

Students belonging to the conservative justice paradigm now constitute a decidedly larger community among those who enroll in the PULSE Program. A sizable though smaller group shares in the liberal paradigm. In this paradigm, the value-priorities revolve around these students' strong feelings of indignation toward what their paradigm regards as the greatest evils: poverty, oppression, suffering, failures to insure respect and dignity, and restrictions upon choice. In this paradigm, justice as a problem-solving endeavor is a matter of eliminating these great evils. Central to their paradigm is the sense that "somebody has to do something" to overcome these evils.

Most of these students, like their conservative counterparts, seek professional or managerial careers, but (with the exception of special education and social work) they do not usually view these careers as having much to do with accomplishing justice. Rather, poverty, oppression, loss of dignity, and suffering, according to their paradigm, have not been solved by the present system of economic rewards because they cannot be solved by it. (That is *their* belief about reality.) Auxiliary systems of human services and governmental protection are believed to be required in order for justice to prevail, and social legislation to fund or enforce such programs is the instrumentation by means of which this is to be accomplished.

Where their conservative counterparts view these problems as peripheral anomalies, the students operating out of a liberal paradigm regard them as the central and urgent measures of injustice. Because these problems are regarded as so pervasive and massive, the instrumentation required to overcome them must be correspondingly massive—large scale government intervention. Ask most of these students "what needs to be done" and they will tell you that the "government" is the somebody that needs "to do something"—pass new laws or fund new social programs. The exemplars for students committed to this paradigm can be someone they know personally, but it is more likely to be a national figure such as Jesse Jackson, Hillary Rodham Clinton, or Edward Kennedy, or a national event such as the passage of Civil Rights or New Deal legislation.

Finally, the great human goods of freedom and happiness are conceived of as what results more or less automatically from the elimination of poverty, oppression, disrespect, and suffering. Hence, *any* structure that requires acquiescence and accommodation—that proposes *any* limitation upon choices—can come to be viewed as oppressive. Such structures, therefore, need to be overcome. Authenticity, defined as expressing one's own self without regard to what others may think, becomes the highest value.

As the liberal students develop intellectually, they begin to articulate their paradigm of justice in terms of equality and respect for human dignity. Interestingly, however, respect for human dignity tends not to entail very much beyond entitlements to economic goods—primarily food, housing, and health care—and avoidance of derogatory speech. Oddly, despite the liberal paradigm's significant divergence from the conservative paradigm, the two views of freedom and happiness are almost identical, stressing absence of economic privation and social-political restraint as the highest human goods. The liberal paradigm augments this slightly with statements such as "I cannot be free until all are free," or "I am happiest when I'm helping others," statements that seldom sound very convincing, at least to me.

A Topography of Paradigms of Love

It is more difficult, I think, to characterize our students as adhering to one or the other of two alternative and competing paradigms of love. Instead, I find it helpful to think in terms of a kind of topography of these paradigms. There is considerable overlap across this landscape of paradigms, with one and the same student committed to two or more paradigms that are not particularly commensurable with one another, though students for a time seem largely innocent of this fact.

One index to the lines of demarcation among these paradigms is the way that a student will use the word "love." The vast majority restricts this word to romantic and domestic contexts—love of boyfriend or girlfriend, spouse, children, immediate relatives. Naturally enough, the exemplars that give substance and meaning to the term are members of their own families. Usually, however, certain figures from literature, cinema, and the arts also provide exemplars that fill out their paradigm of love. Within this paradigm the instrumentation is domestic mutuality of affection and indeed of passion, as well as reciprocity of self-sacrificial deeds. Moreover, domesticity—in the sense of a fairly high level of economic prosperity—is considered indispensable to this vision of love. On the whole, students holding this paradigm tend to be much more convinced of the importance of income to a successful loving relationship (e.g., living together) than they are about the bonds of holy matrimony.

For some students the proper use of the term "love" ends here, and it would be at least anomalous, if not almost immoral to them, to consider love as something taking place outside the immediate context of domesticity. Many other students, however, subscribe at least in practice to additional paradigms of love, although most of them are still uncomfortable with actually using the word "love" in these extended senses. For these students as well, the domestic paradigm remains paramount.

The most common additional paradigm of love has to do with "being nice" to people. It is the closest most students come (initially, at least) to the type of love associated with patriotism in its noblest sense—love of one's fellow citizens. In this paradigm citizen-love reduces to tolerance—the nonjudgmental acceptance of those who are "different" from oneself. The problems of loving crying out most urgently for solution within the purview of this paradigm are problems of how to get more people to be more accepting of others. This paradigm's exemplars are usually certain peers and teachers—and here exemplars who are not "nice" are just as illuminating as those who are. Because of the importance attached to being nonjudgmental, however, the mutuality and reciprocity characteristic of domestic love are not part of the instrumentation of this paradigm. Tolerance is a kind of "live and let live" paradigm, which tends to foster a high valuation of independent action, with an accompanying abhorrence for the messiness that is inevitable in human mutual commitments.

As long as strict boundaries exist between the spheres of domestic love on the one hand, and being nice on the other, students can maintain allegiance to both paradigms. If those boundaries weaken, however, marital and familial relationships themselves tend to become construed according to criteria of tolerance. If this happens, marital love becomes conceived of as "two free and independent selves who make no demands upon one another," as one of my students put it. It is a shallow vision of marital love, as the authors of *Habits of the Heart* and the late Allan Bloom have aptly shown.[3]

A third type of paradigm of love has as its focus what used to be called "acts of charity"—except that now students call it "helping." This paradigm is quite common among PULSE students, for most of them come wishing to "help" others through their field work efforts, though "helping" is not very clearly thought out. Usually helping is understood in relationship to some exemplar, and here their religious backgrounds often are important. Their exemplars can be someone they know personally—clergy, teacher, relative, or less frequently, a parent—or a more famous figure—Mother Theresa, Martin Luther King, Jr., or Archbishop Romero, for example.

Helping tends to share something in common with domestic love—it requires face-to-face contact. Indirect institutional activities—food drives, fund raising, efforts at organizational and financial background support to a service agency—fit uneasily into this paradigm's vision of helping. Helping also tends to share some of the basic values of the liberal and conservative paradigms of justice, for "help" tends to mean giving people a portion of the basic economic goods (food, clothing, shelter, medical care) or giving them something that will enable them to acquire these goods (e.g., through education or rehabilitation). Giving one's time, or listening attentively, or agonizing over someone else's plight do not seem much like help from the perspective of this paradigm. Thus, helping also tends to be one-way—from the helper to the helped—and if the helper receives something in return, this would tend to mitigate the degree to which this act could be regarded as genuine help (love).

Students' commitments to the helping paradigm of love are often in an uneasy coexistence with "being nice," since helping causes dislocations with regard to being nonjudgmental. It is hard to think of oneself as helping another without entertaining the judgment that the other is in need of help. Still, this dual commitment is possible so long as one does not have to try simultaneously to help and to be nice to a person who severely taxes one's ability to do either—the kind of people PULSE students often encounter at their service placements.

A fourth kind of paradigm of love is what I would call the "empowerment paradigm." Although this paradigm is usually one arrived at after a crisis of incommensurability occurs between the helping and the tolerance paradigms, a small number of students already subscribe to this paradigm when they register for the PULSE Program, and so I include it here. In this paradigm there is an attempt to resolve the tensions between helping and being nonjudgmental, which is often expressed through the symbolic generalization of "helping people to help themselves." Instrumentations for this paradigm may include education and rehabilitation programs, but greater emphasis is placed upon efforts such as community organizing, consciousness raising, and dramatic "events" intended to attract public and media attention.

This greater emphasis reflects a fundamental belief about reality: Power, not affection, is the fundamental human *desideratum*. Genuine concern for the other is properly manifested in working to help them achieve power over their own lives, and this usually means wresting power from someone or some institution that has more than its fair share. Affection is all right, as long as it does not become the vehicle for duping people out of their rightful claims to power over their lives (which is what usually happens, according to this paradigm). In this paradigm, therefore, there is a kind of neo-puritanical circumspection about affection: Let it not grow too intense.

Missing from this topography are paradigms of love more prominent at other times and places, paradigms such as those having to do with patriotism, or *philia* (love of friends in the manner portrayed by Plato and Aristotle), or the Chivalric or Romantic visions of love as a deep longing and an arduous quest, or the direct nonviolent action of Mohandas K. Gandhi and Martin Luther King, Jr., or the paradigm of genuine Christian agapic love. Rarely if ever are students aware of such alternative paradigms of love, or aware that such paradigms signify something different, grander or more inclusive than their own paradigms.

I certainly do not intend these brief sketches of the paradigms of justice and love as a complete or comprehensive social psychological analysis of our students. Although these paradigms certainly are held by large numbers of our students, it is also true that many students do not fit easily into these categories. My intention here has been, rather, to show the value of transposing Kuhn's work into the field of service learning in helping us to notice and to think about the ways our students regard justice and love—to "touch them where they live," as one of my colleagues put it. In addition, this transposition of Kuhn's ideas can suggest a connection between service education and paradigm shifts, which is the topic of my next section.

Crisis of Paradigms

One of the characteristics of paradigms, Kuhn observed, is that they are largely unarticulated. Scientists *practice* their paradigms with great ease, and yet would be very hard-pressed indeed to give a nontrivial account of what they are doing. The same holds true for paradigms of justice and love. The need to articulate a paradigm becomes intensified in a period of "crisis," according to Kuhn, and this effort at articulation itself frequently contributes to the process whereby a paradigm shift takes place. Moreover, as Kuhn noted, "novelties of fact" and "novelties of theory" are particularly effective ways of inducing paradigm change (1970, 52). Taken together, these Kuhnian observations about the conditions that promote paradigm shifts offer a way of thinking about the PULSE model of service learning.

To put things simply, the PULSE Program is primarily concerned with bringing about a change in students' paradigms of justice and love. It seems that a prerequisite to this change is that students gain a clearer understanding of the paradigms they currently hold. This means giving them many opportunities to articulate their paradigms, opportunities that for us have included (a) regular supervisory sessions conducted by the field supervisor; (b) small weekly discussion groups conducted by the professor; (c) weekly journal assignments; (d) periodic papers on a topic relating field and course material.[4] Yet, if these assignments do assist our students in appropriating and transcending their paradigms, it is primarily because their field work presents "novelties of fact" and the classroom presents "novelties of theory" that provoke a need for paradigm articulation and change.

The students' field encounters have proven especially effective in provoking reflection and reassessment of their paradigms of justice and love. One conservative student's paradigm was challenged when his desire to instill the value of "fair competition" was challenged as he coached a street-hockey team in a low-income neighborhood. A kind of crisis occurred for him when the boys let him know what they thought of "American sportsmanship." In the end, he said, all that he really accomplished was giving the boys something to do to replace their otherwise listless afternoons. The fact that he could actually begin to discern a value in doing just that was a shift for him.

Other students have been confronted with their visions of "the good life" in their service to multiply-handicapped children who, they gradually realize, will never "make a contribution to society" by holding a lucrative or prestigious job. This is a "novelty of fact" for them; it provokes a crisis insofar as they can no longer hold that their paradigm will eventually solve this anomaly. Through this discovery, these students have been prompted to seek a vision of life that holds a place not only for the children they serve, but also makes a different kind of sense of the career paths they themselves had been pursuing.

Still other students have become perplexed by the fact that people they work with are poor, not because of laziness or a lack of talent, but because they are defeated, or not proficient in English, or simply old. They encounter not poverty, but poor people in all their human complexities, and the encounter creates pressures for new ways of "being realistic."

Service encounters can lead to crises in the liberal paradigm as well. One enthusiastic Big Sister encountered a girl who wanted only a good time from her, not her help. This Little Sister's resistance to her efforts challenged her sense of what the worth of her efforts might be. Another volunteer, who had done all the paperwork to enable an elderly woman to move to better housing, was dumbfounded when the woman changed her mind at the last moment. The depth of her attachment to home and neighborhood—the woman's sense of place—was quite anomalous to my student. Other liberal students have been disconcerted by the continual regression of alcoholic men and women they befriend and counsel, despite all the efforts they and the professional staff have made. Others experience a crisis in their paradigms when they are confronted with the high rates of recidivism in correctional institutions where they volunteer. Many are shocked when they realize that housing programs for the poor or economic and medical assistance for the elderly have made their overall plight worse.

Equally disruptive of their conservative and liberal paradigms are their positive discoveries. One student found the elderly, isolated, blind man she visited to be "the happiest man I know." Another discovered a gentleness, care, and a kind of altruistic morality in the way "street women" treated each other within the walls of a house of hospitality, in contrast to the coarse and aggressive ways they dealt with the outside world. Yet another saw "beauty" in some of these same women. They have at times discovered life among the dying, happiness among the poor, joy and hope among the oppressed, and nobility among the suffering. They encounter intransigence where their paradigms expect success; they find happiness, freedom, creativity, and love where their paradigms predict none. These field encounters provide irreplaceable stimuli for paradigm change.

Equally important to this process of change, however, is the theoretical material treated in the courses. Here we have been greatly influenced by contemporary scholarly assessments of ethical and political theory. Some of that scholarship argues that modern paradigms of social, political, and ethical practice arose from a deliberate and dramatic break from classical norms. It traces the conservative paradigm to concern with power and "rational calculation" in Hobbes and Locke, and the liberal paradigm to Rousseau's and Kant's preoccupation with a certain vision of dignity, autonomy, self-expression, and authenticity.

It likewise traces the origins of both of these traditions to Machiavelli's despair of the efficacy of faith in a transcendent good—a good beyond the satisfaction of passions and the allaying of fears—and his substitution of force as the primary human reality. In our discussions of classical and modern authors, we try to provide frameworks within which students can articulate their own paradigms. From our critical discussions of these authors, we try to help students recognize the limitations of their paradigms. Socrates' insistence in the *Gorgias*, for example, that the happier person is one who, if confronted with the option, "suffers injustice rather than doing injustice" is disconcerting to both the conservative and liberal paradigms, both of which equate happiness and justice with the absence of privation.

Study of Rousseau's account of the "state of nature," set as it is in contraposition to the commercial life, disturbs some conservative students' sense of complacency about their paradigm.[5] Liberal students, on the other hand, find Rousseau's account gives them apt language to express aspects of their own paradigm. They are therefore all the more disturbed when this ideal of the state of nature is set alongside Jane Jacobs's account of the long-range social consequences it has had upon urban life.[6] Jacobs's analysis of the intricate and subtle social patterns in neighborhoods that give rich meaning to people's lives, along with their own first-hand volunteer experiences, provoke crises in their own American-bred sense that "humans are by nature asocial."

Again, Max Scheler's scathingly critical assessment of "humanitarian love"—which bears a remarkable similarity to the students' paradigm of "helping"—elicited this response from one student: "Well, if *that's* humanitarian love, what am *I* doing volunteering at the hospital?"[7] On the other hand, our discussion of the role of the Hebrew midwives in the grand drama of *Exodus* challenged for some students the notion that great political power is required to bring about justice. Or Aristotle's discussions of friendship in the *Nicomachean Ethics* have opened up reflections upon loving—and betraying—clients they encounter at their service placements, as well as their dorm-mates, in ways they'd never previously considered.

"Novelties of fact" and "novelties of theory" came together in one of the most poignant moments I have witnessed in my teaching in the PULSE Program. Nancy Cantu enrolled in my PULSE course as a junior, majoring in French and political science. She volunteered in the education department at a temporary detention facility for male juvenile offenders. In one of her journal entries Nancy recorded an encounter she had had with a detainee I'll call Tom. Tom had been arrested for dealing drugs and was bragging in front of the other juveniles in Nancy's tutoring group. "He could not stop bragging about his own apartment, his stereo system and all the cars he has bought," Nancy wrote. "I let him talk about all these things without interrupting, because I thought it would make him happy."

But the word "happy" triggered a connection with classroom discussion:

> I started to think about Plato's and Aristotle's definitions of happiness and its true meaning. It was then that I realized that even though Tom was very proud of his material possessions, he was not happy with them nor with the way he had acquired them—with drug money. During my conversation with Tom I came straight out and asked him, "Tom, were you happy doing what you were doing? Were you satisfied with earning money from the dealing of drugs?" Tom turned away from me and said, "Well, man! It was good money!" I told him he was avoiding my question. "What do you think?" he replied. "Of course I'm not happy, but you wouldn't understand anyways." I told him I did understand. I told him something of my life and the difficulties I went through in coming to the United States. [She had moved with her family from Mexico a few years before.]

Four weeks later, after Tom had been placed in a permanent program, he wrote to Nancy, thanking her for listening to him. "No one ever really listened to me before. I've thought a lot about what you said and I'm thinking about going back to school so I can get a job." Nancy was not convinced that he would be able to carry through on his resolution, but her encounter with Tom made Plato's and Aristotle's standard of living justly more than an intellectual curiosity for her. The shift to a paradigm of just living differently from her own was made possible by the intersection of theory and practice, in a way that neither theory nor practice alone would have accomplished.

To date, courses in the PULSE Program have tended to rely upon philosophical and theological texts to introduce these "novelties of theory," because our courses have been offered primarily by the philosophy and theology departments. Robert Coles has recently shown, however, the tremendous potentialities of great works of literature to accomplish much the same sort of thing in connection with service activities.[8] These novelties of fact and novelties of theory bring about considerable articulation and reflection among our students. For some, the novelties induce a crisis situation—the need for an alternative paradigm.

Limited and Unlimited Paradigms

According to Kuhn, a crisis in a paradigm eventually leads to a "conversion," to "faith" in a new paradigm (1970, 150–59). This way of speaking has led his critics to charge him with making paradigm choices ultimately an irrational and relativist enterprise (1970, 191–206). The force of such accusations depends a great deal on what one means by "conversion," and how one understands its relationships to reason. Unfortunately, the way that Kuhn himself has construed both reason and conversion does indeed make him vulnerable to those charges.

This is not inevitable, however; nor must a model of service learning dedicated to shifting paradigms of justice and love be arbitrary or irrational. For both the biblical tradition and the tradition of ancient philosophy suggest that conversion may be indispensable for the pursuit of true wisdom. The central moment in Plato's *Republic*, for example, is a conversion of intellect and affect. In the Cave Allegory, the prisoner of shadows is "compelled to stand up, to *turn around* his neck, to walk and look up toward the light" (515c). Likewise, the climax in the *Book of Job* is a conversion (42:6), which takes place when Job is faced with the revelation of Yahweh's surpassing wisdom: Yahweh, who created the cosmos out of wisdom, nevertheless replies in a personal way to Job's complaint. Such sources suggest that conversion is intrinsic to reason because true wisdom concerning justice and love superabounds in intelligibility and surpasses finite comprehension. Hence, genuine dedication to the truths about justice and love entails a shift from finite modes of thinking about them toward ways of thinking and behaving that preserve the transcendent mysteriousness of justice and love.

Given this way of conceiving of the relationship between conversion and wisdom, I would like to speak of a contrast between limited paradigms and an unlimited paradigm of justice and love. The legitimacy of a model of service learning dedicated to shifting paradigms of justice and love depends upon *what sort of* alternative paradigm one shifts to. If the shift is from one limited paradigm to another, then the shift is indeed arbitrary and relative. By and large, what usually takes place in American education is a shift from one limited paradigm to another. Most frequently the shift is from conservative to liberal, or from "helping" to "tolerance" or to "empowerment."[9]

For Christians, however, conversion, *metanoia*, has always meant not merely change, but change to something unlimited, indeed change to a participation in Divine life: "I have come so that they may have life and have it to the full" (John 10:10). Taken in this radical sense, "conversion" objectively denotes a shift from a limited to an unlimited paradigm. An unlimited paradigm of justice and love is evoked by symbolic generalizations such as "His works are great, beyond all reckoning, his marvels, past all counting" (Job 9:10) or Paul's assertion that the *dikaiosune* (righteousness or justice) of God—God's way of rectifying evil—is the free sacrificial gift of loving grace in Jesus Christ (Romans 3:24).

Hence, the beliefs about reality according to an unlimited paradigm of justice and love hold that the most basic reality is the reality of the mysterious, transcendent activity of God's goodness, in which unlimited justice and love, reason and truth, are one. It is a paradigm in which what Johann Baptist Metz has called the "dangerous memory" of the history of God's saving activity makes us aware that God's justice and love encompass those who have succeeded as well as those who have failed, the oppressed as well as the oppressors. Such a paradigm finds problematic, and not merely anomalous, any order that stops short of that vision. It stimulates its adherents to draw upon all the intellectual and spiritual resources of the human-divine community and to work at all the problems necessary for the achievement of an order that is the fulfillment of that vision.

Our efforts at integrating theory and practice in the PULSE Program are oriented toward bringing to light the limitations of prevailing paradigms of justice and love. In that sense, we are endeavoring to do what Christians down through the ages have always done—to draw upon all the intellectual and interpersonal resources we can to unveil narrowness, and to broaden students' awarenesses about all that is truly entailed in both love and justice in the fullest senses. While this way of thinking about service education is explicitly informed by our Catholic and Jesuit tradition, the "novelties of theory" are appropriately drawn from non-Christian classical and modern texts as well as Christian writings, since the challenges to prevailing limited paradigms come from a multiplicity of sources.

Sometimes the "crises" lead to dramatic conversions, but more often they lead to the strengthening of the tentative commitments to an unlimited paradigm already present in the students. Through our classroom assignments, students are encouraged to consider the testimony of religious authors and to probe their intellectual honesty through dialogue, writing, and comparison with authors of opposing views. Through their encounters with their field projects, our students are led to wrestle with the possibility of a meaningfulness to human life that transcends limited paradigms of human purpose. In any case, the faculty plays a key role in the way that it guides the student's reflections. The crisis of a paradigm opens up untapped dimensions of human personality—the dimensions where grace operates. Yet such breakdowns can be frightening, and students cannot be pushed or given easy substitutes for difficult answers. Hence, there is a need for intellectual dialogue and prayer—for the means of a continuous conversion—among the faculty members themselves, in order to deepen their own appropriations of the unlimited paradigm and gradually to root out vestiges of limited paradigms.

One particularly striking example of the problem faced by justice educators was related to me by a priest friend who is involved in spiritual direction. A young woman came to him who is a manager in a computer firm. She volunteered her time to certain social service projects most generously. Yet she was deeply troubled because, although she loved her work, she couldn't see how it could be contributing to God's work of justice and love. Is the production of computers an act of love? Is it just? Could it be? Are we to say that justice and love have nothing to do with such work? If so, are we not operating out of some limited rather than unlimited paradigm of justice and love?

If our paradigms are dependent upon overt manifestations of suffering and oppression, does this mean that justice and love themselves are contingent, that they would cease to be possible in a world free of suffering?[10] These are questions that the faculty in the PULSE Program and those engaged in service learning in general need to debate among themselves if they are going to be of genuine service to their students.

Notes

1. See Max Weber, "Science as a Vocation," in H. H. Gerth and C. Wright Mills, eds., *From Max Weber: Essays in Sociology* (New York: Oxford University Press, 1946), 129–56. The debate over whether theory or practice is the

highest form of human life, however, traces back to Plato and Aristotle, especially *Nicomachean Ethics*, x. 7–8.

2. Thomas S. Kuhn, *The Structure of Scientific Revolutions*, 2nd ed. (Chicago: University of Chicago Press, 1970). The debate sparked by Kuhn is well presented in two volumes: I. Lakatos and A. Musgrave, eds., *Criticism and the Growth of Knowledge* (Cambridge: Cambridge University Press, 1970); and F. Suppe, ed., *The Structure of Scientific Theories*, 2nd ed. (Urbana: University of Illinois Press, 1977). For Kuhn's broad influence, see, for example, the numerous listings under "Kuhn, Thomas S." in any recent edition of the *Social Science Citation Index*.

3. See Robert Bellah et al., *Habits of the Heart* (Berkeley: University of California Press, 1985), esp. chs. 4 and 5, and Allan Bloom, *Love and Friendship* (New York: Simon & Schuster, 1993).

4. See Jane E. Zimmermann, "Journals: Diaries for Growth," *Synergist*, 10, 2 (1981): 46–51.

5. Jean-Jacques Rousseau, *Discourse Concerning the Origins of Inequality* (1974).

6. See Jane Jacobs, *Death and Life of Great American Cities* (New York: Modern Library, 1993).

7. Max Scheler, *Ressentiment* (New York: Schocken, 1961).

8. See Robert Coles, *The Call of Service* (Boston: Houghton Mifflin, 1993) and its companion, Robert Coles, *The Call of Stories* (Boston: Houghton Mifflin, 1989).

9. Clearly the distinction between limited and unlimited paradigms is a complex question, which cannot be adequately treated in the present context. Kuhn himself has no adequate way of conceiving of such a distinction. Bernard Lonergan, however, has suggested ways of speaking about conversion, in a nonrelativistic fashion, as intrinsically related to a manner of knowledge-seeking that is unlimited and unrestricted. See Bernard Lonergan, *Method in Theology* (New York: Herder and Herder, 1972), pp. 104–24, 237–44, 251–53, 267–71.

10. For a theoretical treatment of these issues, see my "Ressentiment and the Preferential Option for the Poor," *Theological Studies* 54 (1993): 213–71.

University–Community Collaborations: Shaping the Vision of Catholic Higher Education

Karen Caldwell, Mary Domhidy,
Sharon Homan, and Michael J. Garazini, S.J. *

The new-found priority on collaboration—on the linking of education, health, social services, and other supports that children and communities need—is one of the most significant developments for the well-being of children and families in the United States at this time. Recent federal legislation creating empowerment zones and enterprise communities calls upon communities to develop comprehensive, locally determined strategies for creating healthy communities in which families can flourish.

In recognition of the rich resources urban universities can bring to bear on the problems of the communities surrounding them, the Urban Community Service Program was developed by the United States Department of Education. Such efforts reciprocally shape not only the community but also higher educational institutions that are engaged in collaborative efforts with the community. Catholic institutions have unique contributions to make in these collaborative processes because their explicitly value-centered education provides a tradition within which to engage the challenges of collaboration.

Neighbor-to-Neighbor illustrates such a collaborative effort. Building on previously developed partnerships, nine departments at Saint Louis University and three community organizations in the midtown St. Louis

*Karen Caldwell is assistant professor of counseling and therapy at Saint Louis University, St. Louis, Missouri. Mary Domhidy is associate dean of the School of Professional Studies and associate professor of public policy studies at Saint Louis University. Sharon Homan is associate professor of health instruction at Saint Louis University. Michael J. Garazini, S.J., is Academic Vice President at Saint Louis University. This article first appeared in *Current Issues in Catholic Higher Education* 16(2) (spring 1997): 63–71.

The tension between theoretical reflection and practice has been evidenced in the history of Saint Louis University. Saint Louis University came to its present location, then the outskirts of St. Louis, in 1888. The University shared the boom, decline, and redevelopment of the midtown area. In the 1960s leaders chose to stay in midtown rather than move to a West County location.

Paul Reinert, S.J., was president of the University at the time, and he had developed his philosophy of higher education during his study at the University of Chicago.[5] Robert Maynard Hutchins, the president of that institution from 1929 to 1945, served as spokesman for a philosophy of higher education that posited a radical opposition between the search for truth on the one hand and scientific research and social action on the other. This view of the university has had enormous influence on the culture of those institutions where graduate education and research have been prized and cultivated.

One negative effect of Hutchins's views has been the suspicion of many within the university that utility and service are at odds with liberal learning. At minimum we can say that there remains a tension between the search for truth, regardless of its utility, and a desire to prepare people for service and to provide the wider community with scientific knowledge and insight.

Father Reinert was shaped not only by the high standards of the University of Chicago but also by the experiences of seeing the University of Chicago respond with increasing isolation to the changes in its surrounding neighborhood. His biographer writes that "the process of deliberate isolation, and the inevitable hostile reaction of the community to an educational institution that seemed to want to have nothing to do with it, convinced Father Reinert that the university was continuing in its failure to fulfill a major obligation to society."[6] Having decided on the importance of the "university as servant," Father Reinert could face the tensions inherent in the decision he made during his tenure as president that the University stay in its midtown location.

This tension was most noticeable when the University actively took on the role of developer in the 1970s as part of the New Town in Town redevelopment. Unlike other planned new communities in suburban areas, New Town in Town targeted existing neighborhoods in urban areas. On the one hand, the University is a significant stabilizing presence, and on the other residents express concern about the University's expansion and displacement of neighborhoods. President Lawrence Biondi, S.J., has more recently invested in the beautification of the campus, and there have been collaborations with neighboring Harris Stowe State College in the development of the area east of the University.

Mutuality, Capacity, and Resilience

How, then, do we build just relationships among university and community participants? The very asking of such a question illustrates the explicit value dimension of the education process. Neighbor-to-Neighbor builds on the premise that the University and the community are interdependent and our relationships are best built on a sense of mutuality. This mutuality involves not only a sense of being understood and valued but also of sharing and being with another. Only recently, and then in limited numbers, have urban universities taken to heart the injunction that the plight of those around them is their own plight. While Jesuit colleges and universities have been exceptions to the trend to seclude campuses from the "world outside," many other urban institutions have preferred to see the city and its inhabitants as sources of possible harm rather than as potential resources for both academic and social pursuits of the faculty, students, and staff.

Our misunderstandings of one another, our ingrained prejudices, our suspicions cannot be glossed over or easily set aside without real struggle. We need to recognize that we are divided by class, by race, by opportunity, and by the perception of opportunity. We are divided by a belief of some within the academy that the wider community, especially the poor, will distract us from our essential purpose. Some feel the university ought to be cautious about entanglement with problems beyond its immediate borders, saying that these are the province of government and social agencies.

One of the guiding philosophies of Neighbor-to-Neighbor has been the Capacity-Focused Alternative Model for Developing Community Capacity devised by John McKnight and John Kretzmann of the Center for Urban Affairs and Policy Research at Northwestern University.[7] This model advocates an approach to addressing community needs by developing policies and activities based on the capacities, skills, and assets of low-income people and their neighborhoods. Historic evidence indicates that significant community development takes place only when local people are committed to investing themselves and their resources in the effort.

This emphasis on capacity and mutuality has involved a revision of Jesuit education, which, as also is the case in other religious orders, was sometimes marked by types of paternalism where the educated believed that they knew what was best for service recipients. All that service recipients had to do was to be compliant with the service providers and their social experiments. The poor and the marginalized were seen as social projects and the objects of research.

Neighbor-to-Neighbor, on the other hand, involves a methodological revisioning and reformulation. We can no longer see persons as the objects of our inquiry or as compliant recipients of services.

Early in the process of collaboration, neighborhood representatives made it clear that they were not interested in being used as research subjects by University scholars. They had been involved in other research-driven projects that one community representative referred to as "taking from the community and not giving anything back." Another community group had been very vocal that they did not want their children used as "guinea pigs." Instead, members of the community wanted long-term relationships with the University as a resource to the community, with the community serving as a resource to the University. The collaborative focus of Neighbor-to-Neighbor has meant heeding the invitation of one of the community representatives to "leave all those ideas you have about who we are and come down and be yourself. Be one of us. You're not better than us and we're not better than you."

To do so requires that we see and encounter others in the mutuality of our personhood, or our intersubjectivity. We are persons with stories, hopes, wishes, fears, dreams, knowledge, and wisdom. Indeed, the entire collaborative experience can be described as "multistoried," an experience in which many different narratives develop about what we are doing because of differences in disciplinary backgrounds, personality, and position in the University or community. In our collaboration we are called to be agents of transformation with and for one another. This collaborative spirit is expressed by people in the community telling their stories and articulating what they believe will make their lives fuller and more substantial. This requires that those who operate out of the educational community listen to the narratives of other communities as they speak from the authority of their experience. And the community must also listen to researchers who seek to bring critical acumen to asking questions and offering possible responses.

Some of the most powerful lessons the university can learn from the community are the lessons of resilience in the face of difficulties. Many of those in the community we collectively serve are models of strength of character and personal conviction and commitment. Through Neighbor-to-Neighbor, we are able to work with many leaders in the wider community whose personal resources are their chief asset, and we have a great deal to learn from them.

Research in the field of psychotherapy with survivors of dysfunctional homes provides clues to what the personal resources and strategies are in those who experience debilitating circumstances, have few of the advantages that most enjoy, and yet continue to carry on.[8] Children from debilitating backgrounds are not "invulnerable" to the influence of negative parenting and unhealthy surroundings, as earlier researchers thought. They are affected in serious ways—in terms of physical, psychological, and spiritual health. But, at the same time, they do more than survive. We call these children resilient because they are able to muster the courage and insight to overcome both terrible conditions and the constant message that they will amount to no more than the people who surround them. They learn to take their cues for who and what they are from positive forces that they locate themselves.

What we know of resilient people can be descriptive of many of the individuals and organizations we encounter in our neighboring communities. They have learned to locate allies outside their immediate family and circle of friends who can assist them in achieving their goals, and they build their self-esteem by little successes, beginning with the areas of their lives they can control. They have learned to work at relationship-building, seeking out healthy people and working to stay connected, and they take initiative in problem-solving, taking pleasure in finding solutions to difficult dilemmas.

Resilient people also are creative and have a strong sense of humor. If creativity is the art of making something out of nothing, then humor is the art of making nothing out of something. One small example of this kind of creative problem-solving was shown by a nine-year-old child at the elementary school that is one of the community sites for Neighbor-to-Neighbor. She came to school having completed her math homework on paper towels because there was no other kind of paper in her home. The school staff members praised her resourcefulness and her commitment to learning became a source of inspiration for many involved in the project from the community and the University.

Interprofessional Work

Concern for just relationships extends to concern for just and appropriate strategies to address issues raised by collaborative members. These concrete, real-world problems encourage genuine interprofessional cooperation. The social problems of our urban communities are complex, deeply rooted, interdependent phenomena that force us to think and require holistic strategies and support mechanisms. Collaborations between communities and the various disciplines of the academy are required. Yet collaborations, according to Groark and McCall, "require talented and competent contributors who work together with mutual trust and respect toward a common goal, sacrificing in the process considerable independence, personal control, and personal recognition."[9] These requirements go against the typical training of researchers who are taught to work independently, maintain control, and achieve in a context that rewards individual efforts.

A number of authors have noted that departmental and disciplinary divisions have served to increase the isolation of universities from the community. A 1982 report from the Center for Educational Research and Innovation pithily noted that "communities have problems, universities have departments."[10] Lawson and Hooper-Briar refer to the "culture of professionalism" that results in each profession becoming more insular, concerned with its status as a specialized, separate arena of knowledge and skills."[11] Each helping field has sought autonomy by claiming a unique body of scientific and scholarly knowledge to be used in defining problems and proposing solutions. Yet most of the pressing questions of society do not fit nicely into single disciplines. Questions relating to the alleviation of poverty, support of children's development, and reduction of violence do not belong to single disciplines. Interprofessional education is needed to emphasize the common denominators of vision, mission, knowledge, language, values, norms, and skills for all the professions dedicated to relieving pressing urban problems.

Interprofessional education is more than preparing students to perform more than one role. Rather, it involves making the professors aware of their interdependence in order to increase their effectiveness as they function together to serve the larger community of which the university is a part. If university faculty do not model collaborative attitudes and behaviors, it is unlikely that future providers will understand the importance of such coordination or be prepared to function in emerging systems that are community-based and empowerment-oriented.

Fostering independence is challenging. The process can leave us vulnerable to feeling misunderstood, threatened, or confused. Our conceptual and experiential maps tune us into different landmarks and sometimes make conversations about our next step slow and cumbersome.

Conclusions

University–community partnerships can redirect our understanding of the university's mission by emphasizing service to the community. One of the fundamental ways we serve both students and the wider community is through our teaching and through the production of liberally educated leaders and participants. Our first duty is to prepare individuals to participate in their communities with insight and sensitivity, to instill in them habits of leadership and service.

Community-university partnerships bring us face to face with the ethical issues our communities face, challenge us to sharpen our critical problem-solving skills, test our theories, stretch our interpersonal and communication skills, and refine our insights into what it means to be a university committed to service for others for the greater honor and glory of God. For those of us within the academy, there is a desperate need for a fresh look at the role of the university in the lives of citizens both within and outside our immediate borders. There is need of a fresh vision for how we might pool personal and community resources to assist all of us in advancing the health and well-being of every citizen, especially the most vulnerable. Community-university collaborations are one avenue for generating just such a vision through the practice of a praxis methodology, through the building of relationships with the community based on mutuality, and through interprofessional work.

Notes

1. David J. O'Brien, *From the Heart of the American Church: Catholic Higher Education and American Culture* (Maryknoll, NY: Orbis Books, 1994), 110.
2. D. Kolb, "Learning Styles and Disciplinary Differences," in Arthur W. Chickering, ed., *The Modern American College: Responding to the New Realities of Diverse Students and a Changing Society* (San Francisco: Jossey-Bass, 1981), 232–55.
3. Cornel West, *The American Evasion of Philosophy: A Genealogy of Pragmatism* (Madison: University of Wisconsin Press, 1989), 201.
4. Patrick H. Byrne, "Paradigms of Justice and Love," *Conversations* (spring 1995): 5–17.
5. Paul C. Reinert and Paul Shore, *Seasons of Change: Reflections on a Half Century at Saint Louis University* (St. Louis: Saint Louis University Press, 1996).
6. Ibid., 8.
7. John McKnight and John Kretzmann, *Managing Community Capacity. Report of the Neighborhood Innovations Network* (Evanston, IL: Center for Urban Affairs and Policy Research, Northwestern University, 1990).
8. Steven J. Wolin and Sybil Wolin, *The Resilient Self: How Survivors of Troubled Families Rise above Adversity* (New York: Villard Books, 1993).
9. Christina Groark and Robert McCall, "Building Successful University-Community Human Service Agency Collaborations," in C. B. Fisher, J. P.

Murray, and I. E. Sigel, eds., *Applied Development Science: Graduate Training for Diverse Disciplines and Education Settings* (Norwood, NJ: Ablex Publishing Co., 1996), 237–51.

10. Center for Educational Research and Innovation, *The University and the Community: The Problems of Changing Relationships* (Paris: Organization for Economic Cooperation and Development, 1982), 127.

11. Hal Lawson and K. Hooper-Briar, *Expanding Partnerships: Involving Colleges and Universities in Interprofessional Collaboration and Service Integration* (Oxford, OH: Danforth Foundation and the Institute for Educational Renewal at Miami University, 1994).

Measuring Moral Development:
A College-Wide Strategy

Margaret G. Kender*

A major objective of the third Ten-Year Plan of Allentown College of St. Francis de Sales was to develop greater social awareness and heightened moral consciousness among students. In 1986 Daniel Gambet, O.S.F.S., the College president, asked the chaplain and the vice president for student affairs to design a College-wide plan for spiritual growth and moral development. This essay summarizes the methodology of the project, lists its key recommendations, and assesses its impact on the College community ten years later. Other Catholic colleges and universities may profit from the strategies it uses.

Allentown College is a young institution. Founded by the Oblates of St. Francis de Sales in 1965 and located in Pennsylvania's LehighValley, it enrolls 1,400 young men and women in a program that brings together career-oriented majors and a strong liberal arts core. The Christian humanist philosophy reflected in the writings of Francis de Sales, its patron, is central to the College mission. His spirituality was optimistic and expansive, centered on the innate capacity of humans to love. He insisted that the ordinary person has the potential for doing great good, for leading a life of transcendent meaning while centered squarely in the world. The College Planning Committee believed that it was important to implement strategies that would actively promote this and other relevant aspects of the institution's mission.

While the notion of Catholic identity had not assumed its current strategic importance when this project began, voices critical of higher educa-

*Margaret Kender is vice president emeritus of student affairs at Allentown College of St. Francis de Sales, Allentown, Pennsylvania.

tion and its ability to prepare undergraduates to fill the growing need of a troubled society were being heard. By the beginning of the 1990s, reports like that of the Wingspread Group on Higher Education challenged institutions to assure that "next year's emerging students will graduate as individuals of character, more sensitive to the needs of the community, more competent to contribute to society, and more civil in habits of speech, thought and action."[1]

Method

A committee of eight—the two administrators, three faculty, and two student leaders—invited Paul Philibert, O.P., to join them as a consultant for the early stages of the project. Father Philibert was at that time associate professor of religion and research and an associate of the Center for the Study of Youth Development at Catholic University of America. He began by defining moral development as a movement within psychology and education that seeks the evolution of the natural capacities of each person. He presented a history of the moral development movement, reviewing the important cognitive approaches of Piaget and Kohlberg, and emphasized what was at that time a growing trend toward viewing the subject in a more holistic way.

Philibert asked committee members to write their own priorities for moral development at Allentown College and to share their thoughts in a round-robin response session. Specifically, each person was asked to think in terms of "what we need more of" and to list those perceived needs in priority order. Responses covered a wide span of concerns, but after some lively discussion, the following themes emerged:

- Students need to develop a heightened moral sensitivity, a greater ability to take a hard look at personal and social issues, and a willingness to stand up for what they believe to be important.
- All members of the community should feel a greater sense of affiliation and involvement.
- The faculty and administrative staff should explore ways in which the College's values, as articulated in its mission statement and other documents can be integrated into the curriculum and the entire fabric of campus life.

As a result of this discussion Father Philibert recommended that the Moral and Spiritual Development Project should next seek community-wide agreement on a fundamental list of values that the curriculum should try to achieve. The committee determined on four categories for curriculum design: goals for the self, for personal relations, for civil society, and for relations to the Church. These goals were to affirm a holistic rather than strictly cognitive approach to moral development; they were also to recognize the needs and opinions of students, faculty and professional staff.

This step required creation of an instrument that would probe the priorities of all three groups in order to agree on a fundamental list of values that the curriculum and co-curriculum should strive to achieve. Philibert agreed to develop an instrument for this purpose; this became the project's chief assessment tool, The Academic and Community Values Inventory (ACVI).[2] During the following semester he interviewed faculty and student leaders to determine their priorities for personal development, attitudes toward the College, and levels of satisfaction. Using that information as well as value statements from College documents and publications, he drafted an instrument that was pre-tested, revised, and finally distributed to a random sample of 151 faculty, staff, and students. Using a five-point scale ranging from greatest importance (5) to no importance (1), it asked respondents to acknowledge the relative importance of fifty-two value statements.

Results were more than encouraging. An average value of 4.00 or better was reported for thirty-three of the fifty-two goals listed in the inventory. In addition, there was overwhelming agreement from all constituencies on eight goals, which are marked (with an asterisk) on the complete survey values list that follows:

Survey Values List

Allentown College ought to teach toward and otherwise support and develop:

1. *Confident mastery of basic communication skills, including reading, writing, speaking, and listening.
2. Mastery of information and skills needed for adult social interaction.
3. *Mastery of the foundations in a chosen field of academic or professional specialization.
4. The ability to understand and interpret numerical data and symbols.
5. Word processing and computer literacy skills.

6. Familiarity with the history, art, music, and the personalities of Western civilization.
7. *Ability to think independently, logically, critically, and creatively.
8. Familiarity with the history, methodology and current state of the art of one of the physical sciences.
9. Familiarity with the history, methodology, and practice of some branch of the social sciences.
10. Familiarity with the Bible, its principal narratives, its sources, and its religious teachings.
11. A recognition of the cultural and humanistic dimensions of religion.
12. Knowledge of the Christian gospel.
13. A familiarity with contemporary Roman Catholic theology.
14. Capacity to evaluate popular cultural values in the light of Christian values.
15. An orientation toward career or life's work based on an ideal of service or ministry to the human family.
16. A rich and varied experience of religious rituals and symbols.
17. An appreciation for the dignity of non-Catholic religious traditions, including non-Christian religious literature and values.
18. A coherent knowledge of and respect for principles of Catholic doctrine and morality.
19. A sensitive commitment to academic freedom out of respect for differences in philosophic and religious traditions.
20. Shared experiences of faith in action through works of service, compassion, and celebration.
21. A respect and appreciation for the natural world and its ecology.
22. Ability to understand, appreciate, and function effectively in social institutions.
23. An informed Christian conscience, especially as related to the ethical problems of one's chosen field.
24. Integration of knowledge from the various disciplines of study.
25. A disposition toward lifelong learning.
26. Personal responsibility for health and physical fitness through good nutrition and exercise.
27. An orientation toward satisfying group activities in sports, committee work, and social life.
28. A recognition of one's particular capacities for leadership and social initiatives.
29. *A personal sense of self-worth and self-confidence.
30. Commitment to a definite, personally chosen frame of values.
31. An awareness of and respect for mystery and the depth of human experiences of love, awe, and beauty.

32. The importance of a peer network for mutual help, growth, and enjoyment.
33. A growing respect for individual differences.
34. *A capacity to stand up for values against contrary pressures.
35. Coherence between one's social network of relationships and one's life values.
36. *Capacity for loving relationships, trustworthiness, and loyalty.
37. Understanding of and respect for law.
38. Capacity and taste for work.
39. Concern for fairness emerging from a personally felt vision of justice.
40. An international or global vision of the moral, political, and economic orders.
41. Involvement in the College community with a sense of belonging.
42. A capacity to communicate personal thoughts and feelings.
43. Responsible and reflective attitudes toward student life—sharing in the stewardship of the common good.
44. Awareness and recognition of significant transition in personal feelings, attitudes, and values as a function of human development across the college years.
45. An environment of trust within the context of a definite Christian and Salesian tradition.
46. Explicit recognition of the dimensions of responsibility and morality in all areas of academic and community life: a sensitivity to the moral domain as it touches everyday experience.
47. Increased access to faculty-student and administration-student social interaction.
48. Life experiences related to one's chosen field through work, internships, supervised apprenticeship or the like.
49. *An experience of Jesus as God and friend.
50. Social, intellectual, professional, and religious synthesis through both classroom and extra-curricular reflection and integration.
51. A readiness to seek a helping relationship when appropriate, whether for psychological or academic counseling, moral guidance, career exploration, or the like.
52. *Awareness of a need to grow spiritually throughout life.

The data revealed comparisons by groups consisting of faculty, professional staff, and students, and by academic major of students. Results were instructive—and in some cases predictable. For instance, students scored the highest average value among groups for values relating to the person's level of socialization and sense of community. Faculty gave the highest average value to items centering on academic achievement and learning. Professional staff responses were closer to student responses than were faculty responses.

Members of the committee were very pleased with the degree of affirmation and consensus revealed by the data. However, they felt it important to broaden the base of the study. A Survey of Religious Beliefs, Attitudes, and Practices created by Michael Donovan, O.S.F.S., the College chaplain, had been given to seniors over a four-year period.[3] The committee decided to compare those survey results with data from national surveys conducted by the Gallup Organization and *U.S. Catholic* magazine[4] and with two questions from The College Student Experiences Questionnaire, which was administered in 1988, 1989, and 1990. A final phase would involve a series of interviews with seventeen students, all of them active in the life of the College.

The Survey of Religious Beliefs, Attitudes, and Practices revealed a gradual decline in those beliefs and attitudes characterized as Catholic and a decline as well in faith practices in classes from 1987 through 1990. However, on average the responses of Allentown College seniors to items like the importance of personal prayer, regular Mass attendance, and living together before marriage were comparable to those reported on the *U.S. Catholic* and Gallup surveys. On some issues, such as abortion and the importance of religion in their lives, seniors revealed attitudes that were much more in line with Catholic teaching.

The CSEQ asked students to estimate their gains in two areas: developing your own values and ethical standards and understanding yourself—your abilities, interests, and personality. In both areas gains reported by seniors were higher than those reported by freshmen to a statistically significant degree.

Finally, four groups of students were asked to respond to two questions:

- If we as a College were to be successful in implementing a College-wide plan for spiritual growth and moral development, what would success look like?
- What kinds of changes would need to take place in order to bring about the success model you have just described?

The last exercise was in many respects the most revealing. But the time had come to review all the data. This task fell to the chaplain and the student affairs officer, who formulated conclusions and recommendations. The committee then discussed and approved their report, which was sent to the President and the College Planning Committee. A summary of the report follows.

Program Conclusions

- Relatedness is key to moral growth and development.
- Students seek spiritual growth through communities of friends and respected adults who demonstrate openness to their concerns.
- They feel a strong need to be affirmed.
- They feel that many friends seek affirmation in unhealthy ways, and they hope that the College can help with this problem.
- Their commitments to other persons are limited but loyal, and they are easily deflated when commitments fail them.
- They expect that they will be permitted to grow as persons and are angry when they feel that their freedom to grow (and make mistakes) is seriously limited.
- They feel impeded by the social forces around them and believe that it will be difficult to change the attitudes of their peers.
- Many have a sense of powerlessness about their ability to discipline themselves in ways that will help them move away from unhealthy relationships.

Recommendations

The College should:

- Continue to maintain a core group of faculty and staff who know the Catholic and Oblate traditions and who will play an active role in the orientation of new professionals.
- Make trust-building a conscious process.
- Give fiscal priority to building renovations that will enhance a sense of community.
- Weave campus ministry activities into student leadership expectations.
- Extend opportunities for team-building weekends and include a spiritual component in each.
- Consider adding or revising cultural symbols on campus as statements of core values.
- Increase hall funding for moral education programming efforts.
- Emphasize community service activities among all student groups.
- Use the values identified in the ACVI as the cornerstone of student development at the College.

Outcomes

Allentown College is a very different place today than it was in 1987, and the moral development project has played only one small part in the institution's evolution. However, in the years since the recommendations were accepted by various constituencies, many new emphases, curricular adjustments, physical plant initiatives, and programs have been put in place as a direct result of the project. Some representative examples follow.

- The faculty introduced values seminars for juniors and seniors based on topics that speak to central issues in the moral life of young adults and of society in general. For instance, Theology 478, Body Talk, considers the contemporary cult of the body with its emphasis on youth, beauty, and perfection. It explores the Christian vision of the body, which serves as a reference for treating such themes as health, sexuality, and wholeness. Other seminar topics include the world of evil, the feminine, friendship, love and sexuality, and alcohol.
- Community service is now connected to membership in student organizations as an expectation for membership, and resulting service hours have increased dramatically.
- Introduction to Philosophy has added a strong debate component.
- A nationally recognized faculty artist, Michael McGrath, O.S.F.S., was commissioned to paint murals for the reception area in two freshman halls. The paintings represent two gospel messages that speak to the modern concerns of youth.
- The Ethical Leadership Series, inaugurated in 1987, has been presented to more than 300 students. Outstanding faculty, staff, and alumni are presenters. Each session centers on a different leadership topic and concludes by setting an ethical problem for consideration.
- Two freshman residence halls have undergone a $2.6 million refurbishing project designed to heighten a community living atmosphere. Incidents of vandalism have decreased dramatically.
- During the 1995–96 academic year, every major College constituency engaged in the Rites of Passage study recommended by the Commission on Substance Abuse at Colleges and Universities. The College held a major student coordinated symposium, and an educational component was added to the College's standard disciplinary protocol for alcohol violations.
- Attendance has increased at off-campus retreats, and the chaplain has formalized community service in spring break trips for work

with Habitat for Humanity in the U.S. and with Oblate missions in Mexico.

- Student activities awards are presented along with academic honors awards at the annual Honors Convocation to symbolize the seamless nature of the College learning community.
- The director of the Counseling Center teaches Self-Development, a course enrolling freshmen that requires students to undertake a personal improvement project, a self-selected topic recorded in a weekly journal that centers on a personal issue of importance to the student.
- The Health Center has developed an AIDS brochure that provides explicit information and also places that information within the context of Catholic teaching on the subject of human sexuality and our obligations as a society to those who suffer from AIDS.

If this project were begun today, many things would look very different, of course. Some of the values listed in the ACVI, such as computer literacy, are quite minimal compared to current expectations. A significantly larger student body, an increase in major program offerings, and the addition of two new buildings have changed the nature of the institution. It is probably time to begin again—an observation that only emphasizes the fact that a study of this kind must be based on each institution's character as defined in its critical documents and affirmed by its students, faculty, and staff. The methodology can be copied, but the values themselves must arise from the specific institution.

The College-Wide Plan for Spiritual Growth and Moral Development has had a deep and lasting impact on Allentown College. It caused faculty and professional staff to resurrect and reconsider issues associated with the institution's Catholic and Oblate tradition quite some time before the term *Catholic identity* became a national watchword. Its successful implementation as defined by measurable outcomes guarantees its revision and renewal as Allentown College prepares for its transition to the new century.

Notes

1. William Brock, "The Wingspread Group on Higher Education Report," Associated Press (December 6, 1993).
2. Paul Philibert, O.P., "Academic and Community Values Inventory" (unpublished survey instrument prepared for Allentown College of St. Francis de Sales, 1986).

3. Michael Donovan, O.S.F.S., "Survey of Religious Beliefs, Attitudes and Practices" (unpublished survey for Allentown College of St. Francis de Sales, 1986).
4. James Breig, "The Young and the Restless: What Catholic Teens Think About Their Church," *U.S. Catholic*, vol. 53, no. 12 (December 1988), 6–15.

Meeting Religious Diversity in a Catholic College

Joan Penzenstadler *

Truly, my life is one long hearkening unto my self and unto others, unto God. And if I say that I hearken, it is really God who hearkens inside me. The most essential and the deepest in me hearkening unto the most essential and deepest in the other. God to God.[1]

A task of religious education, perhaps the most fundamental task, is to cultivate "hearkening." What is it in listeners that religious educators appeal to in order to attune them to "the music heard so deeply that," as T.S. Eliot remarks, "it is not heard at all"?[2] What forms do we employ that would encourage this music to vibrate into full consciousness?

Many of us teach in colleges or universities grounded in a specific religious tradition, and this fact adds another dimension to the questions just raised. The mission statement of my institution, for example, begins: "Mount Mary College is a Catholic college for women. In the tradition of the School Sisters of Notre Dame, the College provides an environment that promotes intellectual, personal and spiritual development. . . ." But ours is an educational milieu, not unlike many other religiously affiliated colleges, where 50 percent of the students are not Catholic and where exposure to any faith tradition ranges from rich to rigid to spotty to nonexistent. How does one educate religiously, honoring the mission on which the school was founded?

*Joan Penzenstadler, S.S.N.D., is chair of the Department of Theology and Religious Education at Mount Mary College in Milwaukee, Wisconsin. This article is reprinted from *Religious Education* 91(3) (summer 1996): 382–95 with the permission of the Religious Education Association, 222 East Lake Drive, Decatur, Georgia 30030.

Reflecting on certain characteristics inherent within the Catholic tradition, I will explore how religious education can provide a forum where the human drive to know and the religious dynamism that stretches toward fulfillment develop in integration with each other. This means that the work of a Catholic college can never simply be knowledge for its own sake. There is an underlying conviction that authentic knowing is inextricably melded to valuing what is known, and thus desiring to be in union with what is of value.

Education communicates self-transcending meaning and value by creating a space where fidelity to the pure and unrestricted desire to know is practiced and where students learn to affirm and appreciate the Creator-given capacity to know and to love. The religious element is that which prevents the process from closing in on itself. It is the questioning, the pondering, the wondering that continues to call us to something more as it deabsolutizes the images we construct in our search for ultimate meaning. It is the commitment to remain open to the restlessness that questions bring and that will never totally be stilled until we rest in the Mystery of Infinite Understanding Love.

To what do religious educators appeal within their students? The entry point that allows all students admittance, regardless of their religious backgrounds, is one that helps them become attuned to their own experience. In *Insight: A Study of Human Understanding*, Bernard Lonergan states: "Deep within us all, emergent when the noise of other appetites is stilled, there is a drive to know, to understand, to see why, to discover the reason, to find the cause, to explain."[3] This inherent desire is a drive we humans are experiencing continuously, and it is often a breath-catching delight when students become aware that it truly is a dynamic structure within them. Lest the above sound as if knowing is purely a mental activity, let me suggest that the motivating power undergirding this desire to know is love, our whole being stretching toward union with what is of value. The Benedictine author Sebastian Moore put it succinctly in conversation one day: "Desire is love waiting to happen."

Having tapped into our profound human longings, how do we connect these longings with a faith stance? Although content is a basic component in the process of educating in faith, it is shaped and remembered according to the forms through which it is communicated. If our concern for communicating an already-established content overrides the possibility of an attentiveness in students that brings forth further questions and a sense of wonder, then we have sacrificed the religious element in education. *How* something is taught shapes *what* is taught. The principles that form our educative practices play powerful roles in the transformation of persons.

Teaching through some of the foundational principles of the Catholic tradition can engage students from multifarious backgrounds. I will explore three characteristics of a Catholic faith stance that give rise to forms of teaching: the principle of sacramentality viewed as the mediation of the Transcendent through bodiliness; the juxtaposition of faith and reason, which demands rigorous intellectual endeavor leading to deeper realms of believing and valuing; and the value of unity in diversity, from which emerges a vision that is all-encompassing in its scope.

There are and will be faculty at Catholic institutions who do not share the college's undergirding faith stance. What is essential is that there be a significant number who do embody the finest of the faith tradition and that the college community create the space where serious conversation, from varying perspectives, constantly challenges and refines the articulations, decisions, and behaviors that govern the life of the community as a whole.[4]

Attending to the Sacramental Character of Life

The Catholic belief in the mediation of the Divine through finite reality stems from reflection on the person of Jesus Christ. Sacramentality in light of Jesus implies that God, the Source of all being and the Infinite Act of Understanding Love, is accessible to human beings while yet remaining Mystery. The Infinite indwells the finite. Thus, the mystery of Incarnation—God's self-disclosure in tangible, human bodiliness—serves as grounding for a perception of the physical world as the icon of Divine reality. I do not mean to suggest that Catholics have a monopoly on this way of perceiving, but I *am* saying that the sacramental view of creation is at the core of the Catholic Christian tradition and that taking this principle seriously calls for reverential ways of encountering all of creation.

The principle of sacramentality shapes the forms of our teaching and learning. A reverential way of attending to life in all its forms can provide a lens for deeper ways of seeing in any academic discipline, but the two I have chosen as examples are science, through the method of biologist Barbara McClintock, and theology, through the "Search for Meaning," a course required of all students at Mount Mary College.

Barbara McClintock, a remarkable scientist in the field of genetic biology, won the Nobel Prize for science in 1983. Her attentiveness to mystery in kernels of maize developed in her a relationality with the object of her attention that allowed her to see things that others passed by. Her attitude seems to parallel that of Evelyn Underhill, who counseled those wishing to practice contemplation in the Christian tradition: "Do not think, but as it were pour out your personality towards it [the object of attention]: let your soul be in your eyes."[5]

McClintock's implicitly sacramental outlook caused her to remark:

> I found that the more I worked with them [the chromosomes] the bigger and bigger [they] got, and when I was really working with them I wasn't outside, I was down there. I was part of the system. I was right down there with them, and everything got big. I even was able to see the internal parts of the chromosomes—actually everything that was there.[6]

Ever the rigorous scientist, McClintock was drawn into a reality greater than herself: "As you look at these things, they become part of you. And you forget yourself. The main thing about it is you forget yourself."[7] (ibid., 1983, 118).

Throughout history, poets, artists, and mystics have talked about the importance of an attentiveness that is free from all self-consciousness and that impels us to identify with what focuses our attention. Scientists also testify to the state of awareness that draws them to discovery. Einstein described it like this: "The state of feeling which makes one capable of such achievements is akin to that of the religious worshipper or of one who is in love."[8]

A sacramental attentiveness that places us into the Mystery beyond ourselves can be effective in any discipline, but theological studies provide an opportunity to probe the dynamics of divine mediation in more explicit ways. "The Search for Meaning" course, for example, offers readings from a variety of authors who have caught on to the dynamic structure that makes them most human. One of those readings in the theology component of the Search course is Viktor Frankl's *Man's Search for Meaning*. In the book, Frankl describes the importance of nature to the concentration camp victim:

> As the inner life of the prisoner tended to become more intense, he also experienced the beauty of art and nature as never before. . . . One evening, when we were already resting on the floor of our hut, dead tired, soup bowls in hand, a fellow prisoner rushed in and asked us to run out to the assembly grounds and see the wonderful sunset. Standing outside . . . after minutes of moving silence, one prisoner said to another, "How beautiful the world *could* be!"[9]

Focusing attention on this passage, we entertain questions that arise from a sacramental perspective: What would cause starving prisoners to forget their bowl of watered soup and gaze at a sunset? Who or what is speaking to them? What nourishes the human spirit? Questions like these can open whole new horizons for students.

Discussing Alice Walker's novel *The Color Purple*, students quite easily discern the mediation of God's presence to Celie through Shug. As Celie grows in awareness of the goodness of life and her ability to choose what she will make of her life, her less-than-adequate images of God are broken open to reveal a God of all-encompassing love and compassion. The sacramental quality of her search is capsulized in the greeting of her closing letter: "Dear God. Dear stars, dear trees, dear sky, dear peoples. Dear Everything. Dear God."[10]

Calling attention to the revelation of God's presence through the people and "stuff" of creation is a dominant theme in the Search for Meaning course. Perhaps this theme is more powerfully realized, however, in the student/teacher exchange than through the readings themselves. The reverence with which we meet one another, respect questions, and honor differing points of view speaks profoundly of how we view the hidden presence of God in the human, the infinite in the finite.

Viewing the world as sacrament, then, offers a form of teaching that resonates with the Catholic tradition. Becoming attuned to evidences of God's presence penetrating our world and revealing more-than-meets-the-eye is an activity of religious education. We pay attention with an attitude that is waiting to receive whatever is true. And we are motivated to this kind of attentiveness because of our fundamental affirmation of the sacredness of all being.

Relating Faith and Reason

If the purpose of our questioning, our reflecting, our deliberating is to know what there is to be known, that is, to know being, then a notion, an inkling, of what "being" is already dwells at the core of who we are. It is "the spark in our clod, our native orientation to the divine."[11] In other words, the exercise of our reason, our desire to understand, is grounded in an inkling, a hint, of our relatedness to being. Conversely, faith—this confidence in our relatedness to ultimate being—needs to be probed and stretched in light of our desire to know the truth.

The Christian tradition proclaims that the source of meaning and the fulfillment of our stretching to know the truth is revealed in Jesus. Brian Daley expresses this faith-stance: "Christian faith in the Incarnation of the Word is the intuition that order and purpose and intelligibility have been and can be discovered dawning within human history, despite the ambiguity and absurdity that constantly swirl around us."[12] At its best, the milieu of the Catholic college or university is one in which the drive toward understanding and the drive toward ultimacy coalesce.[13] It is not accidental that the Catholic tradition gave birth to the idea of the university in the thirteenth century.

The philosopher Simone Weil has caught the creative tension that exists between faith and reason, love and intelligence. After a profound experience of being in mystical union with God, she wrote in her spiritual autobiography:

> Yet I still half refused, not my love but my intelligence. For it seemed to me certain, and I still think so today, that one can never wrestle enough with God if one does so out of pure regard for the truth. Christ likes us to prefer truth to him, because, before being Christ, he is truth. If one turns aside from him to go toward the truth, one will not go far before falling into his arms.[14]

Weil articulates well the interplay between love of God and critical reflection, an interplay that is a hallmark of Catholic higher education.

It strikes me as a natural consequence of the relatedness of valuing and knowing in the Catholic tradition to take seriously the students' own thought processes and the effects that enhance or impede them. Part of our role as educators is to attune students to the various operations in their own knowing and to act as midwives in their appropriation of values. Many educational reforms today do call for an increased emphasis on values, moral education and citizenship training, but many of these reform programs continue to ignore what we understand by knowing, and thus too easily separate knowing from valuing, which reifies and fragments what is to be known.

The human desire to know in the Catholic perspective reaches its highest spontaneity when we fall in love with Infinite Understanding, that is, with God. But all along the way our yearning for completion, our desire, can be refined and purified in order to set the conditions for the realization of this love. Academic studies, no matter what the subject, can make a significant contribution to this process if the intent is to exercise the pure desire to know rather than merely to communicate an already-established body of knowledge.

This longing to know the truth that is undergirded by a fundamental belief in the ultimate intelligibility of the universe can again be seen through the work of Barbara McClintock. Her attention was poised on the project of her concern as she searched for the means to act, not so much upon what she as a scientist already knew, but upon what she did not yet know. What impelled her to continue was the desire to discover what an organism had to offer for her understanding rather than what meanings she could impose upon it. Perhaps that is why, when her colleagues were sometimes disconcerted by unexpected results in their research, she would continue to delight in the surprise of new data. McClintock remained host to complexity and confusion until she perceived a new organizing scheme that she was confident could be discovered. Her inner vision and her confidence involved the belief that the universe is inherently ordered by an Intelligibility that draws us more deeply into its mystery.

Her commitment to working in relationship with this orientation not only brought about sound contributions in the field of cytogenetics, but it also made her an authentic knower, for she continued to meet further questions. McClintock's biographer, Evelyn Fox Keller, often refers to the love and joy that were catalysts for McClintock's work. McClintock did not have to have answers to spur her on, but she did rely on "the joy of going at it. . . . You let the material tell you where to go, and it tells you at every step what the next has to be because you're integrating with an overall brand new pattern in mind."[15] McClintock's was a horizon implicitly converted to the ultimate good.

In a theology course, this horizon becomes more explicit. Wrestling with the roles of love and intelligence, faith and reason, in the "Search for Meaning" course, we reflect on such figures as Job and Thomas More. Throughout the *Book of Job* the main character grows more desperate in his heartfelt yearning *and* in his rage. His yearning stems from his faith in a God who is trustworthy and his rage arises from the betrayal that all the evidence logically points to. Class discussion revolves around such questions as: Would Job have been more faithful if he had kept silent, not questioned, and continued to believe in God the way he had always believed?

Many students (I would be less than honest to say all!) begin to see that Job's fidelity rests in his refusal to collapse the tension between his love and his intelligence. He will not capitulate to a system that reasons: I am suffering. Therefore, God must be punishing me because I did something sinful. Nor does he create a new system with himself as the focus: I am suffering and I am good. Therefore, there is no loving God. He continues to love even as he questions, and that is precisely what make his search so excruciating. And yet of all the characters in the poem, who meets God in the end? To what does Job ultimately surrender and why?

We also meet Thomas More, a sixteenth-century lawyer and one of the most intelligent men in all of England. He is imprisoned because of his personal convictions that arise from his belief and his love. His daughter tries to convince him to seek a reprieve by arguing that he has already done more than even God would reasonably expect. In the play *A Man for All Seasons*, More responds: "Well . . . finally . . . it isn't a matter of reason; finally it's a matter of love."[16] Pondering this faith-stance, I ask the students: Are reason and love compatible? How do you understand their relatedness? The Search for Meaning course never concludes with definitive answers, but the questions can reveal a relationship between knowing and loving that speaks to students even in an age of disbelief.

In conjunction with the questions put out for reflection, the very atmosphere we create in the classroom promotes or hinders the ability to think critically, to let go of perspectives that are no longer adequate, and to allow new insights to emerge. In a chapter titled "What Is a University?" John Henry Newman describes the educational milieu that promotes the search for truth:

> It is the place . . . in which the intellect may safely range and speculate, sure to find its equal in some antagonist activity, and its judge in the tribunal of truth. It is a place where inquiry is pushed forward, and discoveries verified and perfected, and rashness rendered innocuous, and error exposed, by the collision of mind with mind, and knowledge with knowledge.[17]

Although the images evoked by "antagonist activity" and "collision of mind with mind" do not seem compatible with the person's ability to "*safely* range and speculate," the point is there could not be such intellectual rigor unless the environment were safe instead of adversarial. Students are more likely to enter the crucible of commitment to knowing and loving the truth if the climate is one that invites *participation* in this self-transcending venture. There certainly will be disagreements, a divergence of perspectives, and times that demand detachment from ideas and meanings that can no longer be held intelligently. But it can prove detrimental to the learning process for students to leap into intellectual debate without first having established a basic trust in those with whom they will be engaged.

Thus, both faith and reason, valuing ultimate meaning and exercising intellectual rigor, engage students who are educated in the Catholic tradition. Not only can the courses we teach promote knowing and loving, but even the atmosphere in which learning takes place speaks of the values we believe to be fundamental to human living.

Working toward Inclusiveness

A third principle in the Catholic tradition, albeit one that has been grossly abused within the history of that tradition, is valuing unity in diversity. The very name "catholic" suggests a scope that is all-embracing. Welcoming those not considered part of the accepted system was one of Jesus's main activities in establishing God's reign.[18] All were accepted into the community of Jesus—outcasts, strangers, women, the grieving, the powerless, the persecuted. They were meaningful contributors to the vision of a community based on love, justice, and peace. From this principle of community that is inclusive flows a way of being, teaching, and learning.

The principle of inclusiveness is one of the reasons for Barbara Mc-Clintock's success in cytogenetics. She held a deep respect for individual difference and for the complexity of nature that exceeds the kind of reasoning that merely upholds the status quo. She explained her outlook to Evelyn Fox Keller: "The important thing is to develop the capacity to see one kernel [of maize] that is different and make that understandable. . . . If something doesn't fit, there's a reason, and you find out what it is."[19] She was concerned about an outlook too eager to place all data in neat categories, because she sensed this caused researchers to overlook difference, to "call it an exception, an aberration, a contaminant. . . . Right and left," she said, they miss "what is going on."[20] Even though her primary work was in cytogenetics, McClintock remained committed to an awareness of the organism as a whole, and she criticized others for focusing too rigidly on quantitative analysis.

McClintock's ability to see and to know were intrinsically bound together. Her understanding of organisms was so extraordinary because of the internal vision that shaped her perception. It was a vision that believed in an underlying unity amidst diversity. McClintock and other scientists more interested in the multiple and variegated forms of order in nature rather than in the set of laws to which nature ought to comply come to see nature as an active partner in discovery. This principle of inclusiveness, which is open to the different, the unusual, that-which-does-not-fit, is a vital component in teaching and learning not only in science but in every discipline—from art, to music, to math and philosophy.

The importance of not ignoring alien experiences and drawing all voices into conversation in the search for truth comes through in the "Search for Meaning" course. Students read *The Diaries of Etty Hillesum*, in which a young Jewish woman reckons with her plight in Amsterdam during the Hitler regime. As the Nazis are rounding up the Jews, Hillesum reflects:

> Living and dying, sorrow and joy, the blisters on my feet and the jasmine behind the house, the persecution, the unspeakable horrors—it is all one in me and I accept it all as one mighty whole and begin to grasp it better if only for myself, without being able to explain to anyone else how it all hangs together. I wish I could live for a long time so that one day I may know how to explain it, and if I am not granted that wish, well, then somebody else will perhaps do it, carry on from where my life has been cut short. And that is why I must try to live a good and faithful life to my last breath: so that those who come after me do not have to start all over again, need not face the same difficulties.[21]

What is the source of Hillesum's strength? What are the things that make life worth living for her? How would you explain "how it all hangs together"? The discussion that evolves among the students often breaks open dimensions of their own experience that they have ignored or discounted. Hillesum's account leads them to deeper understanding (if not appreciation) of the diverse aspects that make life whole.

Another person who stretches us to see the importance of inclusiveness in the human community is Martin Luther King, Jr. Reflecting on his "Letter from Birmingham City Jail," we are struck by his passion and his eloquence:

> Moreover, I am cognizant of the interrelatedness of all communities and states. I cannot sit idly by in Atlanta and not be concerned about what happens in Birmingham. Injustice anywhere is a threat to justice everywhere. We are caught in an inescapable network of mutuality, tied in a single garment of destiny. Whatever affects one directly affects all indirectly.[22]

Discussion can lead to a lively exchange when students contrast King's words with those of others they have so often heard: "Don't get involved. Mind your own business. Everyone should lead the kind of life he or she wants to; who am I to judge?" Are there any traits that lives authentically lived hold in common? Is conscience something that some people have and others don't? To what is King appealing in the human being when he says, "So we had no alternative except that of preparing for direct action, whereby we would present our very bodies as a means of laying our case before the conscience of the local and national community"?[23]

With readings such as the ones Hillesum and King give us, we can develop an awareness of our interconnectedness with all of life and of how essential it is to include all persons in the conversation that looks toward a just and truly human world.

As was mentioned above, the environment in which a course is taught gives strong messages regarding how safe it is for students to participate. Belenky and her associates have convincingly shown in *Women's Ways of Knowing* that "confirmation and community are prerequisites rather than consequences of development."[24] Teachers intent on developing an educational milieu of confirmation and collaboration do not focus on their own knowledge. This focus belongs to the lecturer. Though there are times when teachers do assume the role of lecturer, the primary concern is to draw the student into the conversation. Although the development of community and confirmation are certainly the ideal, confirmation rings hollow if it is not based in honest acknowledgement of the person's skills and desires. Nel Noddings makes this point clearly when she states, "It is not confirmation to pronounce someone better than he (she) is at something if he (she) has no inclination toward that something or cannot achieve the goals we expect of him (her)."[25]

Nevertheless, forms of teaching that flow from the desire to develop inclusiveness search out ways to help students connect with ideas that have not yet come to light and enhance the joy of learning together. Collaboration involves sharing and reflecting aloud, revealing to students our own thought processes and the further questions that are yet to be answered. "So long as teachers hide the imperfect processes of their thinking, allowing their students to glimpse only the polished products, students will remain convinced that only Einstein—or a professor—could think up a theory."[26]

When we seek to relay a sense of confirmation and collaboration to our students, we make it more probable that they will intensify their dynamism toward knowing and loving, because the environment is conducive to their wonder. A sense of wonder, the desire to entertain life's most basic questions—Who am I? What can I know? What is my place in this world? What is the most I can hope for? What ought I to do?—these fundamental questions within the core of education cannot be explored under the pressure of relentless need or fear. They arise when we are free to pause, to think, to ponder, and to ask questions.

Not all courses are geared to contemplating questions of depth, ultimacy, and meaning in human life, but any teacher can, in some way, structure courses to promote confirmation of the student as a knower and develop listening skills that invite the student into conversation with the subject matter.

Conclusion

This paper began with Etty Hillesum's reflection on the importance of "hearkening." Attuning students to the most profound and abiding rhythms in their lives is a challenge that is as imperative as it is daunting in an age of disbelief. Educating in the Catholic tradition offers openings to in-depth hearkening that can be accessible to students of diverse backgrounds. Teaching and learning with a sense of the world as sacrament, we may catch the vibrations of the Infinite within the finite. Grappling with the link between knowing and loving, we begin to realize that without loving our knowing is skewed, and without knowing, we cannot truly love. Committing ourselves to developing a community of scholars that honors the diversity each has to offer draws us into a wholeness and a sense of unity that our world so desperately needs. Through our efforts to educate in the Catholic tradition, we trust that the world can be changed through the transformation of persons.

Notes

1. E. Hillesum, *An Interrupted Life: The Diaries of Etty Hillesum 1941–1943,* trans. J. G. Gaarlandt (New York: Washington Square Press, 1985), 214.
2. T. S. Eliot, "The Dry Salvages," in *Four Quartets: Complete Poems and Plays* (New York: Harcourt, Brace and World, 1952), 136.
3. Bernard Lonergan, *Insight: A Study of Human Understanding* (San Francisco: Harper and Row, 1957), 4.
4. See B. Daley, "Christ and the Catholic University," *America* 169, 6 (1993): 6–14.
5. Evelyn Underhill, *Mysticism: A Study in the Nature and Development of Man's Spiritual Consciousness* (New York: New American Library, 1974), 301.
6. E. F. Keller, *A Feeling for the Organism: The Life and Work of Barbara McClintock* (New York: W. H. Freeman and Co., 1983), 117.
7. Ibid., 118.
8. Ibid.
9. Viktor Frankl, *Man's Search for Meaning* (New York: Pocket Books, 1972), 62–63.
10. Alice Walker, *The Color Purple* (New York: Washington Square Press, 1982), 249.
11. Bernard Lonergan, *Method in Theology* (New York: Seabury, 1972), 103.
12. Daley, "Christ and the Catholic University," 8.
13. See Michael Buckley, "The Catholic University and its Inherent Promise," *America* 168, 19 (1993).
14. Simone Weil, *Waiting for God,* trans. by Emma Craufurd (New York: G. P. Putnam's Sons, 1951), 69.
15. Keller, *A Feeling,* 33.
16. R. Bolt, *A Man for All Seasons* (New York: Random House, 1962), 81.
17. Quoted in F. Crowe, *Old Things and New: A Strategy for Education* (Atlanta: Scholars Press, 1985), 18.
18. See especially M. Borg, *Jesus a New Vision* (San Francisco: Harper San Francisco, 1987).
19. Evelyn Fox Keller, *Reflections on Gender and Science* (New Haven, CT: Yale University Press, 1985), 163.
20. Ibid.
21. Hillesum, *Diaries,* 161.
22. Martin Luther King, Jr., "Letter from Birmingham City Jail," in J. M. Washington, ed., *A Testament of Hope: The Essential Writings of Martin Luther King, Jr.* (San Francisco: Harper and Row, 1986).
23. Ibid.
24. M. F. Belenky, B. M. Clincy, N. R. Goldberger, and J. M. Tarule, *Women's*

Ways of Knowing: The Development of Self, Voice, and Mind (New York: Basic Books, 1986), 194.

25. Nel Noddings, *Caring: A Feminine Approach to Ethics and Moral Education* (Berkeley: University of California Press, 1984), 196.

26. Belenky et al., *Women's Ways of Knowing,* 215.

Behavior to Consciousness . . . A Paradigm Shift

*Paul Stark, S.J. **

A "text," the dictionary tells us, may be much more than a printed document or a manuscript. We may also define it as "a reference used as the starting point of a discussion." A text, then, is both precursor and guide to an action. We stand a good chance of succeeding in any action if our reference—our *text*—accurately reflects our circumstances and surroundings. Any "text" without a "context" is merely a "pretext."

Today, one of the central texts at most American universities is the system of ideas and programs broadly characterized as "student development." Understandably, student development efforts bear special weight at Catholic universities, which view the cultivation of students' intellectual, spiritual, and moral growth as a sacred mission.

As a Jesuit priest at a Catholic and Jesuit institution, I want to introduce a new text in student development, one deriving from my context as an educator at Saint Louis University. Based on the mission and goals of Saint Louis University, this text reflects a paradigm shift, a philosophical response to the challenge of educating young men and women in a rapidly changing world.

I draw upon the example of St. Ignatius of Loyola, founder of the Society of Jesus. Placing himself at the Pope's disposal, Ignatius founded the Jesuits in the early 1500s. Equipped with a keen understanding of the world around him, Ignatius was a dynamic individual willing to shoulder any task required in God's service. Regardless of any particular job he was called to do, though, Ignatius had only one real purpose: *to change the world*. I believe that we, in student development, can—and must—implement that same purpose, with and for the students we serve.

---

*Paul Stark, S.J., is vice provost for student development at Saint Louis University, St. Louis, Missouri. This article was previously circulated as an unpublished paper (1997).

Building a Genuine Sense of Community

My reflections are driven by changes we see in the world at large, as well as the world of the university. At Saint Louis University, we have seen that the two worlds cannot be separated. Students come to us from all over America, reflecting what we as a culture are experiencing: economic shifts; changes in jobs and the nature of work itself; corporate re-engineering; and, of course, the confusion students face choosing what they will do as well as who they will *be*.

Americans are clearly concerned about the effects of these changing times on our nation's young people. Educators in particular are concerned about the measures our country and culture take to address their needs. What we now do with and for our young people will ensure what *we*—as a culture and as a nation—will eventually become.

Educators typically respond to the challenge by attempting only to understand and address students' *behavior*. Frankly, this will not provide the answer. Additional policies, more programs, punitive or restrictive measures—none of these will serve our society's larger, long-term needs. At best, slogans and quick-fixes are nothing more than a *pretext*.

The real answer—the only answer, I firmly believe—is to join in building *communities* that reflect our interest and involvement in our students and their lives. We need to invest real time with our students, to cultivate and strengthen their innate assets, and to offer them a real and substantial stake in the society they will help create. At the same time, we must reestablish the credibility of the institutions in which many young people have lost faith—our families and businesses, our churches and schools, and, yes, our universities. Only sustained and significant involvement, on a personal level, can make this happen.

This reflection—this text—necessarily constitutes a work in progress, since I directly address other works in progress, namely, the students attending our universities; the men and women we hope to "develop;" the people whom, in the most fundamental and real sense, we *serve*.

The best path is one that fully engages young people. At Saint Louis University, we embrace a series of primary goals and responsibilities to engage young people—and other members of our academic community—by helping them consider the *context* of their lives, circumstances, and personalities. These goals and responsibilities—certainly shared by all Catholic universities, I believe—are best summarized in the following three ways:

- To *inform*—to educate, to develop an intellectual competence; to instill a body of knowledge and skills sufficient for survival and success in the changing workplace—the changing world for which our students are preparing

- To *form*—our students and faculty, staff and administration by cultivating their character, values, and respect for one another, with a heartfelt, integrated understanding of our mutual *connectedness*—our interrelatedness, each to the whole. As we consider ourselves in the context of our relationships, this *information* and resulting *formation* shape the values we share with others, the values our students will carry with them, long after they leave us. However, this process requires an intentional and institutional commitment to reflect on our experiences, examining not only *what I am doing*, but, more importantly, *what I am learning* from *the experience, about the experience, about the people I'm serving, and about myself.*

  This total process often requires something more than simply the availability of various service opportunities. At Saint Louis University, I have found this effort strengthened by theology and religion classes, in addition to such structured religious opportunities as retreats, prayer groups and Masses, and our University-wide SLU MAKES A DIFFERENCE community service day—all typical of Catholic, Jesuit institutions such as ours. *Formation* also requires the opportunity to discuss our faith lives as a real part of our daily lives with members of our communities.

- To *transform*—St. Ignatius of Loyola had no less than the transformation of the world as his goal. Isn't that—can't that be—OUR goal? Isn't that the most profound legacy we can leave those who follow us? But before we attempt anything so bold and outrageous as a trans-formation of the world, mustn't *we* change, mustn't *we* be transformed? Once I have engaged in the experience, and have learned from the experience, *what results do I integrate into my own life from the experience and my reflection?*

Our universities themselves must lead the way in any effort of such magnitude. To direct our individual and institutional transformation at Saint Louis University, we look to the direction provided by our president, Rev. Lawrence Biondi, S.J.:

Guideposts for Change: The President's Vision for Saint Louis University

My vision is to establish and maintain Saint Louis University as the finest Catholic university in the United States, wherein the entire University community is actively engaged in student formation and the generation of new knowledge. Challenged by outstanding faculty and a modern, value-centered curriculum reflecting the Jesuit tradition, students are fully prepared to contribute to society and to be effective leaders of social change based on the ethical values and principles taught in the Saint Louis University tradition.[1]

Isn't this vision—this goal and direction—fundamentally one of *transformation*, speaking to our deepest selves and calling us to be more than we've yet experienced? Isn't this vision a call to *each* of us, to *all* of us, to transform our culture and our attitude, not only as individuals, but as all of us engaged in the enterprise of developing men and women to take our place, to lead our world, to create a *kingdom* well beyond us?

Together, our institutional goals and commitments form the cornerstone of our process of transformation. Not only do they provide specific standards and expectations of performance, with some potential for quantifiable results; they also serve as idealistic, vision-oriented, directional guideposts that can reflectively shape how we do what we do. Taken together, each of these directions—which are essentially *one* direction—help us to achieve our vision. Their strength reflects a fundamental refinement of—and change from—merely behavior-directed approaches to *consciousness*-directed approaches.

The heart of this proposal is a call to *conversion*, to a new understanding of what it means to be a university in our time. This conversion demands more than simply an intellectual acceptance or understanding: it requires a connection between our minds and our hearts. We are, I sincerely believe, challenged to deepen our solidarity with the students we serve. We are called to be one people, interdependent on each other, recognizing and responding to the undeniable connection between what we *do*, who we *are*, and who we can *become*. We are called to address the basic and profound statement of "the common good" not just as educators but

Figure 1. Institutional Goals: Changing the Paradigm.

as educators dedicated in God's service. Indeed, the call to a common good permeates Catholic social teaching, promoting our national health through adherence to a faith that truly serves humanity.

So far at Saint Louis University we have identified and articulated five areas that we consider a mandate for, and a responsibility of, our institution—five areas we consider inescapable as we meet our threefold responsibility to the students we serve and the faculty and staff we employ. Each of these guidelines alone, and all of them collectively, issue a challenge that we take very seriously at Saint Louis University. This challenge, which is reflected in every aspect of life at our university, embraces our goal and our responsibility to *inform, form,* and *transform* our students and our selves.

To meet the challenge, we must cultivate the following qualities:

- *Competence*: This refers to the intellectual component, the primary educational responsibility, of every university. By emphasizing academic ability and achievement, we must be able to impart knowledge and cultivate skills so our students can compete, successfully, in the workplace.
- *Conscience*: By emphasizing conscience, we help socialize our students, faculty, and staff, raising their consciousness and awareness of personal, professional, and cultural issues on and beyond our campus community. We encourage each other to be responsible with both a personal and a corporate conscience. Through a developing conscience we educate our students to be "women and men for others."[2] Philanthropy, volunteerism and community service are encouraged, with an understanding that they are only three of many progressive ways we can intensify our response and responsibility to others.
- *Compassion*: This is an essential aim of a Christian education. Compassion is a genuine caring and concern for our brothers and sisters, locally, in our own communities (on campus, in the city), and in the world at large. We express this concern through ongoing community service, either in our professions or through service agencies in our communities. Through individual and personal respect for each person, we can provide the environment in which students truly learn what it means "to suffer with others." Guided reflection focuses the work and emphasizes its worth, far beyond the immediate task of service.
- *Community*: Of course, an appreciation for community starts with our immediate surroundings (residence halls, the larger campus, our home, our workplace). We then apply this experience and understanding to the city and the world in which we now live and will live, especially the people with whom we live and work. This is a process

that sensitizes our students—indeed, each of us—to our opportunity and our obligation to serve as active members of those communities, responsive to our responsibility to those with whom each of us comes in contact.

- *Commitment*: The four C's we outline above necessarily reflect, and require, a fifth, and that is an active, *life* commitment that encompasses several elements: the *choice* made by this University; the *challenge* we issue to our students, faculty and staff; and the *call* for each of us to respond to our University's Catholic, Jesuit, human tradition. Accepting all this, we must then translate and transfer that experience as we prepare for our future. In these ways, we create a *connection* between who we are, what we learn, and what we do.

All education takes into account the progressive stages of individual growth. So doing, all education can contribute to the formation of men and women who will put their beliefs and attitudes into practice throughout their lives. We challenge and strive to inspire our community to put into practice—into concrete *action*—the values we cherish, the values we subscribe to and teach in their formation. Thus, *text* and *context* lead to constructive action.

University Goals and Student Development Theory

As educators, we are all familiar with the developmental theories of, among others, Perry, Kohlberg and Chickering.[3] Their theories are hallmarks in the field of student development. For a long time they have told us what to expect from young adults in regard to *behavior*. We already know, for example, that many of our students will struggle with identity issues, including racial and cultural awareness, sexuality, and the fundamental struggle of "Who am I? What am I going to do? Who am I going to be?"

We also know that our students are searching and experimenting. Their search is part of their effort to establish autonomy from their parents, often through sexual experimentation, drinking, the rejection of their religious upbringing, falling away from church, religion, and faith. Their "journeys" manifest themselves in myriad ways. We do not always get excited with green or blue hair, or earrings in places most of us don't usually exhibit in public. We often expect, tolerate and even dismiss a wide variety of behaviors as part of "growing up."

We also know that many of our students see only a "right" answer, or a "wrong" answer, and little or no ambiguity. Life for them is black or white—there is no gray area. More often than not, young people will test the values they've long lived with, having been given them by their parents. Consistent with their stage of cognitive development, they will now try to make decisions about which values to keep, which to discard, and which to reshape and re-define for their own use, as they begin to take a much more active role in making their own lives.

Given that knowledge and background—and the expectations of the students we serve—our institutional goal is to use that information to develop and offer experiences of formation. Through this process, we strive to inspire and call our students to personal experiences of transformation. These are not "either/or" shifts;, they are "not only/but also" propositions in the broader context of the University and our efforts to develop students. How can we nuance and fine-tune our focus to understand our *real* goals? One way is to effect and realize the shifts shown in Figure 2.

Beyond a purely religious context, retreats are opportunities for planning, or a break in the routine. Rather than *retreating*, however, can't we emphasize an "advance" in all departments, colleges, and schools in our university? Moreover, while we must be concerned about students' reactions, can't we be more focused on and concerned about their reflections? After all, it's reflection that leads to growth, progress, and long-term development—for them and for us.

When I first entered student development, I felt overwhelmed by the sheer numbers of activities, programs, policies, positions, and reactions to behaviors, and the emphasis on "success." Allegedly these aims were on behalf of students, but with as many shadings of meaning as there were people speaking about them.

Peering through this thicket of activities, policies, and procedures, I also was able to see our students themselves. They seemed to be moving, to be sure, but their movements lacked a concrete or reflective direction. So we spent more and more time on planning more and more activities, to address more and more behaviors. Yet, to our chagrin, the very behaviors we tried to address usually recurred. Little or nothing changed, substantially.

The essence of "development" is change, progress, *growth,* no matter what we're talking about. I realized that while activities, events, and programs were important, our real goal must also be to *touch* and to *impact* our students' attitudes, rather than simply addressing individual behaviors (which their attitudes reflect and often cause). "Student development," then, must emphasize an ongoing, dynamic approach to our students, rather than simply being the static designation of our division. At the same time, although we often can legislate behavior—formulating policies, sanctions, and rules—we will meet with only varying degrees of success. To call forth a long-term change in behavior, to *really* form our students' lives—to change the world, in fact—demands an accompanying

FROM	TO
Activities	*ATTITUDES*
Programs, policies, procedures	*PEOPLE*
Material things	*THINGS THAT MATTER*
Position	*DISPOSITION*
Success	*SIGNIFICANCE*
Reaction	*REFLECTION*
Money	*MEANING*
"Retreat"	*ADVANCE*
Reaction	*REFLECTION*
Persona	*PERSONALITY*
Impression	*IMPACT*
Potential	*PERFORMANCE*
Discipline	*DEVELOPMENT*
Behavior	*CONSCIOUSNESS*

Figure 2. Significant Paradigm Shifts.

change in *consciousness*—in the attitudes from which behavior arises. Obviously, we cannot legislate or regulate a change in consciousness. We can only call it forth, lead our students and ourselves into it.

"Development" must, in fact, be *formation*. If our goal is to change the world through the lives of the students we serve, then our *activities* must address and touch their *attitudes*. We must have policies and procedures, but we must always remember that policies and procedures affect *people*. They must never impede the growth of the people they were designed to serve.

We need, therefore, to shift our thinking from how we help our students achieve success to how we can help our students to *significance*. Ultimately, they must be able to choose a career not only on the basis of money, but also by reflectively considering its longer-lasting *meaning* for their lives.

What I am convinced we must stand for, and strive for, is significance in life, impact, and meaning. I refer to a far-reaching significance that will include success while also transcending it. If we seek significance as our goal, then the guideposts we often view as leading to success will also shift; they will become more refined, less transitory, more meaningful and fulfilling.

This significance recalls and reinforces our Jesuit, Catholic tradition and history, the reasons for which we were founded. It enables the women and men of Saint Louis University to contribute to, and—more importantly—to *transform*, the world of which we are all a part.

Do we want "success" for our students, for ourselves, for each other? Absolutely. But it is a special kind of success, one that

- Embodies service
- Encompasses *significance*
- Mirrors *reflective choices* we've made during our time together at Saint Louis University
- Derives from, and fully returns, the investment made by Saint Louis University and our benefactors, present and past, on whose shoulders we stand, on whose gifts and prayers we rely, and of whose faith we are stewards
- Exposes our students not only to the ideals of Catholic, Jesuit education and of Saint Louis University, but also as importantly, to the reality of what they can achieve, and how they can live, as they graduate *from* us and *beyond* us; in this way we can help them to form themselves.

I speak, then, of a success that leads to *significance*. For if we *are* what we have been created to be, and if we *do* what we have been created to do, then, in fact, we *are* a success. Our success rests upon our recognition and realization of our individual purpose—our *significance*, not only to ourselves, but more importantly to our world. *Then* we have begun to fulfill our purpose on earth.

So, do we want *success* for our students? Absolutely. But not without significance. Catholic universities—like Saint Louis University—can provide and embody human relationships grounded in a faith-centered context, involving each individual student, professor, and staff member, as together we respect, develop, and help form individuals of integrity for their future and our world. These relationships need to be nurtured and encouraged, as does any reality of enduring value, throughout the course of one's university career—throughout the course of one's life.

In this reflection, I have attempted to *inform* you with my ideas, overriding goals and suggestions. Now, in a context of *formation*, I hope that together we will reflect upon the matter, attempting to understand and digest its implications. This shift could take root in any department, at any college or university. Every educator can dare to help shape students' attitudes, to really touch their lives. I would like to share examples of some ways in which Saint Louis University has tried to promote this transformation—to address this shift—in our environment.

Morning of Recollection

Our directors and assistant directors in the Division of Student Development participated in a full morning program of recollection on Ignatian spirituality, methods of prayer, and decision-making. The program was designed specifically for student development staff to deepen their own understanding and experience of Jesuit and Catholic spirituality, and to give them a model for application and integration in their personal lives and daily work with our students.

As *information*, directors and assistant directors were introduced to the Jesuit *Examen* of Consciousness (a method of prayer practiced by St. Ignatius) and to the Ignatian paradigm of experience, reflection and action. On the level of *formation*, participants experienced a guided meditation on the Examen and an exercise in which they applied the paradigm of experience/reflection/action to professional issues in their departments. Our institution's *transformation* will be realized gradually, as we address and transform the culture of the Division of Student Development and the University, person by person.

Our staff will continue to review and reinforce the paradigm; address hiring practices as we hire to the Catholic, Jesuit mission of the University; examine Church documents that address issues of justice; and reflectively consider the specific nature of what it means to be a Catholic, Jesuit university in these times. All these tools provide a context of real substance for our efforts.

New Programming Model in the Residence Halls

We aggressively apply the "5 C's" and the shift from *behavior* to *consciousness (inform, form, transform)* as programming vectors in all of our residence halls. We also incorporate these principles in our training sessions for student and professional staff, through formation teams and more intense programming efforts. These efforts, too, are a work in progress. Not only do they encompass a variety of experiences; they also present each of our students with a challenge to personal involvement, a stake in their own growth, a share in their own lives.

The Discipline Process

We are incorporating a more reflective form of William Glasser's *Reality Therapy* into our discipline system.[4] Glasser's approach emphasizes clear definitions, personal responsibility, and value judgments in a more personal context. He emphasizes developing relationships with the students we serve. We are reevaluating our discipline code and judicial system, bringing it in line with the developmental focus of our mission, the relationships we strive to develop with and among our students, the 5 C's, and the shift from behavior to consciousness.

Of course, because we realize that some students may not yet be ready to change, or be open to growth at this time, we also run a traditional discipline system. It takes some time to change the culture from *behavior: punishment* to *behavior: growth*. This combined process, though, makes students aware of our higher expectations. Our twofold approach is a call to them, at once collaborative and intentional. Ultimately, this approach poses questions that compel students to join us in the effort to promote a beneficial personal transformation:

- What are you doing?
- Is what you are doing helping you or hurting you?
- Do you want to change?
- How and when will you change?
- How can I help you implement this change?

Through this necessary and more targeted collaboration among faculty, staff, and students, we begin to see our high expectations transformed into a new student culture. This culture, I believe, will promote a greater awareness of our students' interrelatedness, of their individual and collective contexts, as they picture themselves rising to the call to conversion.

Co-Curricular Transcript

A "Co-curricular transcript" is an official document issued by the college or university that accompanies a student's academic transcript to employers or other requesting agencies. Many colleges and universities use this document to verify, officially, a student's participation in extracurricular, service, and learning-center participation. The document can take the place of a student-generated activities resume, and can enjoy the benefit of independent verification by the issuing authority. This reflective, long-term process emphasizes each activity of an individual's university career in terms of a larger goal—putting *what* we do in a larger, more formative context. The effort sees personal involvement in the larger community as a formative aspect of our lives, through

- *Experience*
- *Reflection*
- *Action*

Philanthropy, Volunteeerism, and Community Service[5]

Over the last several years, Americans have embraced the spirit of volunteer work. Cutbacks in business, reductions in government support, increases in the cost-of-living, job loss, and economics in general require a different look, a shift in how we "do business." This shift also reflects, I believe, a craving for meaning, application, and substance in what we do, as well as a search for the *connection* between what we *do* and who we *are*. As a result volunteer organizations now abound; virtually every campus, company, and organization has a volunteer coordinator. Service learning is evident in every sector, both public and private. Many of the services we once paid for, or took for granted as being supplied, are now provided by countless men and women, high school and college students, all over the country.

In terms of a broader, more formative, more *transforming*, and longer-lasting purpose, I suggest a fundamental objective difference between *philanthropy, volunteer work* and *community service*:

- *Philanthropy* usually involves a donation of money. Affluent people contribute to organizations designed to serve the poor, such as religious institutions, educational programs, and other not-for-profit causes; thus, philanthropy is concerned simply with material resources—money, buildings, real estate, etc. On our campuses, philanthropy is most often practiced by fraternities, sororities, and individual departments

    Unlike volunteers and community service participants, philanthropists often have little contact with the people their generosity benefits. The very nature of donating money, clothing, buildings, or food, connects philanthropist to beneficiaries solely through the items of donation. Direct human contact is unnecessary in philanthropy.
- *Volunteerism* is most often considered a task to be completed, an end in itself. It involves a good act, performed and appreciated by the organization, and perhaps by the persons served by the organization, to be sure, but finished when the specific task is completed. Though generally motivated by charitable or humanistic values, these are optional and only more or less essential. Volunteerism per se does not question values or the relative justice or injustice of a particular situation; nor does it necessarily seek to change or serve any but immediate and presenting needs. This type of service—though noble, important, and beneficial to the functioning of society—is also not designed to achieve change in any structure or institution in society.

- *Community service*, in a Catholic, Jesuit context, is understood as *a means to an end*. An expression of faith, it also is motivated by a search for, an expression and understanding of, justice. This search is more far-reaching than a particular service opportunity or individual organization. Community service is constitutive and integral to an educational and human experience designed to live long beyond the books and tests and papers. It is designed to provide opportunities for learning from the persons being served; thus, it enjoins us to re-direct our own lives, based on the reflection required by the experi-ence. At St. Louis University, we believe this type of service is vital to an educational experience that prepares individuals for *life*, rather than simply for college life. In the broad sense, none of our students are called simply to be great college students; they are called to be great men and women.

  This approach to service can stimulate the profound questions, courses, and papers that reflect a university education worthy of the name. As educators, we must address our students not only as *stu-dents*, but also as our *responsibility* in the effort to develop men and women in service to others. This approach to service responds to the social justice teachings of the popes, the American bishops, and the Society of Jesus. This approach to service is appropriate to a Catho-lic, Jesuit education. It reflects a "faith that does justice."

Experience, Reflection, Action

From our *experience*, we reflect on our participation, our response, and the context in which we act. We engage in *reflection* on the personal, faith-centered responses we derive from the experience. Finally, we are moved and called to *action*—to address the problems we see and to en-large ourselves for future service to our brothers and sisters, in a context motivated by, and supportive of, faith. What we do is not an end in itself but the beginning of a lifelong process of inserting ourselves into the ex-perience and lives of people around us.

To Change the World . . .

How will we do this? How will we change the world? Among other things, I believe that faith must be implicit in this process; and I think we can all agree that it is often difficult to maintain faith in these times. But if we start with faith, maybe the times will change. Some readers (and many of my staff) may feel that we are trying to "build Rome in a day." Yet, considering the lives of the people we touch—people who will lead *us* into the future, and shape *our* future—and knowing that time is of the essence, then perhaps we *should* strive to build Rome in a day!

Our task, then, is to change the world. That, for some, may seem overwhelming, ambitious, even daunting. But let us think of Mahatma Gandhi, Martin Luther King, Jr., Dr. Tom Dooley, and Mother Teresa. Let us think, particularly, of all those people we each know who may not be famous for any particular reason, but who give their time, talent, or treasure every day. Finally, let us think of all the individuals, great or small, who have changed *our* lives, and through us have changed the world. How did they *reach* us? How did they *touch* us? How did they *change* us? As a result of those people, whom will *we* strive to reach? Who will we touch? Who and what will we change?

Let us look further. Did they touch our *conscience*? Did they impart knowledge that made us more *competent*? Did they reach out their hands and their hearts in *compassion*? Are our world and life richer because we are part of their *community*? Are we standing upon and relying upon their sense of *commitment*? Given my context as a Jesuit priest—my text—what I suggest is not restricted to me, exclusive of others. Rather, in the most profound and fundamental sense, what I suggest is open to all, and reachable by all. What I suggest is *informative*, and *formative*, *transformational*.

As capable as we might be, each of us, of course, is just one person. Yet each of us has each other, and by extension all others. Each person who has touched and transformed us is just one person. Mother Teresa is just one person, formerly unknown, certainly not wealthy, generally pretty ordinary, just one person; yet she changed our world, as we know it, through her *commitment* to the unloved, her care for the marginalized, and her unconditional acceptance of the rejected. Mother Teresa touched our hearts and our *conscience*, with her clear and simple statement, her moving example of *compassion*. How did she do it? By lifting one dying man from the gutter, and then another. She took into her home and her life one rejected child, and then another, and another, one person at a time.

I am not Mother Teresa; we are not Mother Teresa. Yet we need not be. Each of us can derive strength from her faith, inspiration from her example, purpose from her experience. Each of us can change and affect one person at a time, beginning with ourselves, starting with the person next to us.

How will we do this? We will do it the same way every significant event begins: we will change our world, one student at a time, in whatever capacity we serve them—students who have come to us, needing *information*, and seeking *formation*, so that we might all experience *transformation*.

That's how we'll change our world.

Epigraph

I cannot believe that the purpose of life is to be "happy." I think the purpose of life is to be useful, to be responsible, to be compassionate. It is, above all, to matter; to count; to stand for something; to have made some difference that you lived, at all.

Leo Rosten

Appendix I: How Campus Ministry Works to Enhance the Roman Catholic Identity of Saint Louis University

Retreat Program and Spiritual Development

- *SLU Encounter Retreat:* a weekend opportunity for students to explore the foundations of faith in God and Jesus Christ. Community-building experiences are provided through small group discussion, prayer, and fellowship. Catholic in nature, this retreat is similar to the TEC, Kairos, and Search retreat models. The opportunity for sacramental reconciliation is also provided.
- *Journey Retreat:* scripture-based weekend experience of prayer using Ignatian models, spiritual reading, and silence. A preliminary experience to the Ignatian Silent Retreat.
- *Ignatian Silent Retreat:* four-day silent retreat based on *The Spiritual Exercises* of St. Ignatius of Loyola. An opportunity to experience in solitude intimacy with God and Jesus Christ. This individually directed retreat is designed for those students with a more developed spiritual life.
- *Twilight Retreats:* offered in Lent and Advent, these evenings provide the opportunity to share a simple meal and to pray in the context of the liturgical season.
- *Urban Plunge Retreats:* offered twice each year to expose students to local and global communities. Discussions focus on one's personal experience of service and the Jesuit themes of "option for the poor" and "faith that does justice."
- *Bridges Program & 19th Annotation Retreats:* a method for faculty and staff to experience the 30-day Spiritual Exercises of St. Ignatius while continuing with their normal daily life and responsibilities.

- *Christian Life Communities:* small groups of students who wish to grow in their experience of Christian faith and Ignatian spirituality are invited to contact a campus minister to join an established group or for help in forming a new group.

Social Justice

- *Saint Louis University Christian Action Program (SLUCAP):* provides an opportunity for direct service with those in need, and to integrate that service with the challenges of the Gospel and the documents of the Church on the issues of social justice and the corporal works of mercy. Students and campus ministers volunteer their spring break time to assist the poor in different geographic or cultural regions. Participants discover the social factors that contribute to poverty and powerlessness. They work side by side with the poor and reflect on and pray about the experience of living and working with God's poor.
- *Pax Christi:* the University chapter of the national Catholic peace movement offers regular opportunities for reflection on the ideal of Christian nonviolence and projects to help students focus those ideals in specific situations in our community.
- *SLU Food Drive:* an opportunity every November for every sector of the University community to participate in a month-long drive for food and funds that includes educational opportunities about world hunger, spiritual reflection on the call of the Gospel and the challenge of Church documents, and the experience of giving and soliciting on behalf of others.

Education

- *Etchings:* Each issue of this quarterly published by the campus ministry student intern confronts a different problem of social justice, individual morality, or theology that challenges students in our contemporary world. Recent topics have been service, abortion, right to life, and the "seamless garment".
- *Shared Vision:* This program, based on three Saint Louis University-produced videos, helps students, faculty, and staff integrate into their experience of the University the Roman Catholic and Jesuit values that impelled the Society of Jesus to found and to sustain its

institutions of higher education, so that every constituency of the University can internalize and promote these timeless values in the modern world.

Residence Hall Ministry

- Each residence hall has a Catholic campus minister—clergy, religious, or lay—assigned and often in residence. Working with the residence life and counseling staffs, these ministers are available to students for pastoral counseling and to arrange prayer opportunities, bible studies, and liturgies.

Appendix II: SLUVision

The Jesuit spiritual goal is "to find God in all things." The SLUVision program takes this goal as its operative principle. God is sought both in the classroom and in the interaction with the people the students serve. We ask students and faculty to reflect on how the subject matter of the course (theology) and the service outreach in which they participate are part of the goal.

Students reflect formally with the instructor in several ways. First, they write a weekly paper. Sometimes they use the course material as the starting point to reflect on one aspect of their service. At other times, they might be asked to assume the identity of the people they serve and to reflect and write about what it might be like to encounter themselves—students of the University in a role of service.

Second, students articulate to each other, in guided reflection, the specifics of their service; how it's going, what's occurring within them. In these question and answer and reflection sessions, students provide a supportive group learning experience for one another. Regular course work, which often refers to these formal and informal discussions, becomes more integrated through the common class experience.

Sensitive attention to their own feelings, personally and about their faith development, challenging questions to their intellect, and an analysis of the social situation of the people they serve, call the students "to find God in all things," not only for their present, but also for their entire lives.

Appendix III: University Goal (from the Strategic Plan)[6]

Maintain and enhance the Catholic, Jesuit identity of the University

Saint Louis University is an institution of higher education inspired by the values of the Catholic, Jesuit tradition. These values guide the vision and mission of the University, inform the choices that it makes for its operations, and require faithful attention to this heritage in all the University does. Everyone in the University, particularly in positions of leadership and governance, contributes to the embodiment of the Catholic, Jesuit identity of Saint Louis University, which is not merely an intellectual ideal but a living spirit guiding the University. This Catholic, Jesuit identity offers opportunities to those who join the University as students, staff, or faculty to bring the distinct contribution of their own religious tradition to the enhancement of the University's Catholic, Jesuit identity in new and changing circumstances. Each planning unit must regularly consider the ways in which this distinct heritage guides its operations and insure that it continues to do so. Students at Saint Louis University must experience the integration of their spiritual, intellectual, social, and professional lives as part of the distinct Catholic, Jesuit heritage of the University. Faithful to the Ignatian tradition of "finding God in all things," Saint Louis University encourages and supports research and scholarship that explores the interaction among knowledge, culture, religion, and the Catholic, Jesuit tradition.

Essential Objectives

1. All governance decisions will contribute to maintaining and enhancing the Catholic, Jesuit identity, ideals, and values of the University.
2. The recruitment, advancement, and recognition processes for all University personnel will contribute to maintaining and enhancing its Catholic, Jesuit identity.
3. All academic units will periodically assess and improve their contributions to the University's Catholic, Jesuit ideals and values.
4. All student educational support services will assist students to ex-

perience the connection between the University identity and their lives.

5. The University will support research on the ways in which discipline areas, religious concerns, and its Catholic, Jesuit identity intersect.
6. In its self-presentation, the University will regularly promote an appreciation and support of its Catholic, Jesuit identity, values, and ideals.

Core Strategies across the Objectives

Individual Unit Planning Responsibilities

1. Recruit faculty and staff who are in support of the mission and philosophy of the University.
2. Promote ways in which our religious traditions can interact intellectually with our cultures, especially ways in which our Catholic and Jesuit intellectual heritage can continue to interact with and contribute to culture. Explore ways in which our culture can shape and authentically call forth both religious life and the life of the mind.
3. Advance a complementarity of the religious, intellectual, and social lives of all students, faculty, staff, and administrators.
4. Recruit faculty, staff, and administrators who can contribute out of their diversity to the further development of academic interest in the Catholic intellectual and cultural heritage.
5. Give particular attention to issues of equity and justice concerning women and minorities at Saint Louis University.

Multiple Unit Planning Responsibilities

6. Establish comprehensive in-service programs for staff, faculty, administrators, trustees, and regents promoting the University's identity and mission, its intellectual and spiritual tradition, and the history of Jesuit education.
7. Promote ways in which our heritage regularly can be made obvious in art, ritual, symbol, and public events.
8. Clarify and strengthen the University's relationship with the local, national, and international Catholic Church and other organized religions.

Notes

1. Lawrence Biondi, S.J., Saint Louis University, "A Shared Vision and Commitment to Excellence" (June 8, 1996), 12, 13.
2. Father Pedro Arrupe, S.J., former General of the Society of Jesus.
3. Lee Knefelkamp, Carole Widick, Clyde A. Parker, *New Directions for Student Services* (San Francisco, CA: Jossey-Bass, Inc., 1978), 1968.
4. William Glasser, *Reality Therapy* (New York: Harper and Row, 1975).
5. I would like to thank Rev. Denis Daly, S.J., assistant vice provost of Mission and Ministry, Saint Louis University, for his discussion and ideas about these issues.
6. Saint Louis University, *A Shared Vision and Commitment to Excellence.*

Strategies for Change

Introduction

Irene King

In the mid-1980s, notes Donald Kirby, the faculty and administration of Le Moyne College were concerned about "whether the college experience yields a graduate who is sensitive to the values dimensions of problems, and who perceives the values questions as at least as important as the technical questions." A working group began meeting to design a senior seminar "that would help students to integrate the liberal arts and the Jesuit emphasis on socially responsible values into their major disciplinary field." The group had the insight to realize that isolated efforts to raise issues of values would not carry enough weight to change student perspectives; the goal must involve the entire Le Moyne community and stop at nothing short of transforming the culture of the college.

The result of this effort was the creation of the Values Program, the mission of which is "to engage the college community in a campus-wide education effort." It is a well-designed model for other colleges seeking strategies for change.

The program has three primary goals:

1. To create an atmosphere that promotes serious reflection on values;
2. To encourage faculty and staff to explore the relationship between teaching methods and the encouragement of moral sensitivity in students; and
3. To bring students, faculty, and staff into continuing analysis and criticism of values.

The Values Program has three components: the Summer Institute, the Academic Forum, and Assessment and Research. Every summer, the

Summer Institute invites faculty, administration, and staff for a one- to three-week forum on a values-oriented topic. The institute assigns readings, facilitates discussion groups, and brings in outside speakers and consultants. These institutes have been very successful in stimulating a sense of community. The sharing that occurs there has been a catalyst for new initiatives at Le Moyne, including a service option in political science courses. Kirby says, "The collegial experience fostered by the institute empowers participants to return to the college community with renewed vigor to tackle the tough task of values education."

The annual Academic Forum is organized to facilitate reflection and discussion by the college community on values. The theme often springs from the fertile Summer Institute discussions. The Summer Institute has also spawned such other Values Program events as the Leadership/ Scholar Awards. This appellation is given to ninety first-year students "based on their academic record and promise as leaders." Leadership projects for these students are now facilitated in part from a Values Program perspective.

Kirby attributes the success of the Le Moyne Values Program to several factors—factors easily adapted by other colleges and universities:

1. "We engaged the community in a college-wide educational effort." Kirby asserts that it is critical to bring every aspect of the college community into the process. Le Moyne was able to engage a large percentage of the community for two key reasons: (1) "the need for values education touched a profound human hunger and resonated with a very deep chord," and (2) linkages spanned disciplines and institutional roles.

2. "We transformed the institution's culture." The intention was to build upon the positive Jesuit foundation already in place, to produce "highly gifted, intelligent, and creative students" and "imbue in them a sense of values recognized as good by the best of the religious and philosophical traditions." The Le Moyne Values Program, Kirby asserts, stands as a symbol of "who we are and what we stand for."

3. "The program strengthened the College's commitment to a student-centered focus." The Summer Institute and Academic Forum "empower faculty to design courses and student-life activities to help students shape socially responsible attitudes and values."

4. "A clear set of goals and means for assessing success keep the program on track." The program continually measures its impact and strives to meet changing needs and interests in the college community through an empirical evaluation process and constant self-reflection.

5. "The program manifests staying power; it is not a one-shot deal." By building on existing strengths and connecting itself to the College mission, the Values Program has stayed strong for thirteen years. Donors were needed during the start-up phase, but Le Moyne has since incorporated the program into its own budget.

6. "We have always set our sights beyond the Le Moyne campus," and as Kirby says, "Our ultimate goal has always been the education of responsible citizens for the society beyond campus. Our students come to us from that wider world, and they leave us to rejoin that world. Through consulting and through dissemination of our ideas we hope to act as a catalyst to transform other institutions similarly committed to values education for socially responsible citizens."

Yet another valuable model for galvanizing campuses around the issue of values education comes from John Wilcox and Susan Ebbs, who guide colleges and universities in reflection on values, implicit and explicit, within their communities. Once a community recognizes its values, its members can constructively envision a different future culture for their community. A Values Audit is a tool for promoting such an ethical campus climate.

A Values Audit is "a collaborative process that offers a means for bringing about institutional sensitivity to the mission of higher education." The audit "systematically assesses beliefs, goals, standards of choice, and the manner in which these are lived or enacted; it also helps formulate recommendations according to the values proclaimed and practiced." The culture of a community is examined with an eye toward such issues as "administrative use of power, honesty in student recruitment, retention of athletes, and racism and sexual harassment on campus." The audit becomes a catalyst for discussion about ethics, values, and campus-specific challenges.

Process is the most important element of the Values Audit, say Wilcox and Ebbs: A two-year communal exploration of the explicit and implicit values underlying decision-making "can lead to reformulation and reaffirmation of the values system and to better decision-making." A sample of an audit done at a religious-affiliated college in the Northeast gives readers a sense of the components and breadth of this process.

Wilcox and Ebbs outline seven recommendations and lessons learned from their work with the Values Audit. These insights would prove useful to any campus community.

1. The Audit committee "consisted of volunteers from among administration, faculty, staff, and students." Broad representation al-

lows for divergent points of view and creates college-wide ownership. But Wilcox and Ebbs also cite the importance of a single individual directing the various aspects of the audit.

2. Student participation that is consistent and spans all age groups is essential.

3. The support of the president and high-level administrators is also essential.

4. A variety of opportunities to engage community members is important: small group discussions, individual interviews, surveys, and larger community forums all generate valuable information.

5. Follow-up is needed to ensure high rates of return on surveys.

6. It is important to ensure the participation of support staff. These members of the community are often the first line of contact with students and faculty and have valuable insights.

7. The timing of the audit is crucial; the sample audit occurred shortly before an accreditation review, providing valuable information for that study as well.

A Most Promising Road to Take: The Values Program Process

Donald J. Kirby, S.J.*

A colleague sat in a room filled with religious discussing an upcoming presidential search at her college. A member of the founding religious group asked if the search committee was actually open to accepting a lay person as president. The room became alive with anxious energy as this question was discussed from widely differing perspectives. A lay trustee said that this change would not work without an effective process for intertwining the institution's mission and identity continually into every thread of its fabric of experience.

In one sentence, she reduced the challenge to its essence. The important question is not who will be the next president, administrator, or faculty member. The important question is: Does an instrument exist to sustain the identity and mission of the institution effectively and constantly?

The Values Program, as administered by the Center for the Advancement of Values Education at Le Moyne College in Syracuse, has implemented just such a process. In a variety of contexts and cultures, the process is adaptable to most educational institutions. The Values Program is successful because it identifies and articulates for an entire institution a profoundly felt need that is critical not only to institutions of higher education but to society in general. That need is to assure that an institution's graduates understand and act upon the realization that values issues are at least as significant as technical issues.

The Values Program at Le Moyne embarked upon an ambitious dream: to have a major impact on values education and development at

*Donald J. Kirby, S.J., is professor of religious studies and director of the Center for the Advancement of Values Education (CAVE) at Le Moyne College, Syracuse, New York. An earlier version of this paper appeared as "The Values Program at Le Moyne College," *About Campus* (February 1998). Krystine Batcho, Ph.D., professor of psychology and director of assessment and research for CAVE, provided critical assistance in the writing of this essay. Theresa Coulter also assisted in preparation of the essay.

Le Moyne. In doing so it would have an impact eventually on the culture and ethos of the entire institution. It also created effective strategies that are adaptable to different types of educational institutions. The power and promise of the process developed by the Values Program at Le Moyne College is suggested by the following:

- The College Board of Trustees selected the Values Program and the Center for the Advancement of Values Education to receive a $1,000,000 endowment in the College's current capital campaign.
- The Report of the Middle States Accreditation Team on its visit to Le Moyne in 1995 singled out the Values Program for special recognition, calling it a model of teaching and learning that brings eminent distinction to Le Moyne.
- In an age of few religious and members of the founding religious group, the Values Program allows for religious identity in a sophisticated university environment.
- The program has strong support from the vast majority of faculty; to date, more than 85 percent of the college's 127 full-time faculty have participated in the program's Summer Institutes.
- The program has proved to be of lasting value over a ten-year period. It has a carefully thought-out system of organization and consultation, and a sophisticated assessment process.
- Because the Values Program and its process have proven themselves transferable to many different types of institutions, the Center is also actively involved in the dissemination of our process and research findings (1988–1999).

To borrow an ancient Chinese saying, "Only those with a clear understanding of the past can have a vision for the future." As a Catholic, Jesuit liberal arts college, Le Moyne College was founded in 1946 with a very strong, centuries-old tradition. Yet what the tradition and the founding assumptions mean today must be constantly examined and reinterpreted. Le Moyne's 1984 Values Audit asked what gaps existed between the College's assertions and assumptions and its reality. The Values Program continually forces the college to reinvestigate such gaps.

The Birth of a Process

In 1986 seven Le Moyne faculty members began to dream an ambitious dream: to have a major impact on values education and development at Le Moyne. Could we transform the culture of the college? Could we weave the fabric we desired? How could that be done? We didn't know, but we committed ourselves to a process of discussion and discovery. In 1990, Parker J. Palmer wrote that people at Le Moyne "are willing to walk into their fears for the sake of a more humane vision . . . the result is an increase of vitality, humanity, community, and a sense of purpose on the Le Moyne College campus."[1]

This article tells the ten-year story of this process, which began as a grassroots movement, and explains how and why it works. It is a story of a successful effort to discover how to engage the commitment of an entire institution to an ambitious dream. It is the story of a new paradigm for values education.

The story began in 1985. Seven faculty members met to create a senior seminar to help students integrate liberal arts and the Jesuit emphasis on socially responsible values into their major disciplinary fields. By the spring of 1986, this working group realized that attempts to address the need for values education would be ineffective if they were limited to isolated courses or programs. In order to weave disparate threads into a new fabric of experience, the group recognized that it would be necessary to engage the entire college community if students were to integrate their learning with their values.

We faced many of the same challenges already raised in this volume. We thought about encouraging academic freedom, affecting the very culture of the institution, and responding to the changing needs of the students. But how do you maintain the delicate balance: respecting the academic freedom of individual professors and their individual rights while promoting the academic freedom of the institution as a whole and allowing the institution to assert its own identity?

At Le Moyne the challenge looked like this: How could the college be true to its mission and purpose (that is, be Jesuit and Catholic), stress values inquiry, and continue to respect the pluralism and diversity of its faculty, students, and administrative staff, all without yielding to an empty relativism? It was—and remains—a tough question, which we resolved to keep alive as we went along.

The performance of higher education is not immune from the influences of the highly secular, materialistic culture in which it functions. Decades of research have yielded an image of the college graduate as an intelligent, verbal, knowledgeable, and questioning adult.[2] The ideal graduate is prepared to apply reason as well as technical knowledge and skills to professional problems.

What remains unclear, however, is whether the college experience yields a graduate who is sensitive to the values dimensions of problems, and who perceives values questions as at least as important as technical questions. Today's challenge is to build a process that helps students acquire the values of both social and individual responsibility.

As academics, we turned to the literature on values education and be-gan to look at other institutions and programs. We found that, as teachers of values, we were not the first to aim our sights at the entire institution. We may have been the first, though, to attempt to arrive there through a college-wide, interactive model. We hoped to build on students' experi-ences inside and outside the classroom.

As our discussions progressed, we became confirmed in our opposition to any educational practices designed to indoctrinate students into ac-cepting one particular set of theories or beliefs. We were not all Jesuits in mufti; neither are we relativists. Our aim was to create an institution that helps students both to become aware of values issues and to fashion val-ues frameworks that are consistent, defensible in themselves, and in keep-ing with the best of human traditions. Furthermore, when we had accomplished this, we wanted our students to have the moral courage to act on their principles.

We understood that anything other than an institution-wide effort would be doomed. Experience verified that the institution would reject a one-shot program, like bringing in an outside speaker, or involving only one or two faculty or administrative offices. "Any change in the college's perception of the role of values would require the efforts and commit-ment of the entire community, especially the faculty, and an unqualified commitment of time, money, and energy from the top level administra-tors over a considerable period of time (3–5 years)."[3] We know now that it takes more than double the time of our original estimate.

The mission of the College is to produce highly gifted, intelligent, and creative students. The college must also give students a firm sense of the right values as they are understood by the best of the religious and philo-sophical traditions.

The Values Program is the Jesuit tradition in modern garb. It stands for all the things that contributed to the original thrust at the founding of the College. Jesuit education is value-oriented, and the Values Program has made this assertion a reality. Because of the Values Program, values education truly stands at the center of the Le Moyne experience. The Values program is not just an add-on; it permeates the entire institutional culture.

The Values Program at Le Moyne

The mission of the Values Program is to engage the College community in a campus-wide education effort. Its intentions are threefold: to dis-cover and implement ways to help students heighten their awareness of issues that involve values, to develop a comprehensive framework for addressing these issues, and to strengthen students' moral courage to act on their principles.

Some might worry that the program engages in indoctrination. In fact, it initiates a process of serious inquiry. Our aim is to assist students in fashioning frameworks of values that are consistent, defensible, and in keeping with the best of philosophical and religious traditions. The primary goals of the Values Program are to create an atmosphere that promotes serious reflection on values issues; encourage faculty and staff to explore the relationships between teaching methods and their professional roles and the growth of moral sensitivity in students; and engage students, faculty, and staff in an ongoing analysis and criticism of values.

Three major components comprise the program:

1. The Values Institutes
2. The Academic Forum
3. Assessment and Research

It is pivotal to understand that the components of the program work not as the sum of separate parts, but as interactive forces in an integrated, dynamic system.[4] Each component not only serves a particular purpose but also supports and strengthens each of the other components.

The Values Institute

The Values Institute brings together about twenty faculty, staff, and administrators for one to three weeks. Participants explore a values-laden theme foundational for the integrative nature of the program, and plans how to bring what they learn back to students in vital ways. Since 1988, themes have been:

- Economic Justice
- Peace and War
- Families and Public Policy
- Science–Technology and Values
- Values Education across the Curriculum
- Valuing Diversity
- Discovering the Sacred in our Midst
- Education and Public Policy
- On the Edge: In Search of Values for the New Millennium.

After becoming familiar with the relevant literature, participants identify and discuss pertinent values. The institute is effective because participants are actively engaged in exploring how values questions apply to their own professional and personal lives. Its primary purpose is to support participants as they formulate realistic action plans for implementing the fruits of the institute. The institute gives support by providing resources, such as expert outside facilitators and select readings, and by nurturing the deep sense of community that develops among participants. The collegial experience fostered by the institute empowers participants to return to the college community with renewed vigor, ready to tackle the tough task of values education.

For example, in 1999 Values Institute faculty and staff worked together to enhance the freshmen orientation experience. Before arriving, incoming students were required to read an assigned text related to the search for values for the new millennium. During the early weeks of the first academic year, faculty, administrators, and staff led small group discussions on the texts. Discussion leaders were recruited from the institute. This orientation activity, directly related to the 1999 Values Institute theme, brought many members of the campus community together: students, personnel staff, the Academic Dean's Office, and faculty. The gap between what have been traditionally viewed as academic and non-academic realms was bridged.

Influencing students from their first arrival, we set the expectation that values concerns are a priority at Le Moyne. From the beginning, students anticipate that their evolving valuing skills will be an important component of their undergraduate experience. This values component is now integrated into the weekly advisement schedule by Advisement Director Bruce Shefrin, one of the founders of the Values Program, who coordinates closely with Barbara Karper, associate dean for student affairs and director of campus activities.

To date, more than 85 percent of 127 full time faculty have already participated in Values Institutes. Favorable reactions to the experience have been as individual as the faculty members themselves. William Miller, a mathematician, says, "I gradually came to realize what now seems obvious; there is no way I can avoid revealing what I value highly as I teach." Biologist Andrew Szebenyi, S.J., says, "As a scientist I wanted to be objective. As a result, my teaching was very colorless. Now that I include my own opinions and discussions of value issues, my students' response is very good." In his genetics class, Szebenyi not only leads a discussion of the effects of a damaged chromosome, but also shows a film about a Downs Syndrome child and his family.

New lines of communication have inspired innovations by departments as well as individuals. The institutes provided a catalyst for the political science department to reconceptualize its focus from an abstract study of politics to an emphasis on preparing students for lives as active and informed citizens. Important to this shift of focus is the curricular change introduced with the addition of a service option to existing courses.

Two examples demonstrate the potential of the strategy of the Values Institutes as an instrument for enhancing the institution's identity and mission among the faculty.

The first relates to a major Institute goal, to make it legitimate for faculty to make values education a priority. In every college there are those who actively and with careful thought wish to take a responsible role in the mission of the Church. The Values Program gives them the courage to act on their calling. Since values education is a documented priority in the mission of the institution, faculty members who work to become proficient in values education are now esteemed. They are valued and respected by their colleagues, who may not have appreciated their concerns before.

The second example has to do with the Values Institute's concern for pedagogy and techniques for teaching effective values education. As faculty return to classrooms with their sharpened teaching tools, students are encouraged to ask questions from their own experience, and to be active in their own educational process. In an institution where values education is legitimate, students want to make connections between their values and deep faith priorities. The faculty are now trained to respond to students who are concerned about these issues. Faculty understand that dealing with values issues is part of their professional responsibility. Faculty are thus better prepared to understand their students. They are skilled in using techniques that allow for good values and religious education to take place.

The goals of the Values Program are universal in their accessibility and their adoptability. As a colleague at a major university remarked, "You have created a process and a language that is accessible and intelligible to all the secular disciplines." From an Asian perspective, another colleague calls the program "the most promising road to take"—an example of teachers turning to each other for ways to improve the quality of education without waiting for an answer from the school administration or the Ministry of Education or the equivalent.[5]

Academic Forum

One dictionary definition of "forum" is "an assembly for the discussion of questions of public interest."[6] In that sense, the Academic Forum is well named, since it consists of diverse assemblies discussing questions of inherent public interest. Missing from the denotative label, however, is the active dimension of the forum that facilitates the *implementation* of ideas. As current interests and purposes change, the specific format of activities varies to meet individual needs and spur continuing creative growth.

The main function of the Forum is to help students discover connections between classroom material and the world outside the classroom. Professors incorporate content learned in the Values Institute into their classroom teaching; students find common ground in forums outside the classroom.

Because the Values Program evolved within the culture of Le Moyne's Catholic and Jesuit tradition, we soon recognized the need to extend our values research into the spiritual dimension that gives rise to and nurtures those values and values processes. In 1990 we received funding to research the connections and differences between values education and religious and spiritual education. We wanted to discover how to adapt and implement our strategies and techniques accordingly. This project was successful and we learned much.

In 1994 the College was inspired to choose "The Spiritual Dimensions of Higher Education: Attending to the Sacred in Our Midst" as the institution-wide theme. We spent two years on the project, the first creating and planning, the second implementing strategies and techniques. These years gave us hope that religious and spiritual dimensions were an important evolution for our program.

The principal goal of the "Spirituality" values events was to bring the entire Le Moyne community into a vital exploration of paths for attending to the sacred in our lives. Philosophy Professor Katharine Rose Hanley explained, "The program extends responsibility for initiative and leadership to all components of the College, including especially alumni/ae and student leaders of residences and various campus organizations. The program develops informed concern for values through one's life and service in the human community."

Some Academic Forum events related to the spirituality theme were college-wide. For example, a major event in 1995 was the Spring Spirit Fair, modeled after a Renaissance Fair. The fair was the brainchild of a faculty member who wanted to celebrate the lived forms of spirituality extant within the Le Moyne and wider communities. The Spring Spirit Fair celebrated diversity, pluralism, and freedom, but it also gave those interested in being truly Catholic an opportunity to do so without being intimidated. It offered all members of the community an opportunity to sample some twenty activities that nourish the spirits of people at Le Moyne College. With each event lasting about an hour, the fair extended from morning through late evening and incorporated every sector of the College:

- "Ignatian Spirituality" was a presentation by scholastic Steven Spahn, S.J., of distinctive features of a life centered in Christ incarnate in the tradition of St. Ignatius of Loyola.
- "Tae Kwon Do: Exploring the Mental, Spiritual, and Physical Aspects of Tae Kwon Do" included demonstrations of board breaking.
- Sister Joan Kerley presented "Journeying Together: Reflections on the Process of Spiritual Direction." Religious Studies Professor Mary MacDonald used weaving net bags as an image of the creativity of person, culture, and cosmos.
- Philosophy and Education Professor Tom Curley delineated "Meditation Practice," where an introduction to the benefits of meditation was followed by a mindfulness meditation, a guided healing meditation, reflection, and discussion.
- In "Gospel Spirit," the College group Voices of Power praised God in song and in the power of the Spirit. They reflected on aspects of the history, style and spirit of Gospel music, giving the community an opportunity to hear and sing together.

Such participatory events made the sacred visible in ways that had not been evident before.

Just as ripples spread when a stone is tossed into a pond, so too energy in techniques and new-found legitimacy spreads throughout the entire campus. It spreads to dormitories, non-traditional students, student life, campus ministry—all aspects of the institution's culture. This is one way we answered our question, "How can we weave the fabric we desired?" We didn't know, but we committed ourselves to a process of discussion and discovery.

Renewed energy from the institutes also stimulates creative use of existing resources. For example, the Values Program took a fresh look at the leadership/scholar program. Each year, the Admissions Office provides some 90 incoming freshmen with Leadership/Scholar Awards. Students are chosen for high school achievement and promise as leaders. These awards present an excellent opportunity to build connections from academics to leadership outside the classroom. In 1996 a position was created within the Values Program for a graduate assistant who would work specifically on the leadership project.

This effort has already begun to bear fruit. In Fall 1997 some of the previous year's leadership group elected to take a core course in ethics offered by Robert Flower. The course explores human dignity as understood by Aristotle through Kant. Due to the participation of so many

Leadership/Scholars, Flower modified the course content to focus on characteristics that make for leadership. Some students in the class "already have a chemistry of community that is exciting," said Flower. He believes that this community of learners is a result of the efforts of the Values Program to reach students. "This experience is distinctive; it is not your average experience. I don't remember when I was in a community quite as energized as this one," he said. For him this was a quality example of values study and values education: "They are not just doing philosophical theories, they are trying to give voice to something percolating within them, a real value experience."

Values Program events have become catalysts for many other activities that are now part of the institutional fabric. Patricia Schmidt, assistant professor in education, explained how the program has enriched her productivity: "I felt supported and mentored by the colleagueship generated by the program. It gave me confidence to go forward and attempt novel projects." One such project was a spinoff from her participation in the Spirituality Institute. Schmidt, students, Sharon Topp, associate director of continuous learning, and Karel Blakely, technical director of the College Firehouse Theater produced "Let's Talk," a forum conceived by students to open dialogue with faculty on issues important to students. From these encounters, issues of campus diversity emerged: "These issues related to my teaching and research in multicultural education, and also to the Values Program's concern about sending students out into the world as agents of peace, justice, and compassion." Schmidt then designed a course on diversity for resident advisors. With assistance from students, faculty and administration, she presented diversity appreciation programs in residence halls. Carl A. Thomas, director of the Higher Education Opportunity Program (HEOP), worked with Schmidt to implement retreats where diverse groups of students spend a day or two relaxing and reflecting on human similarities and differences.

After the Mass of the Holy Spirit, a traditional liturgy at the beginning of each College academic year, a faculty workshop is held. In 1996 the workshop gave faculty the opportunity to hear the student perspective on whether Le Moyne College delivers on promises to its students. This exchange grew out of earlier "Let's Talk" experiences. Eight students were chosen for the panel, which simulated a late-night discussion in the dormitories. Careful preparation assured that the students had thought through their dialogue. Professional facilitation by a faculty member also assured that students felt secure enough to be spontaneous and truthful in their comments. It was an example of empowering the student to provide moral-valuing leadership.

Six successful Town Meetings provide an example of a long-running Academic Forum event with great power. These were originally created by Professor Robert Flower to celebrate the bicentennial of the Constitution. Combining showmanship with scholarship, the Town Meeting program was adapted to reflect the Values Program theme, to rave reviews. A recent town/gown assemblage, "Spirituality: Personal Journeys, Music, Mystery, Meaning," engaged the wider Central New York community. Experience and reflection were shared through song and image, stories and readings, questions and conversations. "It is our hope," asserts Associate Producer Theresa Coulter, "that they will be deeply touched and challenged in their hearts to reevaluate some of their most cherished values and attitudes."

Assessment and Research

The assessment component is critical to the success of our program, which rests upon the assumption that action should always be based on needs and approaches that have been validated empirically. Assessment results are studied to improve program efforts. Given the inherent difficulty of measuring perceptions, attitudes, valuing processes, and outcomes, the originators of the assessment approach, Krystine Batcho and William H. Holmes, designed a strategy of applying independent methods for cross-verification. For example, faculty self-reports of classroom behaviors are compared to student reports of faculty behaviors. Pedagogical techniques, including lecturing, discussion, playing devil's advocate, functioning as a role model, etc., are then correlated with values education outcomes. When possible, self-report measures of outcomes are compared to task performance and behavioral indices.

Special assessment instruments were designed by Professors Batcho and Holmes to evaluate important valuing factors, such as sensitivity to values issues, perceived importance of the values dimension of decisions, and the ability to make well reasoned judgments on problems in different life contexts. A summary of the assessment strategy appears in our book, *Ambitious Dreams*.[7]

Why It Works

The Values Program is successful because it articulates a profoundly felt need critical both to educational institutions and to the wider society. It also creates innovative strategies to meet those needs that are adaptable to different types of educational institutions. Our journey at Le Moyne has been distinguished by a number of characteristics that may offer valuable insights to others starting out on similar ventures.

1. We engaged the community in a college-wide educational effort. Critical to implementing values-based institutional change is the ability to engage the entire community in the process. A number of factors contributed to our success in this respect. First, the need for values education touched a profound human hunger and resonated with a very deep chord. That this program was initiated by the faculty and administrative staff themselves, with no orders from the top, speaks to this profoundly felt need. That this grassroots movement created and has implemented, funded, and maintained this institution-wide effort since 1986 speaks to the commitment people are willing to exercise for a truly worthwhile endeavor. Its grassroots beginnings helped make the program welcoming and nurturing to all, offering a vehicle for those who seem to have no other way to accomplish their values education goals.

2. Collegiality is fostered. A deep sense of community results from the bridges erected across institutional and discipline boundaries. In a time of increasing professional and social fragmentation and alienation, the program is an instrument for rediscovering the institution's communal character. From the very start, we engineered the makeup of the Values Program to insure participation from diverse constituencies. For example, the founding group of seven included faculty from diverse disciplines. The membership of the main policy and implementation group (The Working Group on Values) includes, in addition to faculty, participants from such areas as student life, continuous learning, academic staff, and administrative personnel. The Values Institutes and the Academic Forum events are engineered to include the special assistant to the president, or the academic vice president and dean, or administration and staff from the continuous learning office, student life, athletic department, or the library. It is critical that, from the beginning, we have always included people from different parts of the community.

This builds collegiality among different constituency groups in the institution. As a result, no particular section of the institution feels that it has unique ownership of the program or a particular Values Institute or Academic Forum event. There are few turf battles. The arrangement allows for cross fertilization of ideas. It is cooperative, not competitive. It reflects some of the religious notion of *koinonia*, where each person's talents are respected and nourished and each person is empowered by the community to exercise his or her unique gifts for the common good.

3. We transformed the institution's culture. Our hope was to reinvigorate undergraduate education by permeating the culture of the institution. The program functions as a catalyst to effect cultural shift in a time of cultural drift. Rather than reinvent the wheel, we set out to transform what was already there. Since its founding as a Jesuit college in 1947, Le Moyne's purpose has been not only to produce highly gifted, intelligent, and creative students, but also to imbue in them a sense of values recognized as good by the best of the religious and philosophical traditions. The new academic vice president, Kurt F. Geisinger, made his commitment to the program's goals clear in his inaugural college convocation address in Fall 1997: "I believe the Values Program is the signature program at Le Moyne. That values permeate our entire curriculum is our statement of who we want graduates of Le Moyne to be. It tells the world with clarity who we are and what we stand for."

4. It is possible to sustain the energy of this process in an ever-changing environment. To sustain the process requires people and financial resources. Our dream is indeed ambitious: to make a major impact on values education and moral development at this institution and beyond. This involves transforming the culture of the college so that values education is continually a real priority.

Because the student body changes every four years, and so do a number of faculty and administrative staff, this is a major challenge. The program is thus continually evolving; in some ways it is continually beginning. While this presents a very real problem, it is also the source of real dynamism and an ability to be self-renewing and energizing. Unlike other efforts in an institution that can build a platform and make very few adjustments, with this platform the students (even the culture itself) keep changing. You have to redevelop the program to meet new stresses and crises.

The culture of the College is a living, ever-changing reality; only a values program that is living and ever-changing itself can truly meet the needs of students as they actually are, and not as they once were.

5. The goals of the Values Program have universal appeal. The challenge that has been successfully faced by the Values Program is to create a language and a process that speak to all the secular disciplines. We employed a strategy that is all inclusive, not one perceived as top down. It was a big idea that not only speaks to the core group committed to Catholic issues but appeals to all faculty, no matter what their denomination, if any.

The 34th General Congregation of the Society of Jesus reminded Jesuits, and all religious, that we are to "collaborate with the laity" in the work of our institutions.[8] How do you make that collaboration open and universal? The Congregation recommends we do this by responding to the desire of our colleagues for formation "so that they are able to minister as fully as possible according to their call and gifts," and by helping them to "recognize and discern the apostolic possibilities of their lives and work."[9]

Where the Values Program is uniquely successful is in engaging those colleagues "who think they have gone beyond Christianity or any religious commitment," those who "judge that neither Christian faith, nor any religious belief, is good for humanity."[10] The Values Program strategy has proven its power and promise by discovering ways to communicate about the deepest-felt desires at the core of what it means to be human with colleagues whose "human spirituality becomes detached from an explicitly religious expression."[11]

6. Selecting a common value-laden theme provides for a common ground of experience and base of knowledge. A critical discovery for us is the importance of a college-wide theme. The theme serves as a bridge between student affairs and academic affairs, and gives the community an opportunity to gain knowledge and experience in a central question of life. Only through dialogue between the individual and the community are true values discovered. By concentrating this dialogue the program gives participants a trusting, intelligent, and caring environment within which they can grapple with tough issues. It is safe training for the world outside the college community.

7. Clear goals and ways to assess success keep the program on track. Careful assessment keeps the program addressing current needs. Clear goals and an empirical evaluation process lead to effective strategies to inspire change. We continue to refine our methods of evaluation and use our findings to improve our efforts. We agree with anthropologist Mary Douglas that to be healthy an institution must continually make explicit its understanding of itself to itself.[12] The assessment process helps deepen the understanding that comes from self-reflection.

8. The program manifests staying power; it is not a one-shot deal. By helping faculty and staff grow, and by providing numerous opportunities for students to engage in the valuing enterprise, the program through its interactive and interdependent components continually transforms the educational environment. The ability to adapt to current themes and new constituencies within the institution and beyond is another source of staying power. Addressing real needs with promising strategies and careful assessment attracts funding partners anxious to collaborate; but by using existing resources, the program has not needed constant external funding or levels of energy beyond the community's capacity—though the generosity of donors did help in the initial stages and with special activities.

9. We have always had our sights beyond the Le Moyne campus. Our ultimate goal has always been the education of responsible citizens for the society beyond campus. Our students come to us from that wider world; they leave us to rejoin that world. Through dissemination of our ideas, we hope to act as a catalyst to transform other institutions similarly committed to values education for socially responsible citizens.

Conclusion

William Dych, S.J., has helped me understand an important connection between the methodology of the Values Program and practical theology.[13] In his interview with Karl Rahner a few years after Vatican II, Rahner observed that theology faced the task of transposing the doctrines of our faith (which usually are expressed as theoretical statements) into practical imperatives, so that "the theological as such will become a principle of action."[14] In such a transposition, Anselm's classic definition of theology, *"fides quaerens intellectum"*—"faith seeking understanding"—becomes a matter not of theoretical expression but of practical reason and understanding. The question becomes: "What must be done?" In the context of the Pastoral Constitutions of Vatican II, the emphasis would be less on what I must do and more on what we must do as Church.

From the perspective of this transposition to practical imperatives, the Church would express its true identity not just in accurate theoretical understanding about itself (orthodoxy), but also in the correctness of what it does (orthopraxis). The Gospel of John reflects the insight of this transposition when Jesus asserts that his disciples are identified by their actions: "By this all will know that you are my disciples, that you have love for one another" (Jn.13.25).

Without using specifically theological language, the mission of the Values Program flows from this consciousness. The Values Program takes this basic insight, puts it in a language and a process that is accessible to all the disciplines, and makes it integral to the way this institution educates. The success with which we work with the entire faculty and student body at Le Moyne and in other private and public institutions tells us that our approach is working.

Notes

1. Parker J. Palmer, "Foreword," in D. J. Kirby et al., *Ambitious Dreams: The Values Program at Le Moyne College* (Kansas City, MO: Sheed & Ward, 1990), vii.
2. A. W. Astin, *What Matters in College: Four Critical Years Revisited* (San Francisco: Jossey-Bass Publishers, 1993).
3. Kirby et al., *Ambitious Dreams*, 8.
4. Dr. Krystine Batcho, director of assessment and research for the Values Program, is now writing a book detailing the method and findings of the pro-

gram (1988–1999). The evaluation of the program is both qualitative and quantitative.

5. D. Ross, *Value Development in the University Classroom,* rev. 2nd ed. (Taiwan, Republic of China: Fu Jen University, 1993), 470.

6. *Random House Dictionary of the English Language* (New York: Random House, 1966).

7. K. B. Yaworsky and W. H. Holmes, "Power and Promise: Evaluation of an Evolving Model," in Kirby et al., *Ambitious Dreams,* 161–84.

8. 34th General Congregation, Society of Jesus, Decree 13, #11. (5 Jan–22 March 1995).

9. Ibid., Decree 13, #18.

10. Ibid., Decree 4, #19.

11. Ibid., Decree 4, #21.

12. Mary Douglas, *How Institutions Think (Frank W. Abrams Lectures)* (Syracuse, NY: Syracuse University Press, 1986).

13. During my sabbatical year I was able to explore these ideas with William Dych, who was completing *Thy Kingdom Come: Jesus and the Reign of God* (New York: Crossroads, 1999), a new look at the theology of grace and church, ministry and priesthood.

14. William Dych, "Karl Rahner: An Interview," *America* 123, 13 (October 31, 1970), 358.

Promoting an Ethical Campus Culture: The Values Audit

John R. Wilcox and Susan L. Ebbs*

A Pervasive Approach to Ethics Education

In a time of rapid economic, social, and technological change, institutions in business, journalism, law, and medicine are assessing their shared values and restructuring their organizational cultures.[1] The assessment and restructuring are closely associated with, and have stimulated much scholarly interest in, applied ethics. The Hastings Center monographs document the origins of this renaissance in ethics.[2] The rapid evolution of higher education in the last four decades[3] demands that colleges and universities likewise look inward and assess their own cultures. As a result, the moral life of colleges and universities is receiving increased attention.[4]

Much confusion surrounds the use of terms like *values, ethics, moral life,* and *culture.* According to Morrill, *values* are "standards and patterns of choice that guide persons and groups toward satisfaction, fulfillment, and meaning."[5] Among the values prized by institutions of higher education are academic excellence, respect for individuals, a caring community, and ethical character. The term *values* is comprehensive, embracing aesthetics, economics, ethics, and politics, among many other aspects of life. Awareness of and sensitivity to the values an educational institution and

*John R. Wilcox is professor of religious studies at Manhattan College, Bronx, New York. Susan L. Ebbs is Senior Vice President for Student Life at Manhattan College. This article is reprinted from *NASPA Journal* 29(4) (summer 1992): 253–60 with the permission of the National Association of Student Personnel Administrators (NASPA).

its members hold enhance the decision-making process and moral life on campus. Such awareness and sensitivity also help the valuing process itself.

Valuing captures the dynamic aspect of values, bringing together both knowing and doing. Values discussions in higher education should lead to reflection on mission and assessment, as well as on individual fulfillment and the common weal, and thus to a valuing process on campus.[6] "At no matter what point one penetrates into the life of the self or a culture," Morrill contends, "one finds a structure of values that enforces claims and standards."[7]

Applied ethics is the normative and systematic reflection on our moral behavior in areas such as business, education, engineering, law, journalism, medicine, and ministry. Moral behavior is defined here as the interpersonal dimension of our behavior: how we treat one another (and, increasingly, other species and the environment), individually and in groups. Because of our ability to critically distance ourselves from our own behavior, morality regularly leads to ethics.

Kuh and Whitt define *culture* in higher education as "the collective, mutually shaping patterns of norms, values, practices, beliefs, and assumptions that guide the behavior of individuals and groups in an institute of higher education and provide a frame of reference within which to interpret the meaning of events and actions on and off campus."[8]

As noted earlier, the ethics of higher education itself is a developing area of research and an important dimension of institutional renewal in colleges and universities. The ethical responsibilities of faculty have thus been analyzed from the perspective of the curriculum.[9] Ethical analysis of college and university cultures has been equally important.[10]

Attention to campus culture, a broad category, logically precedes and sets the stage for discussion of ethical issues in the more narrowly defined area of curriculum. On one hand, curriculum is affected by the many aspects of institutional life associated with culture—the student body's race and gender composition may, for example, affect course offerings, or the school's religious or secular identity may affect course requirements. On the other, academic programs—such as fine arts and environmental engineering—may sensitize students to aesthetics or social issues and thus affect student life.

This essay focuses on the culture of the academic institution. Campus culture manifests itself in such areas as administration, admissions, athletics, and commuter and resident life. Specific issues within these areas include administrative use of power, honesty in student recruitment, retention of athletes, and racism and sexual harassment on campus.

The culture of the classroom is another important aspect of campus life, distinguished here from curriculum. Classroom culture embraces both the tone set by faculty and students and the instruction itself. Are the students treated with respect and dignity? Is justice practiced? Do faculty take seriously the pedagogical dimensions of higher education (an aspect of academic life for which very few faculty are professionally prepared)?[11] When developing an ethical awareness on campus, administrators should use an approach that takes classroom culture into consideration and does not equate it with the issue of ethics in the curriculum.

Cultural analysis and ethical reflection can challenge any group.[12] Higher education is no exception, especially given its pluralism of ethical systems and moral stances, both of which are reinforced by the isolation of academic departments. Concern for academic freedom and the individualism of the professoriate are also sensitive areas. The impersonal contractual constraints of the rational organization are often difficult to reconcile with the care and mutuality characteristic of moral concern and ethical reflection.

Discussion of moral life or ethics impels individuals to ask, "What can I do?" Framing the question in this way is part of the problem, not only in higher education but in society at large. Institutional renewal from the perspective of morality, ethics, and values requires a systemic valuing process that goes beyond individual initiative.[13] Frustration and alienation all too often result from individual enthusiasm for renewal. The Values Audit—a collaborative process—offers a more effective means for bringing about institutional sensitivity to the mission of higher education.

Process: The Values Audit

The Values Audit systematically assesses beliefs, goals, standards of choice, and the manner in which these are lived or enacted; it also helps formulate recommendations according to the values proclaimed and practiced.[14] The Values Audit process can foster better understanding of the moral climate, clarify needed changes, and develop an institutional basis for a pervasive approach to ethics across campus and curriculum.[15]

The Society for Values in Higher Education conducted pilot Values Audits at eight diverse colleges and universities—California State at Long Beach, Centre College, Le Moyne College, Southwest Texas State University, Susquehanna University, University of Tennessee at Knoxville, University of Wisconsin at Green Bay, and Willamette University. The process set in motion at these institutions involved institutional self-scrutiny with a particular focus on values and ethics. Recognizing the merit of this process, the American Council on Education Commission on Women in Higher Education[16] recommended the Values Audit as favorable for all institutions. The Council of Independent Colleges has also initiated a Values Audit project for its members.

Public and private colleges and universities alike have employed the Values Audit, using it as a catalyst to stimulate campuswide discussion about values and ethics. On virtually all the campuses that have conducted the audit, both qualitative and quantitative data on new institutional research questions have emerged. More essential, however, has been the audit's role in evoking discussion of crucial campus issues.

The Values Audit's emphasis on moral life and ethical reflection provides a common basis for bringing administration, faculty, staff, and students together around issues of mutual concern in the classroom and on the campus. Examining the explicit and implicit values that motivate decision-making processes can lead to reformulation and reaffirmation of the values system and to better decision-making. The assumption underlying such an examination is that values are the power behind decision-making. Values lead to decisions and policies in all areas of campus life, from the pedagogy in classrooms to the regulations in residence halls. The Values Audit *process* is as important as the data gathered, since it involves discussion and consensus building among administrators, faculty, students, and staff.

The Values Audit project reported below was conducted over a two-year period at a midsize, religiously affiliated, comprehensive college in the Northeast. The process began with a cross-section of administrators and faculty reviewing the procedures and expectations of a Values Audit. With the strong support of this group and the college's new president, a letter was sent to all members of the community inviting their participation in the work of the Values Audit Committee. The 30-member volunteer committee—consisting of administrators, faculty, students, and support staff—met for a workshop conducted by the executive director of the Society for Values in Higher Education (who had conducted similar audits at other institutions). The workshop's goal was to develop a sense of the process and set a direction for the committee.

The committee reviewed documents concerning the college's mission and goals and delineated areas to be addressed, including the mission, philosophy, and tradition of the institution. It also considered the overall campus culture and agreed to a four-part audit process. The process began with structured interviews conducted by two outside consultants with previous experience in this area. Eight administrators, eight faculty members, eight staff members, and twelve students—half of them selected because of their position or length of service and half selected at random—were each interviewed for approximately one hour, with confidentiality assured.

The structured interviews confirmed many ways that the college culture reflected the values of its heritage, including a strong commitment to individual attention to students by faculty. The widely held perception of the college as a "family" was also confirmed, with students sharing concern for each other and women and minority students integrated into the institution fairly well. The interviews also identified problems that need to be addressed, including an apparent lack of concern for issues of peace and justice, consistently negative perceptions about communication, and uncertainty about mission. Concern was also expressed about the quality of campus life for students, especially in regard to integrating academic and extracurricular activities.

The consultants' report generated discussion questions for a series of small focus groups involving a cross-section of 113 campus community members. The small groups were purposely homogeneous to encourage participation and frankness. Administrative groups, which included leadership and professional staff members, had 27 participants; faculty groups had 20 participants; student groups had 42; and staff had 24. Responses were grouped into three categories: philosophy (tradition, religious identity), community (communication, quality of student life), and education (quality of teaching).

All groups confirmed the strength of the religious tradition. Many expressed interest in enhancing Jewish and Christian values while also recognizing the positive aspects of a pluralistic society.

Student groups supported the national trend of considering their own interests and concerns before those who are less fortunate. Negative perceptions concerning communication were a major focus of discussion, suggesting an inability to confront problems. Student groups reported the quality of student life as good but characterized by differences between the lifestyles of commuters and of residents, resulting in two distinct populations.

Faculty commented on a lack of innovation in teaching methods and the need for more effective evaluation, as well as the lack of cultural and intellectual life on campus. Both faculty and student groups expressed the conviction, however, that excellence, honesty, integrity, respect, and the value of education are communicated in the classroom.

The committee used the observations from the structured interviews and focus groups to develop three somewhat different instruments for distribution to faculty/administration, students, and support staff. The instruments asked for demographic information and responses (using a five-point Likert scale) to questions derived from the categories of philosophy, community, and education. Several questions required write-in responses.

This was the first time such a survey was used in a Values Audit. Its major importance was to legitimize and in some ways emphasize and clarify points of agreement, both positive and negative, that emerged from the interviews and focus groups. The Values Committee was careful to ensure that the survey instrument was not equated with the entire project but was employed as an adjunct to the qualitative methods.[17] Some faculty members have used the survey data to develop student profiles and correlations of values among constituent groups. Their work is the impetus for a current research project on student political and educational values.

A summary of the observations and statistical data was circulated both to and through committee members. Thirty administrators, faculty members, students, and support staff representing diverse points of view and various years of experience at the institution, some on the committee and some not, were asked to write a response to the summary. Their responses were then presented to the community at three symposia, allowing for wider dissemination of the information and enhancing the final report and the proposals for change and renewal of campus life. Implementation of the proposals will be the subject of a future report to the community.

Recommendations

Since *process* is the most important element of the Values Audit, several recommendations are crucial to its success. The Values Audit Committee consisted of volunteers from administration, faculty, staff, and students. Such broad representation allowed for divergent points of view and created a sense of college-wide ownership. One individual must, however, be given the time and support to develop and direct the project.

Maintaining consistent student participation was important, but difficult. Ideally, there should be a cross-section of students. Sophomores should be included so students can participate throughout the project. Participation after graduation by some students can also assist with continuity.

Support from the highest levels of academic administration is essential. In the case reported above the new college president gave the project support and followed up on several recommendations.

Individual interviews, small group discussions, a college-wide survey, and symposia were important means of developing diverse critical inquiry. Outside consultants conducting the interviews stimulated greater disclosure. Each phase provided a variety of data and direction for the next phase. Common themes became apparent early on and repeated themselves throughout the process.

Strategies for obtaining higher rates of return on surveys must be developed carefully. The high student response rate (61%) was due to the willingness of many faculty members to administer the survey during class time. The full-time faculty response was also high (51%), and may have been partly due to their administering the survey in class as well as their interest in institutional change. The question of adjunct faculty must also be considered, however. In this case, adjuncts participated only in the college-wide survey and their response rate was low (19%). These faculty need to be considered because they play an important role, yet they are less involved due to other commitments or to their own or the institution's lack of interest.

There was also a low survey response by administrative leadership (35%) and administrative personnel (22%), which may well reflect the political realities and uncertainty of a new presidency. Persistent follow-up must secure a response from these groups. It is also important to develop strong allies in the administration as the Values Audit begins and continues.

Support staff involvement can be a step toward creating a more inclusive community even though female clerical personnel may be the major or only participants. Clerical staff have a unique perspective on the college; are aware of the daily activities of administrators, faculty, and other staff; and may be the first persons to interact with new students and parents.

Finally, timing of the Values Audit is important. Internal or external environmental factors will influence the institution's interest in the process and its use of the resulting information. For the institution in this report, the Middle States Self-Study began shortly after the Values Audit ended; task forces have data from the audit at their disposal. Audit results may also be fed into the strategic planning process to help stimulate change.

Conclusion

Colleges and universities can begin to structure their environments to promote ethical campus climates through a Values Audit. The procedure provides a method for assessing the values professed and practiced within an institution. Remarkable opportunities exist for student affairs practitioners and faculty to work as teams, sharing responsibility for educating students and helping institutions get a clearer focus on basic issues of widespread concern. Specific recommendations can then be made to improve the campus culture. The process itself, characterized by involvement and sharing, is as important as the findings; its continuation, including serious consideration of and action taken on recommendations, can enhance the well-being of any institution that undertakes such a project.

Notes

1. See, for instance, Peter F. Drucker, *The New Realities* (New York: Harper & Row, 1989), and T. J. Peters and R. H. Waterman, Jr., *In Search of Excellence: Lessons from America's Best Run Companies* (New York: Harper & Row, 1982).

2. D. Callahan and S. Bok, *The Teaching of Ethics in Higher Education* (New York: Plenum, 1980), and The Hastings Center, *Monographs on the Teaching of Ethics: I–IX* (Pleasantville, NY: Author, 1980).

3. See Derek Bok, *Universities and the Future of America* (Durham, NC: Duke University Press, 1990); F. Oakley, "Apocalypse Now in U.S. Higher Education," *America* 160 (12) 286–87; W. D. Schaefer, *Education without Compromise* (San Francisco: Jossey-Bass, 1990); and L. Veysey, "Higher Education as a Profession: Changes and Continuities," in N. Hatch, ed., *The Professions in American History* (Notre Dame, IN: University of Notre Dame Press, 1988), 15–32.

4. W. W. May, ed., *Ethics and Higher Education* (New York: American Council on Higher Education/Macmillan Publishing, 1990); J. R. Wilcox and S. L. Ebbs, *The Leadership Compass: Values and Ethics in Higher Education* (ASHE-ERIC Higher Education Report No. 1) (Washington, DC: George Washington University School of Education and Human Development, 1992).

5. R. L. Morrill, *Teaching Values in College* (San Francisco: Jossey-Bass, 1989), 62.

6. D. C. Smith, "Program Improvement through Values Audits," in D. Deshler, ed., *Evaluation for Program Improvement (New Directions for Continuing Education No. 24)* (San Francisco: Jossey-Bass, 1984).

7. Morrill, *Teaching Values*, 72.

8. G. D. Kuh and E. J. Whitt, *The Invisible Tapestry: Culture in American Colleges and Universities* (ASHE-ERIC Higher Education Report No. 1) (Washington, DC: Association for the Study of Higher Education, 1988), 12–13.

9. See A. W. Astin, "The Implicit Curriculum," *Liberal Education* 74(1) (1988): 6–10; S. M. Cahn, *Saints and Scamps: Ethics in Academia* (Totowa, NJ: Rowman and Littlefield, 1986); H. Giroux and D. Purpel, eds., *The Hidden Curriculum in Moral Education* (Berkeley, CA: McCutchan Publishing, 1983); D. Hirsch, "Translating Research into Practice: The Impact of the Hidden Curriculum in Teaching Morals and Values," *Journal for Higher Education Management*, 3(2) (1988): 45–51; G. Meilaender, "The Ethics of Teaching Ethics: Introduction," *The Annual: Society of Christian Ethics* (1989), 229–31; Edward Shils, *The Academic Ethic* (Chicago: University of Chicago Press, 1983).

10. See J. D. Barry, ed., *Ethics on a Catholic University Campus* (Chicago: Loyola University Press, 1980); R. G. Brockett, ed., *Ethical Issues in Adult Education* (New York: Teachers College Press, 1988); H. J. Cannon and R. D. Brown, eds., *Applied Ethics in Student Services* (San Francisco: Jossey-Bass, 1985); Carnegie Foundation for the Advancement of Teaching, *Campus Life: In Search of Community* (Lawrenceville, NJ: Princeton University Press), 1990); D. D. Dill, ed., *Journal of Higher Education: Ethics and the Academic Profession*, 53 (1982); G. Grant, *The World We Created at Hamilton High* (Cambridge, UK: Cambridge University Press, 1988); Kuh and Whitt, *Invisible Tapestry;* M. Moffatt, *Coming of Age in New Jersey: College and American Culture* (New Brunswick, NJ: Rutgers University Press, 1989); and N. D. Wright, ed., *Papers on the Ethics of Administration* (Albany, NY: State University New York [SUNY] Press, 1988).

11. See P. Smith, *Killing the Spirit: Higher Education in America* (New York: Viking, 1990); M. Weimer, ed., *The Teaching Professor*, vols. 1–4 (Madison, WI: Magna Publications, 1987); and B. Wilshire, *The Moral Collapse of the University* (Albany, NY: State University of New York [SUNY] Press, 1990).

12. Robert Bellah et al., *Habits of the Heart: Individualism and Commitment in American Life* (New York: Harper & Row, 1985).

13. Bellah et al., *Habits of the Heart;* Alasdair MacIntyre, *After Virtue* (Notre Dame, IN: University of Notre Dame Press, 1981); Schaefer, *Education without Compromise.*

14. G. M. Galles, "What Colleges Really Teach," *New York Times* (June 8, 1989), A39; D.C. Smith, "Program Improvement"; D.C. Smith, "Values and Decision-Making in Higher Education" (unpublished manuscript prepared for the Society for Values in Higher Education, Washington, D.C.).

15. Astin, "Implicit Curriculum"; Morrill, *Teaching Values;* C. R. Pace, *Measuring Outcomes of College: Fifty Years of Findings and Recommendations for the Future* (San Francisco: Jossey-Bass, 1979); C. H. Reynolds and D. C. Smith, "Academic Leadership Styles, Institutional Cultures, and the Resources of Ethics" (unpublished manuscript prepared for the Society for Values in Higher Education, Washington, D.C.).

16. C. S. Pearson, D. L. Shavlik, and J. G. Touchton, "The New Agenda of Women for Higher Education," in *Educating the Majority: Women Challenging Tradition in Higher Education* (New York: American Council on Education/Macmillan, 1989), 441–58.

17. Kuh and Whitt, *Invisible Tapestry.*

Index